REAL
TALK
about
LGBTQIAP

REAL
TALK
about
LGBTQIAP

*Lesbian, Gay, Bisexual, Transgender, Queer,
Intersex, Asexual, and Pansexual*

Tara Y. Coyt

Joe Barry Carroll Publishing
Atlanta, Georgia
joebarrycarrollpublishing.com

ISBN-13: 978-0-9898373-7-8 (paperback)
ISBN-13: 978-0-9898373-8-5 (e-book)
Library of Congress Control Number: 2019901800

The paper used in this publication meets the minimum requirements
of the American National Standard for Information Sciences—
permanence of paper for printed library materials ANSI Z39.48-1992

Love.

Equality.

Personal Truth.

CONTENTS

"Knowledge is learning something every day.
Wisdom is letting go of something every day."
–Zen proverb

CHAPTER ONE

WHY?

"Ernest [Hemingway] called for everyone to write
truly, to write so that readers would feel themselves in
the stories, to write only about whatever they believed
to be the thing we ought most to care about."
–Meg Waite Clayton[1]

"Why?" was one of my favorite questions when I was a little girl, and as an adult it remains a question I ask daily. *Why do we think this way? Why do we behave this way? Why is this happening?* "Why?" is also a question people ask of *me*, after hearing I've written this book. They wonder why I spent four years researching and writing a book about LGBTQIAP—lesbian, gay, bisexual, transgender, queer, intersex, asexual, and pansexual—when I don't identify as any of those labels. The reasons are many.

I am a curious person who enjoys investigating, researching, learning, and trying to make sense of things. I am also a writer. My curiosity fuels my writing. Combining these factors has made me a writer whose role is to share information and to help others make sense of things.

In part, it was because I had a growing list of unanswered questions. *Why are some people homosexual and others heterosexual or bisexual? What does queer mean? What determines a person's gender identity?* I also had questions about how we respond to and treat each other. *Why would a religious leader preach that someone should be killed because they are gay? How could a parent reject their child for being transgender, gay, etc.? Why is there so much fear of and hate for people because of their sexuality or gender identity?*

Like most people, I had formed some opinions about sexuality and gender identity. Also like most people, I had never taken the time to delve into the details to determine if any of my opinions were misguided. Perhaps this lack of examination is how so many misperceptions have come to exist in the world. Once we begin to examine our feelings and beliefs, we may discover that some are unwarranted. We might discover there's no factual or scientific substantiation for thinking about and treating people with disdain. I wondered what I would discover. How much of what is believed, reported, and propagated about LGBTQIAP is fact-based and what is only propped up by our personal fears and biases?

One way to gain a better understanding is to have candid conversations: to ask questions and to listen. Talking about human sexuality and gender identity can be difficult terrain. Once we put a question out there, we run the risk of hearing a response that we won't like or that will challenge our understanding of the world. There's a chance the answer will offend us. There's also a chance our question will offend someone else. As a result, we are inclined to avoid having the conversations.

I avoided the conversation 30 years ago after my best friend Robyn confided that she had a crush on a female coworker. Robyn and I were "ride-or-die" friends; however, I was reluctant to ask more about her attraction to women because it made me uncomfortable. Though we talked about how things were progressing with this new relationship, I never inquired into Robyn's thoughts and feelings about her sexuality.

A couple of years later, another opportunity for a similar discussion came and went unanswered. That time it was with my housemate Norma, who was twice-divorced and the mother of two adult children. I presumed Norma was heterosexual, until I saw her in an intimate situation with another woman. A few days later, Norma said she and the woman were in a relationship. I wondered if that meant she was bisexual or homosexual. I wondered if she had always been attracted to women. I wondered if that was why she'd gotten divorced.

Instead of asking Norma any of those questions, I did what many heterosexuals do when they want to learn about homosexuality or bisexuality—I asked other heterosexuals. Instead of going to the source, so to speak, I chose to chat it up with people who knew just as little, or less, than I did about the subject. Over the years, I have learned how this approach didn't advance my knowledge and understanding.

The need for a different, more effective approach became increasingly important to me. I realized that if I wanted a better understanding of sexuality and gender identity, one of the first things I needed to do was talk to people whose experiences and identities differed from mine. I would also need to do something my parents often told me to do: "look it up." In order to better understand sexuality, gender identity, and biological sex, I needed to examine history, science, and previous research. That's what I did. I set out on this path expecting to finish within in a year; it took four.

Just a few months before completing this book, I received a holiday greeting card from my mother that seemed to reinforce my pursuit. It read:

Dear Daughter,

My wish for you is that you'll always know a little bit more today than you knew yesterday—about life, about yourself, about what you can do and create in this world.

This value of knowing "a little bit more today than you knew yesterday" is one I inherited from my parents. They were curious and interested in the world around them, in the things they could and could not see. My father was an avid viewer of the local Public Broadcasting Service (PBS) station and enjoyed programs about history, science, and the animal kingdom. Both parents took continuing education courses in their respective fields, and they spent time every day reading the newspapers and magazines to which they subscribed. My brother and I joined them as soon as we could read.

Thanks to my parents' examples, I have been an active learner throughout my life. I was that kid who read books in the summer of my own volition. I routinely plucked an encyclopedia off the shelf and read a random page just to see what else I could learn that day. Discovering something new that expands my understanding gives me a natural high. Knowing a little more each day helps to broaden our perspectives. Understanding a bit more about ourselves, each other, and the world around us can bring us closer. I hope that learning more about LGBTQIAP will help fill the chasms that currently exist between people of different sexualities and gender identities.

This is not my first time tackling a project that required expanding my horizons. Every job I've held has been an adventure that required me to dive in, learn something new, and share the knowledge. I've written books on single parenting from a male perspective, dentistry, 90s West Coast hip hop, basketball, personal development, and Southern culture. I have written articles on wealth management from a spiritual perspective and articles reporting on Food and Drug Administration (FDA) research and regulations.

What distinguishes this book from the others I have written is that I am the sole author writing on a subject that I am passionate about. This is not solely an intellectual pursuit. It is also a pursuit of the heart. What remains the same is that I have always poured a bit of what I've learned about myself, others, and the world around me into my projects. As my mother's greeting card encouraged, I continue to learn something new every day.

Some people have difficulty understanding why a heterosexual woman would get so involved in investigating something that appears not to be her own. Most of us, after all, are not in the habit of sticking our noses into groups, situations, or causes that don't directly involve us. I have a different view. These conversations and issues do involve me because, although not a member of the LGBTQIAP community, I am a member of the human race.

For me, that means I'm as connected to humans who resemble me in various ways as I am to those with whom I do not share common attributes. Additionally, I am committed to equality and the universal pursuit of life, liberty, and happiness. How, then, can I witness LGBTQIAP individuals being denied those rights and not cry out? History has repeatedly shown us that things do not end well when we rationalize or dismiss hatred, discrimination, and violence. When I think about people who remained silent while witnessing crimes against Native Americans, African Americans, Jews, Chinese people, and others, I know that I do not want to be that type of person, turning a blind eye simply because I am not part of the group being persecuted or abused. I would like to think that had I been a white person during the era of chattel slavery or a Gentile during the Holocaust, I would have said or done something to help end the atrocities, but I will never know for sure. What I can be sure of are my actions in this lifetime.

In presenting this book, I hope to give faces and heartbeats to the real people behind the letters LGBTQIAP by exploring and sharing their realities. I have tried to present questions and answers in a way that reflects what people are thinking, feeling, and pondering, even when it might feel uncomfortable or impolite. Some of the answers come from lesbian, gay, bisexual, transgender, queer, intersex, asexual, and pansexual people I have met along the way. Other information comes from studies, articles, healthcare professionals, medical professionals, historians, and LGBTQIAP organizations. This discussion is far too complex for this to be an all-inclusive exploration. While I have tried to be thorough, no examination can be 100 percent complete. There are additional questions and concerns to be addressed. My intention is for this book to be a starting point for further discussion and exploration.

CHAPTER TWO

ASKING QUESTIONS

"The art and science of asking questions
is the source of all knowledge."
–Thomas Berger.[2]

Asking questions is one of the ways we learn. Making assumptions keeps us in the dark. Asking questions is crucial to understanding ourselves, others, and the world in which we live. I recognize that in personal matters such as sexuality, gender identity, and biological sex, asking questions can be tricky and intimidating, as these are intensely personal and emotional matters. Knowing what to ask, how to ask, when to ask, and who to ask presents a daunting challenge. Should you risk offending your child, cousin, best friend, or coworker by asking about their sexuality or gender identity? Or should you leave it be and trade the risk of offense for the cost of relying on your assumptions? I believe we should ask questions of ourselves and others. I hope this book can serve as a framework to make our questions more thoughtful, respectful, and relevant.

I wondered how the people interviewed for this book felt about being approached with questions about their sexuality, gender identity, and biological sex. As with most things in life, there were differing opinions. Some people welcomed questions, viewing them as an opportunity to educate and inform. Other people believed that you shouldn't ask others anything you wouldn't want to be asked. If you would be offended or feel that your privacy had been violated by a question, then how fair is it to ask someone else to endure the same? Similarly, some said that if you wouldn't ask a heterosexual person about an aspect of their sexuality, then why ask anyone else? With regard to questions about their sex life, an anonymous person posting on asexuality.org writes, "It's nobody's business but my own. If I feel I know you well enough to tell you things about my sex life and history, I'll tell you. If I don't, then under any circumstances it's just rude to ask."

The notion of boundaries was echoed by an Atlanta-area doctor who identifies as queer. They suggested that there are limits to the types of questions a person should be expected to entertain.

> *If you want to ask about my experiences, that is pretty personal; and so that is not something I necessarily want to talk about with just anyone. I wouldn't expect someone who is not a close friend to ask those types of questions.*
>
> –Anne, emergency physician, married,
>   gender queer, queer sexuality, 35 years old

Another person I spoke with, a transgender woman who is a former naval officer, seemed more willing to answer questions, but she also had limits.

> *There are certain things I won't talk about. And if they're actually rude questions, like questions about my genitals, questions that you wouldn't ask any other person, then I bluntly turn those away and explain why they're impolite. But generally speaking, I try to be fairly open. I try to understand that they are curious about these things, so I try to meet all questions with compassion, whether or not I am willing to answer them.*
>
> –Vandy Beth Glenn, writer, single,
>   transgender, lesbian, age undisclosed

Then there was Fredis, pronounced Freddy, who welcomed all questions, as long as they were asked in a respectful way.

I'd much rather have somebody ask me than assume. With anything, it's so much better to ask than just assume.

–Fredis, makeup artist, single, cisgender, gay, 35 years old

My impression was that Fredis saw this openness as an ambassadorship of sorts. He also offered the following advice about asking sensitive questions:

If you want to know, then ask a question, and you work out by body language whether somebody is receptive or not. If you ask a question, and you feel like they cringe, then obviously drop the subject and move on because they're not comfortable. If you ask somebody, "Are you gay?" it depends what tone you take with it, if they feel like they're being judged. It's very tricky. Some people will be okay with answering, some are not.

–Fredis

Sometimes, asking questions is necessary to provide proper service to someone or to complete a task. Doctor Isabel "Izzy" Lowell, who founded a healthcare service for transgender and non-binary patients, and established a transgender clinic at Emory University Hospital, had to guide hospital staff in respectful ways to ask questions and communicate with patients.

The best thing you can do is, if you're not sure by looking at somebody who they are, you can say, "What's your preferred gender? What's your preferred name?" And that's an okay question to ask. I think knowing that you're allowed to ask that is all most people need to be able to kind of relax about it. And I say to patients, "Nobody's perfect. My staff may not, you know, adhere 100 percent to what you prefer, and I may not either, but we're all trying, and we're all welcoming."

–Isabel "Izzy" Lowell, MD, Founder, QMed, married,
gender queer, lesbian, 35 years old

An elected official I spoke with noted that she had fielded countless questions over the years in her capacity as a county commissioner, advocate for lesbian rights, and volunteer. She too welcomed questions but added a very important consideration for the person asking those questions.

You have to be comfortable hearing the answer.

–Joan P. Garner, Fulton County Commission Co-Chair, married, cisgender, lesbian, 63 years old

I interpreted Commissioner Garner's observation as saying that if we want to ask a question, we must be willing to listen and then explore and examine new information. In other words, we should approach these discussions with kindness, an open mind, and an open heart. If we are not prepared to take in new information, then why ask? Asking questions suggests that we are interested in learning more about the person and the subject. It suggests that we are willing to consider that things might be different than we previously presumed.

Let's agree to ask questions of ourselves and others and listen to the answers. Learning more about what makes us different can ease the discomfort, doubts, and fears we have about our differences. Taking the time to try to understand our differences can move us from a place of ignorance and fear to a place of knowledge and acceptance of the many expressions of humanity. It can also help us see our inter-connectedness and the things that make us the same.

This world we live in is not simple, and many things are still unfolding, but that does not have to be frightening. Jennifer Finney Boylan, National Co-chair for GLAAD's Board of Directors, observed, "If the world is not as simple as we thought, the world is also more wondrous and full of variety and miracles. And we should celebrate that."[3]

Let's celebrate our differences in biological sex, sexuality, and gender identity.

CHAPTER THREE

WHAT'S THE WHAT?

"[I] many years ago made up my mind never to form
an opinion without knowledge; invariably, when I
have done so, I have made an ass of myself."
–Judge John W. Edmonds[4]

Intro

What are we really talking about when it comes to LGBTQIAP? Judging by many discussions, sermons, and media soundbites, one might get the impression it's about sex, sin, and depravity; however, those are just smoke screens that distract us from the real topic. This is a discussion about human beings. Specifically, this is a conversation about the variety of ways we humans express sexuality, gender identity, and biological sex. Let's start there.

In order to understand LGBTQIAP, we need to understand the meanings of words like biological sex, gender, gender identity, cisgender, and sexuality.

> *Biological Sex.* A person's biological sex, usually thought of as male or female, is assigned based on particular physical and biological factors, like whether they have a penis or a vagina. Medical professionals also consider which reproductive organs (ovaries and testes) and chromosomes (XX and XY) are present. The

label "biological female" is traditionally assigned when features like a vagina, ovaries, and XX chromosomes are present. The label "biological male" is traditionally assigned when features like a penis, testes, and XY chromosomes are present.

Gender. Gender is described as the subjective expectations a society has for a person based on that person's biological sex. For example, society expects a biological male to exhibit a masculine gender—a presumed set of thoughts, feelings, and behaviors.

Gender Identity. Gender identity refers to our personal feelings and perceptions about our own femininity and masculinity. Gender identity is not reliant on biological sex or gender. Someone's gender identity can be the same or different from their gender and biological sex. Often, a person's gender identity coincides with the gender that society expects of them. In other instances, an individual's gender identity does not match society's gender expectations. A person can identify as a boy/man, girl/woman, or neither.

Cisgender. "Cis-" is Latin for "on this side of" or "same." Therefore, cisgender means "same gender." Cisgender is a relatively new term that refers to people whose gender identity is the same as the gender society expects them to exhibit. For instance, my gender identity is feminine, which is the same as the gender society expects me to have as someone whose biological sex is female. Although most people's gender identities and gender are the same, that is not always the case.

Sexuality. Human sexuality is about who a person is sexually, emotionally, and/or romantically attracted to. Some people refer to this as sexual orientation. Sexuality, however, refers to more than just sexual attraction. Sexuality also involves our thoughts and feelings about sex and the ways we express ourselves as sexual beings. Heterosexuality is one type of human sexuality. Other sexualities include homosexuality, bisexuality, asexuality, and pansexuality.

One letter that is not represented by LGBTQIAP is H for heterosexuality.

Heterosexuality. This is one type of sexuality or sexual orientation found in humans and other animals. With heterosexuality, a person is sexually, emotionally, and/or romantically attracted only to people of the opposite sex. It is estimated that approximately 97 percent of Americans identify as heterosexual.[5]

Why are heterosexuals called "straight"?

Thinking about the term "straight" makes me think about the word "crooked," which sparks a memory of my grandmother, Ma' Dear. If we were watching one of her favorite soap operas or our favorite detective show, *Columbo*, Ma' Dear never failed to warn anyone in earshot to, "Watch out for that man. He's crooked." For her, a crooked person was always some sort of swindler, murderer, or thief. As a result, I grew up associating crooked with anyone intent on causing harm to another person. When I began to think about labeling heterosexuals as "straight," I couldn't help but wonder if it was implying that those who aren't straight are crooked. I decided to look it up.

The term "straight" is reported to have originated within the gay community in the United States as early as the 1940s. That was the era of World War II, Japanese internment camps, and eventually, the beginnings of McCarthyism. It was the time of Captain America, Humphrey Bogart, Tupperware, and pin-up girls. Most Americans held restrictive ideas about what constituted good and wholesome behavior. Homosexuality was taboo during that time and completely hidden from mainstream society. If a person came out as homosexual in the 1940s, they would be ridiculed and ostracized from mainstream society. In many cases, coming out meant giving up one's family, friends, and career. People who came out as homosexual in that era were commonly fired from their jobs, institutionalized, assaulted by fellow citizens, and/or brutalized by the police.

This harsh reality was too steep a price to pay for many people. Others feared less for themselves than they did the collateral damage that their loved ones would endure. These dire circumstances led many people to conclude that perhaps it would be better to follow the "straight and narrow" path of pretending to be heterosexual than to sacrifice almost every other aspect of their lives. If a gay man came out and at some point went back to pretending he was heterosexual, his return would be referred to as "going straight." Tragically, until the prior century, and still today in some places, there were only two bleak options for some people: live a "straight and narrow" lie or die an outcast.

LGBTQIAP Defined

The acronym LGBTQIAP includes people of all races, ethnicities, nationalities, religions, ages, and economic backgrounds. They are grandparents, mothers, daughters, fathers, sons, sisters, brothers, etc. They are students, teachers, doctors, librarians, bus drivers, waitresses, judges, faith leaders, and members of every other profession on the planet. People who identify as LGBTQIAP are parents who strive to take care of their families. They are individuals and families who want to live in safe neighborhoods. They are people who want life, liberty, and the pursuit of happiness. They are also people who are all too often denied those rights specifically because they identify as LGBTQIAP.

Each of the letters in the acronym will be discussed at length later, but for now, let's begin with brief explanations of each one.

L = *Lesbian.* A lesbian is a homosexual girl or woman who is sexually, emotionally, and romantically attracted only to people of the same sex.

G = *Gay.* The term gay can refer to boys, girls, men, and women who are homosexual, and therefore are sexually, emotionally, and romantically attracted only to people of the same sex.

B = *Bisexual.* The prefix "bi" means "two." The term bisexual refers to a person who has the capacity to be sexually, romantically, and emotionally attracted to people of the opposite sex and the same sex.

T = *Transgender.* The term transgender describes a person's gender identity. It does not describe their sexuality or sexual orientation. "Trans-" means "opposite," and transgender refers to a person whose gender identity is the opposite or across from the gender society expects them to exhibit. For instance, a person assigned a female biological sex would be expected to identify as a girl/woman, and have a feminine gender identity. If that biological female instead identifies as a boy/man, then that person is a transgender male. Likewise, someone who was assigned a male biological sex would be expected to have a boy/man gender identity. If that biological male instead has a girl/woman gender identity, then that person is a transgender female.

Q = *Queer or Questioning.* The terms queer and questioning can refer to a person's sexuality and/or their gender identity. When "Q" represents "questioning," it refers to a person who is trying to figure out which label best describes their sexuality or gender identity. "Q" can also represent "queer," which has different meanings for different people. Some queer people equate queer with being homosexual. Others use queer to mean they are something other than heterosexual. There are others who use queer to describe their gender identity as being neither masculine or feminine or some mixture of masculine and feminine. And for yet others, queer is used to describe their sexuality *and* gender identity.

I = *Intersex.* The term intersex refers to a person's biological sex. The prefix "inter" means "between." Intersex refers to a person whose biological sex, which is based on things like genitalia, hormones, and chromosomes, is not clearly male or female. Intersex individuals have what medical professionals refer to as "intersex conditions" that lead to atypical development of physical [biological] sex characteristics.[6]

A = *Asexual.* This is another type of sexuality. The prefix "a" means "without," as in without sexual attraction. Someone with an asexual sexuality does not experience *sexual* attraction to other people. An asexual person may or may not, however, experience other types of attraction, such as romantic and/or emotional.

P = *Pansexual.* The prefix "pan" means "all" or "every." A pansexual person, therefore, can experience sexual, romantic, and emotional attraction to other people regardless of the other person's sexuality, biological sex, or gender identity. A pansexual person may find themselves attracted to someone who is male or female, transgender, queer, etc.

The above are all labels used to describe different sexualities, gender identities, and relationships to biological sex.

Why are there so many letters in the acronym?

While some people feel an acronym with eight letters is cumbersome, I have come to understand and appreciate why every letter is warranted. It's about identity—what we call ourselves and what we would have the rest of the world call us. Being identified as who and what we are is important.

This was instilled in me at a young age. As a child, I remember adults frequently saying, "Don't let anybody call you out of your name." This was a warning that some people might refer to us by names we did not choose or did not prefer because they were demeaning or ignored an important aspect of our identity. This warning was also a call not to accept labels and names we did not identify with or that were insulting.

For years, much of the LGBTQIAP community was being called out of their names. In the 60s, everyone who didn't fit society's expectations of heterosexuality and a cisgender identity was lumped together and called "gay." Bisexual men and women were considered gay, even though they are not. Transgender men and women were considered gay, although being transgender is about gender identity and not about sexuality.

Consider this: Lumping everyone under the "gay" umbrella would be like holding a conference for American Southern states and naming it the Alabama Conference. Identifying the conference by only one state's name ignores the identities and existence of all the other states. Georgia, Louisiana, Florida, Texas, and the other Southern states might initially go along with it, but eventually, each one would reasonably demand to be identified and to have their particular concerns addressed. That is what has been happening with all the people who were initially placed under the "gay" umbrella. As each group of people has decided they want to be called by their name, another letter has been added to the acronym. What was labeled as "gay" became LG, then LGB, LGBT, LGBTQ, LGBTQ+, and LGBTQIAP.

There's something else to consider. Although individual recognition is important, many people who identify with one or more of these letters have merged under the LGBTQIAP acronym because they are all being marginalized by society for not complying with a certain set of expectations.

Many believe uniting as a single entity will help them acquire the rights and privileges that society and governments readily make available to heterosexual, cisgender people.

Is it true that the number of LGBTQIAP people is increasing?

It's difficult to answer this question with certainty. To know if a population is growing, there has to be a reliable benchmark or past number to compare with a current number. There would have to have been a "count" of LGBTQIAP people at some point in the past that we could compare to today's "count." No such count exists. There has never been an "official" count of people based on their gender identity and/or sexuality. The United States Census has never explicitly asked respondents to identify their sexuality or gender identity. The closest they've come was to begin offering estimates of the number of same-sex unmarried partners in 1990. Some companies, like Gallup, a reputable survey provider, are able to offer estimates of the number of LGBTQIAP adults based on surveying smaller populations of people across the country. Yet even if Gallup had been gathering this information since they began operating in 1930, they could only offer less than one hundred years of data. That's not much considering humans have existed for more than 200,000 years.

It's also important to note that the percentages offered for populations who are gay, straight, bi, etc. are estimates. Surveys can only provide estimates because 100 percent of the population doesn't take the survey; they are conducted on a sample size of the population. The percentages offered might also be skewed because of the people answering the questions. Many people answering surveys, regardless of the topic, are unwilling to reveal certain information. Some who answer the survey may not be truthful. The survey also can't account for those who haven't come out to themselves, and therefore are not likely to out themselves in a survey. Additionally, some people will refuse to take the survey. Yet surveys are still our best way of approximating the percentage of the population with children or with incomes of less than $50,000 or with LGBTQIAP identities.

According to a Gallup January 2017 report, more adults are *identifying* as LGBT than ever before. (Gallup does not use the LGBTQIAP acronym.) The distinction of "identifying" is important. More people openly identifying as LGBTQIAP doesn't necessarily mean that a larger percentage of the population is gay, bisexual, transgender, etc. What it does indicate is that more people are willing to openly accept their sexuality and/or gender identity regardless of society's expectations than in the past.

The steady increase of social acceptance over the years is one reason more people are "coming out" or refusing to hide or deny their identities. The reality of more people *identifying* as LGBTQIAP is not the same as more people *being* LGBTQIAP. For example, seven percent of the population may have always been homosexual, but because society made it untenable for them to be out, it might have looked like only one percent of the population was gay or lesbian. While it may seem like the LGBTQIAP population is increasing, what is more likely is that more people are willing to accept that they are not heterosexual or cisgender, and are able to be more open about their gender identity and sexuality.

When I spoke to a sociology professor about this and many other topics, he offered another reason for the growth in those willing to identify themselves.

> *There was a* USA Today *survey a couple of years ago that showed that the number of people under the age of thirty who identified as gay or lesbian was almost three times as high as people over the age of thirty. I think it's because a lot of people in earlier generations didn't feel comfortable coming out because they never saw it visible.*

–Eric R. Wright, PhD, Sociology Professor, Georgia State University, married, cisgender, gay, 53 years old

We may never know if the number of LGBTQIAP individuals is increasing. What we can expect is for the number of people *identifying* as LGBTQIAP to continue to increase as society becomes more accepting of human experiences. This creates a self-perpetuating cycle of increasing visibility, because as more people decide not to hide their true sexuality, gender identity, or biological sex when they see those aspects of themselves reflected by other members of society, the resulting amplification of visibility then empowers even more people to do the same, and the process continues.

Our "Need" for Labels

Identifying ourselves and others in terms of certain attributes and experiences, such as political affiliation, race, sexuality, and gender identity, is the process of labeling. Humans use labels because they help us define relationships with each other and the world, according to Fritz Klein, author of *The Bisexual Option: Second Edition.*[7] Using labels is a sort of shorthand, a method of instant communication. Professor Wright also explained why labels help humans communicate.

> *We create labels because our brains are programmed to categorize; because that basic categorization system is how we communicate. Whether you're talking about a gay label, lesbian label, or straight label, we use that because it's shorthand to describe experience, so you and I can communicate.*

–Professor Wright

Labels can be beneficial because they can help us identify aspects of ourselves and others. Klein further explained that labeling is self-reinforcing because it "is a tried-and-true method of eliminating the threats of uncertainty, ambiguity, [and] fear." For instance, when encountering someone for the first time, we want to know how we are alike or different. We then use this information to assess a threat or determine a level of comfort. Generally, when we perceive a person as similar to ourselves in ways we deem important, we assign a low or null threat level. When someone differs from us along those lines, we are more likely to conclude that they could or would pose a threat.

Labels have been helpful to humans as a survival mechanism, facilitating the quick response time required by our fight-or-flight mechanism. Now that we have evolved beyond rudimentary tribalism and live in an integrated world, wouldn't we be better off to explore an extended thought process that lends itself to discernment and compassion? Rather than continuing to rely on labels as a shorthand to identify friend or foe, wouldn't it be better for us to look deeper into the person, as we would want them to give us deeper consideration before equating our particular differences to something bad?

As Professor Wright pointed out, part of the problem with labels is that Western culture tends to force everybody into one of two boxes. This habit of only allowing two choices, known as binary options, has shaped our thinking. Klein also noted that our labeling limits us to either-or scenarios rather than allowing for infinite possibilities and uniqueness. Binary systems of thought only allow for two options, such as on or off, black or white, gay or straight. The problem with this labeling system is that many things, including sexuality, gender identity, and biological sex, have far more than two states of existence or modes of expression. When it comes to our identities, binary label options do not allow room for the nuance and layers of the human experience. That is perhaps why some people resist being labeled by a particular attribute, such as sexuality or race.

When asked which labels they identified with, some of the people interviewed readily identified with a particular label. Others, like Jazmyn, who initially responded "lesbian," went on to express a resistance to labels:

> *I actually try to avoid any kind of labels. I find that a really challenging question. And at some level, I feel like I don't want it to be an important question, and yet, clearly it is. People want to know.*

–Jazmyn, entrepreneur, committed relationship, cisgender, bisexual, 61 years old

Jazmyn, until a few years ago, spent her life dating men. Now that she is in a loving, committed relationship with a woman, should Jazmyn have to accept the label of lesbian simply because society doesn't want to allow for bisexuality or no label at all?

One man explained that some of his friends don't necessarily identify with a gay or transgender label:

> *I have some friends who don't consider themselves in that category, even though they live a gay life. They consider themselves who they are by their name, and this is the way they are, but they don't consider themselves gay, transgender, lesbian, et cetera.*

–Demetrius, analyst, single, cisgender, gay, 55 years old

I recognize the necessity of labels in certain circumstances. They can be a great place to start. What I find troubling is the inclination to rest on labels rather than use them as entries to deeper introductions and discussions. Labels describe one aspect of a person but can never offer the rich, full experience that can only be gained through mutual understanding, respect, and acceptance of each other's individuality and humanity.

The Meaning of "Normal"

A common presumption about heterosexuality is that it is "normal." A similar term that crops up is "normative behavior," which is interpreted as behavior that is good, desirable, or permissible. This practice of designating certain behaviors as normal and others as abnormal shows up in almost every aspect of our lives, especially when it comes to sexuality and gender identity. Unfortunately, many people take this line of thought a step further. The perception that heterosexuality is normal, and therefore righteous or correct, has given rise to the belief that anything other than heterosexuality is wrong or incorrect. Let's explore why this could be misguided thinking.

What does "normal" really mean? And why do we assume that what is normal must be good and that anything abnormal is bad? These were some of the first questions I asked Professor Wright to answer from his perspective as a sociology and public health researcher.

> I'm not sure there's really a normal, other than in a statistical sense or what's the most common path. One thing I've learned as an academic is that there's always an average, which is sort of how I think of normal. In some ways, normal is more about what's visible, and so people tend to interpret what's normal from what's visible.
>
> –Professor Wright

I would like to explore the three ways for determining normality that Professor Wright mentioned: statistical average, common practice, and visibility. A statistical average is calculated by adding the values of each member of a set and then dividing the sum by the number of members in that set. To determine the average height of an American man, for instance, I would add the height of every man in the country together, and then divide that sum by the number of men in the country. According to averageheight.com, the average American man is 5'9.5" tall.[8] Does that mean that any shorter or taller man is bad, wrong, or incorrect? No, of course not. It simply means that said man is not the statistical average.

The second method that Professor Wright mentioned was to define normal as the "most common," meaning that it occurs most often. Being common does not indicate whether something is good or bad. Consider that there was a time when enslaving black people was common and therefore considered normal. Nothing, however, could ever make slavery a good or acceptable practice. Another example is that the most commonly spoken language in the world is Chinese.[9] (The English language ranks third[10].) Few, especially those speaking English, would suggest that Chinese is the only acceptable language simply because it is the most common. Nor would they conclude that English is bad or wrong because it isn't the most common language. Why? Because being the most common instance or type might make something the norm, but it does not make that thing good or correct, nor does it mean that everything else is bad or wrong.

Professor Wright's last approach to defining normal status was visibility. As he explained it, what we *see* is often what we deem normal. Relying on the visibility barometer can trick us into thinking that what we are accustomed to seeing in our environments is the same everywhere else, or the universal norm, and therefore good or correct. Someone who grows up in a society where everyone prays three times a day, every day, might think that is the norm because that's what they see. To those people, praying three times a day is normal, but that doesn't mean that people who only pray on Saturday or Sunday, or people who never pray, are wrong.

Visibility confirms the existence of a situation, behavior, or thing, and it can imply that something is, to some degree, common. Visibility, like the preceding measures of commonality, does not necessarily coincide with something being good/correct or bad/wrong. Heterosexuality has long been considered the norm because, for many people, it's the only visible expression of sexuality that they encounter directly. All too often, this has occurred because people who aren't heterosexual have hid their sexuality.

Then there are the things we don't or cannot see. We can't see the air we breathe, but no one would conclude that the lack of visibility makes air wrong or bad. Using what we see as the gauge for what is normal, and therefore right, is obviously flawed. Concluding that bisexuality is wrong, for instance, because it is not something we see and therefore is not normal is also flawed.

What is considered normal is subjective and changes over time, as do the people who define it. Often, as societies grow and gain more knowledge of themselves and the world around them, the definition of normal expands to allow more expressions of a given trait or behavior. For example, in early twentieth-century America, it was not normal for women to wear pants or for white women to be employed outside of the home. Today, these are standard practices accepted as the norm. No matter how we define normal, we should not automatically equate being normal with being good, correct, or acceptable.

Sexuality

"There is nothing new under the sun."
–Ecclesiastes 1:9 (NAS)

When it comes to the topic of sexuality and sexual orientation, it seems few people can clearly define it, yet everyone has an opinion about it. These factors combine to leave us with frequent conversations about sexuality that are often poorly informed. Many of the people who insist that only one sexuality is natural are unable to explain what sexuality is and have made no attempts to learn anything about human sexuality. How can such a person be relied on to offer guidance when they have none to offer? They can't. How can any of us be sure that a particular sexuality is natural, wrong, or a choice if we don't know how human sexuality is determined? We can't.

What do sexual orientation and sexuality mean?

One way to think of sexual orientation is that it describes to whom we are attracted. Sexual orientation, according to the American Psychological Association (APA), "refers to an enduring pattern of emotional, romantic, and/or sexual attractions to men, women, or both sexes."[11] They go on to say that sexual orientation is "closely tied to the intimate personal relationships that meet deeply felt needs for love, attachment, and intimacy. In addition to sexual behaviors, these bonds include nonsexual physical affection between partners, shared goals and values, mutual support, and ongoing commitment."

Sexuality isn't just about to whom we are attracted. Sexuality goes beyond attraction and, as the University of Wisconsin, Parkside's Agents for Liberation puts it, "includes how and what we enjoy and desire intimately and sexually."[12] Human sexuality, according to the organization Sexual Health, also includes how we feel about sex, what we think about sex, and how we express ourselves as sexual beings. Human sexuality includes things like sensuality, intimacy and relationships, sexual health, sexual identity, and gender identity.

No two people express their sexuality the same way. Each of our thoughts, feelings, and behaviors differ. Some people, for example, view sex as natural. Others see sex as an expression of love. Some people view sex as sinful or dirty, while others think sex is a duty, and still others consider sex a sport. Each individual is also sexually aroused by different things. Some people are aroused by breasts or feet or teeth. Some find themselves aroused by flirting or caressing and others by long passionate kisses or being spanked or watching pornographic movies. There are also people who never experience sexual arousal. Other differences in how we express our individual sexuality include our preferred sexual positions, whether or not we like to talk during sex, and what we like to say or hear during sex. Our sexual feelings, thoughts, and expressions are as individual and inexplicable as the way we dress, the music we enjoy, or the friends we are drawn to. Just as we cannot explain exactly why we might like or dislike these things, so it goes with our sexuality. "It is what is."

Sexuality is not monolithic. If we are to be honest with ourselves, we must admit that nothing about humans is monolithic. We are all different and express ourselves differently. It makes sense then that there would be more than one expression of sexual attraction, desire, feelings, and thoughts. In some respects, sexuality is like a fingerprint. We are all born with fingerprints and sexualities that are different and unique to each individual. There is no changing a fingerprint, just as there is no changing a person's sexuality. There is no wrong fingerprint, and there is no wrong sexuality.

Scientists, medical doctors, and mental health professionals believe that each of us is born with a specific sexual orientation that cannot be changed. What they do believe changes as we grow, develop, and experience the world is the way we *express* our sexuality.[13] This fits with my experience, and if you give some thought to it, you will likely find it fits with your own. Every way in which we express ourselves, including sexually, has evolved in tandem with the growth and development of our minds, bodies, and experiences, and the changing world around us.

Consider that we begin our lives with no conscious awareness of sexual orientation or other aspects of sexuality, then at some point, we become aware of who we are sexually attracted to, how we think about sex, what arouses us, etc. My thoughts, feelings, and behaviors as a ten-year-old differ dramatically from those of the twenty-two-year-old Tara, and many of those thoughts, feelings, and behaviors changed again by the time I was thirty-five, and so on. For me, the type of men I am attracted to, the way I express my attraction to men, the way I derive sexual pleasure, the way I think about sex, and the way I express myself sexually have changed over the years and continue to change now as I enter my fifties. Those are aspects of sexuality that expand and contract as we mature, experience new things, and learn more about ourselves.

How many sexualities are there?

There are differing answers to this question. Some would say "There are three basic types of sexual orientations: monosexual, polysexual, and asexual."[14] This description offers a general categorization for the types of sexualities. The most common labels for specific sexualities are: asexuality, bisexuality, heterosexuality, homosexuality, pansexuality, and queer sexuality.

Is it natural for a person's sexuality to be something other than heterosexual?

Yes. Natural describes something that exists or is formed in nature. When something is natural, it is not manufactured or engineered. Experts report that all human sexualities exist in nature and are formed in nature and are, therefore, a part of human nature. They also agree that we are born with our sexuality, no matter what that sexuality might be. Sexuality, whether hetero-, homo-, bi- or otherwise, is natural.

Some have argued that homosexuality is not natural and is therefore wrong because two people of the same sex can't produce children. The naturalness of a sexuality does not rest on procreation. Natural refers to whether something occurs naturally or is artificially produced. Sexuality is not constructed or contrived. Secondly, if procreation determined whether a sexuality was natural, then heterosexuality could also be considered unnatural because there are heterosexuals who have sex without the ability to procreate.

Furthermore, procreation has never been the sole purpose of sexual intercourse. Sex satisfies several vital physical, psychological, and emotional human needs. "Sex serves several of life's basic purposes: pleasure, stress reduction, formation of our identity, intimate connection, and procreation," according to John T. Chirban, PhD, ThD, Harvard Medical School. Of all the reasons humans have sex, procreation has the shortest shelf life, yet these other purposes for sex can be experienced from the time of puberty until death for many people. For a human woman, conception can only occur for the few days each month when that woman is fertile, and procreation is only possible for a limited number of years of a man or woman's life. On the other hand, there is no time limit on when men and women can experience the other benefits of sex. Stress reduction, identity, intimacy, and pleasure are natural and vital to our individual survival, development, and fulfillment. Even when two people can't conceive a child—because of menopause, sterility, or some other condition—it is still natural for them to need, desire, and have sex because sex satisfies important emotional, physical, and psychological human needs. Labeling a particular sexuality as unnatural because it doesn't lead to procreation is misguided, in part because procreation is not the only reason humans experience sexuality.

What causes or determines a person's sexuality?

Before answering this question, I can't help but wonder why we would ask what makes a person homosexual, bisexual, asexual, or pansexual but not what makes a person heterosexual. Perhaps it stems from the often-held belief that heterosexuality is normal and other sexualities are not normal. We are not in the habit of questioning things we perceive as normal. If homosexuality were perceived as normal, then I doubt we'd be questioning the "cause." (Similarly, we are also inclined to wonder when a person realized they are homosexual but don't ask when someone realized they are heterosexual.) As we make our way through the who, what, when, how, and why of human sexuality, let our purpose be to gain a better understanding of the human experience without judgment or condemnation.

After years of research, studies, and examination, those who study human development, biology, genetics, psychology, and human behavior have not been able to isolate one singular element that determines a person's sexual orientation or sexuality; there is no one "thing" that causes or determines anyone's sexuality.

There is agreement among experts that an unknown combination of factors influences our attraction to other people. According to the APA, extensive research has examined genetic, hormonal, developmental, social, and cultural influences on sexual orientation with no conclusion that any particular factor or set of factors determines our sexuality. Additionally, the American Academy of Pediatrics Committee on Adolescence (AAPCA) says all sexuality is determined by biological and environmental factors and involves a complex interplay between nature and nurture. [15]

Many theories about why someone is gay, bisexual, asexual, or pansexual have been proposed, explored, and found to be unsubstantiated. There have been theories about a "gay gene" and that homosexuality is the result of a genetic mutation. Despite attempts to locate and identify a "sexuality gene," genealogists have been unable to find one. The notion of genetic mutation has been debunked by geneticists. Professor Wright also offered insight on this theory:

> *To say it's a mutation is not accurate because homosexuality is part of the natural variation. If you look across species, you find examples of it all over the place.*
>
> –Professor Wright

There seems to be a prevalent belief that one act or experience can change a person's sexuality, even though this has been disavowed by experts who study sexuality. One popular misconception is that sexual abuse or molestation changes a person from being heterosexual to another sexuality. I have heard this belief espoused by people of all ages and backgrounds. One young woman in her late twenties told me the few gay people she knew said they had been sexually assaulted. She therefore believed that sexual assault, abuse, or molestation must cause homosexuality, even though none of those people said they believed the sexual assault changed their sexuality, nor did any of them say they were heterosexual before the assault. I also know of a grandmother who believes her adult granddaughter is bisexual as a result of being "messed with" during childhood, even though there is no indication of an assault.

There is no evidence to support the claim that sexual assault, abuse, or molestation change a person's sexuality. Years of research and study by medical and mental health professionals have found no evidence or indication that sexual assault, abuse, or molestation will "turn" a person from straight to gay, or any other sexuality. What they have found is that these experiences can affect *aspects* of our sexuality and personality, including self-worth, ability to trust, intimacy, desire for sexual intercourse, and views about sex. Despite the substantial influence of sexual assault, abuse, or molestation, these acts do not make a straight person gay, a gay person straight, etc.

If sexual assault caused homosexuality, for instance, might it not follow that everyone who has been sexually assaulted would be gay? You likely know someone who is a heterosexual and a victim of sexual assault. If sexual assault causes homosexuality, then why isn't that person gay? Why didn't their sexuality change? Sexual assault can lead to a number of responses from the assaulted individual, however changing their sexuality is not one of them because, as experts have stated, nothing changes a person's sexuality.

Let's also look at the numbers. Since 1998, at least 17.7 million American women have been the victims of attempted or completed rape.[5] If we follow the notion that rape causes homosexuality, and that all these women were heterosexual, then there should be at least 17.7 million gay women in America. The number of gay women in the United States is estimated to range from six to ten million. Then there's the reality that not all lesbians are survivors of sexual assault. According to the Centers for Disease Control (CDC), 13 percent of lesbians report having been raped. Among the gay and lesbian women with whom I spoke, only one person reported that she had been raped, while the others were adamant they had never been assaulted in any way. If these women have never been sexually violated, then how did they get to be homosexual? They were born that way.

Another suggested "cause" of homosexuality is that if a child has a sexual encounter with a person of the same sex, even with another child, that act will "turn" them gay. Medical and mental health professionals have not found any evidence to support this notion. If it were true, then there would likely be a larger population of homosexuals because in many instances, a child's first sexual encounter is with another child of the same sex. That's not necessarily a harbinger of sexuality but is more likely a result of proximity and overall sexual curiosity. It is more likely that little boys will befriend and play with other little boys, and girls will do the same with girls. When sexual curiosity emerges in children, the first avenue of exploration is often with their playmates. A heterosexual woman I know recalled having such an experience when she was around middle-school age.

> When I was about ten or eleven years old, one of my female friends and I [were] pretending one of us was the husband and the other was the wife on our wedding nights. We had no idea what we were doing, but we were curious about sex and knew that it was supposed to happen on our wedding night. That was my first sexual encounter, and it was with a girl. It wasn't about either of us being attracted to each other. We were heterosexual then, and we are heterosexual now.
>
> –Yvette, writer, single, heterosexual, cisgender, 49 years old

Fredis agreed that this type of roleplaying is common for boys and girls and does not influence a person's sexuality.

> If you think of experimentation when it comes to sexuality, then we all experiment with our same sex first. Why? Because when you're a little girl, your momma will leave you to do whatever you want with the little girls. When you're a little boy, same thing. When you're young, you experiment.
>
> –Fredis

There are also people who believe a positive sexual experience with someone of the opposite sex can change a person from homosexual to heterosexual. I hear this most often from men who say something like, "All he needs is one night with the right woman," or something like, "One night with me, and I'll make a real woman out of her." The premise here is that a person is homosexual because they haven't had "great sex" with a person of the opposite sex, and that once they have wonderful heterosexual sex, they will forever be straight.

Perhaps one of the reasons some heterosexual people really believe this is because for them, heterosexual sex is delicious. They cannot imagine how anyone could not enjoy it or would want any other kind of sexual experience. Perhaps they should consider that homosexual sex is just as delightful for homosexuals as heterosexual sex is for heterosexuals. Some homosexuals who've had opposite-sex sexual experiences say they were unfulfilling—lacking sexual desire, pleasure, and/or orgasm. Others say the experience was downright unpleasant and might leave the person physically ill or feeling under duress.

Another point is that for a gay or lesbian person—who is not sexually attracted to or aroused by the opposite sex—the prospect of having sex with a person of the opposite sex would not be appealing or enjoyable. It is difficult to place ourselves in the other person's shoes or sexuality, but that should not be cause to dismiss their sexuality.

> I can still look at a man and think he's good looking. I can clearly see whoever the latest heartthrob is and think, 'Oh, he's beautiful.' Do I desire one? No. Do I want him? No.
>
> –Tiffany, realtor, married, cisgender, lesbian, 45 years old

Some might wonder how some homosexuals could have had relationships with or marry someone of the opposite sex if they are truly gay. Doesn't that mean they *are* attracted to the opposite sex? No. It could mean they tried to do what society and their parents expected. It could mean they were in denial about their sexuality. It could also mean they didn't realize they were attracted to the same sex until later.

Many homosexuals who've had same-sex and opposite-sex experiences report that it wasn't until they had same-sex relations that they realized how wonderful sex could be.

> I had several relationships with guys in high school, but it was never very fulfilling. When I was with guys, or in a physical relationship with guys, I always felt guilty, dirty; like this doesn't

feel right. This doesn't feel like I should be in this place. My first experience with a woman was when I was in college. I didn't have those negative feelings, and that was kind of the lightbulb moment, "Oh, it doesn't have to be a bad situation." You can feel connected to somebody, and it feels good.

–Karla, Lieutenant, metropolitan police department, married, cisgender, lesbian, 39 years old

This leads me to another one of the circumstances that has been said to change a person's sexuality: "bad relationships." You may have heard people say things like, "I think she turned lesbian because she had a bad relationship with the last guy she dated." Think about how rarely you've met someone who has never had a bad relationship. Heterosexual women, including me, have been experiencing bad relationships with men for thousands of years. If bad relationships made straight people gay, then there probably wouldn't be any straight people. Commissioner Garner agreed:

If that was the case, then 99.9 percent of us would be lesbians. I never really had negative experiences with men. I think we are born the way we are born.

–Commissioner Garner

Commissioner Garner reported trying to follow the expected path of dating and even marrying the opposite sex. She realized something was missing or not quite right, but it took years to put her finger on it.

I was thirty-two when I realized I am lesbian. I had been married to a man for five years. After my husband and I divorced, I continued to date men, but I was never really happy or satisfied in the relationships. When I was exposed to lesbian women and started hanging out with them, I realized there was just this affinity there that I felt was comfort. Once I started dating women, it felt right. That thing that had been missing with men was no longer missing.

–Commissioner Garner

Some anti-gay folks have insisted that gay parents turn heterosexual children gay. Again, research does not support this; a person's sexuality cannot be changed. Similarly, there are those who believe that homosexuality is somehow "contagious" and that just being around a gay person will "turn" a child gay. If homosexuality is contagious, then wouldn't it follow that heterosexuality is also contagious? If one day Little Johnny, whose parents are straight, visits Little Jane, whose parents are gay, then Little Johnny would presumably "catch" their homosexuality. If this were true, then wouldn't Little Johnny "catch" heterosexuality when he returned home to his straight parents and be reinoculated the next day at school when he interacts with his straight friends and straight teachers? The reason this does not happen is because sexuality is not contagious.

Is sexuality a choice?

No. There is a consensus among scientists and health care professionals, like those of the APA, that sexuality is not a choice. They insist that sexuality is a human feature that each of us is born with and is the result of a complex interaction of biological, environmental, and cognitive factors.

Not only do we not choose which sex we are attracted to, we can't even choose the type of person that draws our attraction. Did you choose to be attracted to tall men or curvaceous women or is that just the way it is?

> It's who I am. It's not a choice. I don't believe it's a choice for anyone. This is a tough life, and I don't know that anybody would willingly accept the hardships that come with being LGBT. People who say it's a choice are off base.
>
> –Alex Wan, Atlanta City Councilmember, married, cisgender, gay, 50 years old

Saying that you don't act on your attractions is not the same as claiming that you don't feel the attraction. We all have the opportunity not to act on our attractions, but that does not negate the attraction. It simply means we are denying ourselves the opportunity to act on our attraction. An ordained Unitarian Universalist minister I spoke with reiterated that our sexuality is not a choice. He also made the distinction that what we *do* about our sexuality is a choice.

There was a moment, and this is what I think is confusing for folks, when I made a choice; it wasn't a choice about my sexual orientation; it was a choice about whether I would deny my sexuality or embrace it.

–Reverend Duncan E. Teague, Founder, Abundant
Love Unitarian Universalists Congregation of Atlanta,
cisgender, gay, 54 years old

Fredis also addressed the notion of choice and the dangers of trying to ignore or deny one's sexuality.

You can have a choice in terms of what you can have for breakfast, but in terms of sexuality, you can't. If you try to go against what you feel deep inside, it's just going to lead to depression and more problems like suicide because you don't accept yourself.

–Fredis

If you didn't choose whom you're attracted to, then why presume anyone else can choose?

What does it mean when people say that sexuality exists on a spectrum?

Spectrum refers to a range of different positions between two extreme points. One definition of "spectrum" is "a broad range of varied but related ideas or objects; the individual features of which tend to overlap so as to form a continuous series or sequence."[16] It might be helpful to think about things we once thought of as binary—only having two options—before being exposed to multiple options.

For example, at birth, we only see the world in black, white, and shades of gray, even though many other colors exist. As our eyes and brains develop and mature, we begin to see a spectrum of colors, including red, orange, yellow, blue, indigo, and violet. There was also a time when we thought there was only right or wrong, and then we discovered there can also be a myriad of "extenuating circumstances."

Another example is the light switch. There was a time when we only had the binary options of on or off, either light or dark. Then the dimmer switch came along, allowing us to experience varying degrees of light. Just because there was a time when we weren't aware of the color spectrum or the light doesn't mean they didn't exist. It simply means we weren't aware of them. The same is true for the sexuality spectrum; it has always existed, even if it is just coming to your attention now.

When many people talk about sexuality existing on a spectrum, they mean that there is a broad range of sexualities expressed by humans, rather than just one or two, and that those sexualities overlap. The sexuality spectrum, as we know it today, ranges from having no sexual attraction to having the capacity to be attracted to all sexes, genders, sexualities, and gender identities. There also may be other sexualities on the spectrum that haven't yet been named. Those inclined to dismiss this notion of a sexuality spectrum might consider what scientist Bill Nye says: "We have to listen to the science, and the science says we're all on a spectrum."[17] As Nye observes, looking at sexuality this way is more complicated, but, "It's also a lot more honest."

Has humanity always expressed more than one sexuality?

We don't know. We may never know. Anthropologists, scientists, biologists, and historians have reason to believe same-sex attraction has likely existed since humans' first days on earth. To date, no definitive evidence has been found to prove or disprove this supposition. This absence of proof, however, is not proof of absence.

One of the most obvious reasons for the absence of early evidence is that homosexuality doesn't leave the same kind of "proof" as heterosexuality. Reproduction, for instance, offers proof that heterosexual behavior has always existed because heterosexual sex produces babies. If heterosexuals didn't produce offspring, then we'd have to look for other forms of proof, such as written or pictorial documentation, e.g. love letters, laws, legal documents, and art. Those are examples of the types of things that historians and archaeologists look for as evidence of early homosexual sex and relationships. But those things did not exist until humans began to draw, write, establish governments, and create laws—ages after modern man first walked the planet.

Another reason for this absence of "proof" could be that all sexualities were accepted as natural aspects of human behavior, and so no special effort was made to make note of them or to distinguish one group from another. On the other hand, there is also the possibility that at some early stage, any human who wasn't heterosexual realized a need to keep their sexuality hidden, which would also result in a lack of documentation.

One reason experts believe it's very likely other sexualities existed in early humans is the existence of other sexualities in other species. Homosexual and bisexual behavior, including sex, courtship, and long-term relationships, is well-documented throughout the animal kingdom—in fish, birds, reptiles, and mammals, including apes. The existence of homosexuality throughout the natural world, including in the animals that most resemble humans, provides experts with reason to believe homosexuality, bisexuality, etc., existed three million years ago in our early human predecessors and in modern man, who began roaming Earth 200,000 years ago. In other words, a spectrum of human sexualities has likely always been a natural part of human life.

Are any of the sexualities considered a mental illness?

No. According to the American Psychiatric Association, the American Psychological Association, and the World Health Organization (WHO), sexuality is not a mental illness or disorder. It doesn't matter if the sexuality is hetero-, homo-, bi-, pan- or a-; none of them are considered a mental disorder.

A mental disorder is a condition of the mind characterized by disturbances of thought, emotion, and behavior that negatively affect an individual's ability to care for themselves, relate to other people, or have intimate relationships. Examples of mental disorders are schizophrenia or depression. Sexuality does not reflect this definition. In fact, sexuality can have the opposite influence. Unlike mental disorders, sexuality can encourage us to take better care of ourselves, improve our relations with others, and enable intimate relationships.

Unfortunately, there was a time when homosexuality was treated as a mental illness.

It was not okay to be gay in those years. It was against the law.
It was considered a psychiatric disease, so I had therapy in college

> to "cure" myself. In the 60s, it was just the thing to do, to go "fix" yourself. I didn't have any of that conversion therapy that they talk about today. It was psychoanalysis. It was talk, and the therapist would listen. I went for at least six years, and the entire time, I was looking for and dating women. The gay people I knew at the time all went to be "cured." Some of those people are very active in the LGBT world today.

–Marilyn, retired chief of audiology and speech pathology, single, cisgender, lesbian, 75 years old

It's hard to imagine that this intelligent, passionate, and fierce woman who earned a doctoral degree and retired as Chief of Audiology and Speech Pathology at a major US veterans' hospital would be considered mentally ill because of her sexuality. That is what happened for Marilyn and many others, particularly after 1952 when the American Psychiatric Association published the first version of *Diagnostic and Statistical Manual of Mental Disorders* (DSM), which listed homosexuality as a mental disorder. Twenty years later, the realization that homosexuality did not meet the criteria for a mental disorder led the American Psychiatric Association to remove homosexuality from the DSM with the explanation that "homosexuality per se implies no impairment in judgment, stability, reliability, or general social or vocational capabilities."[18]

Can a person's sexuality be cured or changed?

No. Sexuality is not a mental disorder, illness, or disease and, therefore, does not need to be cured or changed.

Suggesting that a cure is needed for any sexuality presumes there is something wrong with it rather than accepting it as a natural expression of our humanity. "There is no medical illness or mental defect condition associated with being LGBT. We know that being gay or lesbian does not need a cure,"[19] said Hudson County Superior Court Judge Peter Bariso Jr. in a ruling that a New Jersey conversion "therapy" practice, Jews Offering New Alternatives for Healing (JONAH), was fraudulent.

The APA and the American Medical Association (AMA) maintain that our sexuality cannot be changed and reject using so-called "conversion therapy" to attempt to alter a person's sexuality. They are adamant that these therapies do not change a person's sexuality, and go further, warning that these types of therapies can cause substantial emotional and psychological harm, such as depression, anxiety, and self-destructive behaviors, including suicide.

State and federal laws have been drafted to outlaw conversion therapy. The Therapeutic Fraud Prevention Act introduced in 2015, and its companion bill introduced in April 2016, seek to ban all advertising that claims a "therapy" can successfully change a person's sexuality or gender identity. The proposed laws would classify conversion therapy as a fraudulent practice that would be illegal under the Federal Trade Commission Act.

Proposing that a person change their sexuality to make you feel comfortable is not in their best interests. Asking someone to be the sexuality *you* want them to be disregards their humanity and personal freedom. Subjecting a human being to conversion therapy to force them to change something that is innate and cannot actually be changed sounds like a form of mental and emotional torture. And as has been proven, torture is an inherently flawed tool in that at some point, victims will comply with any demand to end, or even pause, the torture regardless of their personal truth. Similarly, the children and adults subjected to conversion therapy often say or do whatever they are instructed to do to end the horrible situation. They may even convince themselves that what they are saying is true. The kicker is that saying they are no longer homosexual or transgender does not stop people from being who they are. It simply means they have chosen to pretend to be someone else, to deny who they are.

> *I don't buy it. I believe it can help you think you're cured, but I think you are what you are.*
> –Tiffany

A person who accepts their sexuality would not try to change it. Likewise, a person who voluntarily undergoes conversion therapy has not yet accepted who they are.

When do people realize which sexuality they are?

The moment of realization varies for everyone. Many people discover which sexuality they are somewhere around puberty, but realization can come earlier or much later. Medical and mental health experts report that people may become aware of their sexuality at any point in childhood, adolescence, or adulthood. A Pew Research Center survey reported that the average age for a man to first think of himself as gay was ten years old, and lesbians are most likely to self-identify for the first time around the age of thirteen. For bisexuals, the median age to first self-identify was thirteen. The average age when bisexuals were sure about their sexuality was seventeen. For lesbians, it was twenty, and for gay males, it was fifteen.[20] The survey did not include asexual or pansexual respondents.

Realization and acceptance can come later in life for some people because there wasn't a readily available label to match their experiences. That has been the case for many asexuals and pansexuals. Some people who are pansexual say they recognized their attraction to people but didn't know what to call it because they had never heard the word pansexual. Some asexual people may have recognized during adolescence that they were not experiencing the type of sexual attraction they heard their peers discussing or saw in the movies, but they didn't immediately think of themselves as asexual because the term "asexual" was not on their radar. Some people don't discover that there's a name for asexuality until they stumble across an article or talk to someone like a counselor or medical professional. In a post on asexuality.org, one person writes, "I never had the desire to kiss or do anything physical. It occurred to me that I was different, but I didn't have a name for it quite yet." When asked why they didn't date, the anonymous author said, "I tried to explain how I didn't experience any sexual attraction. He then suggested I may be asexual. That was it!"

Realization of sexuality may also come later for asexuals because they might be led to think they are "late bloomers" or that they just haven't met the right person yet. Julie Sondra Decker, author of "The Invisible Orientation: An Introduction to Asexuality" says when she didn't enjoy kissing her first boyfriend, she was told it was because she was too young. "I could barely think of an experience I'd enjoyed less. But whenever I told people I thought so, they'd say, 'You're fourteen. One day you'll like it.'" But she didn't. Two years later, with her second boyfriend, Decker still wasn't interested in sex. "At age sixteen, I left my second boyfriend perplexed and frustrated. I liked him as a person, but I wasn't interested in him the way he wanted me to be: definitely not sexually, and not even romantically."[21] Decker says her lack of interest wasn't because she was afraid of sex or getting pregnant or that she thought it was immoral. "I simply had a complete lack of interest in sex and anything related… I'd just never been sexually attracted to another person. Not my boyfriend, not the hottest people in school, not the heartthrob movie stars. I wasn't interested. Period." That has never changed, and Decker says she has made peace with it.

The age of realization and acceptance varied among the people I spoke with. Perry, for instance, recalled that some form of realization likely began by the time he was in first grade.

> *I think there's a realization and then there's a process by which you come to accept it. The first signs were there right at twelve to thirteen with some dreams that were kind of out of nowhere. That was probably the first time I was like, 'What?' It made me, even then, look back [and] realize I was never like most of my friends. There was even some realization when I was five or six that I was a little bit different.*
>
> –Perry, realtor, single, cisgender, gay, 32 years old

Others reported being aware of and understanding of their sexuality at a young age.

> *I remember being five and liking boys. I think you know when you're gay. I think you grow up faster. You're more aware of things quicker than your straight peers.*
>
> –Fredis

> *It was quite young. I made a pass at a male babysitter when I was probably eight or nine. We were playing Cowboys and Indians, and I was trying to take his clothes off.*
>
> –Professor Wright

Everyone has different experiences. Karla, who grew up in Indiana, attended Catholic schools, and later became a law enforcement officer, didn't initially equate the realization she was attracted to women with the understanding that she was gay.

I got into a relationship with a woman, and when that relationship fell apart, I realized that I'd opened a door that I needed to look through, and I did. I discovered that door worked for me. That side of the fence worked, and I remained there. There was a comfort level there that I'd never felt with a man. It was more than just the familiarity of feminine kinship. For me, it really felt like a key in a lock.

–Tiffany

In a society that claims everyone should only be attracted to the opposite sex, it shouldn't be surprising that being attracted to the same sex or both sexes can be confusing and frightening. Dr. Regina U. Reinhardt, who identifies as bisexual, says, "In childhood, I erotically fantasized about and experimented with both boys and girls. My puberty was entirely void of feelings for girls, and these same-sex feelings did not return until my late teens, at which time they brought to me the recognition of my own bisexuality."[22] For most people, it takes time to wade through this reality, sort things out, and determine what their truth is. Some men and women only become aware when they meet a particular person or when a certain situation arises that leads to the awareness that they are attracted to both sexes. That was the case with several people I spoke to.

I'm in a relationship with a woman for the first time. I've been married to a man and have two kids. I just met someone I liked and was attracted to. We fell in love. It just happens to be a woman, this time.

–Nancy, esthetician, divorced and in a relationship, cisgender, bisexual, 35 years old

Another woman I talked with shared a different story. Vicki met her husband in high school and admitted to having designs on him from the beginning. She initiated their dating and engagement. The two had been married for twenty-five years when she met and fell in love with a woman.

I've always been pretty open, sexually, but I didn't enjoy being in relationships with women that much. And I didn't think

41

I'd ever be in a long-term relationship with a woman. There was no spark with the other women I was with. It was just purely physical. Then I met Sharon. I really felt like I could not visualize myself with any other person, man or woman.

–Vicki, office manager, divorced and engaged, cisgender, bisexual, 59 years old

I also spoke with a woman who was well into adulthood upon realizing and accepting that she was sexually attracted to men and women but romantically only attracted to women.

When I finally realized that I was sexually bi and wanted my main relationship to be with a woman, I was just so excited about the whole thing; how good I felt with Val and how much I loved the fact that she was as wild about me. It was just incredible. It really is. And I'm not saying that it's perfect, we fuss and argue like everybody, but we always come back, and we also know that there's no danger.

–Sheila, entrepreneur, engaged, cisgender, sexually bisexual, romantically lesbian, 59 years old

Does a person's sexuality impact their desire to have children?

I was unable to locate any studies that examined this question. What is available are studies that measure the number of LGBT adults who are parents and those who want to adopt a child. For instance, an estimated three million LGBT adults have had a child, according to the Williams Institute.[23] According to the American Civil Liberties Union (ACLU), "researchers estimate the total number of children nationwide living with at least one gay parent ranges from 6 to 14 million."[24]

It seems that most adults, regardless of sexuality, have a desire to become parents. Many people want to have children so they can love, nurture, and care for another being or because they want to create an extension of themselves. This desire to have children is not negated by a person's sexuality, biological sex, or gender identity.

Anne and I spoke a few months after her wife gave birth to their first child. The thoughts and feelings she shared about wanting to have children resembled the reasons I've heard other parents offer.

> *I knew that I wanted kids, although I didn't know exactly how that would work. I wanted kids for many reasons, but one reason is how amazing it is to teach someone about the world, but then at the same time, they are teaching you with their questions and the way they are putting things together. I just think it is one of the most amazing experiences to watch the development of a human being and be so intimate in that process. There is something about the circle of life, getting to experience what my parents experienced, now that I have a baby. Getting to watch my mom give my baby a bath and know that is exactly how she bathed me. That is just really moving and powerful. Also, the way I am just going to drive my kid crazy. In twelve years, he is just going to think I am so annoying. What is more amazing than helping to shape a new human being, to be a decent man or woman? Whoever he or she is is going to be very lucky, because we are going to love them no matter what.*

–Anne

Does a person's sexuality make them unfit for parenthood?

No evidence exists to indicate that someone is unfit to parent simply because of sexuality, biological sex, or gender identity. There is also no scientific support for fears about children of lesbian or gay parents being sexually abused by their parents or their parents' gay, lesbian, or bisexual friends or acquaintances. Additionally, there is also no evidence to support the misconception that a parent's sexuality, biological sex, or gender identity harms children in any way. In fact, according to the ACLU, reputable research has found that "Good parenting is not influenced by sexual orientation. Rather, it is influenced most profoundly by a parent's ability to create a loving and nurturing home—an ability that does not depend on whether a parent is gay or straight."[25] Good parents love their children, make sacrifices for them, and nurse them when sick. Good parents do homework with their children, cook for them, and encourage them, etc. Good parents come in all ages, races, religions, cultures, biological sexes, sexualities, and gender identities.

Additionally, the ACLU reported that research has found that "There is no evidence to suggest that lesbians and gay men are unfit to be parents," and that "The children of lesbian and gay parents grow up as happy, healthy, and well-adjusted as the children of heterosexual parents." The Academy of Pediatrics reported "the conclusion drawn from these studies was that children raised by gay and lesbian parents did not systematically differ from other children in emotional/behavioral functioning, sexual orientation, experiences of stigmatization, gender role behavior, or cognitive functioning."[26] Children of gay and lesbian parents enjoy a social life that is typical of their age group in terms of involvement with peers, parents, family members, and friends.

Sexual Intercourse

Since we're discussing sexuality, we should also discuss sexual intercourse. For many of us, sex is a very important part of our lives. Sex provides a way for us to connect with others, express our feelings, relieve stress, experience pleasure, and procreate. Yet it's an aspect of life that can present individuals with many conflicting messages and feelings. For example, sex may be perceived as desirable or dirty, pleasurable or painful. On one hand, we are told sex is natural, and on the other sinful. We've been taught to think it's okay for men to be promiscuous but not women. These conflicting ideas impact how we approach our own sex lives and those of others.

> *There's the conflict of Puritanism versus overt sexual behavior. We can't talk about it, but we like it. And so, it creates this inherent contradiction.*
>
> –Professor Wright

This inherent contradiction, as Professor Wright puts it, impacts the way we understand and experience sex, personally and socially. Thousands of years spent refusing to talk about sex has also made us more likely to fear sex and sexuality. Our conflicted feelings, beliefs, and perceptions about sex may also make us reluctant to talk openly and honestly about it or to learn more about sex and sexuality. Perhaps we could gain a better understanding and acceptance of sex, and sexuality, if we engaged in honest and thoughtful discussions about these topics.

When it comes to having serious discussions about sex, many people avoid it. We're afraid to say what we like or dislike and afraid to ask questions about what's happening or not happening. Not talking about sex strengthens the taboo of sex, which is passed from generation to generation. If adults won't talk to each other about sex, it's a good bet they won't talk to their kids about it either. This lack of communication helps to perpetuate the conflict, contradictions, and a general lack of knowledge. Instead of providing children with facts about sex, parents tend to create fairytales like the ones about the stork or the cabbage patch, or avoid the subject completely. My father's advice during my teen years was, "Don't get in trouble." When I asked what that meant, he said, "You know what I mean." Parents tend not to talk about intimacy, emotion, erogenous zones, foreplay, or sexual positions. This lack of discussion is echoed in many homes.

> *We never talked about sex things in my family, ever. I didn't want to know about sex with them, and they didn't want to know about sex with me and my sexual things, so we never addressed it.*
>
> –Sheila

The conversations we're most likely to engage in keep us in the dark rather than bring us closer to enlightenment. Some people like to brag about sexual conquests, real or imagined; others readily talk about their sex companion's physical endowments or complain about their shortcomings. Our most robust sex discussions often occur when gossiping or conjecturing about someone else's sex life. We are not shy about speculating on who's doing whom and providing our opinion on it. This fascination with what other people do sexually is often heightened when it comes to heterosexuals speculating about homosexual, bisexual, asexual, and pansexual activity. It's as if we forget that all humans have the same body parts—arms, legs, fingers, toes, tongues, lips, and genitalia—and can and do participate in some of the same sexual activities, including oral and anal sex.

Do we have to follow the rules about sex?

Many societies, religions, and parents are willing and very eager to pass down a certain set of rules regarding sex. There are rules about when to have sex, who should have sex, how old you should be when you have sex, how old you should be when you stop having sex, where sex should occur, which body parts should be used, how you should feel about yourself after having sex, and what to think about other people who have sex. And I also heard of other rules growing up: Self-pleasuring was wrong; sex toys were perverted; oral sex was dirty, anal sex was forbidden. My parents, like many others, cited the rule that "good girls" don't have sex until marriage but said nothing about what "good boys" could do. One of the most common rules is that sexual intercourse should only occur between one man and one woman.

I've noticed that somewhere along the way, an increasing number of people have decided to bend, break, or ignore these societal and religious rules themselves, while in many cases still applying them to others. Many people, even those who preach "no sex until marriage," have engaged in premarital sex. The Catholic Church taught that sex outside of marriage and sex with young children are sins; all the while, some Catholic priests were raping young boys. There are those who believe that under no circumstances should two men have sex together, yet some of those same people accept sex between two women, especially if it's done for the pleasure and entertainment of a man. Some people consider oral sex and anal sex acceptable between heterosexuals but unacceptable between homosexuals. This hypocritical approach to rules about sex suggests that many in heterosexual society want the freedom to bend the rules to fit their libidos but refuse to allow anyone else to do the same.

I understand an individual's need to create rules to define their own sex lives; what baffles me is why we feel justified forcing our rules on other people. We would never want someone else to do that to us. It's as if we expect the personal freedom to define our own personas, morals, and lifestyles, and we expect other people to share our definitions. That is unreasonable and unfair. It is not my place to make you adhere to my personal rules or share my values and goals. For instance, I exercise six days a week because I like the way it feels, and it helps me stay a size six, which also feels good to me. It wouldn't make sense for me to demand that you follow my routine. Wanting to dictate our rules to other people is more about *us* than it is about *them*; that is, it's about our ego and self-importance. Insisting that someone else follow our personal rules is akin to saying, "Who I am, what I want, and what I believe are more important than who you are, what you want, and what you believe." It's another way of saying, "I am better than you."

None of us has the right to demand that another person adhere to our feelings, beliefs, rules, and practices about sex. The need to enforce personal rules on others directly contradicts the ideas of individuality and personal freedom that characterize modern society. Being your authentic self and expressing who you are is a personal freedom that every human being should be allowed to have.

Why are we so deeply concerned about whom other people have sexual intercourse and relationships with?

Part of the reason we're even having this discussion is that many people claim to be concerned about other adults' sexual, emotional, and romantic relationships, to the point that they try to control what others do and punish people who don't comply with their rules. What is at the root of this need to get involved in other people's lives in such a restrictive and punitive fashion? Is it superiority, insecurity, jealousy, fear, ignorance, or something else? As a medical sociologist with specific interests in sexual health and public health, Professor Wright was able to shed some light.

> *The sex research community generally agrees that part of the problem is our culture is based on labeling impure values. It's a human drive. I also think our interest in other people's sexuality is partly because we haven't really reflected on our own sexualities. We're constantly looking at other people wondering, "Am I normal? Is this normal?"*
>
> –Professor Wright

This need to label impure values that Professor Wright mentioned can be seen as the need to judge another person. It's assessing their behavior and categorizing it to determine if the behavior, the values represented, and the person are impure and therefore bad. If I can point a finger at you and say you are bad and therefore wrong, then there's usually a good chance I am also tacitly saying, "I don't do the bad things you do; therefore, I am good, and what I do is correct." It's a false way of validating and elevating ourselves based on uncorrelated comparison. To prove our "goodness," we must identify someone else's behavior as bad. To do that, we establish a code of conduct, which is usually based on things we have never done, or no longer do, and other concepts drawn from our existing behaviors and belief system. It's easier to label a behavior as bad if I'm not likely to ever participate in that behavior or if I have "overcome" that behavior. It's also easier to assign myself a higher status because I don't participate in that behavior I have deemed as bad. And that might make me feel better about myself. This superiority might also convince me that I have the right and the duty to stop others from engaging in that bad behavior. And if I really want to make myself feel superior, I can go on a crusade to stop others from engaging in what I deem as bad behavior.

Another reason Professor Wright mentioned is that we don't reflect on our own sexualities. This is an extension of our reluctance to have meaningful dialogues about sex. It stands to reason that if we aren't willing to have a forthright discussion about sex, then we won't have one about sexuality either. Many people have never taken the time to learn about human sexuality in general, let alone to explore their own sexuality specifically or the sexuality of others. Rather than seeking a better understanding of our own sexualities, we often find it easier to divert our attention to other people's sexualities. Instead of doing the heavy lifting of learning about the spectrum of sexuality, many people find it easier to condemn anyone who differs from them. For instance, it's all too common for people who know very little about bisexuality to make blanket statements that bisexuality is wrong or that bisexuals are just promiscuous.

Jealousy offers another motivation for people to want to control or restrict other people's sexual lives. I'm not suggesting that one person is jealous of another's sexuality; rather, a person may be jealous of someone who dares to be themselves. Some people are afraid to be themselves, especially if it means going against societal norms and expectations. Going against societal norms and expectations is exactly what it takes for LGBTQIAP individuals to be their authentic selves. This can be unsettling for those who never dared to express their true selves or to follow their dreams, not just in sex and relationships, but in any aspect of their life, from their profession or faith to the clothes they wear. For some of those people, it is unsettling to witness a person who dares to be different, because it is a reminder that they chose to acquiesce. This reminder may push a person toward the uncomfortable realization that they regret not listening to their true selves and therefore not going against societal expectations. That regret can evoke jealousy of people who possessed the courage to break with convention in some aspect of their lives, such as refusing to adhere to the false notion that there is only one sexuality.

Coupled with that jealousy may be the feeling of guilt for denying or tamping down their true nature or desires. This is not a far-fetched notion. Many of us have, at times, felt some degree of jealousy for people who are freethinkers or behave boldly and are enjoying their lives because of it. Sometimes the other person's boldness is a reminder of our own weakness or failing, which leaves us feeling bad about ourselves. When that happens, our ego's job is to protect us. The response is to reverse those feelings and project them onto others in an attempt to feel better about ourselves. Before we know it, and many times without knowing it, those bad feelings have been projected onto the other person. When someone's accomplishments make us feel bad about our lack of accomplishments, initiative, etc., we might view that person with contempt. Instead of wishing them well, we might wish them harm, or at least try to curtail their behavior. We might think, "If I had to follow the rules, they should too." We may try to convince ourselves that what they've done is bad or that they are bad people for not following society's rules. Some people may even go a step further and say, "They must pay a price for going against the grain. They must be punished." This can also be the reaction to people who openly express a sexuality that isn't heterosexual.

> *It also bothers them that a gay person has the balls to live their own life, regardless of the repercussions that one may suffer, and they don't have the balls to live life how they want to live. So, therefore, it's like an anger they have inside; they're mad at themselves.*

–Fredis

This thought pattern can manifest as prejudice. People use prejudice to justify saying horrendous things and committing despicable acts against anyone they perceive as different. All prejudices have three principal features: 1) Prejudice is an evaluation or judgment, 2) It is directed at a social group and its members, and 3) It is negative, involving hostility or dislike. Sexual prejudice is based on the notion that one person is good and correct and better than someone whose sexuality differs from theirs.

Sexual prejudice, according to Gregory M. Herek, PhD, "refers to all negative attitudes based on sexual orientation, whether the target is homosexual, bisexual, or heterosexual. Given the current social organization of sexuality, however, such prejudice is almost always directed at people who engage in homosexual behavior or label themselves gay, lesbian, or bisexual."[27] Sexual and other prejudices can be rooted in feelings of inadequacy, which people may project outward onto others to avoid addressing within themselves. When someone else's behavior disturbs or irritates us, it is usually more about our own thoughts and feelings than it is about the other person. A person who is at peace with themselves, their sexuality, their relationships, their financial status, etc. is not likely to intrude on or attempt to regulate those aspects of another person's life.

> *When something impacts you that hard, you need to take a look at why. Why does that make you so angry, or why does that repulse you? Or why is it okay for you to decide how everybody's supposed to be? I think it's about honesty and being honest with yourself and being able to look at yourself.*
> –Sheila

Perhaps if we spent more time looking at and learning about ourselves, we would be better equipped to appreciate others.

> *If we would invest in ourselves to appreciate ourselves more, then I think we could appreciate others more. But we first have to appreciate ourselves. I think that leads to a lot of the ignorance that is displayed among all genders and all sexes because we don't appreciate ourselves. We don't even know who we are. We're insecure and not comfortable in our skin. So how are you going to be comfortable with someone else? You're just going to*

pass judgment on that person, instead of looking at yourself, and looking within, and saying, "Who am I? Why am I so critical of this person? Why? Why is this person bothering me [enough] that I have to talk about this person that I don't even know?"

–Demetrius

Wouldn't we be better off turning our gazes to ourselves and focusing on our own thoughts and behaviors? After all, at the end of the day, the only person one can truly change is oneself. And the only person one has a right and a duty to change is oneself. The only actions we can truly control are our own. Therefore, if it disturbs you seeing two men or two women kissing, for example, then do what is within your power—close your eyes or look away. Focus on controlling your body and your actions instead of trying to control someone else. Everyone has as much of a right to be themselves as you, me, and the next person.

How much better would the world be if we followed the advice of actress Ellen Pompeo who said, "Check yourself before you check somebody else?"[28] If we invest in ourselves and spend our time trying to understand ourselves and take responsibility for our own actions and lives, there would be little, if any, time to try to exert control over other people's identities and lives.

Love

"Tis a human thing, love."[29]

Anyone trying to wrap their heads and hearts around the varieties of human sexuality and gender identity will benefit from examining the importance of love. Love is, as psychologist William Meeks, PhD, says, "one of the most central components to human life."[30] Love is intrinsically tied to this discussion for several reasons. Love of self, familial love, love for friends, romantic love, and love for humankind are inextricably connected to this exploration of sexuality and gender identity.

Self-love emboldens us, providing the inner strength and determination to be who we are, even when the world insists we be something else. In Shakespeare's *Hamlet*, Polonius advised, "This above all: to thine own self be true."[31] This truth is the love that inspires a person to come out as gay, transgender, bisexual, etc. despite the social risks. Remembering that self-love means being true to ourselves and wanting to be our self-defined best selves, even when others disagree or disapprove, can prevent us from insisting that LGBTQIAP individuals deny who they are.

Familial love is the love many of us benefit from simply by being born with a parent or parents, maybe even grandparents, who love us from the moment of conception. If we are fortunate, our family loves us for who we are. Focusing on the importance of familial love can help us love family members who identify as LGBTQIAP.

There is also the love that exists between couples, which can include romantic love and committed love. Evolutionary psychologists and biologists report that the early stage of romantic love is ingrained in us and stems from an internal biological drive to pursue mates. Meeks explains romantic love as "the stage where people generally describe being 'in love' or 'falling in love,' the stage of 'courting' or being in a state of 'fusion.'" When we are in romantic love, our sympathetic nervous system causes our heart to pound. It produces that feeling of butterflies in the stomach and can even make some people sweat. Psychologists and anthropologists also say that romantic love can be expressed in innumerable ways, including "emotional dependence, elevated sexual desire, sexual possessiveness, obsessive thinking about the person of our desire, craving for emotional union with this preferred individual."[32] When we are in romantic love, we experience an intense motivation to obtain and retain that person as a love/life partner or spouse.

Because romantic love comes from an internal drive, romantic love is *not* an intellectual decision. We do not choose the person for whom we will have romantic feelings. Yes, we can have thoughts about the prospect of romantic love, and even tell ourselves what we want that person to look like or be like, but those thoughts may be very different from the actual experience of romantic love. For example, when the notion of romantic love first invaded my twelve-year-old mind, I imagined that the man of my heart would be physically molded after my father, probably because he was my primary example of what a "man" and husband should be. My heart, however, rarely followed the image that my mind had constructed. I, like the rest of us, had no control over my romantic attraction and romantic love. Romantic love can, and does, blossom where we least expect it.

When any of us experiences romantic love, it can include sexual attraction, romantic attraction, and attachment. Each aspect of romantic love results from feelings rather than an intellectual decision. Sexual attraction involves a desire for a sexual relationship with someone. The romantic attraction element of romantic love is characterized by the desire to share feelings and aspects of ourselves, to give and receive affection, to know more about the other person, and to share time, space, and experiences with that person. When we are romantically attracted to someone, we might desire to be close them—to date them, live with them, marry them, and build families with them. The attachment element of romantic love is described as the feeling of a deep union with a long-term partner. It's what inspires us to want to spend a lifetime with one individual. It can compel us to move beyond desire to commitment. Attachment often results in taking the vows of marriage, and for many, having children.

Psychologists agree that romantic love is not limited to heterosexuals. Romantic love, and all of its elements—sexual attraction, romantic attraction, and attachment—can be experienced between people of any sexuality or gender identity.

In many instances, romantic love fades and the relationship ends. In other instances, romantic love can grow into committed love. Those desires for attachment experienced during romantic love become solidified in committed love. Committed love can include marriage, raising children, buying a home, caring for a sick partner, forgiving infidelity, etc. Committed love is considered to be deeper than romantic love because it lasts longer and goes beyond infatuation and includes more of the 'heavy lifting' required to sustain relationships. The psychological community also agrees that committed love is not the sole domain of heterosexuals and can exist between two people, regardless of sexuality or gender identity.

Most of us look forward to having committed love relationships. It is something we cherish, which is why it's difficult for me to understand why anyone would want to deny that same cherished experience to someone else. Perhaps remembering how vital and uplifting it is to be in a romantic or committed, loving relationship will compel us to want that same experience for other people, regardless of their sexuality or gender identity. I was reminded of this during a conversation with Jennie, a woman I met while waiting to board a flight. In chatting about our travel destinations and work, we also discussed this project, which was in its infancy. Jennie said, "Aahhh, perhaps that's why we met today." Among the things she shared were that she has been in relationships with men and women, and that her life partner is a woman. Jennie also revealed that for many years, her father refused to accept her sexuality, until he remembered how valuable love was in his own life.

> *Then one day he said, "You know, I think it's grim to be alone in this world, and I think that everyone deserves to be in a relationship." It was his way of saying, "I think it's important that people find their companions, no matter who they are."*
>
> –Jennie, entrepreneur, committed relationship,
>   no labels, 49 years old

As the Doobie Brothers put it, "Without love, where would you be now?"[33]

Let us not forget love for humankind. This love compels us to want the best for people we may never meet—for future generations and for people who live on the other side of the country or the other side of the world. Love for humankind is also supposed to prevent us from wishing ill or inflicting harm on others, even people we don't know or understand or who differ from us. Shouldn't our love for humanity spark us to insist on freedom and equality for everyone, regardless of sexuality, biological sex, or gender identity?

Relationships

The discussion of love leads me to the topic of relationships. It can be difficult to wrap our minds around how a relationship that doesn't work for us could work for someone else, especially those involving people whose sexuality or gender identity differs from our own. Some heterosexuals, for instance, are convinced that there is something fundamentally different about homosexual relationships, and many cisgender people can't imagine why someone would be in relationship with a transgender person. The awe and speculation surrounding other people's relationships is usually unwarranted. Every relationship has different challenges, arrangements, and understandings, and most relationships have fundamental similarities, regardless of the partners' sexualities or gender identities.

We are more similar than we are different. Speaking to people of different sexualities, gender identities, and biological sexes affirmed this belief for me. Most human beings need and desire some level of interpersonal relationships. Most of us seek a companion, and many of us seek to create families. How that plays out will differ from person to person and couple to couple, but those differences often have less to do with sexuality and gender identity than other factors like personality, culture, religion, etc.

CHAPTER FOUR

LESBIAN & GAY

"I say that homosexuality is not just a form of sex, it's a form
of love—and it commands our respect for that reason."
–Christopher Hitchens[34]

Intro

Individuals who identify as lesbian or gay have a homosexual sexuality. The prefix "homo-" is Latin for "same," and the term "homosexual" refers to people who are only attracted to people of the same sex. The word homosexuality was coined in 1868 by German psychologist Karoly Maria Benkert. As explained earlier, the term lesbians can refer to girls or women who identify as homosexual, and "gay" can refer to homosexual girls, boys, men, and women.

Of all the groups under the LGBTQIAP umbrella, "lesbian and gay" is thought to be the largest. Relative to the overall US population of 327 million people, it has been estimated that homosexuals represent somewhere between 5.5 million people and 9 million people, which equates to 1.7 percent to 3.0 percent.[35, 36]

Perhaps the most visible symbol of homosexuality is the rainbow flag, also known as the gay pride flag or the LGBT pride flag. It was created in 1978, a time when few homosexuals were living openly. The flag was designed by Gilbert Baker for San Francisco's Gay Freedom Day

Parade at the request of Harvey Milk, a gay San Francisco City-County Supervisor. Milk, California's first openly gay elected official, was assassinated later that year. Baker conceived meanings for each color in the flag: red for life, orange for healing, yellow for sunlight, green for nature, indigo for serenity, and violet for spirit. Baker's flag quickly became a symbol for the Gay Freedom Day Parade, and its use began to spread throughout California and eventually across the country as a symbol of homosexuality. Today, the rainbow flag is recognized around the world.

What are acceptable ways to refer to people who identify as homosexual?

Aside from "homosexual," the two most widely known and accepted terms are "gay" and "lesbian." There are other words people within the community might use as self-identifiers.

> *I used to identify myself as a "rebel gay dyke." I often say "gay woman" to get people's attention. The reason I don't use the word "homosexual" is because I don't go around using the word "heterosexual," because that puts emphasis on my person as a sexual being. I am more than that. I want people to see me as a human being first, and then as a woman, African-American, lesbian.*
>
> –Commissioner Garner

Terms like "queer," "sissy," and "bull dyke" were initially meant to insult and have now been reclaimed by some lesbian and gay people. When used by members of this community, these terms can reflect positive meanings, much like other groups have renovated pejorative terms once used against them, giving them new meanings.

As a general rule, it is never a good idea for someone outside of the community to use a pejorative that has been re-purposed by the community it was originally inflicted upon. The fact that some people have reclaimed the word in a positive light doesn't give those outside the community license to use it. Author Ta-Nehisi Coates cautions that just because a word has been re-purposed doesn't eliminate the negative impact it can have when spewed by someone outside of the group. He offers examples: "My wife and her girlfriends will use the word 'bitch.' I do not join in... Dan Savage had this idea for a show he was going to call, 'Hey Faggot.' I'm not going to yell 'Hey faggot' at Dan Savage. That's not my relationship with the LGBT community, and I understand that. And I'm okay with that. I don't have the desire to yell out the word 'faggot.'"[37]

To be respectful, and to avoid hurt feelings—yours and theirs—the best approach is to ask a person how they would like you to identify them rather than assigning a term on your own. Even if you've heard people within the community use a particular word, it's best that people outside of that community refrain from using it. It is disrespectful and demeaning to dismiss another person's wishes, feelings, or concerns when it comes to how they want to be addressed or referred to. Shouldn't we all strive to be respectful of the labels people feel are acceptable and unacceptable?

The list of pejorative and, therefore, unacceptable names used against homosexuals includes "faggot," "punk," "carpet-muncher," "fairy," "pansy," and "sodomite." These words are used with the intention of dehumanizing and belittling people. One of the most memorable quotes from the Oscar-winning film *Moonlight* occurs when a child asks his mentor what the word "faggot" means. The heterosexual mentor responds, "'faggot' is a word used to make gay people feel bad." I hadn't thought of it in that way before. Lobbing pejoratives at someone is an attempt to make them feel bad. It's an attempt to make that person absorb the fear, disdain, and hatred the speaker feels for them. Far too often, these verbal assaults are directed at children who may not be old enough to know what the words mean or to fully understand their sexuality.

The use of derogatory terms is especially present in educational settings. It was disturbing to discover how frequently hateful terms for gay and lesbian people are spoken in the American secondary education system.

> In school, you hear words like "gay" and "faggot" and "you're so gay." One of the things our students in the Gay Straight Alliance did for a week was to document what words were said. Each day, ten participating students heard an average of twenty-three

anti-gay remarks. There were over 700 different remarks in a five-day period, reported by ten students. Even teachers were participating in the anti-gay remarks.

–Ryan Roemerman, Executive Director, LGBT Institute,
   Center for Civil and Human Rights,
   cisgender, homosexual, single, 32 years old

That equates to a child hearing four hateful, derogatory, or insensitive words each hour, or one every fifteen minutes (based on the national average of a six-hour school day). Some might be tempted to dismiss this, by saying that many people are called derogatory names, but, as we discussed earlier, just because something is common, doesn't make it good, correct, or acceptable.

According to the National School Climate Report, 86 percent of LGBTQIAP youth reported being harassed at school, which included the use of derogatory terms, compared to 27 percent of students overall.[38] This suggests that harassment of LGBTQIAP youth is much more extensive than harassment experienced by the student population in general. The severity of the situation is compounded by the fact that, as Roemerman noted, sometimes teachers are among the perpetrators. If you've ever been harassed because of your race, sex, weight, or some other personal attribute, then perhaps you know that this torment can diminish self-esteem, lower academic performance, incite depression, and leave lasting scars.

As an adult, imagine what it would feel like to hear three hateful, derogatory, and insensitive statements about your sex, sexuality, race, religion, etc. every day, without fail, when you enter your workplace. Would you look forward to going to work, or would you dread it? It's likely you would be on guard, never knowing when the verbal or written assault would come. You might begin eating in your office or in the car. Your productivity might suffer. You might wonder why your co-workers or supervisors won't treat you fairly. You would likely wonder why they can't see that you are a human being with feelings and that their words hurt you. Now, imagine your ten-year-old or fifteen-year-old self in that situation, except instead of three terms, your young mind is hit with twenty-three or more derogatory statements. What impact would that have on your developing emotional state, your self-esteem, your sense of safety, and your ability to focus on your education? The fact that children are subjected to this sort of hostile environment should upset all of us.

The takeaway from this discussion is that words have complex meanings that carry weight. If you think that a word might be hurtful, then don't use it. It might be helpful to consider that name-calling is often an opening to do something inhumane to the target of your insults. Dehumanizing a person is how we rationalize granting ourselves license to treat them as we choose rather than as they want to be treated.

Are all butch women lesbians and all effeminate men gay?

"It's absolutely not true," answered Professor Wright. The way a person looks, dresses, or behaves is not a reliable indication of their sexuality. These are stereotypes, as are the ideas that all feminine women and masculine men are straight. The stereotype that all effeminate men are gay has resulted in some straight men being labeled homosexual because they don't measure up to society's masculinity quotient. We have been conditioned to associate so-called feminine behavior with women and so-called masculine behavior with men. Therefore, when we witness a man exhibiting what has been deemed effeminate, the immediate assumption is "he must be gay." We also apply the same rules to women we perceive as masculine, assuming that they must be lesbians. The reality is some effeminate men are gay and some are straight. Some so-called "butch" women are homosexual and some are not.

Demetrius refuted some of the stereotypes he has heard about gay men.

> I've heard people say a lot of them. "All gay men can decorate." That's not true. "All gay men know how to dress." That's not necessarily true. There are a lot of gay men who are good and skillful at coordinating, arranging, creativeness, et cetera, but there are a lot of gay men who are not. There are gay men who are professional, who are attorneys, doctors, accountants, auditors.
>
> –Demetrius

Perpetuating these stereotypes is harmful.

I have counseled quite a few straight men who would be considered effeminate. They have been suicidal because they are so stigmatized. It causes as much, if not more, psychological distress than coming out... One of my students... told me the story about how she met her husband. I've met him, and he's one of those guys people would assume is gay. He likes theatre. He loves to cook. He's very sensitive. He's helping us with the pride stuff, and he's very comfortable with gay people. For years, she didn't think he liked girls. Then one day, she asked him out, and now, they're married and have been together for five years...

–Professor Wright

When we take a closer look at the activities and traits that often lead people to label a man effeminate, and therefore gay, we often realize these activities and traits apply to men and women.

It's unfortunate that those behaviors or characteristics are used to determine whether a man is gay or straight. Because if a man is single, he has to cook, he has to take care of himself, he wants to be well groomed, well presented to the public, workplace, etc. Just because he's well groomed, and polished, and likes the theater, the arts, and knows how to cook, doesn't necessarily mean he's gay.

–Demetrius

We also allow different degrees of latitude for what is considered appropriate behavior for men and women.

Women have a much wider latitude in terms of what's gender-appropriate behavior, so it's easier for people to be more gender-lenient with women. Women can wear pants, they can have their hair short, all those little things that would be gender normal in the female context would be gender abnormal in the male context. There's a much narrower range for men. It's amazing how many people are straight that feel abused by that lack of latitude. Some psychologists talk about it as a Western problem because we tend to have dualisms. The fact that we tend to force people into a lot of social categories is dualism—you're gay or you're straight. You're black or you're white. You're left handed or you're right handed. What about everybody who is in between? It's limiting for us because we have to be one way or the other, and when we're not, when we don't fit either mold, what do you call us? Where do you put us? I think that's the origins of distress for a lot of people, because I don't think people fit cleanly into any dualist category.

–Professor Wright

This situation offers another cautionary tale of how stereotypes can be incorrect and hurtful. Presuming a person is something they're not can cause them emotional distress. The need to make people fit our image of them is all about *us* and disregards the other person's humanity. We may be missing the opportunity for great friendships and loving relationships by holding on to our stereotypes.

For years, I have heard people say that all gay men like Broadway musicals, or that if a man likes Broadway musicals, then he must be gay. Neither is true. I have yet to encounter any one group of people whose every member like or dislike the same thing. For example, not all straight men like football, not all women like shopping, not all black people like rap music, and not all Hispanics speak Spanish. Omar, a graduate of Morehouse College, offered a valuable perspective.

It's a sweeping generalization because that would be like saying all gay men hate sports. The last few men I dated would prefer to go to the Super Bowl than a Broadway opening. Homosexuality doesn't make people like things; that's your personality.

–Omar, production manager, single,
cisgender, gay, 23 years old

There are some instances when generalizing about certain people or groups of people can be helpful shorthand. Sometimes the generalization/stereotype may hold true, and sometimes it does not. We should be mindful of the limitations of stereotypes. The greater challenge for any of us is the danger of holding fast to a particular generalization in the face of a different reality. Using stereotypes to discriminate, reject, and isolate people is a disservice to us all.

How can a real man be gay?

Whether someone is a "real man" is not determined by his sexuality. Some real men are gay. Some are straight. Some are bisexual, asexual, or pansexual. A man's sexuality does not deprive him of manhood.

This fallacy that a gay man is not a "real man" has been spewed from the mouths of men and women for too long. A few years ago, NFL quarterback Kordell Stewart denied rumors that he is homosexual by saying, "I'm a 'real man.'" This must be addressed, refuted, and put to rest by examining what "man" means. According to *Merriam-Webster*, the broad definition of "man" is "the condition of being a human being." A more nuanced definition is "the condition of being an adult male, as distinguished from a child or female." Neither definition measures manhood by a person's sexuality.

Some people associate manhood with certain traits like virility, which relates to having a strong sex drive, or the ability to impregnate a woman. Possessing a strong sex drive is not limited to any one sexuality or gender. The ability to impregnate women and produce offspring doesn't appear to be a good measure of manhood, given that a teenage boy could potentially accomplish this feat. And what about the "real man" who impregnates a woman and then abandons her and the child he created? Many of us would not consider that person to be a "real man." The measure of a man in that situation is taken by what he does after the seed is planted: how he then cares for the child, the mother and child, and himself.

> *What we've gotten lost in is narrowing the definition of masculinity. You hear the same "real man" crap from men who are beating on their wives. A real man wouldn't be hitting on her. For me, it's a lot broader definition. How about you own the space that you occupy, and you take care of the world in a way that's loving and caring, and as a provider, or a protector, or a nurturer?*
>
> –Rev. Teague

I vote that manhood is about the quality of a man's character and conduct, his behavior and actions in his relationships with other people and society at large. I consider a real man to be one who is honest, responsible, and loving. A real man takes care of his family. A real man respects women. A real man respects people. A real man can be gay, straight, bi, etc.

Is it true that anti-gay people are closeted homosexuals?

There is no evidence to support the notion that all or even many of those who oppose homosexuality are closeted homosexuals. Although it may make some people feel better to cast all anti-gay people into this category, this is an unfounded stereotype. It perhaps stems from a small number of prominent anti-gay individuals who have been revealed to have engaged in same-sex relations.

The most newsworthy of them have been elected officials and faith leaders. For instance, North Dakota State Representative Randy Boehning (R) voted against a bill that would extend housing, workplace, and other protections to LGBT North Dakota residents in April 2015, the same month he was caught sending explicit photos on a gay dating app. Puerto Rican Senator Roberto Arango (NPP[39]), an outspoken opponent of gay marriage and gay rights, was found to have posted shirtless photos of himself on the gay dating app Grindr. Eddie Long, a prominent faith leader who developed a ministry to convert homosexuals, including "homosexual cure" programs and a march to ban same-sex marriage, was later accused of having sexual relationships with several teenage and young adult male congregation members.

There are also other instances of people who oppose homosexuality while struggling with the fact that they are homosexual.

> *There was a series of gay-bashings in Portland, Oregon, where I went to school. About fifteen guys… were killed coming out of gay bars. The killers were a bunch of kids who were all 'playing around' with each other. They just didn't know what to do with that, so they decided they'd go and beat up gay men.*
>
> –Professor Wright

Sometimes there are aspects of ourselves that we don't like, haven't accepted, or wish we could change. We can either work to accept those parts of ourselves, or we can rail against them. For some individuals, that railing includes self-hatred, which is likely to spill over into how we treat others. If a person hates themselves for being gay, there is a pretty good chance they may hate others who are gay. If that self-hating person is in a position of power, like elected officials and faith leaders, they might use that power to strike out against gay people. They might believe that this anti-gay behavior will deflect suspicion about their own sexuality, thinking that no one would suspect them of being capable of the venomous hypocrisy required to persecute other people for attributes that they share. They also might believe their anti-gay actions will change their sexuality.

The existence of anti-gay people who participate in same-sex relations is a definite reality; however, there is a danger in suggesting that all anti-gay people are homosexual. The reality is that some are and some are not.

Why do some people flaunt their homosexuality in public?

If by flaunting we mean "to parade yourself," as the dictionary describes, then why not applaud it as we do any other group who parades some aspect of their being? Many people love a parade, as is proven by the barrage of parades that exist for nationalities and holidays. I have never heard anyone ask Irish Americans why they flaunt themselves in the streets and in bars every year. Saint Patrick's Day parades offer annual opportunities for Irish folks to flaunt who they are. There's a Dragon Con parade, a Fourth of July parade, a Christmas parade, and on and on. All of these parades or flaunting activities are about pride in a particular thing, which leads me to ask, "What is wrong about being proud of who you are?"

On an individual scale, flaunting is about outwardly showing some aspect of yourself. Some people use the term "flaunting" to refer to homosexuals openly showing affection, wearing colorful—what some might consider flamboyant—attire, or speaking or walking a certain way. There are some who would say they are opposed to these actions regardless of the actor, suggesting that they aren't singling people out because of their sexuality. There are also those who are only opposed to outward displays by certain groups of people, such as homosexuals. For instance, when a heterosexual couple shows affection in public, some observers might joke about someone "getting lucky tonight" or remark how beautiful it is to see an elderly couple still holding hands. Even in extreme cases of heterosexual public displays of affection, an observer might jokingly say, "Get a room." Never, ever, have I heard someone accuse heterosexuals of "flaunting" their sexuality. Why, then, is it considered flaunting if the two people are gay?

Flaunting is an accusation launched at gay people by those who do not approve of homosexuality. The term "flaunting" seems to be code for disapproval and is sometimes used by straight people who are uncomfortable with homosexuality and don't want to be reminded that gay people exist. What they might really be saying is, "I don't like seeing gay people express sexual attraction, affection, or love." A person who disapproves of homosexuality may not want to see homosexuality expressed around them. It is never the homosexual couple's responsibility to assuage the discomfort of anti-gay individuals.

Every person should be free to be who they are and to dress, speak, and behave as they see fit, as long as it does not endanger other human beings. Suggesting that gay people or anyone else should not express themselves in public is an impossible double standard. It denies them the rights that others expect for themselves. If you want the right to display your personality, sexuality, affection, and love in public, then why not allow others to do so as well?

Relationships

How do lesbian and gay relationships differ from straight ones?

Human relationships share many similarities, regardless of sexuality. We are often driven to seek people with whom we share something in common, such as morals, religion, race, age, socio-economic background, geography, income, or profession. Most people desire companionship, commitment, and family. Most people are concerned about things like stability, health, money, and fidelity. Our relationships go through cycles of attraction, getting to know each other, infatuation, romance, and love. Couples face many of the same issues, regardless of sexuality. Our relationships also face similar challenges including communication, infidelity, finances, estrangement, and divorce.

We have the same issues in our relationships—money, family, sex. It really is no different. It's just two people having a relationship. That's it.

–Tiffany

Others agree that there are similarities and differences.

With two women, you have a lot of hormones, so you have a lot of sensitivities. You have all of the things that we think of as women's issues that come up in the relationship.

–Commissioner Garner

No two relationships are exactly alike. Perhaps all relationships differ more because of the individuals' personalities than because of their sexualities.

What attracts homosexuals to each other?

Homosexuals are sexually, emotionally, and romantically attracted to people of the same sex for the same reasons that heterosexuals are sexually, emotionally, and romantically attracted to people of the opposite sex. Sometimes it's purely physical. At other times, it's personality, or intellect, social status, or financial status, or maybe it's something we can't explain.

My wife is a great conversationalist, and she is super cute. In many ways, opposites attract. She has a very feminine energy, and my energy and my wife's energy are opposite energies. I feel like you learn so much about yourself being in a relationship with someone. Being in a relationship with her allowed me to explore a lot more deeply about myself.

–Anne

I think I was ready. David was cute, and he was President of the congregation, and I liked that. He was running the show. And he was good looking. He had his stuff together. He was a doctor. And when we got together, David held a lot of the values I held.

–Rev. Teague

How do lesbian and gay people find each other?

If that question were asked about heterosexuals, the answer might be that they find each other at church, work, the grocery store, nightclubs, health clubs, concerts, museums, schools, professional events, a friend's home, or online. It can be anywhere. This is no different from how people of other sexualities find dates, partners, and spouses. Most relationships are bound by shared values and interests, so it shouldn't be surprising that we all meet people in the course of our daily activities—when doing things that are necessities or expressions of our personal interests.

> *I met my current boyfriend while on vacation at an annual event. In a hotel, full of men, he was the only one who made me wonder, "Who is that?" We've spent nearly every weekend together ever since, even though we live in different cities.*
>
> –Sam, entrepreneur, single, cisgender, gay, 45 years old

> *We met at a party where we sat down next to each other and had this amazing conversation.*
>
> –Anne

Some people meet at places of worship.

> *We actually met twice. A dear friend was a Quaker, and she had been working tooth and nail for more than a year to get us to meet. Plus, I was already in a relationship, which she somewhat ignored, but later that gentleman had to move out of Atlanta on a job transfer. When we met the first time, I thought David was nice, but I was looking at the guy in the cowboy hat. We did get to meet later... when he let me cut in line at a Friends meeting.*
>
> –Rev. Teague

It is perfectly natural for people to meet in places of mutual interest. Sometimes that mutual interest can be based on sexuality. It is also natural for people to seek spaces where they feel safe and comfortable to express themselves. That space might be a bookstore or a bar.

When I went to open Outwrite Bookstore, we were the largest city in Atlanta—in America—that didn't have a bookstore focused on the LGBT community. At that point the bookstores were a meeting place. I had gone to New York, San Francisco, Boston, and Washington, and every place that you went that was a city had a bookstore that you could go to and find books by, for and about lesbians, gays, bisexuals and transgender. And there was something to do during the daytime. In Atlanta there was no gay life in the daytime. I mean, we had bars, we had a couple of exclusively gay restaurants, but nothing specifically for the community that was open during the day. I thought it was kind of ridiculous that we didn't have one. I really wanted to establish a place that you could get information if you were coming out, if you were moving on to the next step, if you were closeted, and also a place where people could come together and have meetings.

–Philip Rafshoon, founder Outwrite Bookstore,
　Director of Member Engagement at Midtown Alliance,
　single, gay, 53 years old

　　Some heterosexuals frown on the fact that there are spaces where gay, lesbian, asexual, pansexual, and transgender people can go with the express intent and purpose of being around people with shared interests. Why is this so when heterosexuals do the same thing? We all seek places where we can find people who are like us. We have social clubs and interest groups based on nationalities, political parties, religions, etc. There is absolutely nothing wrong with people seeking people with similar interests in an attempt to find dates, partners, spouses, etc. Dating services are popular for this very reason. There are dating sites for men seeking young women, white people seeking other white people, black people seeking other black people, biracial people seeking other biracial people. Why, then, do some find these things unacceptable for LGBTQIAP individuals? Perhaps we should be suspicious of our motives and judgments when we take exception to a group of people doing what everyone else is doing.

Is it true that homosexual relationships begin and end quickly?

There are no statistics that compare how quickly heterosexuals start relationships relative to homosexuals or people of any other sexuality. In some instances, the answer is yes, and in others, no. The same can be said of heterosexual relationships, which suggests that the length of relationships is not necessarily a specific characteristic of any sexuality. Some of the gay men and women I spoke with said they had observed instances where there was a sense of urgency to turn something into a monogamous relationship soon after meeting someone who seemed reasonably compatible. They also warned that it doesn't make those relationships any less genuine, nor does it have any impact on whether those relationships can be long-term or committed.

> *I don't think it is any different than heterosexual couples. If there is a connection, you get together, and you go with it. If there is not a connection, then there's not. Before I got with my wife, I had had two long-term relationships, and before that, I felt like I was out of a relationship more than I was in a relationship.*

–Commissioner Garner

There are other perspectives.

> *Most lesbian relationships, that I know, have started quickfire, and mine started quickfire. I think it's mostly because women are just so intense. After starting quickly, my wife and I broke off, and I'm glad we did. We decided to slow down for a minute. We were doing the whole thing of "I like you, I like you, I love you." I see it a lot more when it's been one woman who has long identified as lesbian and another woman who has recently come into herself as a lesbian. One might be thinking, "I'm finally getting this thing that I haven't been satisfied with. This woman is giving me everything that I think I've been wanting but didn't get from a man." Then you have, "Let's get married," after a month.*

–Tiffany

Yes, our relationships happen really quickly. If it's not meant to be, then things disappear as fast as they start. Nowadays, I have noticed some people are wanting to take it slower, like "I want to date." I think it's very important to have emotional relationships, but if the sexual relationship doesn't match, or you don't have a good sexual chemistry, I don't think it's going to work.

–Fredis

What must be factored in is how we differ from person to person, which impacts our movement in and around relationships. Some people move quickly, others like to take it slowly, and yet others avoid relationships altogether.

Are homosexual relationships easier than heterosexual relationships?

No. The saying "men are from Mars, women are from Venus" suggests that there's a vast difference between men and women, and this difference can create a lack of understanding between the sexes. Because of the differences between men and women, many people assume that a relationship with two men or two women would be easier than a relationship between a man and woman. The presumption seems to be that two people of the same sex will have similar thought processes, understandings, motivations, and emotions. Two men, therefore, would not have to explain themselves to one another the way a man and a woman may need to, and likewise, they wouldn't have to explain what pleases them sexually. The same thinking is often applied to women, assuming they must think the same, have the same emotional temperament, and have the same sexual needs and appetite. While two people of the same sex might share some preferences, we should also keep in mind that they are still two different people, with different backgrounds, experiences, emotions, and thoughts. Some of the people I spoke with had been in same-sex relationships and opposite-sex relationships and didn't find that one was necessarily easier than the other.

I don't think that is necessarily true. Maybe you have more understanding of some things, of the range, but you can't assume that they like what you like. You can't assume that communicating with them the way you want to be communicated with is going to work for them. In fact, nine times out of ten, it's not. I think that's what gets a lot of people in trouble in relationships. That is, in some ways, less about women and women and just differences in people.

–Jazmyn

If a lesbian is attracted to butch women, then why wouldn't she be attracted to men?

The short answer is that lesbians are gay women who are sexually, emotionally, and romantically attracted to other women, not men. A butch woman is not a man, regardless of how masculine she may appear.

> *The first woman that I actually fell in love with was a very butch woman, and I liked the fact that she was a woman. It is just not the same as being attracted to a man.*
>
> –Commissioner Garner

There is a difference in being attracted to a butch woman and being attracted to a man.

> *For me, there's that androgynous appeal. You get the best of both worlds. You get a woman. And you get a woman's mindset, but you get a harder appeal. You get the harder edge of a woman. I think women go out and seek men who look a certain way but might say, "I wish you would get in touch with your feelings more." Okay, what you wish is that you had a man with a very soft side. A woman wants a butch woman, but they want a woman.*
>
> –Tiffany

How do gay couples decide who's going to be the "man" and who will be the "woman"?

Homosexual relationships involve two men or two women, therefore there is no need to decide who will be the man or the woman.

At the core of this question seems to be the belief that every relationship must have a man, who many people generally presume will assume the dominant, controlling role, and a woman, who is generally presumed to be the submissive partner. This presumption conflates dominance with masculinity and submission with femininity, although those characteristics appear in both men and women. This presumption makes it difficult to transcend the notion that every relationship needs a man and a woman.

When considering two men or two women in a relationship, our conditioning urges us to assign the traits and roles that we typically assign to a heterosexual relationship. Many people can't help but wonder how same-sex couples allocate roles that society traditionally assigns based on biological sex. It's as if we expect one person in the relationship to declare, "Me Tarzan, you Jane." A more realistic scene is that individual personalities, careers, interests, skills, and needs guide how a couple interacts with each other, manages their family life, and operates their household.

> *I just don't agree with the stereotypes. Having taken the garbage out my whole life, as a child and as an adult, I really don't think of that as associated with men. I don't think decision-making is either. I know plenty of men who can't make a decision to save their lives and women who will make a decision without thinking twice about it… People have male and female energy. And they have those energies around different things, but that is very different than they have to be "the man" and they have to be "the woman." I am not comfortable with the whole concept that somebody would have to be a man. We are both women, and we are two women in a relationship with each other.*
>
> –Jazmyn

In most relationships, it is likely that one person will be the more dominant of the two, and that person might also be the major breadwinner and the one to take the lead in the relationship. One of my female friends embodies the dominant, take-charge personality often associated with men, while her husband is the mild-mannered, submissive personality often associated with women. What also happens in most relationships, heterosexual, homosexual, or otherwise, is that the leadership role happens organically rather than by an explicit declaration.

There are, of course, relationships where there is no clear leader, or where leadership changes based on the situation encountered. I have observed that every relationship, regardless of the couple's sexuality, has its own ecosystem. That's because different components are required to plant, cultivate, and yield. The most fruitful and happy relationships allow each person to be who they are without forcing anyone into a specific role.

> *There is no man in the relationship. We are both women. There are things that I do and things that she does, and we just kind of, like, share in our household, so there is no particular role that we play. It is about, "What are you adept at doing?"*
>
> –Commissioner Garner

In some lesbian couples, one person might be viewed by others as "the man," although that this is not always the case.

> *I know that people say it all the time, and I do know many lesbian relationships where there definitely is one person who would be considered "the man" in the relationship, but it hasn't played out like that in our relationship. We don't decide who will be "the man." I think because she probably looks more butch, people probably decide that she is the man in the relationship. That's not always the case. I fix the toilet. We live near a nature preserve, so I deal with wild possums and the snakes.*
>
> –Tiffany

Some would stress it is healthier for both people in a relationship to take on both roles of husband and wife.

> *Archbishop Carl Bean said, "If ya'll want your relationships to work, then you need to know when you need to be a wife." I thought, "Whoa, that's a different way of viewing the relationship." So now when somebody asks, "Which one of you is the wife?" I say, "We both are, and we both are the husband." If you want your relationship to work, then you might want*

to adopt this model. At this point, David and I may have one of the longer relationships in the family. Regardless of sexual orientation, and certainly financially and emotionally, we have one of the healthier ones.

–Rev. Teague

How much better might all our relationships be if we abandoned some of the traditional male-female regulations we impose on ourselves, particularly if they are not working for the betterment of the union? What I have found to be most critical in successful relationships is that each person does their part to keep the ship sailing. Sometimes that means taking care of menial tasks in order to free our partners to perform other activities. Sometimes it means doing what you do best, regardless of tradition. At other times, it means performing tasks we don't necessarily enjoy. I doubt that assigning "man" or "woman" is required to maintain a fruitful relationship, family, or household.

Can straight men and women be platonic friends with gay men and women?

Yes. Many heterosexual men and women, including myself, have friendships with men and women who are not "straight." We are friends because we share common interests, similar goals, complementary personalities, etc.

One response to this question, that relates specifically to men, is the presumption that a straight man isn't really heterosexual if he is friends with a homosexual man. That seems to suggest that there's no credible reason for a straight man to befriend a gay man. This sounds like an insult to both sexualities. It suggests that heterosexual and homosexual men do not or cannot share similar interests. It also suggests that neither is capable of platonic relationships with people of different sexualities. It could also suggest that gay men are not worthy of friendship with heterosexual men. These suggestions dehumanize a person because of their sexuality. They ignore the reality that sexuality does not determine personality, interests, intellect, humor, nationality, age, or any of the other human traits that elicit and solidify friendships.

There is another false presumption that gay and straight people can't be platonic friends because gay men want to have sex with every man they meet or that lesbians feel the same way about every woman they meet. That is simply not true. Heterosexuals don't want to have sex with every person of the opposite sex. Likewise, homosexuals don't want to have sex with every same-sex person they meet. It's possible for straight men to have close platonic friendships with gay men without either person being sexually, romantically, or emotionally attracted to the other. The same is true for platonic friendships between heterosexual women and lesbians. This shouldn't come as a surprise to any heterosexual who has platonic friendships with people of the opposite sex. Friendships are about people, not sexualities.

> *I have really amazing straight friends. We're like brothers. Once you get past the part of sexuality, you can see the person as a person. It's very hard to find good friends, people who not only understand you but get you mentally. It doesn't really matter about race or sexuality. It's about seeing the person as a person.*
> –Fredis

A heterosexual friend offered his opinion on having friendships with gay men.

> *I welcome friendships with men and women, as long as we are clear about our intentions. It would be awful for me to miss out on a fulfilling friendship, steeped in our shared values of culture, politics, art, and literature, just because a man is gay, and I am not. I believe that this whole energy people are concerned about is that they are not secure in their own sexuality. I think it also presumes that homosexuals are predators, which is not true.*
> –Joe, retired, single, cisgender, heterosexual, 60 years old

In some instances, there may be a challenge if one friend comes out after the friendship has been established.

> *There are definitely those situations where straight men think they can't have gay friends. I find that men who are straight and who are comfortable with gay men are more often than not some of the most comfortable in their own sexual orientation.*

I think men who protest too much about it might be a little concerned about their own sexual orientation, and they might be projecting a little bit. That's my hypothesis. Straight men are just going to have to recognize that they've been dealing with gay men all their lives; they just have never known it... Let's say two guys are friends, and there's a straight guy who thinks this other dude's been a straight friend. After the guy comes out, they may have a conflict in the sense of, "Okay, what does that mean now?" Ultimately, not always, but I think they can get to a point where they think, "You know what, it doesn't change how I interact with this person." And those are the learning moments.

–Roemerman

This raises a point worth noting. It is likely that every straight person has a gay friend who hasn't come out to them yet. If you liked that person before knowing their sexuality, then why should that change after you find out they're gay? They're the same person with the same intellect, sense of humor, loyalty, etc. The difference is that now you know they're attracted to people of the same sex. The only thing that changed is that now you know something more about them and possibly have an opportunity to be even better friends.

Sex

Can "one good roll in the hay" with someone of the opposite sex make a gay person straight?

No. This myth has been repeated and believed for ages, at times with detrimental results. While writing this book, a heartbreaking story about a father who thought his eleven-year-old son was gay made headlines in the Southeast. This man instructed a woman to rape his child in a restaurant bathroom. All because he thought forcing the boy to have sex with a woman would "make him straight." Situations like these make it imperative that this myth be laid to rest once and for all.

It's worth repeating that, according to medical, scientific, and psychological consensus, nothing can change a person's sexuality. An opposite-sex sexual encounter cannot make a gay person straight, nor can a same-sex sexual encounter make a straight person gay. Therefore, a homosexual man—one who is only sexually, emotionally, and romantically attracted to men—will not be sexually, emotionally, and romantically attracted to women. Not only is a gay man not attracted to women, he might even be repulsed by the thought of having sex with a woman.

Once, when I was in my teens, I tried it and had to run to the bathroom to throw up. It was one of those super embarrassing moments. I was in a girl's bedroom, literally hooking up, and then realizing halfway through that I was going to get sick. I ran to the bathroom. It's a very visceral reaction. It's a visceral reaction to the anatomy of a person that you're not attracted to. It's a physical thing, and there's some part of my brain that will not allow me to go there.

–Perry

This shouldn't be surprising or hard to understand because many heterosexuals say they feel the same way about homosexual sex. A gay man might be physically capable of having sex with women, but being physically able to perform a certain sexual act does not mean he would experience sexual attraction to women.

I feel comfortable enough with some women that I'd sleep with them naked. But I'd never get aroused. My body just wouldn't respond. I had one dream about having sex with a woman. In the dream, we had sex, then I got up, and a baby popped out. That's the only dream I ever had about straight sex.

–Professor Wright

Once we take all of these realities into consideration, it's unreasonable to conclude that a sexual encounter between a homosexual and someone of the opposite sex would "turn" the gay person straight. Just as there is nothing about a same-sex encounter that would make a heterosexual become homosexual.

This lesson is not limited to heterosexuals; some homosexuals have also bought into the myth. Emmy-winning screenwriter Lena Waithe, who identifies as gay, says some teens and adults try to "sex the gay away."

Waithe elaborates, "There's a lot of gay girls that know [they're] gay but don't wanna be. And so, they're like, 'Oh let me try having sex with a guy and be sure. Maybe if I have sex with him, maybe I won't be gay anymore.'"[40] They eventually learn that it doesn't work.

If someone has one same-sex sexual encounter, does it mean that person is gay?

It might, and it might not. Who a person has or doesn't have sexual intercourse with is not necessarily the determining factor for their sexuality. Sexual orientation is defined by who a person is attracted to, sexually, emotionally, and romantically, which may or may not be the same as whom they have sexual intercourse with. For instance, a person can be heterosexual and never have had sex with a person of the opposite sex or any person at all. That doesn't mean they are not heterosexual. Additionally, someone can be heterosexual, even if they have had one or more same-sex sexual encounters. You may be wondering how this can be true.

What determines a person's sexuality is their emotional, sexual, and/or romantic attraction to others.

> There's a whole other dimension to this; there's affection, who you tend to fall in love with, who you find emotionally more attractive, and then there's also this notion of a lifestyle—who you actually want to live your life with, partner with, and all that kind of stuff.
>
> –Professor Wright

> I don't think that if you've had sex once it makes you necessarily gay, because sexual orientation is more about whom you sexually, romantically, and emotionally feel connected to. If someone says, "Well yeah, I've had sex with a guy, but I'm not gay," then who am I to say, "No, you are gay because you had sex that one time?"
>
> –Roemerman

If a heterosexual person has a same-sex experience, such as kissing, petting, oral sex, anal sex, or vaginal sex, but is not sexually, emotionally, or romantically attracted to people of the same sex, then that person is not homosexual. Some people will doubt this to be true; however, there are a number of reasons why someone who is not homosexual might have one or more same-sex sexual encounters.

Earlier, we discussed the notion of sexual experimentation, which is natural for children, teens, and young adults. Youthful experimentation and curiosity are common and might result in a young girl experimenting by kissing her best female friend before kissing a boy. Young heterosexual boys, for instance, might experiment with each other before realizing they are performing sexual acts or as a way to experience an orgasm until they have an opportunity to have sex with a girl. In some cultures, boys are encouraged to have same-sex sexual encounters until they are ready to marry a girl or woman.

Another instance where sexual intercourse may not match the person's sexual orientation is in the case of rape. Rape is about dominance and has nothing to do with sexual, emotional, or romantic attraction. Since rape is not about sexual, emotional, or romantic attraction, this violent sex act should not be viewed as a barometer of a person's sexuality. Being the victim of rape is not a barometer of the victim's sexuality. For example, a heterosexual boy who has been raped by a man or a group of boys is still heterosexual. This is true regardless of whether the forced sex is oral, anal, or anything else. Additionally, a man who rapes another man could be homosexual, but he could also be heterosexual, bisexual, etc. This is true because rape is an act of violence, not an act of sexual, emotional, or romantic attraction.

Most instances of same-sex rape are reportedly between men, and often occur in situations of extreme conflict, violence, or aggression, such as war and prison. In "Sexual Violence Against Men in Armed Conflict," Sandesh Sivakumaran, writes, "Male sexual violence is all about notions of power and dominance."[41] We connect power and dominance to masculinity; therefore, when men are in a situation of armed conflict, sexual violence becomes a form of emasculation. Sivakumaran further explained, "Male-on-male rape is more about taking away the victim's masculinity and making him feel... submissive and not in control." Male-on-male rape has occurred around the world for centuries and continues today. It is even glorified in today's rap lyrics by many men who brag about their heterosexuality. Rappers like Big Pun, Snoop Dog, and DMX, for example, have spouted lyrics that reference taking someone's manhood, forcing a man to perform oral sex, and forcing a man to receive anal sex.[42] Many male rappers who rap about raping men say they are rapping about power and dominance, not sexual attraction to men.

These are just some of the reasons it is misguided to presume that someone who has had one or more same-sex sexual encounters is a homosexual. People have sexual intercourse for many reasons. Some of those reasons are related to a person's sexuality, and others are not.

How can men who repeatedly have sex with other men still claim to be heterosexual?

There are a number of reasons why a man could have multiple intentional acts of sex with another man and still think of himself as heterosexual. This question is usually asked relative to men, but it can be asked of women as well. Again, it is important to keep in mind that sexual orientation is defined by a person's sexual, emotional, and romantic attractions.

There are teens and young adults who participate in same-sex activity as a way to earn money, even if they are not attracted to the same sex. A homeless heterosexual teen boy, for instance, might see prostitution with male clients as his only means of income and survival. If that teen boy is not attracted to men, then he is not gay. The same can be true for women. If a woman participates in sex with another woman solely to earn a living, and she is not attracted to women, then she would not be considered gay.

Same-sex sexual encounters that may not reflect a person's sexual orientation can also occur when people are incarcerated. Many of these sexual encounters are not necessarily a testament to an individual's sexual orientation but rather a testament to a human need. Imagine being stranded on an island where the only food is something you don't like—broccoli, for instance. You would never eat broccoli if the foods you preferred were available. But you are on this island, and that's all you have, so you eat broccoli because not eating the broccoli means you won't survive on the island.

Earlier in the sex discussion, it was pointed out that sex provides humans with some very important things. For many humans, sexual satisfaction, and the intimacy, touch, and connection with other human beings that sex provides, are necessary for survival. Living without those things for three, thirteen, or thirty years can adversely affect a person's mental and emotional health and their will and ability to survive. For someone imprisoned in a same-sex community, the only option to satisfy those needs is a person of the same sex. Kate Johns, a former prison inmate says, "Consensual, same-sex prisoner relationships are common among both male and female inmates. It's not a reflection of their sexuality but more out of pragmatism and as a counterbalance to loneliness. The expression is 'gay for the stay.'"[43]

There is also another perspective. Some people who *are* sexually, romantically, and/or emotionally attracted to the same sex, and have sexual intercourse with people of the same sex, might still tell themselves and others that they are heterosexual. This can occur for a number of reasons. Some men, for instance, are in denial and haven't yet accepted their sexuality, perhaps because being homosexual conflicts with their idea of masculinity. Some have accepted being gay but are afraid of what will happen if others find out. Those men might live out their attraction to the same sex but do it in a way that allows them to create the façade, for themselves and others, that they are heterosexual.

One tactic that some men apply is to only have sex with men but never have an emotional or romantic relationship with men. Another practice is to only participate in certain types of sexual acts. For example, some view being the penetrator during anal sex as the "masculine" role and would therefore never allow themselves to be penetrated, which they view as the "feminine" role. Being on the receiving end of anal sex is also known as being "the bottom."

> For them, as long as they're not receiving, then they're not gay.
> In some countries, virtually all the male prostitutes are always
> bottoms because guys hire a male prostitute, and then they can
> maintain their straight identity.
>
> –Professor Wright

We humans have a unique ability to rationalize anything if it suits our egos and gives us space to do the things we want to do without feeling bad about them. We're particularly good at rationalizing our behavior if we fear that others might think badly of us. Societal norms or religious beliefs have oppressed homosexuals for many years, and some people have not yet broken those chains. The stigma associated with homosexuality can be so deeply internalized that some people lie about their sexuality. Deceiving themselves and others does not, however, change the fact that they are attracted to the same sex. If a man has sex with other men because he is sexually, emotionally, and/or romantically attracted to men, then that man is not heterosexual.

What is meant by the terms "pitcher" and "catcher"?

"Pitcher" and "catcher" are slang terms for the anal penetrator and receiver mentioned in the previous discussion. A pitcher is a man whose penis penetrates another man during anal sex. A catcher is a man who is sexually penetrated by another man during anal sex. Some people choose these positions based on their notions of masculinity and femininity, while for many, it is a matter of which positions bring pleasure and which don't.

> Some guys like being pitchers all the time. They feel more comfortable being in control, and they don't want to give up that control. I've counseled guys who say, "I would never be at the bottom!" Some guys like being the catcher all the time. There are some couples that like to pitch or catch…
>
> A lot of gay couples are just fine having oral sex, and they never have anal sex. It's really about your pleasure.
>
> –Professor Wright

Do all gay men enjoy anal sex?

Assuming that all gay men enjoy anal sex is like assuming all straight women enjoy penis-to-vagina intercourse. It's not true. It's also worth pointing out that people of all sexualities practice anal sex. We each have our preferences about how we have sex and what types of sex bring us more or less pleasure. The different ways we enjoy or dislike having sex are an aspect of our sexuality, because sexuality isn't only about which sex we are attracted to. Some people enjoy foreplay and others don't. Some people like to kiss and others don't. Some people like their nipples to be fondled and others don't. None of these acts are owned by any one sexuality. Ideally, we all explore different ways of having sex until we discover the things we enjoy most, and then we keep doing those things.

Do all lesbians use a strap-on penis during sex?

No. This question seems to stem from the mistaken assumption that all women need vaginal penetration from a penis in order to experience sexual stimulation, which is not true.

> *Some do and some don't. Not everyone is stimulated by or can reach orgasm by the feel of a penis.*
> –Tiffany

As stated in the previous question's response, we all derive sexual pleasure in different ways. Some women, regardless of their sexuality, are not sexually aroused, stimulated, or satisfied by a penis, whether it's real or synthetic. In "11 Things You've Always Wanted to Know About Lesbian Sex but Were Afraid to Ask," Jincey Lumpkin, Esq., Founder and Chief Sexy Officer, Juicy Pink Box, states, "The ways we have sex are as varied as straight couples [sic]. We have oral sex, anal sex, penetrative sex, and everything in between."[44]

Is it true that homosexuals are more promiscuous than heterosexuals?

No, this is a stereotype. There is no proof that homosexuals are more promiscuous than heterosexuals. Promiscuity is characterized by, or involves, indiscriminate mingling or association, especially having sexual relations with numerous partners on a casual basis. This definition can apply to anyone, regardless of sexuality.

A related stereotype is that homosexuals have higher sex drives than heterosexuals. According to medical professionals, a high sex drive is not emblematic of homosexuality. The difference in sex drives is most pronounced when comparing men to women. A high sex drive is more characteristic of men, whether hetero-, homo-, bi-, or pan-. According to WebMD, "Study after study shows that men's sex drives are not only stronger than women's but much more straightforward." They go on to say that the majority of men think about sex sixty times a day. After reviewing several surveys of men and women, Roy Baumeister, a social psychologist at Florida State University, concluded, "Men want sex more often than women at the start of a relationship, in the middle of it, and after many years of it."[45]

Men also say they want more sex partners in their lifetime and tend to be more interested in casual sex. Additionally, in many cultures, boys and men are praised for having as many sexual encounters as possible. It's considered a badge of honor. This can contribute to a culture of highly sexualized males where sexual dalliances are considered the norm for men. In many instances, boys who expect and seek many sexual encounters grow up to be men who do the same. What, then, should we expect the outcome to be when men are attracted to men and both have the sex drives and conditioning described?

In many situations, what we see is that the behaviors more often found in one sex become amplified when both partners are of that sex. For example, in a relationship involving two women, the traits more likely to be found in women are more likely to be present in both women, and therefore, that same-sex relationship would have a higher presence of that trait than an opposite-sex relationship might have. For instance, women are more likely to develop emotional attachments than men, and men are more likely to have higher sex drives than women. Therefore, a relationship involving two women might be more emotionally intense than a relationship involving a man and a woman. Likewise, a relationship involving two men might include a higher frequency of sex than a relationship involving one man and one woman.

> *Put two men who are socialized to think that having sex is part of your masculinity, and you don't have a woman in the mix, what happens is more sex. I don't think it's because they're gay. In gay male couples, there's a real tendency toward non-monogamy. Non-monogamy in lesbians is very low because they commit, they bond, in a different way. In the case of lesbians, it's the female role that's magnified. In male couples, it's the male that's magnified.*
>
> –Professor Wright

I don't think we are more promiscuous than the next person. I think that we have a lot of promiscuity in this country because of being repressed sexually.

–Commissioner Garner

We should also keep in mind that sex, sexual orientation, and sexual practices remain very personal, and there are always exceptions to any generalization.

I've known gay people who've had long-standing relationships. I know gays who have open relationships because both partners enjoy it. For me, sex does not rule everything. Casual sex does not work for me. I am probably a hopeless romantic, which is not an unfortunate thing to be because I still believe in love.

–Omar

Sex is an individual and personal expression. A person's preferences regarding the frequency of sex and the number of people involved have more to do with things like personality, mentality, and emotionality and should not be stereotyped based on sexuality or gender identity.

Are homosexuals more likely than heterosexuals to be child molesters?

No. *Heter*osexual men are more likely than any other sexuality to molest, rape, or fantasize about having sex with children. This behavior is referred to as pedophilia, which is a mental disorder most often observed in men who identify as heterosexual. Approximately 70 percent of men who molest boys identify themselves as heterosexual, according to studies like The Abel and Harlow Child Molestation Prevention Study.[46] It has also been noted that a child's risk of being molested by the heterosexual partner of a family member "is over one hundred times greater" than the risk of being molested by someone who is gay, lesbian, or bisexual, according to a study published in the Journal of Pediatrics.[47]

Not only are heterosexual men the most likely group to sexually assault children, "There is no evidence [to support the] mistaken belief that gay men have more of a tendency than heterosexual men to sexually molest children," according to The American Psychological Association.[48] As for gay women, *The Journal of Psychology and Human Sexuality* concluded that instances of adult lesbians molesting pre-pubescent children "are virtually nonexistent."[49] Joe Kort, PhD, asserted, "In reality, abuse of boys by gay pedophiles is rare, and the abuse of girls by lesbians is rarer still."[50]

The false narrative about gay men being more likely to molest children has led to years of prejudicial treatment of gay men and women, including discrimination, false accusations, and violence. Commissioner Garner noted that this unfounded stereotype made some homosexuals reticent to take jobs around children or get involved in community organizations where children are present.

> *That is the misconception that gay people are pedophiles. Unfortunately, there are a number of gay people that are afraid to get involved with children's groups because teachers are of that perception that you are going to molest them or you are a pedophile.*
>
> –Commissioner Garner

This absurd notion that homosexuals are a danger to children still exists, and until recently, the Boys Scouts of America (BSA) had a policy of prohibiting gay men from being Scout leaders. Fortunately, more people are realizing that gay adults do not pose a threat to children, including the BSA, who lifted their ban on gay leadership and membership in 2015.

Portraying homosexuals as sexual predators serves those who want to perpetuate hatred and fear. The reality is that homosexual men and women are far less likely to commit a sexual crime against a child than are heterosexual, cisgender men.

Marriage

Why is same-sex marriage controversial?

Gay marriage has given rise to public disagreement, which is the definition of controversial. There is a group of people who would deny homosexuals the right to marriage. There is also a group of people who would not stop fighting for the right to have their unions declared legal and official. Thus, the controversy.

Same-sex marriage is controversial because some people believe that somewhere along the way, there was an edict declaring that marriage should only exist between a man and a woman. A little research uncovers no such edict, and actually reveals that marriage has involved a variety of unions for a variety of purposes.

Today, marriage is often viewed as an expression of love and commitment—the union of two people who love each other and have decided to, hopefully, spend the remainder of their lives together. US Supreme Court Justice Anthony Kennedy said, "No union is more profound than marriage, for it embodies the highest ideals of love, fidelity, devotion, sacrifice, and family. In forming a marital union, two people become something greater than once they were."[51] Additionally, marriage delivers social and/or economic status and respect, for some, and provides legal protections for each spouse.

The modern idea and purpose of marriage is, in many instances, drastically different than that of centuries ago. The notion that marriage has always been reserved for one man and one woman is incorrect. There continue to be cultures and religions that practice marriage between one man and several women, or one man and a female child, for instance. In some cultures, marriages were, and still are, arranged between two strangers, regardless of whether the two people approve. There was a time when marriage between siblings was an accepted practice; even marriage between one living sibling and one dead sibling was considered acceptable.

The notion that marriage is universally practiced as a union based on mutual love is thus also incorrect. There is a long and documented history of marriage being used as a tool to strengthen an individual's or family's power, to solidify or increase land ownership, and/or to maintain "pure" bloodlines. Religious involvement in marriage has also changed over the centuries. For much of the early Christian era, religions stayed out of weddings and let the state handle the union of man and woman. Eventually, sometime after 800 AD, weddings became religious ceremonies conducted by various faiths. In many instances, this was the result of church-states seeking to extend their control over citizens, which was primarily an effort to collect additional fees and taxes. A few centuries later, the Catholic Church made marriage one of its sacraments and, some historians suggest, this too was an attempt to strengthen the church-state's control over citizens. The point is that marriage has existed for a variety of purposes and reasons, and in numerous instances, has born no resemblance to the concept of marriage that exists in many modern societies.

Marriage is an important part of the human experience. The idea of someone "to have and to hold, 'til death do us part" is a driving force in Western cultures for many people, regardless of sexuality or gender identity. Some folks get married three, four, or even five or more times, which perhaps speaks to our everlasting hope that marriage can fulfill its life-long promise. According to the 2013 Pew Research survey, the top three reasons heterosexual and homosexual people listed for wanting to get married are: 1) love, 2) companionship, and 3) lifelong commitment.[52]

As compelling as the marriage concept is to the human experience, I struggle to understand why anyone would want to deny this revered institution to two consenting adults who want to love, commit to, and protect each other. Some have claimed that Jesus said marriage should only be between a man and a woman. However, as we will explore in Chapter 12, this is a distortion of Jesus's teaching. While on the subject of the Bible, it should be noted that our modern society does not adhere to or approve of many of the marriages depicted in the Old and New Testaments. For instance, many men in the Bible had multiple wives, as well as sex slaves or concubines. The Bible also tells of men marrying siblings, as Abraham did when he married his half-sister, and of men marrying cousins, as Isaac and Jacob did. If the Bible is to be our guide for marriage, then why don't we adhere to those practices?

The issue of gay marriage also brings up another contradiction. Many anti-gay people want to paint homosexuals as promiscuous. Yet when gay and lesbian people seek the commitment and stability of marriage, anti-gay groups say that's wrong too. It would seem that if you want to dissuade people from what you might deem as promiscuous behavior, then encouraging them to settle down and get married would be the preferred alternative.

In June 2015, the Supreme Court ruled on this controversy, declaring that the US Constitution guarantees the right to same-sex marriage. Though religious entities may continue to deny the religious marriage ceremony to gay couples, local, state, and federal governments in the United States are no longer allowed to do so. Fortunately, the Supreme Court decided that the right to marry was an issue of equality and ruled that, under the Fourteenth Amendment to the US Constitution, states must license a marriage between two people of the same sex and must recognize a marriage between two people of the same sex when their marriage was lawfully licensed and performed out-of-State.[53] In doing so, the United States joined more than twenty other countries who had legalized gay marriage, including the Netherlands (2000), Belgium (2003), Canada (2005), Spain (2005), South Africa (2006), Norway (2009), and England (2013).[54] Regarding Uruguay's 2013 legalization of gay marriage, President José Alberto "Pepe" Mujica Cordano (2010–2015) said, "Gay marriage… it's older than we are. It's an objective reality that it exists. For us, not legalizing it would be to torture people needlessly."[55]

While arguing in favor of gay marriage, Justice Anthony Kennedy said, "It would misunderstand these men and women to say they disrespect the idea of marriage. Their plea is that they do respect it, respect it so deeply that they seek to find its fulfillment for themselves. Their hope is not to be condemned to live in loneliness, excluded from one of civilization's oldest institutions. They ask for equal dignity in the eyes of the law. The Constitution grants them that right."[56]

Prior to the Supreme Court ruling, the United States Federal Government treated gay people as second-class citizens when it came to marriage. Prior to 2015, same-sex marriage was only allowed in a few states. Prior to 2003, same-sex marriage was not legal anywhere in the US. Massachusetts became the first state to legalize same-sex marriage in that year. By 2008, only California and Connecticut had joined MA in legalizing gay marriage. They were followed by New Hampshire (2010), New York (2011), Washington (2012), Minnesota (2013), and Wyoming (2014). By 2015, the list included thirty-four states and the Districts of Columbia and Alaska. Gay couples like Tiffany and Yolanda or Rev. Teague and David, who lived in states such as Georgia that had not yet legalized gay marriage, had to go to another state such as California, or to another country such as Canada, to get married. That marriage would not be recognized upon returning to their homes in Georgia.

Denying the legal right of marriage to adults who are homosexual was determined to be discriminatory and unconstitutional because doing so denied access to rights and benefits that heterosexuals have. As a result of the Supreme Court ruling, gay couples across the country showed up at courthouses for legal marriage ceremonies. Norman MacArthur, seventy-four, and Bill Novak, seventy-six, profiled in a *Yahoo Parenting* story, had been together since their twenties and were married in May 2015 after fifty-two years together.[57] By June 2016, nearly one million adults reported being in a gay or lesbian marriage.[58]

In the US, modern marriage bestows certain rights and protections for the two people in that union.

> *The important reason why there's a federal law in place is because, in addition to the state rights one can get when they get married, they also get 1,049 rights from the federal government. When you get married in Georgia, you get a couple hundred separate individual rights, just because you're married. But there are also 1,049 rights that the US federal government gives to and grants to married couples.*
>
> –Roemerman

How can any American think it's fair to deny a US citizen 1,049 rights?

> *Marriage became more of an issue of fairness. I don't see it as a religious thing but the legal aspects of it and the civil rights aspects. If Emily or I ended up in the hospital, the other person potentially wouldn't have visiting rights. It's one level of protection against discrimination and sort of a societal solidifying of our relationship as a very commonly accepted thing. We wanted the validity that's assumed with marriage, and we wanted the civil rights and protections that come with marriage. Those were the kind of key points that made us think, "Let's get real-married, not skim-milk marriage."*
>
> –Dr. Lowell

Not being allowed to marry can cost couples upwards of thousands of dollars, which many cannot afford.

> *From a legal perspective, there are some things that are a pain in the ass [about not being able to get married]. I had to adopt my daughter, and then Rochelle had to adopt our son Brice, so*

it's stupid. It's like 3,000 bucks we had to pay for adopting our own kids because we couldn't legally be married.

–Karla

If marriage is available to one sexuality, then it should be available to all sexualities.

Why should the church or the country decide what you want to do? If people don't want gay marriage, there shouldn't be straight marriages. Why should it be a difference in terms of sexuality? Why is it okay for men and women to marry and proclaim their love and it's not okay for two women or two men to do that? I think once we get past that, the human race will be a better human race.

–Fredis

I think if you have an intimate connection and you want to live your lives together and you want to build a family, then you should be entitled to get married. You should be able to benefit from that. We should be able to participate like everyone else in terms of the benefits that come with it... The fact that we could get married really solidified that, in the midst of life and challenges, there is no retreating. We had something here that validates our relationship.

–Commissioner Garner

Wanting to deny legal marriage to gay couples seems to be another attempt to separate them from society and punish them for not being heterosexual.

A 2013 Pew Research Center Survey found that 93 percent of LGBT adults favor same-sex marriage,[59] though not all homosexuals are in favor of same-sex marriage.

There's a segment of the population that is saying "you're selling out." There are gay people that don't believe in gay marriages, and there are gay people that believe in marriage.

–Professor Wright

Some people, regardless of sexuality, might not think they want to get married until they meet an individual that inspires them to make that commitment.

> *I never thought I would get married growing up, actually. Then Emily and I started dating, and it was unlike any other relationship I had to that point. We just had such an intellectual and emotional connection that kind of surprised us both. It came out of nowhere, and we had both been dating other people, but it was a totally different connection than either of us had had with anybody else.*

–Dr. Lowell

One of the most common reasons conveyed to me by Commissioner Garner and others was that of validation. To validate is the act of making or declaring something legally or officially acceptable. It also means to recognize or affirm that a person or their feelings or opinions are valid and worthwhile. Who among us does not seek validation? We want the world, society, family, and friends to see us and validate us. This quest for validation extends to marriage. We want the world to recognize that we have found love and love has found us. If that is true for a man who loves a woman, why wouldn't it be true for a man who loves a man or a woman who loves a woman?

Does same-sex marriage weaken the institution of marriage?

No. How can allowing more people to make a legal commitment by getting married weaken marriage? It seems more likely that making same-sex marriage legal reinforces the institution of marriage. When we talk about marriage as an "institution," we are referring to the "established law, practice, or custom" of marriage. It also refers to the aspects of marriage for religious or social purposes.

I can think of a few ways same-sex marriage reinforces the institution of marriage. If we consider heterosexual marriage a legal contract binding two people together, then same-sex marriage fulfills that role of being a legal contract. From a religious perspective, same-sex marriage also fulfills the same purpose as heterosexual marriage. If marriage is considered two people joining together under God, as some religions view it, or as two people making a covenant with God, as the Catholic Church views it, then gay marriage fulfills that role. Gay marriage also furthers the grand and modern idea of love between two people.

There is also something called the "marriage benefit":

> *There's something in sociology we call the marriage benefit. Heterosexual couples who get married tend to have better health than if they cohabitate. What you find is that the benefits that come with marriage actually do something more than simply having the relationship. We know that having a relationship also benefits your health, so people in relationships do better than single people, and marriage does something extra. We've done a paper and found that the health of lesbian and gay couples, the individuals and the couples, is better in states that have embraced same-sex marriage. [Prior to the Supreme Court ruling granting national marriage rights.] I think what's good about marriage, as an institution, is it sanctions a relationship, and it organizes resources that make it easier for them to live their lives.*

–Professor Wright

Denying marriage to gay couples not only denies them the legal rights and benefits associated with marriage, it also hinders their ability to function at their highest level. Why would we want to prevent that? The ability of individuals to perform at their pinnacle benefits individuals, couples, the institution of marriage, and society as a whole.

Same-sex marriage also reinforces the value of commitment that is inherent in our modern concept of marriage.

> *The commitment was very important to me. I've never wanted a series of casual relationships. I wanted a lifetime relationship with a person with whom I was compatible and shared values and purpose. The religious ceremony, I first saw as just a public expression. After we had that Quaker meeting for worship, which was our marriage, there was something very profound*

about it. We not only affirmed our commitment to each other, and our love for each other in that meeting, that marriage, there was a deepening of the commitment after that. The civil ceremony in Canada a couple of years later was a good thing. It was a reaffirmation, but it didn't have the gravity, in my mind, in my heart, that our religious wedding did. At that point, it wasn't clear to me if it would ever come in the United States, but I wanted a legal marriage certificate in our respective pockets. And I also wanted to tell certain people who said, "Well, you had a ceremony of commitment, but it wasn't a real marriage," that it was a real, legal marriage recognized by the Province of Ontario and the Government of Canada.

–David J. Thurman, MD, epidemiologist,
  Centers for Disease Control (CDC), married,
  cisgender, gay, 65 years old

This aspect of commitment is important to many people.

I wanted to commit. I wanted it to be messy for us to separate. I wanted us to have to make that commitment so that it was not easy to fall apart. We wanted the typical thing where you make a promise in front of your community, which you can do as a non-legal ceremony of some sort, but the legal piece is important for us. I want stability.

–Anne

Same-sex marriage also reinforces another aspect of the institution, that if two people truly love each other, they will get married, share property, and build a home and a family. When I was a child, my parents disapproved of living together without the benefit of marriage, something they referred to as "shacking up." Reverend Teague also grew up hearing that shacking up was not desirable; that if a man loved a woman, he would marry her.

My father put it in our heads that we were to not just shack up with a woman—because, of course, we were supposed to be heterosexual. He said, "You go get a license for the dog. How

dare you do less for a woman that you would be living with?" I
always grew up knowing that whomever I was going to be with
significantly, I wanted to be married to. And so, of course, I
wanted to be married.

–Rev. Teague

Same-sex marriage also does not hinder or diminish heterosexual couples from getting married. Supreme Court Justice Ruth Bader Ginsburg pointed this out when she declared that allowing gay marriage is "not taking away anything from heterosexual couples. They would have the very same incentive to marry, all the benefits that come with marriage that they do now."[60]

What kinds of things *do* weaken the institution of marriage? Infidelity, spousal abuse, and divorce are proven to weaken individual marriages and marriage as an institution. Yet those very acts have long been committed by heterosexuals, without anyone suggesting that heterosexuals as a group shouldn't be allowed to get married or that heterosexual marriages weaken the institution of marriage.

We can't do marriage no more harm than what straight folk
have done to it. Isn't straight marriage at a 50 percent divorce
rate? You can't blame us for that.

–Rev. Teague

The Reverend Otis Moss III expounded on this notion. Moss, the son of the Reverend Otis Moss II, writes, "Marriage was under attack years ago by men who viewed women as property and children as trophies of sexual prowess. Marriage is under attack by low wages, high incarceration, unfair tax policy, unemployment, and lack of education. Marriage is under attack by clergy who proclaim monogamy yet think nothing of stepping outside the bonds of marriage to have multiple affairs. Same-gender couples did not cause the high divorce rate, but our adolescent views of relationships and our inability as a community to come to grips with the ethic of love and commitment did... Gay people have never been the enemy, and when we use rhetoric to suggest they are the source of our problems, we lie on God and cause tears to flow from the eyes of Christ."[61]

Parenting

Does having homosexual parents make children gay?

No. Having gay parents will not "make" a child gay, just as having heterosexual parents will not "make" a child heterosexual. It's worth restating that those who study sexuality and human development state that we cannot change a person's sexual orientation. It is something we are born with and come to realize over time. The conclusion from research is clear: sexual and gender identities (including gender identity, gender-role behavior, and sexual orientation) develop in much the same way among children of lesbian mothers as they do among children of heterosexual parents.[62]

If a parent's sexuality determined the child's sexuality, then wouldn't heterosexual parents only give rise to heterosexual children, and conversely wouldn't homosexual parents only give rise to homosexual children? Neither of these is the case. In fact, most children raised by homosexual parents are heterosexual, according to the APA, National Association of Social Workers, American Psychological Association, and the American Psychiatric Association. They also reported that most homosexual adults were raised by heterosexual parents.

> *Dad was an All-American football player and got a doctorate in aerospace engineering and went to Vietnam. Mom was [a] UGA sorority girl. And they produced a gay son.*
>
> –Perry

Additionally, heterosexual, religious, conservative parents have gay children.

> *I've been raised by straight people, very religious people, and yet I like women as friends, but not sexually… Two gay people can raise a child, and if the kid is not into guys, they're not going to go with guys.*
>
> –Fredis

A parent's sexuality doesn't determine or impact a child's sexuality. While having gay parents won't make a child gay, it might make it easier for a gay child to accept their sexuality.

Does it make them open to it, or does it make them gay, or does it just make it easier to accept it if that's in them? If you grow up in an environment where there is variety, it doesn't seem like anything is wrong, and if you discover you're gay, then it's easier to just go on and be you.

–Tiffany

I like the sound of that: "Just go on and be you."

Saying that homosexual parents make children gay is often used as a scare tactic to incite fear of gay people. It is also a way of saying homosexuality is bad.

There is an obvious value judgment in that statement because it is saying underneath it that being gay is bad.

–Anne

Being gay is not bad. Being a gay parent is not bad, nor is being a gay child. Having gay parents is not bad for children. Having no parents is bad for children. Perpetuating the notion that homosexuality will "rub off" on a child is completely unfounded. If we want to look at the kinds of things that rub off on children, perhaps we would be better off paying more attention to things like love and hate, nurturing and neglect, support and rejection, protection and physical abuse, and honesty and dishonesty. Our behavior and character are what rubs off on children, not our sexuality.

What options exist for same-sex couples who want to have children?

The way any couple goes about bringing a new life into their family depends on things like age, fertility, and other health conditions. For instance, some heterosexual couples use in-vitro fertilization or surrogates or pursue adoption, as do some LGBTQIAP couples. Karla and her wife relied on artificial insemination to have their two children.

When we met, we knew we were meant to be together, and children would be part of our life. I've always had a desire to be a parent. We both had the children biologically. My wife carried our daughter. We tried insemination the first time, and she was pregnant right away. Then I tried to get pregnant for about eighteen months, and it happened on the third try with my son. Our children had the same sperm donor.

–Karla

With some couples both partners have the experience of pregnancy and child birth.

I came into the relationship with a child that I gave birth to. And when we had our son, my partner had him; she gave birth to him. She wanted to physically have a child. That has always been a part of our plan.

–Tiffany

Adoption is another option many couples choose. The ACLU reports that same-sex parents in the United States are four times more likely than different-sex parents to be raising an adopted child. "Among couples with children under the age of eighteen in the home, 13 percent of same-sex parents have an adopted child, compared to just 3 percent of different-sex parents."[63] Adoption agencies like Lifelong Adoptions report that nearly two million LGBTQ individuals are interested in adopting children. Sadly, as will be discussed in chapter 11, many states and adoption agencies don't support adoptions by LGBTQ couples.

CHAPTER FIVE

BISEXUAL

"Cancel your subscription to what other people say
about you, because in this life, it ain't what other folks
say about you; it's what you say about you."
–Dr. Frederick Douglass Haynes, III[64]

Intro

"I call myself bisexual because I acknowledge in myself the potential to be attracted, romantically and/or sexually, to people of more than one sex, not necessarily at the same time, not necessarily in the same way, and not necessarily to the same degree," writes Robyn Ochs, author of *Getting Bi* and *Bisexual Resource Guide*.[65] "Bi" means two. Bisexual refers to being attracted to two sexes. A person with a bisexual sexuality has the potential to be sexually, emotionally, and romantically attracted to two sexes: the opposite sex and the same sex.

The idea of bisexuality is often more difficult for people to understand and accept than homosexuality. One reason might be that our society has a habit of insisting we "pick a team." This pick-a-team philosophy appears in many aspects of our lives, including relationships and sexuality. For instance, we are expected to pick one boyfriend or one girlfriend, one husband or one wife, and to be attracted to only one sex. This is an extension of the duality Professor Wright mentioned earlier. We are accustomed to allowing ourselves and others only two options and often further insist that only one of those options can be appropriate. Bisexuality is difficult for many people to understand and accept because it does not adhere to this arbitrary "pick a team" rule. It's one thing to ask folks to consider that some people are only attracted to the same sex, because at least that still fits within the boundaries of "picking a team," but this whole idea of "going both ways," as bisexuality is sometimes referred to, can be too much for some people to wrap their brains around.

> *There are a lot of gay people who feel that way about bisexuals. You have a harder time if you're bisexual because the gays don't understand you, the straights don't understand you, and you know.*

–Rafshoon

As a result, many heterosexuals and homosexuals simply deny the existence of bisexuality.

If you are someone who insists that bisexuality isn't real, please consider that telling a bisexual person there's no such thing as bisexuality is akin to saying, "You don't exist." Fritz Klein, author of *The Bisexual Option: Second Edition,* agreed, saying, "I think it is presumption to tell people they do not exist."[66]

Bisexuality exists. There are an estimated 255 million bisexual people in the world, representing 3.5 percent of the world population. Of that number, 2.25 million bisexuals are estimated to live in the United States.[67] The Centers for Disease Control and Prevention report that 5.5 percent of women and 2 percent of men said they were bisexual.[68] Bisexual people exist all over the world, in varying cultures, classes, races, religions, education levels, and ages. In 1976, David Bowie told *Playboy,* "It's true—I am a bisexual. I suppose it's the best thing that ever happened to me."[69] *New York Times* columnist Charles M. Blow came out as bisexual in his 2014 memoir. Congresswoman Krysten Sinema (D-Arizona) is the first openly bisexual member of the U.S. Congress. Kate Brown, governor of Oregon, is the first openly bisexual person to lead a U.S. state. Rabbi Debra Kolodny is a bisexual rights activist. Add to the list music mogul Clive Davis, actress Anna Paquin, and country singer Vanessa Carlton, who in 2010 announced, "I've never said this before, but while we're here and living out loud as we should every single day, I, myself, am a proud bisexual woman."[70]

According to a paper published in the *Scientific American*, "bisexuality is a natural state among animals, perhaps Homo sapiens included, despite the sexual-orientation boundaries most people take for granted."[71]

Are there certain names we should use to refer to bisexuals?

Bisexual and bi are commonly accepted words to use. The word "bisexual" was first used by neurologist Charles Gilbert Chaddock in 1892 and has become widely accepted, along with the term "bi."[72] A different term, "bi-curious," refers to people who are curious about this sexual orientation as it relates to their attractions and may be trying to determine if they are bisexual.

I don't hear terms used to demean bisexuals and bisexuality as often as I did when I was a kid. During the seventies and eighties, bisexuality was referred to as "AC-DC" or "swings both ways." Neither was used in an endearing way.

There are other terms used by people who identify themselves as heterosexual, even though they are attracted to males and females. The term "heteroflexible" is being used by individuals who identify as heterosexual and say they live a mostly heterosexual life but are also "occasionally" attracted to and have sexual relations with the same sex. There is mixed sentiment about the use and introduction of this term. Some, like Joe Kort, PhD, a *HuffPost* blogger, believe "people can be heteroflexible, homoflexible, and bisexual."[73] Others, like *PRIDE* columnist Zachary Zane, consider "heteroflexible" to be "just a word that perpetuates bi-invisibility and seems to be used by people who are not quite comfortable with the label bisexual (or pansexual)."[74] A related term is "beer-bi," which refers to someone who says they are heterosexual except when inebriated; then they become attracted to people of both sexes. The commonality among these terms is that they associate themselves with bisexuality without actually claiming bisexuality.

What attracts bisexuals to other people?

Bisexuals are attracted to people for many of the same reasons as people of other sexualities. Sometimes a person's appearance sparks the initial attraction; sometimes it's personality, profession, the way a person thinks, or similar backgrounds and experiences. Bisexual relationships also move through the same cycles that other relationships do, including attraction, dating, breakups, commitments, marriages, and divorces. Vicki spoke about why she was attracted to the man she married and to the woman who is now her fiancée.

> I thought my husband was just beautiful. He was real little, like a size-26 waist. I think whether Sheila had been a man or a woman, I would have fallen in love with her, with her energy. They're opposites, just about. He's more feminine than she is and less self-assured. She's more of a man than my husband was, as far as her expertise and her persona. I could see this bright light surrounding her. I had never experienced that before. And when she talked to me, her face lit up. The more we talked, the more I realized our personalities fit. And she's a take-control kind of person. I like that a lot.
>
> –Vicki

Some bisexuals will say the attraction doesn't have anything to do with biological sex; that they are attracted to people regardless of sex.

> I like to think I'm open. I look at the person, being in a relationship with somebody based on who they are. There's definitely a type that I'm more attracted to in a man and a type I'm more attracted to in a female. I have dated a Japanese-American woman, an African-American man, white females, white males, all different ages, some much older, some younger.
>
> –Jennie

Are bisexuals equally attracted to both sexes?

Being bisexual doesn't necessarily mean being equally attracted to males and females. It depends on the person. Bisexual.org, a project of The American

Institute of Bisexuality (AIB) and the Bisexual Foundation, explains that bisexuals do "not have to feel the same kind of attraction or intensity of attraction to all genders."[75] Some bisexuals find themselves more attracted to men, some are more attracted to women, and others feel there is an equal chance for them to be attracted to a man or a woman. *The Bisexual Option* describes the range of bisexual attraction as extremely broad—from almost-complete preference for one sex to enjoying sex with either gender to almost-absolute preference for the other sex.[76] Writer Charlotte Dingle says, "It's not uncommon for bisexuals to have a preference for a certain gender/genders."[77] According to *A Survey of LGBT Americans: Attitudes, Experiences and Values in Changing Times,* 71 percent of bisexual men and 69 percent of bisexual women say they are more attracted to a particular sex. When asked if they were equally attracted to both sexes, only 28 percent of bisexual men and 31 percent of bisexual women say they are.[78] When it comes to actual relationships, 84 percent of bisexuals in relationships have opposite-sex partners, 9 percent have same-sex partners, and 4 percent say they have a spouse or partner who is transgender.[79]

If we consider how anyone's attraction correlates to who they actually have relationships with, then it shouldn't be surprising that the attraction percentages don't match the percentages of actual relationships. Feeling a greater attraction to a certain type of person doesn't guarantee that's who you will meet and develop a romantic attraction to or have a long-term relationship with. Although Angelia is bisexual and has a preference for women, she fell in love with and became engaged to a man.

> *I'm attracted to men and women. I like sex with men and women, and I like relationships with men and women, but if I had to choose one, it would be women.*
>
> –Angelia, truck driver, engaged,
>   cisgender, bisexual, 27 years old

Jazmyn's perspective was different.

> *In some ways, I say that I am bisexual with a preference for a woman. I am saying it really explicitly, so it is not like a preference for women. It is really a preference for this woman.*
>
> –Jazmyn

While bisexuals can be attracted to both sexes and may enjoy sexual intercourse with males and females, some bisexuals say they prefer sexual intercourse with one sex more than with the other. This may or may not align with whom they are more attracted to. Sheila considers herself bisexual and said sex was much better for her with a woman.

> *I was a different person after my first sexual encounter with a woman. It was like I saw the fireworks. I had my first orgasm with a woman. Up to that point, I had tried hard with men, but it hadn't happened.*
>
> –Sheila

Jillian Michaels, of the TV show "The Biggest Loser," doesn't have a preference. She says, "Let's just say I believe in healthy love. If I fall in love with a woman, that's awesome. If I fall in love with a man, that's awesome. As long as you fall in love."[80]

Can bisexuals be attracted to a man and a woman at the same time?

Yes. "They can if they can,"[81] states Regina V. Reinhardt, PhD, of the California School of Professional Psychology, author of *Bisexual Women in Heterosexual Relationships*. Have you ever been at a gathering and had two different people catch your eye? Have you ever dated more than one person at a time because you were attracted to them both, even if you were attracted to them for different reasons? I have. Anyone, regardless of sexuality, can be attracted to more than one person at the same time. For a bisexual person, that could mean being attracted to a man and a woman at the same time or being attracted to two women or two men at the same time.

Is a person considered bisexual if they have same-sex relations while incarcerated and then have opposite-sex relations once released?

The determining factor isn't whether they've had sex with both sexes, the determining factor is whether they are attracted to both sexes. Bisexuality is defined as being sexually, emotionally, and romantically attracted to men and women. An incarcerated woman who has sex with women, and is sexually, emotionally, and romantically attracted to women and men, is bisexual. If that woman is not sexually, emotionally, and romantically attracted to both sexes, then she is not bisexual, even if she has had sex with men and women. The same is true for men.

What is sequential bisexuality?

Sequential bisexuality is when a bisexual person's sexual relationships are only with one sex, males, for instance, at any one given time. Although a bi person has the potential to be attracted to males and females, there might be periods when a bisexual person only dates one sex at a given time.[82] Sequential bisexuality doesn't mean that a person is no longer bisexual.

Is bisexuality a gateway to homosexuality?

No. This mistaken impression likely stems from the fact that some people come out as bisexual before coming out as homosexual. There are a number of reasons this might occur. Some people know they are gay and might openly identify as bisexual thinking it will be easier for parents to digest. Eventually, they decide not to hide their true sexuality any longer and come out as gay.

> *I told my mother I was bi because they probably wouldn't be crushed that I wasn't going to have kids or anything like that. I think that's like the first step. Just like learning how to walk. That was the first crawl for me to acknowledging and being proud of who I am, a gay man.*
> –Fredis

In an interview with *Daily Mail*, Neil Patrick Harris says it took years for him to come to terms with his homosexuality, and that he initially labeled himself bisexual.[83] Harris says that acknowledging he was bisexual seemed like a "half-truth but the only truth" he knew at the time. He eventually told his parents.

Now, there are people who are gay and don't want to come out all the way, who will say they're bisexual. I think I maybe did for a day or two.

–Rafshoon

Bisexuality does not lead to homosexuality. For some homosexuals, like Fredis and Harris, *saying* they are bisexual can be a gateway to acceptance. It should not, however, be construed as something every gay or lesbian person does.

Can you trust a bisexual person in a relationship if they're attracted to both sexes?

Of course, you can, just as much as you can trust a heterosexual person or someone of any other sexuality. An individual's inclination for infidelity is not related to their sexuality. Additionally, there is no data to support the assertion that bisexuals have a higher rate of infidelity than any other sexuality. Infidelity among heterosexual couples is well documented, and most of us know of heterosexuals who have been unfaithful. A 2015 YouGov survey found that 21 percent of men and 19 percent of women admitted that they had cheated on their partners, with another 7 percent saying they didn't want to answer the question.[84] An article in *the Daily Mail* provided a much higher rate, stating, "Some 63 percent of men and 45 percent of women reported having been unfaithful at least once, according to an international study published in 2004."[85]

It would seem that the claim that bisexuals aren't trustworthy is just another attempt to disparage them. In terms of relationships, 68 percent of bisexual women and 40 percent of bisexual men are in committed relationships, compared to 70 percent of the overall population. The bisexual divorce rate is slightly lower than the overall population's rate.[86]

Being bisexual doesn't mean a person cherishes their relationships any less than anyone else. A HuffPost.com article on bisexuality addresses the belief that bisexuals are more prone to cheat or leave their partners and spouses: "People leave their significant others for other people every day, regardless of orientation. To insinuate that bisexuals are more likely to do so than others, and to shun them as a result, is just ignorant."[87]

Fred Klein, author of *The Bisexual Option: Second Edition*, offered another perspective on why bisexuals are thought to be untrustworthy in relationships. He believes bisexuals are viewed as spies and traitors because they are capable of moving freely among both sexes, and this access places bisexuals in a position to know the "secrets" of both sexes. He writes, "The bisexual, in short, is seen as a dangerous person, not to be trusted, because his or her party loyalty, so to speak, is nonexistent."[88]

Some bisexuals, like Kristina Marusic, a writer for *Slate*, may be in an opposite-gender relationship and have an understanding with their partners that allows them to enjoy secondary relationships with members of the same gender.[89]

> *I can be in a serious relationship with a woman and not have to have a man. But when I'm in [relationships] with men, I still have to have women in my life. My fiancé knows that.*
>
> –Angelia

Most relationships and marriages are based on mutual agreements, and sometimes those agreements allow for one or both parties to have relationships outside of the marriage. This can exist regardless of sexuality. In these situations, there is no cheating or lack of trust if both people are behaving within their agreed boundaries. Regina U. Reinhardt, PhD, had such a relationship, saying, "I have spent my adult life happily married while maintaining secondary relationships with women with the full knowledge and consent of my husband."[90] In this and similar situations, there is no infidelity because both members of the couple are aware and have agreed to the possibility of extra-marital relations.

Nonetheless, most people, regardless of sexuality, desire and eventually settle into a monogamous relationship. In the article "12 Things to Never Say to a Bisexual Woman," freelance journalist Charlotte Dingle writes, "I would never cheat on them, and if they cheated on me, I would cry forever. We are as monogamous as it gets."[91] Trust and loyalty are important to most people in relationships.

> *I still sometimes may have some kind of fantasy or something like that but would never act on it. Never. I would not risk my relationship with Val for anybody. The most important thing is*

we share the same values and trust. We have tremendous loyalty and trust. We both know it's forever.

–Sheila

Do bisexuals date straight people?

Yes. When a bisexual person dates someone of the opposite sex, there's a pretty good chance that person will be heterosexual. Consider that bisexuals are estimated to represent 3.5 percent of the overall population, and that heterosexuals represent more than 90 percent of the population.[92] This means that a bisexual person has a greater opportunity for dating and relationships if they are willing to date heterosexuals. Another thing to consider is that a bisexual person who is dating someone of the opposite sex will be presumed heterosexual until they state otherwise. Author Greta Christina states, "When you're bisexual, but you're in a long-term relationship, your bisexuality can become invisible. People often assume that you're gay or straight based on who you're involved with now."[93]

The opportunity for a bisexual woman to date a heterosexual man appears to be greater than it is for a bi man to date a heterosexual woman. There appears to be less stigma associated with a bisexual female than a bisexual male. As a result, a heterosexual man might be more willing to knowingly date a bisexual woman, while a heterosexual woman might be less willing to knowingly date a bisexual man.

Marusic believes the dating pool for bisexuals is predominantly populated by straight people because "a large number of gay men and lesbians still flat-out refuse to date bisexuals."[94] Many bisexuals report that some homosexuals won't date bisexuals because they're viewed as "traitors" for dating the opposite sex. There are some homosexuals who don't believe bisexuality exists; instead, they claim that bisexuals are actually homosexuals who haven't made up their minds.

Do bisexuals get married?

Yes. For most people, regardless of sexuality, marriage is an important part of the human experience. A person's sexuality doesn't eliminate the desire for marriage, and since the 2015 Supreme Court ruling about same-sex marriage, there is nothing to prevent bisexuals from marrying someone of the same sex. In a 2015 survey, the Pew Research Center found that 32 percent of bisexual women and 23 percent of bi men were married, and that 45 percent of bisexuals said they would like to get married someday while 40 percent were unsure.[95]

If a bisexual person gets married, are they still bisexual?

Yes. A bisexual person remains bisexual, whether they marry someone of the opposite sex or the same sex. Their marital status changes, not their sexuality. Several years ago, talk show host Larry King suggested that his guest, actress Anna Paquin, who identifies as bisexual and married her *True Blood* co-star Stephen Moyer, was therefore no longer bisexual. Paquin responded that her being bisexual was not a "past-tense thing."

A heterosexual's sexuality remains constant whether they are single, dating, engaged, married, or divorced. The same is true for bisexuals. Why would we impose a different standard or expectation on bisexuals than we impose on heterosexuals or homosexuals? Marusic observes, "We'd never tell a gay man practicing abstinence that he 'wasn't really gay' just because he wasn't currently sleeping with men."[96]

CHAPTER SIX

ASEXUAL

"Asexuality is like any other identity—at its core, it's just
a word that people use to help figure themselves out then
communicate that part of themselves to others."
–The Asexuality Visibility Network

Intro

The prefix "a-" means "not" or "without." The term "asexual" refers to a person who is not sexually attracted to others. An asexual person does not experience sexual attraction. On asexuality.org, a site where asexual people share their experiences and perspectives anonymously, one person writes, "Theoretically, sex sounds all well and good. But in actuality, it doesn't appeal to me at all." The post's author also explained that they had always felt this way but initially thought it was because they were too young. In an article for *The Guardian* titled, "We're Married, We Just Don't Have Sex," Paul Cox recalls that he has never had sex and has never been interested in sex. "When I was thirteen, my father gave me a book on sex education. I felt as if I was reading about a foreign culture; I just couldn't see why anyone would go to so much trouble just to have sex."[97]

It is estimated that one percent of the world's population, about seventy-six million people, are asexual.[98] That number may be higher given that some people don't want to come out as asexual, others won't admit it anonymously in a survey, and others haven't yet identified themselves as asexual. It's worth noting that asexuality has not been studied to the same degree as heterosexuality and homosexuality, and that most surveys and research do not include asexuality or asexual people.

Asexuality, also known as "ace," might be the least-talked-about sexuality, in part because many people can't fathom that anyone could be asexual. In the hypersexualized world we live in, the general belief is that every adult wants to have sex or is having sex unless they are senior citizens, nuns, priests, or physically unable to have sex. Gaining a better understanding of asexual relationships requires stepping out of our own experience. We are likely to understand more if we don't require everything to line up with what we have known and experienced.

Some people mistakenly equate asexuality with celibacy or abstinence. The difference is that asexuality is a sexual orientation, and celibacy and abstinence are behaviors that a person of any sexuality can practice. Asexuality describes a person's sexual attraction, while celibacy and abstinence describe a person's choice to refrain from sexual activity. The Asexual Visibility & Education Network explains, "Unlike celibacy, which is a choice, asexuality is a sexual orientation."

Do asexuals experience sexual arousal?

Yes, some do. Sexual arousal can exist without sexual attraction, according to Asexuality New Zealand Trust.[99] Sexual arousal is physiological, which means it involves physical changes in the body brought on by physiological processes and hormones, like estrogen and testosterone. In a woman, sexual arousal can begin with dilated blood vessels in the vagina which result in fluid passing through the vaginal walls, increasing lubrication. In a man, it can appear in the form of an erect penis.

For some asexuals, according to AVEN, "Sexual arousal is a fairly regular occurrence, though it is not associated with a desire to find a sexual partner or partners." Some people ignore the arousal, according to Asexuality New Zealand Trust. Masturbation and sexual intercourse are also options some asexuals pursue to address sexual arousal. "These people can still identify as asexual because asexuality is defined by a lack of sexual attraction, not a lack of sexual arousal."[100]

Asexuals who experience little or no arousal do not perceive it as problematic because, "We don't care about sex, asexual people generally do not see a lack of sexual arousal as a problem to be corrected and focus their energy on enjoying other types of arousal and pleasure."[101]

Do asexuals have sexual intercourse?

Yes. Even though asexual people do not experience sexual attraction, and some have little, if any, interest in sex, some asexuals have or have had sex. As discussed in the homosexuality chapter, a person can have sexual intercourse that does not reflect their sexual attraction. One term for this is "sex-positive asexuality."[102] Some asexuals have said that having sex actually enabled them to confirm that they are asexual. Conversely, "some asexual-identifying individuals want absolutely nothing to do with sex," according to the author of "Asexuality and Having Children."[103] This is referred to as "sex-repulsed asexuality." If an asexual "doesn't have strong feelings one way or the other," it is referred to as "sex-neutral asexuality."

Some might wonder if asexuals are sexually frustrated by their lack of sexual desire and sexual activity. The answer is no. The frustration an asexual person might experience regarding sex is more likely to be due to being pressured, judged, misunderstood, and ridiculed.

How does someone know they are asexual?

It varies for each person. Many asexuals report being in puberty when they first recognized that they weren't experiencing the type of sexual attraction their peers talked about. Very few people reported immediately thinking that meant they were asexual, which shouldn't be surprising A teenager or young adult who hasn't experienced sexual attraction might think they are "late bloomers" or haven't met the right person yet.

Making peace with their identity can be the hardest part for some asexuals because of the pervasive societal expectation to be sexual. Many people become upset and frustrated with a person who isn't interested in sex and doesn't participate in sex. In many instances, people of other sexualities will try to pressure or guilt the asexual person they are dating into having sex. If sex doesn't materialize, then the relationship is likely to end. Sexual people may encounter similar scenarios, but they are compounded for an asexual person, because this will never change.

Asexuals also have to face and manage the expectations of family, friends, and society. Males are expected to be interested in sex at an early age and to become sexually active in their teens. People who don't meet those expectations can be labeled as soft, gay, or other terms meant to belittle and denigrate. Women might be considered selfish, prudish, or barren for not meeting their partner's and society's expectations. Women have the additional burden of being expected to get pregnant and have children.

Another reason a person wouldn't immediately identify as asexual is because the term asexual was not on their radar. In a post on asexuality.org, one person writes, "I never had the desire to kiss or do anything physical. It occurred to me that I was different, but I didn't have a name for it quite yet." Some people have said they didn't discover the term asexuality until reading it in an article or hearing it from a teacher, counselor, or medical professional.

Asexuality is rarely discussed, and some people can live their entire lives without hearing the term. The internet has made it much easier to access information and be introduced to new concepts, but that has not always been the case. Even in the twenty-first century, there are many people who will never have access to the internet, a computer, newspapers, or sex education. Where would they hear the term asexuality?

Can asexuals also be straight, gay, bi, or pan?

Yes, according to the Asexual Visibility & Education Network (AVEN). "Asexual people who experience attraction will often be attracted to a particular gender and will identify as lesbian, gay, bi, or straight." If asexuality is a person's sexuality, then how can they also be gay, straight, bi, et cetera?

Sexuality or sexual orientation can include three types of attraction: sexual, emotional, and romantic. Some people who are asexual don't experience any of those attractions. There are others who do experience emotional and romantic attraction. Those asexuals can also be straight, gay, bisexual, or pansexual, depending on who they are emotionally and romantically attracted to. AVEN's website offers this explanation, "Many asexual people experience attraction, but we feel no need to act out that attraction sexually." For some, that emotional and romantic attraction is for a person of the same sex, while for others, it could be the opposite sex, both sexes, or all sexes and genders.

How do asexual relationships differ from platonic relationships?

The answer to this question depends on how platonic is defined. When most people think of platonic, they think of a relationship that does not involve sex, which would also describe the relationships of some asexuals but not all. Some asexuals have sexual intercourse.

Many people think of platonic as just being friends without romantic or sexual attraction. Cox says, "People always ask how our marriage is different from just being friends, but I think a lot of relationships are about that—being friends. We have built on our friendship rather than scrapping it and moving on somewhere else. The obvious way we differ is that we don't have sex, though we do kiss and cuddle."

Platonic has also been described as a "loveless" relationship, which isn't necessarily true of asexual relationships. "Asexuals feel love as strongly as anyone else does; it simply isn't connected to sex for them," according to AVEN.org. Sex is not a prerequisite for love. Just because a couple isn't sexually active doesn't mean they don't love each other, as many couples of other sexualities can attest. Cox says, "Amanda and I have been happily married for nine months now, and we're both still virgins."[104]

Another definition of platonic is "lacking romance, sensual desire, or sex." Again, this describes some asexual relationships, but not all. Asexual relationships can include sex, romance, and sensual desire. There are instances where an asexual person may decide to have sex with their partner. If by romance we mean the "courtship behaviors undertaken by an individual," then those things can and are done by asexual people. Sensual refers to the senses, such as taste, touch, smell, etc. Therefore, sensual desire can exist in a relationship without sex ever coming into play. Asexual individuals can also experience sensual desire, and for those who do, their relationships may not meet this definition of platonic.

To better understand, it might be helpful to consider the things that brought pleasure in your relationship before your first sexual encounter. Perhaps it was simply holding hands or a light caress on the cheek or arm. These are acts of tenderness and affection that can elicit intimacy and pleasure without sexual attraction or sexual activity. Also consider all the ways you enjoy spending time with the person you are coupled with that have nothing to do with sex. In fact, only a very small portion of our lives is spent having sex, and most of the time spent with our partners does not include sex. Of the 1,440 minutes in a day, on average, just a few of those minutes, if any, are spent in sexual activity.

For many asexuals, the few minutes that might be spent on sexual activity are replaced with other activities like talking, watching television, eating dinner, hiking, going to a concert, and all the other non-sexual things any couple might do. This is affirmed by AVEN: "The possibilities for non-sexual intimacy are vast. Intimacy, described as things that are said or done between people who have a close relationship, can include sex but is not synonymous with sex." They continued, saying, "Some asexuals enjoy physical closeness, perhaps cuddling or stroking, with their partner. Some asexuals express intimacy through talking, maybe sharing their innermost fears and secrets, or by making each other laugh. Some asexuals feel intimacy with their partners by sharing common interests and activities or by working together toward common goals. Others experience intimacy in other deeply personal ways or by a combination of some, all, or none of the above."

A lack of interest in sex does not negate the need for emotional connections. In fact, The Trevor Project, a nonprofit organization focused on suicide prevention among LGBTQ youth explains that most asexual people desire emotionally intimate relationships.[105]

The conclusion is that asexuals can have the same types of relationships with friends or romantic interests that sexual people have. "Some asexual people are happier on their own, others are happiest with a group of close friends," according to AVEN. People like to socialize and interact with people who are similar to them in some way, such as common interests, experiences, or backgrounds. Seeking familiarity in our relationships can make those relationships more pleasurable and less stressful. This can be even more true for an asexual person.

Asexuals who choose to mingle with other asexuals can be reassured that sex won't enter the relationship. If the person they spend time with is also asexual, then they don't have to worry about unwanted sexual advances, being pressured to have sex, or feeling bad or guilty about not being sexually attracted to the person they're dating.

Can asexual people have relationships with sexual people?

Yes. Each situation is different, just as each person is different. Having a relationship with a sexual person can be more complicated because most sexual people are not willing to have a relationship with a person who is not sexually attracted to them. These relationships are possible and may require more communication and compromise from both people regarding their sex lives. In some instances, the asexual partner might agree to have sex periodically or agree to perform certain sex acts but not others. The sexual person may have a low interest in sex, or is not physically able to have sexual intercourse. In other relationships, there may be an agreement that the sexual person can go outside of the relationship for sexual satisfaction.

Do asexual people get married?

Yes. The fact that a person does not desire sex doesn't mean they won't want to get married. Some asexuals have no desire or intention for marriage, while others do. According to AVEN, some "asexual people have a desire to form more intimate romantic relationships and will date and seek long-term partnerships." In Cox's case, his relationship began the way many others do. He loved Amanda's attitude about life, thought she was pretty, enjoyed hanging out with her, and would even deliver food when she was hungry. "Two months in, we were at a gig, and it seemed like a good idea to hold her hand. I felt cautious about it but just wanted to. I wondered if I could. Then I found I couldn't let go. That evening ended with us agreeing that our friendship was an important thing. We wanted to commit for life."[106]

Prior to meeting the woman who is now his wife, Cox says he never thought he would get married. "I wasn't interested in relationships or finding a girlfriend and was very sure I didn't have an interest in boys either." He continued, "We like to joke that the longer we're married, the less unusual this is. By the time we've been married five years we'll be just like everyone else."

It is entirely possible to be married and not have a sexual relationship. There are plenty of sexual couples whose marriages, for one reason or another, do not include sex. The absence of sex in a marriage doesn't necessarily indicate the absence of love. Nor does the absence of sex make a marriage any less valid than any other marriage. As far as sex in his marriage is concerned, Cox says, "We've decided that if either of us wants to try sex out in the future, then we will see what we can do. We would both be willing to compromise because we're in a relationship, and that's what you do."

Do asexuals want to be parents?

Some do. Not having a desire for sexual intercourse does not necessarily mean a person won't be interested in having children. It also doesn't mean they are incapable of having children. As the Asexuality Archive puts it, "Asexual people are just as fertile and capable of producing offspring as non-asexual people."

Being asexual also doesn't mean a person is unable to parent, or to love, nurture, and protect a child. Cox and his wife are considering parenthood and say, "When it comes to the future and to children, we're big advocates of adoption. We're not so fussed about passing on our own genes."[107]

CHAPTER SEVEN

PANSEXUAL

"Love is boundary-less."
–Angel Haze[108]

Intro

The term pansexuality is attributed to Sigmund Freud; however, his definition was a description of general human behavior rather than a specific sexuality. The modern-day usage of the term pansexual is presumed to have emerged in the 1990s. The prefix "pan-" is derived from a Greek word that means "all," and pansexuality refers to the potential to be attracted to all sexes, sexualities, genders, and gender identities. Another word for pansexual is omnisexual, in which the prefix "omni-" is Latin for "all."[109]

A pansexual person might be attracted to someone who is male, female, transgender, intersex, or genderqueer, for example. "Pansexual is often conceptualized as a label that denotes sexual or romantic attraction to people regardless of their gender expression (masculinity or femininity), gender identity, or biological sex," says James Morandini, PhD, University of Sydney.[110] Many pansexuals would say they are attracted to whom a person is—based on personality, appearance, energy, intellect, etc. A writer for CNN.com described it this way: "Pansexual is used to describe a romantic or sexual attraction focused on traits other than sex or gender."

Sexologist Dr. Carol Queen, PhD, suggests that "people who identify as pansexual might want to be ready to clarify their own specific 'take' on this identity to people who are confused about its implications."[111]

A woman named Alexa also says her attraction to people is not about biological sex or gender: "I work off energy; if I dig your energy, I dig you."[112] In *Pansexuality and Being Pansexual: Everything You Need to Know*, HB says, "I am attracted to certain personality types and physical features, just like anyone else."[113]

The creator of the website "Pansexuality Is Perfect" states, "The personality, soul, everything in that direction is more important to me… Once I realize how awesome someone is, regardless of what they have as intimate bits, then I probably want to be with them / make love / sing songs to them." Jazz Jennings, a transgender pansexual advocate, says, "Being pansexual basically means to me that you are attracted to anyone, no matter their sex, sexual orientation, gender, gender identity, everything. There're no limits. It's more that I love someone for their soul."[114]

Rapper Angel Haze sees it as love having no boundaries. She told *The Guardian* that to identify as pansexual "means to just want love. To have a connection with anyone you can find it with. Love is boundary-less. If you can make me feel, if you can make me laugh—and that's hard—then I can be with you."[115]

Twenty-eight-year-old Danielle, who has dated asexuals and bisexuals and says she could also see herself dating a transgender person, explains to *Teen Vogue*, "To me, pansexuality feels the most organic way to exist in this world."

No reliable attempts have been made to estimate the number of pansexual adults in the US or in the world. A *Women's Health* article postulates that less than one percent of the population, approximately 3.28 million people in the US, identify as pansexual.[116]

Pansexual individuals have not yet been included in the LGBTQ research and surveys conducted by doctors, scientists, and advocacy groups, presumably because of the relative newness of the term. Doctors at the University of Sydney conducted a small survey that led them to suggest that women are five times more likely than men to identify as pansexual.[117] The study also found that youth, and "those who have a gender identity, gender expression, or gender role that society considers inappropriate for the sex one was assigned at birth" are more likely to identify as pansexual.

Does being pansexual mean a person is confused about their sexuality?

No. A person who identifies as pansexual is aware that their sexuality involves the possible attraction to people of any biological sex, sexuality, gender, or gender identity. In an article for *Independent*, Farhana Khan writes, "Being pansexual doesn't mean that I'm yet to make a choice about whether I am gay or straight, but instead, it means that I'm not restricted in choice of partner because of a person's gender or sex… It's just who I am."[118] If there is confusion, it lies with those who are not pansexual and who have difficulty wrapping their heads around the notion of pansexuality.

How is pansexuality different from bisexuality?

There is a debate among some bisexuals and pansexuals about this very question. Some bisexuals argue that bisexuality doesn't strictly limit attraction based on biological sex, and that it can also describe their attraction to other gender identities, for example. Others, including bisexuals, doctors, and psychologists, however, firmly distinguish between bisexuality and pansexuality. There are also those who insist that pansexuality should fall under the bisexuality description; however, others, like Ritch Savin-Williams, PhD, Director, Sex, and Gender Lab, Cornell University, believe "we should be very careful to distinguish pansexual from bisexual individuals."[119]

The prefixes that define these terms explain the difference: "bi-" means "two" and "pan-" means "all." Bisexuality is based on binary notions of biological sex—that is, male and female. Bisexuals, by definition, can be attracted to males and females. Pansexuals, by definition, can be attracted to more than just males and females. Pansexuality also includes attraction to intersex, transgender, genderqueer, third-gender, and androgynous people, or the many other sexual and gender identities. Pansexuality is open to the spectrum, and therefore goes beyond the binary notions of male and female that define bisexuality.

Is pansexuality new?

No. The newness of the *term* pansexuality is not the same as saying the sexual orientation itself is new. Many people say they recognized their pansexuality long before having a name to associate with it. We don't know when the first pansexual humans walked the earth, just as we don't know when the first homosexual, asexual, or bisexual humans lived, but there is a great probability that the variety of our sexualities has existed for as long as humans have existed.

When does someone become aware they are pansexual?

Most people, pansexuals included, become aware of their sexuality during or after puberty. Awareness of sexuality is not, however, restricted to puberty and can occur when a person is younger or older.

What seems to differ more broadly for some is when pansexuals associate with the pansexuality label. Use of and identification with the term pansexual has been growing since the 1990s, and awareness increased dramatically after singer/actor Miley Cyrus came out as pansexual. Because of its relative newness in our sexuality vernacular, it is likely that although some people realized their pansexuality, they might not have known what to call it. Twenty-five-year-old Alexa, for example, discovered her pansexual identity just after college. [120]

Some pansexuals originally thought they were bisexual until recognizing their attraction to transgender people and those of other gender identities. Others say they had early awareness, but lacked the terminology. According to Khan, "Being pansexual is something I have always known to be true about myself. From a young age, I was always aware that my attraction to people is not limited by their gender or sex, but I lacked the words to explain this." He initially thought bisexuality was the best label, but, "Pansexuality soon entered my vocabulary, and it has stayed with me ever since." [121] Another woman named Jenny says she originally thought bisexual described her sexuality until she became familiar with the term pansexual. "I sat uncomfortably with the word 'bisexual' until my forties, even though it didn't seem to define me. Then I heard about the term 'pansexual' and realized I'd found my 'home' label-wise."

It shouldn't be surprising that the realization comes for some people as they get older, learn more about themselves, and have more interpersonal relations. For pansexuals, that can include learning they are attracted to a wide array of people, regardless of biological sex, sexuality, gender, and gender identity, in addition to learning more about how they think and feel about sex. While most people become aware of their sexual identity early in life, we all learn more about our sexuality as we age and collect more experiences. We discover more about who we are attracted to, our sexual preferences, and how we think and feel about sex.

What kind of relationships do pansexuals have?

Pansexuals have the same kind of relationships that people of other sexualities have, and their sexual and romantic relationships go through the same cycles as everyone else's. Some relationships are short-term, others are long-term. Some relationships begin with physical attraction, others begin with intellectual attraction. Some relationships are just about sex, others are based on friendship and love.

Kimberly O'Sullivan, a social commentator, historian, journalist, and self-identified pansexual, hasn't experienced a real difference. "I'm amazed at how similar it all is, all the normal highs and insecurities—'Am I good enough? Will they leave? Will they ring?'"[122] These are questions that anyone who has ever been in a relationship has likely asked.

Challenges can arise in a relationship after someone learns of their partner's pansexuality. Clinical sexologist and marriage and family therapist Dr. Kat Van Kirk says pansexuals "may find it difficult to date when potential partners don't understand or are intimidated by who they are attracted to."[123]

Is pansexuality an excuse for promiscuity?

No. Sexuality isn't an excuse for anything. No one's sexuality is an excuse for promiscuity. It is misguided to equate pansexuality with promiscuity. Pansexual sexuality is about having the potential to be attracted to people regardless of their biological sex, sexuality, gender, or gender identity. It is not about wanting to have sex with anybody and everybody.

Khan says, "Pansexuals aren't more likely to be promiscuous or unfaithful than anyone else. Just because we are attracted to all kinds of people, it doesn't mean we're attracted to ALL people. Sexual identity and sexual behavior are two completely unrelated things, neither of which influence the other."[124] In the article "Pansexuality and Being Pansexual:

Everything You Need to Know," Dr. Carol Queen writes, "Pansexual people do not desire everybody, they just don't rule a person out because of gender."[125] In the same article, Vera Papisova warns that people often misconstrue pansexuality to mean pansexuals lead a hypersexualized lifestyle, but that is not true.

If we do not presume heterosexuals are attracted to everyone of the opposite sex, then why presume pansexuals are attracted to everyone they meet or see? Papisova says, "It's a ridiculous assumption." She reminds us that we don't say, "If you are a straight man, you must be attracted to every single woman, or if you are a lesbian, you must want to hook up with every girl you meet." I imagine we all know or have met heterosexual men who pride themselves on being promiscuous—having sex with as many women as they can. We do not, however, take the leap to conclude that all heterosexuals are promiscuous.

Promiscuity is about sexual behavior, not sexual orientation. It is characterized by having sexual relations with a number of partners on a casual basis. Promiscuous behavior can be exhibited by anyone, regardless of sexuality. Anyone, regardless of sexuality, can be promiscuous. Conversely, anyone, regardless of sexuality, can be discriminating about their sexual activity.

Do pansexuals get married?

Yes. There is nothing about pansexuality that suggests pansexual individuals want marriage any more or less than people of other sexualities. "Everyone wants love in their lives," says O'Sullivan, who has been married twice. Her first marriage was profiled in a 1999 *Australian Story* episode, "Kimberly's Wedding."

CHAPTER EIGHT

QUEER & QUESTIONING

"Queer has many different facets."
–Hari Zayid[126]

Intro

For some people, "Q" represents a "queer" identity. For others, it represents a "questioning" identity. Each word can refer to a person's sexuality and/or their gender identity. We'll discuss both terms and their meanings, beginning with "queer."

Queer

The word "queer" has held multiple meanings and connotations over the years. The first known use, according to Merriam-Webster, occurred in the 1500s, referring to something that differs "in some odd way from what is usual or normal." In the 1800s, it meant "to spoil the effect or success of" something, e.g. spoiled food. The word later was used to refer to someone who was perceived as eccentric, as well as anyone or anything thought to be peculiar or odd. Queer eventually came to mean "perverse." In modern times, the word has been used in reference to a person's sexuality, and more recently a person's gender identity.

Marissa Higgins, a writer for *Bustle,* explains, "Whether or not someone identifies with and uses the word "queer" is an intensely personal decision."[127] The definition of queer is determined by the person claiming or rejecting it as their identifier.

Queer Sexuality

The first documented connection of the term queer to homosexuality occurred in the late 1800s. By the early 1900s, queer was being used negatively in literature and in the media to refer to gay and effeminate men. Queer could also be found in positive references by homosexuals, including author Gertrude Stein. By the 1950s, queer was most widely used as a derogatory term for homosexuals and homosexuality.

That began to change in the late 1980s, when the label began to be appropriated from its pejorative use.[128] Then, in 1990, an organization called Queer Nation circulated an anonymous flier at the New York Gay Pride Parade titled "Queers Read This."[129]

"In part," it said, the term "gay is great. It has its place. But when a lot of lesbians and gay men wake up in the morning, we feel angry and disgusted, not gay. So, we've chosen to call ourselves queer. Using "queer" is a way of reminding us how we are perceived by the rest of the world."[130] Queer Nation also made the phrase, "We're here! We're Queer! Get used to it!" a popular rallying cry. Over the years, many gay and lesbian individuals have seized this word and recycled it, removing its negative meaning, effectively neutering those who tried to use the term against them.

Many people think of queer as referring to homosexuality; however, that is not the only use. For instance, some people "queer sexuality" as an umbrella term representing anything and everything that is not heterosexual and does not adhere to the binary constructs of sexuality.

> *I've always identified as queer, and I continue to identify as queer even though I have only ever been attracted to women. It means not straight, mostly. It means not heteronormative. Yeah. It is in some ways defined by what it is not, but for me, it is an expansive.*
>
> *I think part of it is allowing space for my partners to identify however they identify because I've been with women who identified as bisexual, I've been with women who identified as*

lesbians, and I've been with women who identified as straight…
Queerness makes that space possible in my mind in a way that
both lesbian and straight don't.

–E.R. Anderson, non-profit executive director,
long-term monogamous relationship, trans masculine,
queer sexuality, 36 years old

Some people identify both their sexuality and gender as queer:

Because I feel in the middle of the gender spectrum; I don't feel
like it is easy to say straight or gay on the sexuality spectrum. I'm
somewhere in the middle of that.

–Anne

Omnes et Nihil, a writer on asexuality.org, says, "I happen to be a queer asexual… It's about reclaiming the mark of outsiderness and using that unapologetically to shake things up."

Acceptance of the word is not, however, universal among homosexuals. Some people continue to find it offensive and do not use it. Even among those who embrace the word as a self-identifier, there is a mixed reaction to whether someone outside of the community should use the term.

Questioning Sexuality

For some, the letter "Q" stands for "questioning" sexuality. In this instance, questioning refers to a person trying to identify which, if any, of the existing labels best fit or describe their expression of sexuality. Some who identify as questioning sexuality might be wondering if they are a specific sexuality. For instance, "Am I bisexual?" Others might have an open-ended question of, "What sexuality am I?" Questioning sexuality does not mean a person is "choosing" a sexuality because, as has been previously stated, we don't choose our sexuality; it chooses us.

Questioning is about the process of discovery. Those who are sure of their sexuality might not understand the notion of "questioning." They might wonder, "How come they don't just know what they are?" This is another instance where recognizing that your particular experience is not universal. What may be clear and unequivocal for one person might be confusing for another. Everyone's situation is not the same. For instance, we don't all go through puberty at the same time or have our first crush at the same time or fall in love at the same time or in the same way.

There are many reasons someone might question which sexuality they are. Because many societies consider heterosexuality to be the norm, some people might be confused to realize they don't fit into that category, and be unsure of what that means. A person who might have thought themselves heterosexual might be confused after discovering they are also attracted to someone of the same sex, and wonder if that means they are homosexual or bisexual or something else. There are also many people who've experienced emotional and/or sexual trauma that has made them fearful of building or reluctant to build relationships of any kind. That type of trauma can cause a person to shut off their sexual, emotional, and romantic attraction as a means of protection. For those people, questioning their sexuality—trying to determine what it is—can be a part of the process of healing from the trauma they've experienced.

For a person questioning sexuality, it could be that they haven't yet been sexually attracted to anyone, regardless of sex or gender, and aren't sure what this means. Or perhaps they've been sexually attracted to people of both sexes but aren't sure what that means. Questioning could also arise if a person hasn't met someone they could be sexually attracted to, and therefore wonders what that means about their sexuality.

In an article for *Elite Daily*, Zara Barrie offers a personal example. "I didn't know if everyone had such big lusty feels for their female gym teacher or if it was just *me*. I wanted to know if the reason I wasn't getting wet for the "hot" boys in school was because I was a late bloomer or because I was a lesbian."[131] A questioning person might wonder if their crush on a person of the same sex means they're gay or bisexual. A person might also wonder if they have a crush on someone or simply adoration for that person's physical appearance, personality, or accomplishments. Barrie also said that for some people, admiration can be so powerful it's almost sexual, and that it is possible for some girls, for instance, to "mix up whether you just want to be this girl or have sex with this girl."

Some might think questioning sexuality is limited to youth, however it is not. An adult, for example, might have been married to a person of the opposite sex and later discovered an attraction to someone of the same sex. Finding themselves attracted to the same sex after years of being in heterosexual relationships could understandably cause a person to question their sexuality, perhaps wondering if this attraction means they are gay, bi, pan, or still hetero.

For a person who is questioning sexuality, it takes time, experience, and self-examination to sort through feelings, attractions, relationships, and societal "norms" to reach a moment of clarity. If you still find this difficult to digest, please consider that we each have something about ourselves we've had to spend time deciphering. It might have been something that another person would look at and wonder why you haven't figured out. It shouldn't be far-fetched to understand that sexuality can be that "thing" for some people. If we honestly consider how our own appetites and dispositions have evolved over our sexual lives, then hopefully we can create the space within ourselves for compassion and understanding for others. I'm all for allowing folks time and space to figure it out for themselves and not insisting that they do it my way or on my schedule.

Queer Gender Identity

> "My gender identity and presentation [are] my
> own, not to be determined by anyone else."
> –Michal "MJ" Jones[132]

"Q" can also stand for "queer gender identity." Before exploring what this term means, it will be helpful to first expound on the meanings of gender and gender identity.

What is gender?

Gender is a word that is often misunderstood and conflated with other terms. Gender is often used interchangeably with biological sex; however, the meanings differ. As mentioned earlier, biological sex refers to physiological characteristics such as whether a person has a penis or vagina, and XX chromosomes or XY chromosomes. Many people also think gender and gender identity are the same thing. They are not.

Gender is defined as feelings, behaviors, and attitudes that a given culture associates with being a biological male or female. Gender is about what society expects of a person. The World Health Organization (WHO) states, "Gender refers to the socially constructed characteristics of women and men—such as norms, roles, and relationships of and between groups of women and men."[133] In other words, gender describes the way a particular society or culture expects a person to think, feel, and behave based on whether they were born with a penis or a vagina. For example, because I was born a biological female, our society expects me to wear dresses, makeup, nail polish, jewelry, and other accoutrement associated with femininity. Society also expects me to present certain personality traits deemed as feminine, like being sensitive, nurturing, and docile, and to have certain interests like shopping, cooking, and parenting.

These constructed gender expectations differ from culture to culture, society to society, and generation to generation. To gain some context, consider how expectations for men and women have changed throughout history in different cultures. Skirts, dresses, wigs, and makeup are currently considered feminine in many Western cultures, but that has not always been the case and has never been universal.

In African, Irish, Scottish, and Eastern cultures, men have been known to wear apparel that resembles Western conceptions of skirts and dresses. In Egypt in 4000 BC, it was considered masculine for men to wear makeup. In the first century AD, it was considered masculine for Roman men to wear blush, face powder, and nail paint. In the eighteenth century, France's King Louis XVI began wearing wigs to hide his premature baldness, which then made it fashionable for men to wear wigs and became a sign of aristocracy. There was also a time when European men wore higher heels than the women. Today a man wearing makeup, a wig, or high heels would be considered feminine and unacceptable in most cultures.

Historians connect some changes to the norms of feminine and masculine behavior back to Queen Victoria, who decided makeup was vulgar, an idea later adopted by the Church of England, which deemed it an abomination. Wearing makeup eventually became associated with femininity, and this association is now accepted in many cultures around the world.

Is gender the same as biological sex?

No. Biological sex is determined by factors like genitalia, reproductive organs, chromosomes, and sex hormones. These genetic and anatomic factors are used to assign a "male" or "female" biological sex when a baby is born. Gender, on the other hand, is about society's perceptions, feelings, and expectations for someone who is biologically male or female. Gender is not biological. Gender is a socially constructed notion based on what a particular society expects relative to a person's biological sex.

What is gender identity?

Gender identity is not the same as gender. A person's gender identity reflects that individual's authentic thoughts, feelings, and behaviors. As the American Association of Pediatrics (AAP) puts it, "'gender identity' is one's internal sense of who one is."[134] Medscape.com explains it as "a personal conception of oneself as male or female,"[135] and Genderspectrum.com says it's one's "innermost concept of self as male or female or both or neither."[136] Medscape.com goes further, explaining, "For example, if a person considers himself a male and is most comfortable referring to his personal gender in masculine terms, then his gender identity is male," regardless of that person's biological sex or society's expectations.

In other words, a person's gender identity has to do with how they identify themselves in terms of being girl or boy, man or woman, both, or neither. Gender identity is personal and not dependent upon society's perceptions, feelings, or expectations. Gender identity is also not dependent upon a person's genitalia, according to healthcare professionals and those who study the human mind and body.

One of the most important things for us to keep in mind is that "variations in gender identity and expression are normal aspects of human diversity," according to the AAP.[137]

What does it mean when people say gender and gender identity exist on a spectrum?

Spectrum refers to a range of different positions between two extreme points. Saying gender exists on a spectrum means gender is not limited to the binary (two) options most societies have traditionally held fast to. The two positions on the gender spectrum that most are familiar with are the boy/man label and the girl/woman label.

Some cultures have acknowledged that gender is not a binary, either-or proposition. Instead, they accept that gender exists on a spectrum, like colors. Viewing gender on a spectrum, rather than as binary, allows us to acknowledge that gender and gender identity are not limited to the traditionally accepted boy or girl options.

In the gender-spectrum model, those two genders exist at opposite endpoints with an infinite number of genders, or points, existing between them. Think of it this way: instead of a person trying to determine whether a black or a white t-shirt is best for them, they look to the rack of t-shirts that contains a spectrum of colors. When it comes to gender, instead of trying to fit into one of two gender/gender identity options—boy or girl—some people recognize the broader spectrum of options that includes more than just boy and girl.

The idea of a gender spectrum is a new concept for many of us and can be difficult to grasp. My friend Lois, one of the most informed, open-minded people I know, was left saying, "I don't know what that means" when we discussed this topic. We've grown up in a society that teaches gender and gender identity as binary, and breaking out of that binary box of understanding can be difficult.

In the earlier discussion about a sexuality spectrum, color and light were offered as examples of things that exist on a spectrum. We should think of gender identity similarly. When you think about it, none of us expresses gender identity in exactly the same way. The ways I think, feel, and behave as a woman differ from those of my mother, my cousin, my best friend, etc., which means we each occupy a different position on the gender identity spectrum. And in a comparative pairing, each one of us would be viewed as more feminine than the other, while the other is seen as more masculine, which means we each occupy a different position on the gender spectrum.

To visualize this more clearly, draw a straight, horizontal line. At one endpoint, place society's ideal of the feminine gender, and at the other end, place society's ideal of the masculine gender. Now think about yourself in relation to one of those gender ideals. Are you an exact replica of society's ideal? How far away from the ideal would you place yourself? Identify that point on the line and write your name. If you're a woman, and you are an exact match for the feminine gender ideal, then place yourself at that end. If, however, you possess 90 percent of those feminine gender characteristics, and some masculine characteristics, then move yourself

10 percent away from the feminine end. If it's 80 percent, move farther away, and so on, based on how well your feminine gender identity matches society's gender ideal.

I don't know anyone who fits neatly into the binary options of all things feminine or all things masculine. If I had to assign percentages for myself, I might say I feel 70 percent feminine and 30 percent masculine. For example, on one hand, I exhibit many of what society considers feminine tendencies. As a little girl, I enjoyed playing with dolls, jacks, and the Easy-Bake Oven. I loved going to the hair salon and wearing ribbons, lace dresses, and patent leather shoes. As an adult, I know the lyrics to many of the great love songs, I cry at sad movies, and my feelings are bruised when someone says something mean to me. On the other hand, I also exhibit what society considers masculine tendencies. When I was younger, I played basketball, football, and baseball with the boys in my neighborhood. Instead of taking Home Economics or Sewing classes in high school, I opted for Woodshop. Many would consider my personality bold or even aggressive in contrast to the meek and mild mannerisms society more often associates with women. I certainly feel like a woman and have never considered myself to be anything other than a woman, but it is also obvious that my placement on the gender spectrum would be several ticks down the line away from the girl/woman endpoint.

Now, think about your parents, children, siblings, best friends, and neighbors, and place them on the line based on how they relate to society's ideal gender. What you are likely to find is that people fall in different places on that line, and few people fit at either ideal end. Most people have some mixture of gender expression—behavior, mannerisms, interests, and appearance that are associated with gender. Some women, for example, have a small portion of what society would consider masculine, while other women have a larger portion.

My explanation of the gender spectrum is just one example. Sabrina offered a simpler explanation.

> *You see females who are not girly-girls, and you see men who are not macho men. So, there is that spectrum.*
>
> –Sabrina, construction project manager, ordained minister, divorced, transgender, heterosexual, 60 years old

I think that a lot of people could put themselves on a scale. I have a friend who is a professor of Women's Studies who asks that of her students. She says it is really rare, if ever, that people put themselves in the far end of the baskets. So, most people do appreciate in themselves a dual energy. I think it is being a little bit more at the center of the spectrum where it gets hard. If you feel 80 percent woman and 20 percent man, then you probably feel comfortable sitting in the woman box. But if you feel 50/50 or 60/40, then maybe it is a little harder to say you fit neatly into that category. It creates a little bit more friction.

–Anne

There is absolutely nothing wrong with where any of us lands on the gender spectrum. My place on the gender spectrum is just as acceptable as yours or anyone else's, even when it's not what society has taught us to expect, which under closer examination, is the case for most of us.

When do humans become aware of their gender identity?

Doctors and mental health professionals who study human development agree that most humans become aware of their gender identity during toddler years, which spans the ages of twelve months to three years. As a general guideline, this holds true regardless of what the gender identity is. There is also agreement that toddlers can verbalize and demonstrate their gender identity regardless of what that identity is.

It is also common for children to verbalize and demonstrate gender identity at later stages of development. The *Pediatrics* report also cites a 2009 *Journal of Adolescent Health* issue that stated that children who later identify as transgender recall first having recognized their gender as "different" at an average age of 8.5 years; however, they did not disclose such feelings until an average of ten years later.[138]

The ability to understand our gender identity, or to articulate it, increases the older we get and the more we discover about ourselves and the world around us. This is confirmed in *Pediatrics*, which states, "Self-recognition of gender identity develops over time, much the same way as a child's physical body does."[139]

What is the difference between cisgender, transgender, and genderqueer?

The prefix "cis-" means "same." The term cisgender "is used if someone identifies and expresses a gender that is consistent with the culturally defined norms of the sex that was assigned at birth," according to the AAP.[140] For cisgender people, their gender identity happens to be the same as the gender society expects. An example of a cisgender person is someone assigned biological female, and a feminine (girl/woman) gender, and who also possesses a feminine (girl/woman) gender identity.

The prefix "trans-" means "opposite" or "on the other side." The term transgender refers to people whose gender identity is opposite or does not match the gender society associates with their biological sex. An example of a transgender person is one who was assigned biological female at birth, and a feminine (girl/woman) gender; however, that person possesses a masculine (boy/man) gender identity.

A general definition of queer gender identity is "an umbrella term for people whose gender identity is outside of, not included within, or beyond the binary of female and male," according to "7 Things Queer Gender People Want you to Know."[141]

What is queer gender identity?

"A 'queer' gender identity may fall outside of, fall in between, or fluctuate among the binary gender categories of man and woman," according to "What Does it Mean to Identify as Genderqueer?"[142] In other words, those who identify as genderqueer may not feel they fit into the binary boy or girl gender boxes. "Transgender people can also identify as genderqueer and vice versa,"[143] although a report from the APA says members of the genderqueer community "typically reject the term 'transgender' because it implies a change from one gender category to another."[144]

"Being genderqueer isn't limited to what you look like or how you physically present," as writer Marissa Higgins stresses.[145] It's all about how a given person understands their own personal identity.

> *Your gender is some way that you identify, some way that your brain kind of feels you exist in the world. I usually identify my*

gender as queer. I use it to mean I am somewhere in between. On the gender spectrum identifying as woman or man, I'm sort of in the middle, so I'm genderqueer. I perceive a masculinity in myself. I feel like I have a sort of masculine energy. I feel it in the way I think about things and problems, the way I walk and talk, and how I interact with people. I also have a softness and an access to emotionality and things that sometimes men in our society get really cut off from.

–Anne

The definition and expression of a queer gender identity will differ for each person.

When does a person realize they are genderqueer?

As mentioned earlier, most humans become aware of their gender identity during toddler years. The same applies to someone who is genderqueer. The realization can also come later in life, during or after adolescence for instance. It's also important to note that being aware of gender identity does not necessarily mean a person is immediately able to understand or articulate that identity.

Ever since age three, I wouldn't wear a dress, and I've always been kind of a tomboy. I think nobody thought much of it, but nobody was surprised when I came out as a teenager. I've always kind of inhabited the gender identity that I have. I've always just kind of been who I am, and people don't seem to care too much or mind. I started thinking about gender probably in high school, when I started getting mistaken for a boy. It took me by surprise at first, but then I kind of got used to it and made it my own a little bit more. And I did a photo project regarding my own gender identity, exploring that a little bit. It was displayed for the whole college to see, and some people were upset by it, but most thought it was really cool. I never cared that much what people think of me, and that in itself seems to make people like me better.

–Dr. Lowell

What pronouns apply to someone who is genderqueer?

We have come to associate the pronouns "she" and "her" with someone who identifies as a girl or woman and the pronouns "he" and "him," with someone who identifies as a boy or man. Many genderqueer people, who do not feel they fit into the gender binary options of boy/man or girl/woman, prefer pronouns like "they" or "them."

It is becoming more common for genderqueer individuals to make their preferred pronouns known to prevent being assigned an inaccurate, gender-specific pronoun. Take the case of someone like Dr. Lowell, who identifies as a woman but, to some people, appears to be a man. The use of Dr. Lowell's preferred pronouns "she" and "her" can help others eliminate any confusion about her gender identity. Meg Zulch, author of "7 Things Genderqueer People Want You to Know," counsels, "There is no way to tell someone's pronouns or gender identity by simply looking at them."

Anne offered insight into when and how pronouns might be brought up in conversation.

> *If we are talking one-on-one, you are never going to have to use my pronoun, so you don't have to ask immediately. You aren't going to need to use it... Let's say I was meeting somebody for the first time, and they wanted to make sure they were using the right pronouns, which is a big way gender-variant folks get silenced, because they never get asked. "What pronouns do you prefer?" is a really respectful way.* I use it at work. I think that asking about preferred pronouns works in pretty much any setting if you are meeting someone.
>
> –Anne

If a person identifies as genderqueer, then referring to them with a gender-specific pronoun like "she" can be inappropriate and disrespectful. For instance, if I was writing about or talking about a genderqueer person who preferred the pronouns they or them, then it would be disrespectful for me to say or write, "She said..." or "He thinks..." Zulch, who uses they/them pronouns, says, "I am consistently invalidated through mis-gendering, with the constant use of 'girl,' 'woman,' and 'Miss'... even after I correct people. It's disorienting, frustrating, and often makes me feel invisible." If you feel inclined to dismiss a person's preference for pronouns, please consider how important your identity is to you and how being misidentified by name, gender, marital status, race, etc. makes you feel. Recall what it feels like when someone calls you "Ms." instead of "Mrs."; or Chinese instead of Japanese; or Jim instead of James.

When the need to refer to someone using a pronoun like "he," "she," or "they" arises, it is best to ask the person's preference. Zulch points out, "there are also those gender-nonconforming individuals who don't change their pronouns from she/her or he/him." Everyone is different, and we should avoid making broad generalizations.

What kind of clothes does someone who identifies as genderqueer wear?

"It depends on the person!" according to Suzanne Samin, editor at Romper. "Not every non-binary person chooses to dress differently from their socially prescribed gender." Samin, who identifies as gender fluid, is most comfortable presenting as her biological sex, which is female. She adds, "For me, clothing does not play an important role in how I express my gender identity. However, for others, it is crucial."[146] Michal "MJ" Jones wears traditionally masculine clothes most of the time but is also inclined to present as his version of feminine. As Jones explains, it is possible for a person who may identify with the pronoun "he" but was assigned female sex at birth "to wear short skirts, makeup, and other presentation that society tends to label as 'feminine.'"[147]

I can't help but notice that when it comes to how we dress, our society enforces more than a few contradictory notions. For example, often, people are more comfortable with a woman wearing masculine attire than with a man wearing feminine attire. Why is that? It's acceptable for women to wear "boyfriend jeans," men's shirts, loafers, and other things that have traditionally been labeled as men's clothing, yet we denigrate men who feel comfortable in what has been traditionally viewed as women's fashion, like earrings, skirts, makeup, and heels. Is there any logical reason for this? This societal custom seems to disregard the personal preference and comfort of a genderqueer or non-binary individual.

What does gender non-binary mean?

Non-binary means "not relating to, composed of or involving just two things," according to dictionary.com. Gender non-binary is a broad term that can mean different things to different people. It can be used to describe people whose gender identity does not adhere to the two gender options of boy/man or girl/woman. The concept of offering only two gender options is an example of a binary, a set of two, which has previously been discussed.

Aida Manduley, MSW, a sex educator and therapist, defines a non-binary person as "someone who does not identify as a man or a woman or solely as one of those two genders."[148] Psychiatrist Dr. Meredith R. Chapman, MD, explains, "Non-binary people may feel some mix of both male and female, somewhere in between, or something completely different."[149] And according to healthline.com, "Non-binary can also be used as an umbrella term, encompassing many gender identities that don't fit into the male-female binary."[150]

Some individuals who identify as gender non-binary may refer to themselves as "agender." Here, the prefix "a-" means "no," and therefore, "agender" means no gender. A teenager named Kelsey explains that being agender isn't about being a tomboy or wearing certain clothes or having certain personality traits. When asked what gender they are, Kelsey replies, "I would say I'm neither. Both... I don't want to be a girl wearing boy's clothes, nor do I want to be a girl who presents as a boy. I just want to be a person who is recognized as a person."[151]

Some people who identify as non-binary also associate themselves with a gender. Writer Suzannah Weiss, for instance, identifies as a non-binary woman "because, to me, this identity acknowledges both that I don't have an innate identification with any gender and that I've been socialized as a woman."[152] Weiss also referred to another person who identified as a non-binary woman "because she loves her female-coded body but doesn't always feel it accurately represents her."

If, at this point, you still find yourself wondering, "Why can't they be like everyone else?" it's because they're not. In fact, who is truly "like everyone else?" No one. Each individual is like themselves and should be free to identify themselves as they see fit. Just as it is your prerogative to figure this out or ignore it, everyone should be able to figure out who they are for themselves and then be that person.

Which bathroom do genderqueer or gender non-binary people use?

This is another matter of personal comfort. "Non-binary people will use whatever bathroom they feel comfortable in," according to Samin. Dr. Lowell prefers to use the ladies' restroom, even though her appearance leads some people to perceive her as a man. Dr. Lowell is not obligated to use the men's restroom simply because someone perceives her as a man. She, like the rest of us, is obligated to do what is best for her.

If you encounter a genderqueer person in the restroom and feel it is your duty to send them away, Samin cautions, "If you see someone in a bathroom who looks different than you, ask yourself this one, very important question before confronting them or consulting an authority: Are they doing anything to make the people around them uncomfortable other than simply using the same bathroom? If the answer is no, then mind your own business and let them mind theirs."[153] Obstructing a person from using the restroom because their gender identity makes us uncomfortable seems equivalent to hijacking that person's identity and denying their humanity.

Another individual's identity is not about my comfort or your comfort, it's about theirs, just as my identity is about me, and yours is about you. A genderqueer person has as much right as anyone to be who they are and express who they are, and to move through this world, as long as it does not harm another person. It would be just as offensive and absurd for an able-bodied person to insist a physically challenged person leave the restroom because they are uncomfortable with that person's presence, or for a man to insist I leave a restaurant because he is uncomfortable eating near a woman.

What is gender fluid?

The word fluid suggests motion. "For some people," according to the AAP, "gender identity can be fluid, shifting in different contexts." This can mean that a person feels their gender identity is not stagnant, that it flows along the gender spectrum between man and woman. For instance, at one point in time, a person might feel more masculine than feminine and, at another time, feel equally masculine and feminine.

In an article on cnn.com, a twenty-six-year-old named Lee says that they might wake up as a man or as a woman, sometimes as both, and sometimes as neither.[154] Theresa, a thirty-seven-year-old, expresses gender fluidity in her behavior. She describes behaving more masculine when challenged. "The tone of my voice does change. It comes a little bit more forward. My voice drops a bit," she said. "I have been told that I walk really masculine, and I puff my chest out when I'm walking."[155] When feeling safe, Theresa says, "I am in touch with my feminine side, I feel soft."

What do "gender normative," "gender conforming," and "gender nonconforming" mean?

Gender normative refers to feeling, thinking, and expressing a gender identity that is in alignment or agreement with society's notions of gender. It means a person's gender identity is considered normal, which, as discussed earlier, can mean it is the average, or most common. As an example, I might be considered gender normative because for the most part, my gender identity matches the gender society expects of me, and my feelings, thoughts, and behaviors align with society's view of what is normal. The ways that I might exhibit more masculine gender traits are not so glaring that they would cause society to point at me and say, "Hey, you're abnormal. Your gender is not what we expect." While there is a range for what can be considered gender normative, most people fall into this category because they do not stray too far away from societal guidelines for gender.

A gender-conforming person has a gender identity that conforms with the gender society expects of them. To conform means to comply with the rules, standards, or laws. Halle Berry might be considered "gender conforming" because she was born a biological female, and she identifies as a woman, and, it appears, with many of society's feminine gender expectations. Most people are naturally gender conforming, meaning they are being their authentic selves and that authenticity happens to conform with expectations. There are others, however, who force themselves to conform, denying their authentic selves in order to conform.

Individuals whose gender identity does not conform to society's expectations are considered gender nonconforming. The farther away we move from society's gender expectations, the less we are conforming to those expectations, and the less normative we are. Societal norms will typically tolerate a certain amount of nonconforming behavior if it isn't very obvious and as long as the person primarily conforms to gender expectations. When it becomes obvious that a person is not conforming to gender expectations, society often sends the message, "This is not acceptable."

Think back to the line we drew earlier, with a boy gender on one end and a girl gender on the other. The farther away a biological male, for instance, moves away from the boy gender point on the end, the more nonconforming they become. A biological male whose gender identity sits firmly at the middle point on the spectrum might think, feel, and behave in ways that would be viewed as nonconforming.

One gender-nonconforming example that comes to mind is when actor Will Smith's son, Jayden, posed for a Louis Vuitton apparel campaign wearing skirts and dresses. This was met with huge disapproval and disdain by many people. His behavior was labeled as wrong, abnormal, effeminate, degenerate, and homosexual because it did not conform to society's notions of gender. Many men and women said they would do horrible things to their son if he dared to dress in such a blatantly gender-nonconforming manner. Actor Jada Pinkett Smith, Jayden's mother, recalled that initially even his father, Will Smith, had said, "No, my son is not supposed to be in a Louis Vuitton ad wearing skirts." Her response was, "It's what he wants. It's his expression."[156]

Females who are gender nonconforming don't always experience the same degree of disapproval. Some people are willing to acknowledge that presenting masculine gender attributes can gain a woman some of the benefits society often reserves for men. As Professor Wright mentioned earlier, society is much more accepting of women presenting masculine gender traits than of men who present feminine gender traits.

I identify as female, but I can pass fairly easily as male, and it's always fascinating to me. This started happening in high school, and since then, I can tell right away if somebody thinks that I'm male or female, not because I've said anything that would gender me, but just in how people interact with me. I think it gives me a pretty cool perspective. I get to see both sides, and it certainly comes in handy. I'm in business school, and most of my classmates are high-powered men used to getting what they want. The way that I can relate to them is very different than the way that most of my other female classmates can relate to them. I'm like buddies with them in a way that they don't see many of my female colleagues.

–Dr. Lowell

The experience Dr. Lowell had with male classmates does not mirror society's typical reaction to gender-nonconforming people. Many people find themselves unsettled and disturbed by the notion and certainly the presence of people who do not conform to society's gender expectations. Part of this is because nonconforming people force us to look beyond the gender labels we've grown comfortable using. As discussed earlier, labels tend to give us comfort because they help us quickly categorize people and establish a set of expectations. When people don't adhere to those traditional labels, we don't know what to expect and can feel disoriented, groundless.

Encountering a gender-nonconforming person may be disconcerting because we are unsure of their identity, and thus our expectations of them. But the more deeply unsettling part of our encounter may actually stem from how it provokes an internal dialogue about our concept of gender and our own gender expression and identity. One way we may seek to dispel this uneasiness is to cling to the known, familiar gender perspective and conclude that it is not acceptable to step outside of the binary that has given us so much comfort. Rather than doing the heavy lifting and examining our parameters for gender, we might decide there's something wrong with people who don't conform. This experience becomes more about our own internal discomfort than it is about the nonconforming person. Making our internal discomfort someone else's fault removes the weight and burden from our shoulders and transfers it to the person who doesn't conform.

We should ask ourselves: What is so wrong with not conforming? What is wrong with a person naturally being who they are? If we are comfortable with who we are, then it shouldn't bother us that someone else is comfortable with their own gender identity and expression. For example, Anne's identity and expression of gender has no bearing on how I live my life. I can still earn a living, love my family, possess my own gender identity, and do anything else, regardless of whether Anne or anyone else is gender conforming or nonconforming.

It appears that the greater harm is in not allowing a person to possess and express their gender identity the way they see fit. Not allowing them to do so infringes on their individual freedom. Instead of trying to force individuals to conform and pretend they are something different, why not have a society that accepts and even embraces our different gender identities and expressions?

Questioning Gender Identity

The "Q" in LGBTQIAP can also represent "questioning" gender identity, which, as PFLAG explains, is "a term used to describe those who are in a process of discovery and exploration... of gender identity, gender expression, or a combination thereof."[157] PFLAG also notes that questioning can mean a person has "a feeling they might be different but are still in a process of exploration."

An individual who doesn't see themselves fitting neatly into the traditional gender binary may then find themselves trying to figure out what their gender identity is, how to describe it, and what to call it. A gender-questioning person is trying to determine which, if any, label on the gender spectrum best describes them. As a gender-questioning person learns more about gender, gender identity, and themselves, and becomes more comfortable expressing themselves, they may eventually move out of the questioning state and identify with a specific gender identity, or no gender identity.

Anne recalled a period of questioning during which she sought the aid of a therapist.

> *The gender question, like am I a man or am I a woman?* Am I trans or queer? *It is a vulnerable question to ask myself. Therapy was definitely helpful in having just someone to let you be whoever you want to be.*
>
> -Anne

The question of "Who am I?" is a rite of passage that is asked and answered in different ways for every individual. It should be understandable that someone could be in a state of questioning some aspect of their identity, gender or otherwise. Most, if not all of us, have things about ourselves that we must try to figure out.

Questioning can occur at any point in a person's life, even after several years of identifying solidly as one gender or another, according to the University Library, University of Illinois at Urbana-Champaign.[158] They also advise that questioning "can last for any length of time, can co-occur with any other identity categories, and does not necessarily have to end in a coming out process."

CHAPTER NINE

TRANSGENDER

"I can understand you not understanding it, but don't deny it exists."
–Unknown

Intro

People who identify as transgender have a gender identity that is the opposite of their biological sex and therefore the opposite of the gender society has likely assigned them. Think of someone assigned the male biological sex. Society would say this person's gender is masculine, boy, or man, and would also expect that person to have the same gender identity. If this person's gender identity is feminine, girl, or woman— opposite the gender society has assigned—then this person would be labeled as transgender, specifically a transgender woman. Olympic medal winner Bruce Jenner was born a biological male, has the gender identity of a woman, and is now known as Caitlyn Jenner. That makes Jenner a transgender woman. On the other hand, Chastity Bono was born a biological female and has the gender identity of a man. Bono, now known as Chaz, is a transgender man. Transgender identity is not defined by whether a person has made changes to their attire or physicality. A person can be transgender without making any physical changes.

"I still don't get it." That's what my friend Bryan and many others have said. "Sex is objective," he continued. "Your sex is either male or female.

If you're born a male, you can't just say your gender is female." Where it seems Bryan and many people get stuck is in distinguishing between biological sex, gender, and gender identity, and recognizing that they are three different and separate things.

Biological sex is based on observable biological and physiological factors like the presence of chromosomes, gonads, and hormones. Biological sex is objective because, as dictionary.com describes, objective means "of or relating to actual or external phenomena as opposed to thoughts, feelings, etc." Gender is based on society's thoughts and feelings about how a male or female should think, feel, and behave; therefore, gender is subjective rather than objective. Gender identity, as the APA states, "refers to a person's internal sense of being male, female, or something else."[159] This means that gender identity is also subjective rather than objective. Gender identity is personal; it is not dependent upon biological sex, nor society's mandates.

I was ten years old when Toni, a 6'4" transgender woman, attended a party at our home. Toni worked with my mother, and this was not the first time we'd met; however, on our previous introduction Toni had been a man. I was puzzled, and prodded my mother, a nurse, with plenty of questions, which she answered to the best of her understanding.

"Why is Toni dressed like a woman?" I whispered to my mother.

"Toni wants to be a woman instead of a man," she said.

"Why does he want to be a woman?" I asked.

"Toni says he feels like a woman," Mommy replied.

"But *how* is he going to become a woman?" I persisted.

"Toni is taking something called 'hormones'—"

"What do hormones do?" I interrupted.

"Hormones will change Toni's voice. And make breasts grow." After a pause, she then said, "Toni also plans to have a surgery to change his penis into a vagina."

Mommy was an operating room nurse and was not in the habit of sugar-coating

these things, even to a child. She also explained the surgical procedure to satisfy my questions.

"But why wait? Why can't Toni just do it now?" I asked.

"These things don't happen overnight, Tara. It takes time for the hormones to work, and Toni has to meet with psychiatrists, who will have to approve the surgery," Mommy answered.

"Oh," I said, satisfied for the moment, and ready to move on to another activity.

I only saw Toni a few more times after our first meeting and did not bear witness to her full transition. Even after I discovered that society didn't approve, I still thought it was cool that Toni was willing to pursue what she felt was her true identity. What I did bear witness to was my parents' behavior. I never heard either of them say a disparaging word about Toni or any other transgender person. Nor did they warn my brother or me to be afraid of or to steer clear of her. Perhaps that is why, as an adult, it was not difficult for me to accept the reality of transgender identity, even when I didn't fully understand it.

Why are some people cisgender and others transgender?

Medical professionals haven't reached any definitive conclusions and continue to search for answers as to why some of us are cisgender and others transgender. "We know that there is a significant, durable biological underpinning to gender identity. What we don't know are all of the biological factors at play that explain gender identity," according to endocrinologist Dr. Joshua D. Safer, executive director of the Center for Transgender Medicine and Surgery at Mount Sinai Health System in New York.[160]

Evidence points to the brain and its interaction with other biological forces such as genetics and biochemistry to shape an individual's gender identity.[161] In studies of twins, for example, if one is transgender, the other is far more likely to also be transgender if they are identical, rather than fraternal twins. This supports the connection between gender identity and genetics, because identical twins are near matches genetically. There is also agreement among researchers that our gender identity is not determined by genitalia.

There is some indication that gender identity is determined during fetal development. Harvard University professor Catherine Dulac, who studies masculine and feminine identity in the brain, believes something happens during fetal development that causes one identity to be blocked and the other to be activated. This is one of the theories that Sabrina has heard and finds plausible.

> *I've heard numerous other theories. One theory was that it was environmental, that you grew up with basically no father figure around and you were around women all the time, and they sort of just pushed femininity on you. That really wasn't the case for me, so, that theory doesn't apply. My dad was very strong and still is like, 'You're going to work hard. You're my son. Men are men.' The second theory was that you grow up in a community that encourages feminine men, and I didn't grow up in that, and that sure wasn't the way Detroit was. The other idea was that something happened in the womb, and the theory is that your body sex develops at one time, and then later your brain gender or brain sex develops, and that something happens between those two that your body and your brain sex get mixed up. That made the most sense to me. That made a very plausible argument that there is a real possibility that okay, here my body is a male body, I see it, everybody else sees that I'm meant to be a boy, and they expect me to act that way. I don't think of myself as a boy; I don't see myself that way.*

–Sabrina

Author and activist Jennifer Finney Boylan thinks we shouldn't be overly concerned with the "why" of transgender and should embrace it as a human reality. Boylan, National Co-chair for GLAAD's Board of Directors, says, "I think what's behind this question of brain function and being born this way is a sense that if it's about neurology, then it's not our fault, and we want to say it's not our fault because on some level we're ashamed, or it must be bad to be trans." She encourages transgender people to "let go of that shame, let go of trying to find a reason other than our own—the nature of our own souls for why we are the way we are. And in fact, we should be grateful, we should embrace ourselves, and we should celebrate all the diversity of gender and sex and life itself."[162]

Boylan presents an important perspective. We are not in the habit of questioning or distancing ourselves from what we view as positive or acceptable or what we deem as an achievement. Most cisgender people are likely to be proud of their gender identity without asking why they are cis. If we view transgender as a problem to be "solved," then that can send the message that it's not a good thing, and certainly nothing to be proud of.

As a former pre-med major and science geek, I understand and appreciate that searching for the "why" could be helpful, by providing a better understanding of the human body and its development. In the meantime, perhaps we are best served to view transgender identity as just another part of the life process, another path on the map of human experience. In an ideal world, we might adopt the philosophy of the Bugis culture in Indonesia. They acknowledge five genders, including transgender women (*calabai*) and transgender men (*calalai*), and believe that all five genders must harmoniously coexist.[163] I agree with the perspective of celebrating all gender identities and sexualities, and life itself. We are all different in some way. How cool would it be to realize we all deserve to be here?

Have transgender people always existed?

Possibly. At this point, no one knows the answer to this question. Nothing has been found to prove or disprove that transgender people have always existed. "There's no reason to believe that trans people haven't been around since people have been around, just like any other variation in human biology," according to Dr. Stephen Rosenthal, co-founder and medical director of the University of California San Francisco (USCF) Child and Adolescent Gender Center.[164]

The fact that we haven't yet been able to definitively prove that the first humans included transgender people doesn't mean they didn't exist. This lack of proof should not be misconstrued as proof of absence. Nor should it give us ammunition to dismiss the present reality that transgender identity is part of our human expression.

How many people are transgender?

The number of people who are transgender can only be estimated. In the US, the estimate is that 1.4 million or 0.6 percent of adults identify as "transgender or gender nonconforming."[165] The estimated number of teens between the ages of thirteen and seventeen in the US who identify as transgender is approximately 150,000, or 0.7 percent.[166] The organizations that provide adult and teen estimates do not offer estimates for the number of transgender children.

Is being transgender a mental disorder?

No. A mental disorder, as described by mental health professionals, is a condition that affects the mind in such a way that it prevents a person from caring for themselves and interacting with other people. Transgender people are as capable of taking care of themselves and having interpersonal relationships as cisgender people.

In 2013, the American Psychiatric Association stopped referring to transgender identity as a "gender identity disorder," and began using the term "gender dysphoria." In this instance, dysphoria relates to a person who is in a persistent state of anxiety, discomfort, or dissatisfaction with the gender they have been assigned. The organization's fifth edition of the *Diagnostic and Statistical Manual of Mental Disorders* (DSM-5) explains gender dysphoria as "a marked difference between the individual's expressed/experienced gender and the gender others would assign him or her."[167] With this new label and definition, mental health professionals have acknowledged that transgender identity, or gender dysphoria, is a difference and not a disorder.

Is being transgender just about wearing a dress or pants?

No. No person's gender identity is not just about the clothes we wear. For any of us, what we wear is only one expression of our gender identity. Most people seek to wear clothes that express various aspects of their identities. As a cisgender woman, for example, I wear slacks, jeans, dresses, skirts, shorts, jewelry, etc. that reflect my gender identity, and the way I feel that day, the way I want to be perceived, my desire for comfort, etc. Some of my clothes might be deemed feminine, others masculine, and others neutral. The same is true for many people, regardless of gender identity.

I dress appropriately to being the person that I am and doing what I happen to be doing that day. I had a conversation that came up with a college student who said, "I can't imagine getting up in the morning and putting on a blouse or dress and your hair and makeup to go out and cut the grass." I laughed and asked, "Why would I do that? What woman do you know that puts on a dress, heels, makeup, and jewelry to cut the grass?" He said, "Isn't that what it's all about?" I said, "No, it's not. If I am going to get up on a Saturday morning and go out and cut the grass, I am going to put on a pair of jeans and sneakers, and I am going to pull back my hair in a ponytail. I don't have to put on makeup, but it doesn't change the person that I am. I am still the same person wearing the jeans and the sweatshirt cutting the grass as I am when I go out to dinner later that evening and I put on a dress, heels, makeup, and jewelry. I am the same person."

–Emily, engineer, separated,
   transgender, heterosexual, 60 years old

While wearing a dress does not define who a person is, being able to do so can be important.

To me, to be able to dress as a girl was kind of a fulfillment and part of the actualization of embracing who I was. When I couldn't do it, I was still that same little girl just going through life wearing blue jeans, sneakers, and a sweatshirt. I was still that same person, but when I had the opportunity to wear a dress, that gave me the ability to present myself in a way that really showed the rest of the world who I was. I like the dress and clothes, but it's not about pretending to be a girl; it's about being a girl.

–Emily

What are acceptable ways to refer to or address a transgender person?

The best way to address a transgender person is in the way that they prefer. Pay attention to the way a person introduces themselves or writes their name, or ask them about preferred titles, e.g. "Ms." or "Mr." We can also ask about preferred pronouns.

So, my actual preferred pronoun in my ideal world is they, they/them, non-binary pronouns, but the world is just not often very fluent in that or able to do that. So, they/them or he/him, those are both totally fine. People use those sort of interchangeably for me, and that's fine.

–Anderson

In far too many instances, I have heard people refer to transgender individuals in very unpleasant ways. It seems the most offensive situations occur when people are intentionally callous, cruel, or condescending. If you don't think highly of someone, then you're not likely to treat them with respect, which includes the way you speak to that person or about them. There are other instances when the disrespect might reflect someone's personal state of confusion or discomfort. For instance, someone may think, "I don't understand how a man can be a woman or how a woman can be a man," or, "This person says they're not a man, even though they were born male. But I'm not comfortable referring to them as a woman, so I'll stick to what makes me comfortable instead of what they want." Some people who think this way use their discomfort as an excuse to be disrespectful.

Most of us have been on the receiving end of someone refusing to ask or learn our name or refusing to address us by the correct title, such as Mister, Miss, or Doctor. It might sound like a small thing when you aren't on the receiving end, but when it's done *to* you, it can feel insulting, dismissive, and hurtful. Placing ourselves in the other person's shoes is a good first step to figuring out if what we are saying is disrespectful. Consider whether the term you are about to use would make *you* feel emboldened or belittled if directed at you. Is the title you are about to use intended to minimize or equalize?

If unsure whether to refer to someone with "he," "she," "they," "sir," "ma'am," etc., then consider doing as the Trans Awareness Project suggests: respectfully ask which words a person uses to identify their gender. Having the conversation about appropriate and inappropriate words is likely to be uncomfortable for both parties, but it is worth the effort if it means everyone can be addressed with respect.

Disappointingly, I have also heard more than one individual refer to a transgender person as "it" rather than "he" or "she." Using derogatory words helps us separate ourselves from people we don't approve of or understand. It is clear to me that this is done in an attempt to belittle trans people. Belittling words support our view of them as less than us and less than human. On the other hand, if we view transgender people as human beings whose feelings can be hurt, just like ours, then we should strive to use kinder, more appropriate terms.

The word "tranny" has been used with negative intent, and it has also been re-purposed by some in the transgender community. Some transgender people find this word offensive because it has been used to demean them, yet others have reclaimed it with the idea that it has a friendly meaning when those inside the community use it. This does not give cisgender people the license to use the word, because it can be viewed as a pejorative when issued by someone who is not transgender.

On the other hand, "trans" is an acceptable term that is used and generally accepted by transgender individuals. Instead of saying "transgender man," for instance, once might say "trans man."

What's the difference between transgender, crossdresser, transvestite, and drag queen?

The terms crossdresser, transvestite, and drag queen have different meanings, none of which are synonymous with transgender.

Crossdresser can refer to a male or female, but according to GLAAD, a crossdresser is typically a cisgender male who occasionally wears clothes, makeup, and accessories culturally associated with women.[168] They also explained that crossdressing is not about gender identity, and that crossdressers do not want to change their sex or gender identity or live full-time as women.[169]

The term transvestite refers to the way a person dresses and is not the same as transgender. "Vestite" is an Italian word that means "dress" or "dressed," and "trans" means "across from" or "opposite." The *Merriam-Webster* dictionary defines transvestite as "a person who wears clothes designed for the opposite sex." They also say it is "an older term for crossdresser." For many years, transvestite was used to describe a person who likes to cross-dress for emotional or sexual gratification. Today, some in the crossdressing community find transvestite antiquated and offensive, while others accept the term.[170] Kristine Johnson, the secretary of the Australian Transgender Support Association of Queensland, finds the word transvestite offensive "mainly because that was used as a psychiatric term for crossdressers, those that were heterosexual men who got a thrill out of dressing up in female clothing."[171] While Johnson acknowledged that some people cross-dress for sexual pleasure, she insists, "It's not perverted; they don't go out looking for sex everywhere." While some continue to use the term transvestite, others don't feel the sexual pleasure distinction is accurate, and they prefer the word "crossdresser."

"Drag queen" is another term often misconstrued to mean transgender. A drag queen is not a transgender person. Drag queens, also called female impersonators, are cisgender men. These cisgender men enjoy wearing women's clothes as a form of fashion or entertainment. For drag queens, dressing as a woman and performing as a woman is considered a talent. Some drag queens like RuPaul have turned it into a career. RuPaul, likely the most famous drag queen of our time, is a cisgender gay man who became famous for the TV shows *The RuPaul Show* and *RuPaul's Drag Race*. Many drag queens are gay men; however, drag queens might be straight, bi, or any other sexuality.

When does someone realize they are transgender?

According to psychiatry.org, many people may not express feelings and behaviors relating to being transgender, also known as gender dysphoria, until puberty or much later. Other people become aware they are trans before the age of four years old. This might sound absurd until you recall that most humans become aware of their gender identity around the age of two or three, according to pediatricians, child psychologists, and scientists. It is at this age when we human beings begin to show independence and become self-aware of our body parts, our gender, and our gender identity. Those who study human development also say that once our cisgender or transgender identity is developed, it remains stable over time.[172] *Pediatrics* also reports that research shows children who assert a transgender or gender diverse identity "know their gender as clearly and as consistently as their developmentally equivalent peers who identify as cisgender."

This was surprising to me at first, until I also learned that doctors and psychologists who study human development say our sense of self becomes apparent during our toddler years; that sense of self develops as our brains and bodies develop and as we begin to build connections between ourselves and other people. It includes how we think and feel about ourselves and how we see ourselves, and is also impacted by how others see, think, and feel about us and themselves.

One aspect of our sense of self is our gender identity. Hence, it is possible for a toddler to be aware of their transgender identity and to recognize that it doesn't match their biological sex. If you find it difficult to believe that a three-year-old child can be aware they are transgender, consider that you, too, likely became aware of your gender identity around the same age. You might be asking, "Why don't I remember it?" It's probably because nothing made it stand out in your mind. For those of us who are cisgender, it was not jarring to realize our bodies matched our gender identity. The challenge occurs when a person's gender identity does not match their biological sex.

Some people have tried to dismiss this by likening a child's gender dysphoria to a child having fantasies of being a princess or a superhero, but that is a vastly inaccurate comparison. A child becoming aware that their gender identity does not match their biological sex and the gender society expects is not the same as a child pretending to be a princess or superhero. The key word is "pretending." Mental health professionals explain that when children pretend to be a fantasy character, they generally know it is pretense. On the other hand, when a child becomes aware that their gender identity differs from their biological sex, it is not a fantasy game that they can stop playing; it is their permanent reality. That child is not pretending to be something or someone else.

The APA explains that in children, gender dysphoria or transgender identity must be present and verbalized, and must continue for at least six months, to be pronounced. They also say the characteristics of transgender children are "a pervasive, consistent, persistent, and insistent sense of being the other gender and some degree of gender dysphoria."

Diane Ehrensaft, a psychologist at UCSF Benioff Children's Hospital says, "We are now much more commonly hearing very little children speak up, 'Please let me be the gender I am rather than the gender you think I am.'"[173] Parents of transgender children confirm these occurrences. One mother says as soon as her child, who was assigned biological female at birth, and therefore assigned a girl's gender, could speak, they would scream, "I'm a boy!" Another mother recalls her five-year-old announcing, "When the family dies, I will cut off my hair so I can be a boy."[174] Lisa Raman, the mother of a trans man, looks back now and recognizes that her child exhibited early recognition, although it was not verbalized until later.

> *My child would not keep female clothes on. They would literally pull things out of their hair and off their body and spent most of their time wearing a diaper or pull-ups or shorts. Then as my child got older, rather than wanting to behave "girly," they moved into boys' sports and played on the boys' baseball and hockey teams. We just figured we had a tomboy on our hands. Then, at eighteen, my child told me, "In my head, I'm a boy, but my body says I'm a girl."*
>
> –Lisa Raman, Cofounder and Co-President,
>   Transgender Health and Education Alliance
>   Plus (THEA+), committed relationship,
>   cisgender, heterosexual, 52 years old

Jazz Jennings, a teen transgender activist, came out as transgender at age five and says, "When I was two years old, I asked my mom, 'When is the Good Fairy going to come and change my private parts?'"[175] Dr. Ben Barres, MD, PhD, who was assigned the sex of female at birth and transitioned to a transgender male in 1997, says strong feelings that he "felt more like a boy" began to occur around the age of four.[176] Barres, formerly Chair, Department of Neurobiology, Stanford University School of Medicine says, "I felt like a boy. I played with little boys. I preferred boys' toys. I remember dreadfully wishing I could be in the Cub Scouts and Boy Scouts." Recognition of being transgender also set in around the age of four or five for Emily, even though she didn't know the terminology for it. Similarly, Sabrina, who was born a biological male, remembered becoming aware that her biological sex and gender identity didn't match around the age of four or five:

> *I was four or five when one day my sister was going through a bunch of old clothes, and there was a pinafore that I asked if I could put on. It fit me perfectly, and I knew when I put it on that*

'this is right, this is me.' When I saw myself with that dress on, I saw the image of what I saw myself as. I just knew in my heart, this was how it's supposed to be. And nobody else saw me this way.

–Sabrina

It is understandable that parents might respond with fear and confusion. But it might be helpful to also consider the repercussions of telling a child they are wrong or bad and insisting they adhere to what society deems normal. Forcing them to live counter to their inner self can be detrimental. When a transgender child expresses how they think and feel, it should not be ignored or minimized. Mental health professionals suggest that, in the long run, it can be more beneficial to give the child credit for knowing themselves and being unrelenting in their self-knowledge and self-expression. Being transgender is not a phase a person passes through; it is their life.

For Vandy Beth Glenn, the realization that she didn't feel like a biological male came during puberty:

It was around puberty, so I guess that was eleven or twelve. I was reading a Mad Magazine, *and on one of the pages, there was a picture of a girl, a shapely young woman wearing a leotard, and I remember being struck by the effect that it had on me. I was experiencing a desire to be the girl in the picture. The shape of her face, the curves of her body. Everything about her seemed like something that was appropriate for me.*

–Glenn

For others, trans identity can have a longer development ramp.

My gender identity has developed and changed over the course of my life. I've always been masculine from the time I was a child. I was assigned female at birth but never really felt that comfortable with that label. And so, when I was about thirteen or fourteen years old, I found the word 'butch' and I was like all right, that sounds close enough. But I didn't really like it. A lot of people say butch lesbian, and I didn't really like the lesbian part of that. I was always just fine with butch. Then as society evolved and language evolved, I knew trans men, but mostly the trans men that I knew identified as transsexual in the '90s. They knew they had been born in the wrong body and had the very kind of early narratives that were very binary. I would be like, I don't feel wrong. I feel whole, complicated but whole. So, I can't call myself a transsexual. And then language around transgender identity has continued to develop over the last twenty years, and there was room to call yourself trans-masculine. There was room to call yourself transgender, which is a little bit more of an umbrella term. But I think, for me, what I've kind of most comfortably settled on is trans-masculine because it implies a gender that is not firmly male but is masculine. It implies a sense of identity that is broader than just male or female. So that's a long answer to your question, but it is a complicated trajectory.

–Anderson

How do children deal with gender dysphoria?

Each child manages their situation uniquely. Many of us think of childhood as this magical, carefree time in our lives, yet for a transgender person, childhood can be scary and confusing. Feelings of safety, love, and support can be replaced with fear, confusion, guilt, threat, depression, isolation, and even betrayal.

Darlene Tando, a licensed clinical social worker and gender therapist, says, "A lot of times, kids don't say anything, or they keep it hidden or they modify their behavior based on the wishes of those around them. But when they start getting feedback from others about how they should dress, which line they should stand in, or what activities they should be involved in, they may start speaking up. And that's when they may start asserting themselves."[177]

Glenn and many others reported trying to suppress their feelings:

> *I suppressed it for as long as I could. It's a difficult part of yourself to accept. I didn't tell anybody. I was afraid of their reaction.*
> –Glenn

Being transgender is something that many people feel they can't talk to anyone about.

I was the only one who saw me this way, and nobody else did, and I couldn't really explain it. I didn't understand why I was like this. I kind of said some stuff to my sister, and she was real negative about it. She would let me dress up a little bit, as time went on, but would say, "Boys don't do that." I was a little embarrassed. My family was somewhat religious, so I was told that this was wrong; that it wasn't right. I didn't know what to do. If I mentioned anything, everybody said, "No, no, no, no." So, I knew better than to push it. I could see that it was not the right thing to say.

–Sabrina

Emily was also reluctant to tell anyone that the boy child they saw actually felt like a girl.

The conversations that we had were very brief and very guarded and more along the lines of talking to them about why I was interested in having a tea party and playing with dolls and with the girls in the neighborhood. My parents didn't understand why I would want to do that. We never got in depth about me coming right out and saying, "It's because I think I am a girl." I kept that part inside of me, because on a day-to-day basis, I was exposed to the societal and cultural pressures that are there to try to force me to fit that mold of being a boy.

–Emily

Like most of us, transgender children often develop methods of coping with whom they are and with the negative messages received from family and society.

The boys gave me a hard time. They would beat up on me for being with the girls all the time. I didn't know what to do. I was like, okay, boys don't do this; this is wrong. So now, what do I do because I feel this way? I was very perplexed. I decided I would be kind of a loner. I did that for a while, and I couldn't take that, so I did what a lot of us people as transgender do. I overcompensated. I thought 'if you can't beat them, join them,' and that's what I did. I was as masculine as I could possibly be. I decided that I would be the meanest, rottenest, dirtiest boy anybody had ever seen. I didn't have any problem getting down and dirty. If someone wanted to fight, I would fight. I was not afraid of anything. It took everything in the world to do it, but I didn't back down from anything. My dad had finally gotten a son, and I did everything in the world to please him. I did everything I could to please him since I didn't want him to know. He worked at Ford Motor Company and he had a landscaping company. I worked very hard in landscaping, and that kind of work was very dirty. I lived up to all of his expectations.

I struggled. I struggled a lot, and it was very, very, very, very hard. When I was alone and by myself, I would try to be me. I did that most of my life. I had portrayed this masculine identity to please everybody. I thought I would probably never be able to do anything about what I was feeling, and I would just have to keep doing what I was doing.

–Sabrina

My heart breaks for Sabrina. That this child or any child would have to suffer and pretend to be a completely different person seems the height of cruelty. Demanding that another person be whom we want them to be just so we can be comfortable is unfair, unjust, and inhumane. Their pretense might make us feel better, but it comes at their expense, making them unhappy, depressed, and possibly suicidal.

Some people are able to embrace their transgender nature, even in the face of adversity.

You have this great fear of what the repercussions are going to be if you come out and say, 'No, I am supposed to be a little girl.' One of the benefits I have had embracing myself as Emily the whole time was I was able to experience the things in life that little kids, adolescents, young adults experience. I had to fight hard to be able to do that. For me, that was very rewarding and very fulfilling.

–Emily

For some transgender children, puberty becomes a more stressful time because that's when their bodies change, creating a more drastic and visible difference between their gender identity, biological sex, and society's gender expectations. When a trans child enters their teenage and adult years, some behaviors that might have been accepted or overlooked are no longer tolerated. Boys playing with feminine toys might be overlooked during childhood, but in teen years, masculine behavior is expected to be more pronounced and is much more intensely reinforced.

While a trans person might internally accept who they are, they may make efforts externally to meet familial and societal expectations.

> *There is always a part of you that even though you accept yourself for who you are, you are surrounded by what is always there confronting you in terms of the social norms and expectations. As a boy, I was always extremely competitive and just over the top in terms of trying to demonstrate my masculinity in everything that I did. I played in sports and did quite well in several of them because I was so driven to live up to the expectations that were presented to me to do that.*
>
> –Emily

Another experience some transgender people have communicated is an underlying hope, particularly during their youth, that one of life's events—moving to a new city, changing schools, or going through puberty—will change them.

> *You think that something is going to happen, and it is going to "correct" you. It's going to "fix" you, for lack of a better word… About a third of the way through my senior year in high school, I went through puberty. When I started, I was 5'9" and weighed 130 pounds. Months later, I was 6'3" and weighed 185 pounds. At that point in time, part of my thought process was, "This is the 'fix.'" But it didn't "fix" me.*
>
> –Emily

If communication from today's transgender youth is any indication, more transgender people are moving into a space of acceptance earlier in life. This does not eliminate challenges, confusion, and fear, but it can offer a greater sense of peace and more of an opportunity to live authentically.

How does the situation change as transgender people move into adulthood?

As a transgender or gender dysphoric child grows into their teens and young adulthood, the conflict between their gender identity and what society instructs may continue to grow. For many, the hope persists that these feelings will go away, and they can instead be cisgender.

> *The next big opportunity after getting out of high school was going into the military. Even going through all the experiences of basic training didn't change the person that I was. I was still struggling to deal with that and to understand it.*
>
> –Emily

It is not unusual for many gender-dysphoric individuals to continue receiving messages from others that being transgender will not be accepted. Many trans people are told God doesn't approve of them, which only intensifies feelings of doubt and confusion.

> *I was so perplexed about this idea of being a woman in a man's body, and I had this moral war going on inside. I was told that God doesn't like this, and this doesn't please God. I sort of felt that if I served God, if I had the right relationship with Him, that He would take this away.*
>
> –Sabrina

How people respond to society and manage their internal conflict differs from person to person. Some double down on their relationship with God and religion.

> *Later, I went to a Bible college. I worked in youth ministry, and then I went into pastoring small churches, and I still kept a secular job. I did that for thirty years until I decided to transition.*
>
> –Sabrina

Acceptance eventually becomes a reality for many transgender men and women. They no longer hope for something to change them.

> *I am okay with the person I am. I like me, and I accept me. I am okay with who I am, and I like me as a person, and I accept me as a person, and I am doing okay in life. I am doing a lot better than a lot of transgendered guys and girls because, situationally, I have been able to make it work for me. A lot of transgender people never quite get to that point because they are battling a lot of things in their lives. There are a lot of guys and girls out there that go through a lot more on a day-to-day basis just to survive in life than I have ever had to deal with. I feel extremely fortunate for the life I have had.*
>
> –Emily

Coming to a place of acceptance can be empowering. It doesn't make everything right in the world, and it doesn't eradicate many of life's challenges, but it can offer a certain strength and peace of mind that can help one to better face those challenges.

> *I think that I did realize what I experienced as just sort of a low-level degree of dissatisfaction with my body... I assumed that dysphoria was the water that everyone was swimming in, so it didn't occur to me that my relationship to my body might actually be unique, not unique but different than what other people were experiencing. So, it wasn't just difficultly with my body. It was like I don't recognize myself... The more stories, the more people came out and were visible, the more I was able to be like actually, yeah, that is true. I don't feel at home in my body.*
>
> *The other thing that was going on is that I was an alcoholic, and I was suppressing a lot of the bodily dysphoria that I was feeling with alcohol. I quit drinking when I was thirty, and then all of this stuff rose to the surface. And I was like right, that's all been there this whole time, and I have not dealt with it. And it was this low-grade hum underneath that I had not*

addressed because I was pushing it down with drinking. And so right around when I was thirty, it was like [explosion sound].

I got sober, and there was nothing to quiet how loud the world was, and so all I could do was be with myself. What kept coming to the surface was you are unhappy with your body in lots of ways. You are unhappy with how you move in the world and how people see you, and there's a disconnect. And so that, coupled with more and more stories of people who did not have a standard binary transition, meant that around the age of thirty, thirty-one, I started being like huh, what could I do?

–Anderson

Being transgender in a predominantly cisgender society is stressful and challenging. My hope is that those of us in the cisgender population will not add to this stress.

Transitioning

What is transitioning?

Transitioning is the process a transgender person goes through to acknowledge, accept, and live as their gender identity. For someone born a biological male, transitioning is a process of visibly and possibly physically transforming from boy/man to girl/woman, or as it is sometimes referred, male-to-female, also known as MTF, MtF, or M2F. For someone born a biological female, transitioning is a process of visibly and possibly physically transforming from girl/woman to boy/man, or female-to-male, also referred to as FTM, FtM, or F2M.

The transitioning or gender affirmation process can include social, legal, medical, and surgical aspects.[178,179] The social aspect of transitioning can include selecting a different name, changing preferred pronouns, and modifying appearance with things like clothes, jewelry, wigs, and makeup. Legal aspects can include changing the name on one's driver's license and birth certificate. Medical interventions can include laser hair removal and hormone replacement therapy. Surgical measures can include breast implants, Adam's apple reduction, and procedures to alter genitalia.

A more recent term for transitioning is "gender affirmation." The reasoning is that it is an affirmation and acceptance of who a person has always been rather than a transition from one gender identity to another.[180] People who prefer the term gender affirmation might also refer to themselves as affirmed men or women rather than transgender men or women.

Transitioning can occur over several years as individuals become more in tune with their gender identities and more comfortable presenting them. Boylan compares transitioning to moving.[181] "There's just a lot of people that you have to notify that you're not at the same address anymore." She also says she felt a sense of victory when she got the paper that "outwardly verified the thing that I had known to be true within [me] for most of my life."

What prompts a person to transition?

The details vary but can be summarized as "it was time." According to Crystal Raypole, Editor, *Good Therapy*, "Typically, people transition to align their physical appearance and characteristics with their gender identity."[182] Another reason that transgender individuals transition is so their gender identity is accurately perceived by others.

Many transgender people see transitioning as a liberating process, one that allows them to say goodbye to a way of life that once held them captive, and farewell to the way others have perceived them. When Diane Sawyer asked Caitlyn Jenner, "What are you saying goodbye to?" the answer was, "I'm saying goodbye to people's perception of me and who I am. I'm not saying goodbye to me because this has always been me."[183] That sounds empowering to me, and I suspect that many of us have done that with some aspect of our lives or wish we could.

Those who are parents have said they waited until their children became adults. Some have said they were tired of being miserable. Others have said they were tired of pretending. And yet others have said it was the only way they could survive. At the core of anyone's decision is a desire to live as they see themselves.

Some people, particularly those born in the 60s or earlier, say they weren't aware that transitioning was an option when they were younger.

> *I heard about Christine Jorgensen, and that she had transitioned;*
> *that she used to be George Jorgensen, and George became*
> *Christine. And that was the first time in my life that I heard it*

was possible, and that was like, the first ray of hope, that this could actually be something that could actually happen in my life. From that moment on, it was like a dream. It was a hope that I could actually have the chance or have the opportunity to be me, to be whole, to be who I really am.

–Sabrina

There are those who would say they decided to transition because they could no longer ignore their gender identity.

Gender dysphoria's like a ringing in the ears, and eventually, it gets so loud that you can't ignore it anymore. I shared it with a few select friends prior to that time, but it wasn't something that I talked about regularly or even openly acknowledged with the people I had told. It just didn't seem like there was any point until I was ready to do something about it. It provided some relief to have caring and understanding friends, but it wasn't a solution. I reached the point in my life where I only saw two solutions. I decided to transition because that was the solution that kept me alive.

–Glenn

Once the decision is made to transition, is it every day, all day?

Some people present their identity every day early in the transitioning process, while others might gradually work their way up to it. For example, some people might start by expressing their identity in the privacy of their home, and then expand by presenting their identity to friends, before eventually presenting themselves to the rest of the world. Others might select specific places to present their gender identity and work their way up to expressing it everywhere, every day, all day.

Some transgender people limit where they present their gender identity to avoid retaliation, exclusion, or job termination.

On a day-to-day basis, I live myself and my true person that is Emily. I have been living in that role for the past fifteen years since my wife and I separated. It has become more and more important for me to do that. I would like to say that I live and present myself as Emily twenty-four-seven, but I am not in a position to be able to do that. I have to present myself differently in order to accommodate society and the practicality of having a job and earning a living. I work as a consulting engineer, and I am able to do quite a bit of my work from my home office, but on the days that I do have to go into the office and meet with the people there, I have to go to the back of the closet and put on a three-piece suit and look presentable as a guy so they will accept me, and I can keep my job and earn a living. Those are the days I feel like I am crossdressing because I have got the wrong clothes on.

–Emily

I am struck by how destabilizing that must be for Emily. She has transitioned and expresses her feminine gender identity daily, except on those two or three days each month when she reports to the office. Instead of being Emily, she must flip to being Bruce, or else risk being fired. It doesn't seem fair that any transgender person must deny themselves so profoundly just so everyone else can be comfortable.

It should be a crime that Emily could be fired for expressing her identity at work. It's not that she can't perform the duties, nor is she hurting anyone. It's simply that other people wouldn't be comfortable with her. That doesn't seem fair, just, or equitable.

How does hormone therapy fit into the transitioning process?

One medical aspect of transitioning may include hormone therapy, which can alter the body's appearance and reproductive functions. Hormones are present in all humans and help our bodies develop in many ways. They impact growth, metabolism, mood, sexual function, and reproduction.

Testosterone, the main sex hormone found in males, controls the development of male physical features. It affects the growth of the penis and testes, as well as facial, pubic, and body hair, and the deepening of the voice. Testosterone also builds muscles and strong bones and influences height. Women have testosterone too, but in much smaller amounts than men.

Females have the sex hormones estrogen and progesterone. Progesterone serves several purposes related to conception and pregnancy. Estrogen is responsible for female physical features such as growth of the breasts as well as pubic and underarm hair, and reproduction processes, including the start of menstrual cycles. Men have estrogen, too, but in smaller amounts.

Doctors prescribe hormone therapy for cisgender as well as transgender individuals in order to add or block hormones. Cisgender women with excess amounts of estrogen might undergo hormone therapy to reduce the amount of estrogen in their bodies. This can prevent or counteract weight gain, fatigue, and loss of sex drive. Hormone therapy for cisgender women is also prescribed to regulate their menstrual cycles or to counter the adverse effects of menopause. Cisgender men might also undergo hormone therapy when their estrogen is too low, which can cause excess belly fat and low sexual desire, according to hormone.org. High levels of estrogen in a man can cause breast development and infertility. Hormone therapy can regulate these conditions.

Birth control pills are also a form of hormone therapy prescribed to manage painful menstrual cramps, and to prevent pregnancy.

> *She said, you know, I take birth control to help even out some of the hormonal issues that I have, and that could be considered gender-affirming hormone treatment for myself as a woman, but we don't think of it like that because that's just normal. Lots of women take birth control to keep their cycles different or whatever, so I think you should think about hormone therapy, however you need to think about it...*
>
> –Anderson

Doctors can recommend hormone therapy for transgender people to help their bodies match their gender identity. Hormones can have physical, physiological, and emotional effects. Crystal Raypole, editor of GoodTherapy.org, says, "Hormone therapy helps people develop secondary physical characteristics that reflect their true gender."[184] According to a medical journal article about hormone therapy for transgender patients, "Cross-sex hormone therapy has been shown to have positive physical and psychological effects on the transitioning individual and is considered a mainstay treatment for many patients."[185] The article also noted that the World Professional Association for Transgender Health (WPATH) and the Endocrine Society have created guidelines to help medical professionals provide this type of healthcare for transgender patients.

Estrogen therapy for transgender women is based on treatments used for postmenopausal cisgender women. Estrogen might be prescribed to a transgender woman—born a biological male but with a woman's gender identity—to help grow longer hair, enlarge breasts, feminize voice, soften facial features, and modify moods. Christine Jorgensen, who gained national attention in the 1950s after transitioning, describes the results of hormone therapy: "The first step towards becoming a woman was a long course of female hormones."[186] As the hormones began to take effect, Jorgensen's doctor noted the changes. "The first sign was an increase in size of the mammary glands, and then hair began to grow where the patient had a bald patch on the temple."[187] Later, the doctor reported, "Finally the whole body changed from a male to a female shape."

Guidelines for hormone therapy in transgender men are based on the current recommendations for cisgender men. When testosterone is prescribed to a transgender man—born a biological female but with a man's gender identity—it can stop ovulation, help shrink breasts, grow facial hair, deepen the voice, and alter his mood.

Before I was on testosterone, my brain was like I-285 at rush hour, just in positive and negative ways. The biggest tradeoff that I see is that I feel less capable of multi-tasking and less capable of holding multiple truths at once. I don't want to over simplify because it is only my experience. It is like going from 285 to a two-lane country road, and there is something magical about that in terms of my anxiety levels and my sense of peace and my own, like, quiet in my brain, but there is a loss, too, because it has really changed. I feel very much like a uni-tasker, like I'm going to do this thing, and I'm going to do this thing. It makes listening harder, and it makes having conversations harder.

And then, physically, I've been able to put on more muscle, which was a goal and has made me happier. It has actually made my diabetes be better controlled, which has been better.

It has also made me more invested in my overall health. I think if you have a contentious relationship with your body and don't really feel like your body represents you in the world, it makes it a lot harder to do all of the very heavy-lifting stuff you have to do to care for a chronic illness. And being, like, it is not even about I think I look good, it is like my body looks like what I think I look like, which is a very hard concept for cisgender people to get, right? It is not about thinking you look cute. It is thinking you look like yourself. I don't know. I don't know if that always comes through. It is not a vanity thing.

So, there are tradeoffs, right? Okay, that's a tradeoff, but it is worth it if your sense of self, if you look in the mirror and you don't see a ghost. And that's kind of how I felt both consciously and unconsciously for so much of my younger life.

–Anderson

Hormone therapy was administered to Raman's trans teen, with her consent.

Within three months, he sprouted this nice, thick, fuzzy beard, and he started growing hair all over his body. His female shape turned into a male shape, and because he was so young, his body just soaked it up and his brain did too, and he needed that. It changed his personality; it changed everything.

–Raman

She also explained how hormone therapy affected her transgender partner's genitalia.

Transgender men who take testosterone, their clitoris grows and becomes erectile tissue. As they take testosterone, the clitoris goes from being this tiny little bud that cisgender women have to being maybe two inches. They get a lot of erectile tissue from the testosterone.

–Raman

The effects of hormone therapy vary from person to person and cannot be precisely predicted or controlled. Once begun, the treatments typically continue for the remainder of a transgender person's life, unless that person chooses to stop the treatment. Tristan Reese, a transgender man who was taking testosterone, stopped the treatment in order to become pregnant. In 2017, Reese gave birth to a son, saying, "I'm okay being a man who has a uterus and has the capacity and capability of carrying a baby."[188] Stopping treatment can result in the reversal of some changes but won't reverse all changes that the therapy inspired.

So, I took testosterone for about a year. I experimented with a lot of different doses to see what was right for me, and I've been lucky to have great doctors who were very thoughtful about allowing me to trust my body and communicate with them about that. At one point, I was, like, let me go off this for six months and see how I feel. I really want to make sure this is what I want to be doing. I went off it for six months, and I did not feel well at all. I just physically felt terrible because one of the things testosterone does physically for you is it gives you a lot more energy. I mean, one of the things is you are physically stronger pretty quickly, so you go to pick up a five-pound bag of sugar. I remember I was probably on testosterone for four or five months. I had been an athlete when I was younger, played sports my whole life, but I went to pick up a five-pound bag of sugar and almost threw it across the room. I was like, oh, this is changing. So that part was hard, but it also just made me emotionally really feel off. So, all of that is to say you can certainly, and I have known lots of people who have happily stopped taking hormones for various reasons, both estrogen and testosterone, depending on what they were doing, and some of the changes go away or lessen.

So, your voice. If you were taking testosterone, your voice lowers permanently but does go back up a little bit because your vocal chords thicken and stretch out, which is the same thing that happens in cisgender boys at puberty. But it will go a little bit higher, so you don't go back to your original vocal range, but you do kind of move back into a slightly more gender-neutral vocal range. Or a lot of the people do.

Facial hair, if you have been on for a while, you will always grow facial hair, but it will get fine again. So, your body somehow knows that you started to grow hair here; you are going to continue to grow hair here, but it is not going to be coarse. Your body sorts some stuff out. Your body fat pattern will redistribute to a female body fat pattern. There are lists of all these things online that are pretty normal for people. But your abdominal fat, if you have it, shifts to the front for men, and it will go back to the hips and butt if you stop taking it. Stuff like that.

You don't grow your hair back… One of the frustrating things is being thirty-six, being on testosterone for not that long and immediately going bald, and being like oh cool, all right. All of the men on both sides of my family are bald. All my cousins are bald in their twenties.

–Anderson

They also addressed some of the myths:

I think there are a lot of myths about testosterone, like making people angry or making people more sexual, and I think like alcohol or like anything else, testosterone exacerbates what already exists within you. If you are not inherently angry, you're not going to be angry. I think all that kind of stuff, it doesn't change the core of who you are.

–Anderson

Also worth noting is that, in most states, transgender individuals seeking hormone therapy need a letter from a mental health professional confirming the presence of gender dysphoria and recommending hormone therapy.[189]

What is a sex-change operation?

The term "sex-change operation" is considered an antiquated term and has been replaced with "genital reassignment" or "genital reconstruction."

These procedures, also referred to by plastic surgeons as "bottom" surgeries, reshape a person's genitalia to match their gender identity. For a transgender man, the transmasculine bottom surgery can help make the vagina look and function more like a penis. For a transgender woman, the transfeminine bottom surgery transforms a penis into a vagina. Genital reassignment surgery is just one of the numerous types of surgeries a trans person might undergo during their transition and is the least frequently performed. According to the American Society of Plastic Surgeons, genital reassignment surgeries account for less than 0.05 percent of all gender-affirming surgeries performed.[190]

The terms "gender-affirming," "gender confirmation," or "gender reassignment" surgery refer to the various types of surgeries a transgender individual might undergo to make their body match their gender identity. The American Society of Plastic Surgeons lists the following categories of gender confirmation surgeries: facial feminization, facial masculinization, transfeminine top (enhance breasts), transmasculine top (remove breast tissue), transfeminine bottom (transform male genitalia into female), and transmasculine bottom (transform female genitalia into male). It's worth noting that some of these surgical procedures are also performed on cisgender individuals. It's also important to note that none of the gender reassignment surgeries is required for transitioning. Some people feel genital reconstruction surgery is necessary and others do not.

> *It depends upon what you feel you have to have to fit into a role and a lifestyle that you are comfortable with. I have friends who are sixty and seventy years old and want surgery because they feel that they have to have that to achieve the fulfillment that they need as a person. There are some girls that have facial feminization surgery so their facial features appear more feminine, or they will have breast implants. They will have other surgical procedures done to affect their posture, their bone structure, to give them the bone structure to get the curves they want. Then as a final step, they might decide they have to have sexual reassignment surgery. There are all levels and degrees of it, and it is not a one-size-fits-all for everybody.*
>
> –Emily

Lili Elbe, a transgender woman, is believed to be the first person to undergo male-to-female reassignment surgery in Germany in the 1930s. Laurence Michael Dillon, a transgender man, is believed to be the first female-to-male transgender surgery recipient in the 1940s. Christine Jorgensen, mentioned earlier, underwent male-to-female reassignment surgery in the 1950s.

For some people, their transition isn't considered complete without genital reconstruction.

Well, for me, I want to completely transition. First of all, it really messes with my gender dysphoria. I also think it's asking quite a lot from somebody who might want to be in relationship with me. I would really like to be in a relationship, and I think it's kind of unfair to go into a relationship when the top part of my body is female and the bottom part is male. There are some people that can deal with it, but it's already a hard thing to deal with someone that's transgender, but to ask that is asking a lot.

–Sabrina

Transsexuals feel that in order to fulfill their life, they have to have the sexual reassignment surgery in order to have the sexual organs associated with their gender.

–Emily

Emily's use of the word "transsexual" bears further discussion. Transsexual has been defined as a transgender person who transitions from one sex to another.[191] The medical community has traditionally referred to transgender people who've undergone reassignment surgery as transsexuals, but that is also changing. The Stanford University website explains, "Among the younger transgender community, the word is considered archaic and is more common within medical discourse." The International Society for Sexual Medicine (ISSM) advises, "Some feel that the word transsexual should not always refer to physical changes. And some transsexuals no longer refer to themselves as such after they have finished their transition. They call themselves either men or women."

Why don't all trans people have genital reassignment surgery?

There are a variety of reasons a person might not have reassignment surgery. As mentioned earlier, genital reassignment surgery is not required for a person to transition. Also, transitioning is a personalized process and each person crafts that process based on what makes them feel whole, what they can afford, and what their health allows.

As mentioned in the response to the preceding question, very few gender-dysphoric individuals have surgery to change their genitalia. According to a survey by the National Center for Transgender Equality, only 11 percent of transgender women and 12 percent of transgender men say they've had reassignment surgery to alter their genitals.[192]

Transgender people, for any number of reasons, don't feel that they have to have the sexual reassignment surgery in order to live their life in the gender that they identify with. The sexual reassignment surgery, the restructuring of the genitalia, is the most traumatic, the most involved, and can be the costliest.

If the state of society, culture, and medical knowledge and understanding existed forty years ago, then I would have had surgery immediately after high school. Do I need to do that today? No, I don't. There is still a part of me that says, "Yeah, I would like to," but I don't have to. I am sixty years old now, and I have grown to be comfortable with who I am, my situation. A lot of it is wrapped up in my level of understanding and acceptance of who I am and my relationships with other people who say I don't need to go through that to have a happy and rewarding lifestyle. That doesn't mean there aren't going to be some struggles because of that, but I can deal with that.

–Emily

Trans men and women who desire bottom surgery may be faced with financial challenges that make it impossible. The survey also found that almost 50 percent of trans women say they want reassignment surgery but can't afford to pay cash and don't have insurance that will cover the cost.

We do have some companies, bless them, like Starbucks and AT&T and Apple, Chase Bank. They actually pay for their employees to go through gender reassignment surgery, because they know in the long run, it's going to save them money, and they're going to have happy employees and healthier employees, but we have a long way to go still on that.

–Raman

Without the help of insurance, plastic surgery of almost any kind is an expensive venture. Consider that the average cost of breast augmentation surgery is $3,719, according to 2016 statistics from the American Society of Plastic Surgeons.[193] For trans patients, that cost is increased by a number of requirements. Prior to the surgery, transgender patients must also receive counseling that can cost more than $5,000 for one year.[194] There is also hormone therapy, which can be up to $2,400 for one year. Gender reassignment surgery to reconstruct genitalia can cost $15,000, according to health.costhelper.com.

Even if more employers' insurance plans covered this type of healthcare, it would still be unattainable for most transgender people because of the precarious employment situation they face. Many transgender people are fired from their jobs after coming out, which can leave them without income and health insurance. Many are then unable to find a new job after coming out, which means they are not in a position to benefit from an employer healthcare plan that might cover reassignment surgery if/when they are ready.

Health concerns can also prevent genital reconstruction surgery from becoming a reality, particularly for older people.

The other part of it is going through sexual reassignment surgery, there is a lot involved and it is not easy. It is so hard on the heart.

–Emily

Younger people may opt out because they feel conflicted about genital reassignment surgery.

When my son was around nineteen, he wanted the surgery more than anything. He had this pervasive sense that he needed to get rid of his organs, and he needed to get his breasts removed. At that time, surgery wasn't covered under insurance, and we did not have the money, so as long as he took the testosterone and it took the menstrual periods away, we could kind of keep him content for a while. After about two years of waiting and us planning for it, now he's saying, "I don't want my organs taken out yet. I just don't want them gone yet, because if I had been born a cisgendered male, like I should have been born, then I would have been happy not being a mother." You have to kind of put yourself in their position. They have a body and they have hormones that give them opposing messages. He has female organs, and sometimes, the feelings of, "I wish I could be a parent, I wish I could have a baby, I wish I could maybe give birth." He also has this brain that says, "You're a man." So, it's not so simple.

–Raman

Surgery is not the be-all and end-all option for transgender men and women. There are many other ways gender-dysphoric people live out their true identities.

Some people ease their dysphoria simply by dressing differently or by asking people to use a different name or a different set of pronouns. Other people will take many sorts of interventions up to and including genital surgery, and that's going to be different for each individual. For myself, it's not something that I discuss in detail.

–Glenn

The fact that some people don't feel the need for body-altering surgery suggests that being a man or woman is more about how we feel than what our physical packaging provides. A cisgender woman isn't any less of a woman after a hysterectomy or because she has small breasts. A cisgender man isn't any less of a man after a vasectomy or because he has a small penis. In a perfect world, we would all have the breasts or penis and other physical features we desire, but not having those attributes doesn't diminish who we are. And as the medical community has asserted, genitalia do not define gender identity.

I'm not going to define it for anybody else, but I have always known myself to be female, despite physical evidence to the contrary. My body, for most of my life, did not conform to my inner understanding of my correct gender. Eventually, I was diagnosed with gender dysphoria, and I began steps to transition my gender presentation from male to female, and I think the presentation has as much to do with it as anything else, including psychologically, intellectually, and emotionally. I have never thought, and I don't think, it's a fair assessment to argue that your genitals dictate what your gender identity is.

–Glenn

Many cisgender people expect for transgender people to divulge whether they've had reassignment surgery; some even act as if they have a right to know this information. They do not. Each of our medical histories is personal. We should afford trans men and women the same privacy we demand for ourselves. We should understand that a transgender person would be uncomfortable with others asking into their medical history just as we would not feel comfortable with a stranger asking if we've had breast implants, a vasectomy, or any other surgery.

There are other reasons why this obsession with a trans person's gender surgery is disrespectful. Elite model Carmen Carrera says people "always focus on either the transition or the genitalia, and I think there is more to trans people than just that."[195] Actress Laverne Cox says, "That preoccupation… objectifies trans people, and then we don't get to deal with the real lived experiences. The reality of trans peoples' lives is that, so often, we're targets of violence. We experience discrimination disproportionately to the rest of the community, and our unemployment rate is twice the national average… When we focus on transition, we don't get to talk about those things."[196]

Let us not become Peeping Toms or voyeurs in our fascination with gender reconstructive surgery. General discussions about medical and surgical procedures are important parts of the discussion, however wanting to know which body parts someone has or does not have is disrespectful.

Transgender individuals who do not undergo genital reassignment surgery will have the genitalia they were born with, as well as some or all of the respective reproductive organs and functions. A trans man—born a biological female and transitioning to a man—could have a clitoris, fallopian tubes, and uterus, and may continue to menstruate. As a result, a transgender man could need some of the same medical care as a cisgender woman, such as an annual pap smear and breast exam. A trans woman— born a biological male and transitioning to a woman—could still have a penis and testes and would need to seek the same general medical care that a cisgender man would seek.

How does hormone therapy and/or reassignment surgery affect a person's ability to have sex?

Hormone therapy and genital surgery can produce numerous changes to a person's sex organs, reproductive organs, and sex drive, all of which can impact sexual activity. Studies have found that frequency and sexual satisfaction can be impacted if a transgender person is undergoing or has had gender confirming treatment (GCT), such as hormone therapy or genital surgery. Generally, trans women reported experiencing increased frequency of sex after GCT, and trans men experienced either the same or increased frequency of sex after GCT.[197] Many transgender women and men also report increased sexual satisfaction after hormone therapy or genital surgery.

Before examining how these treatments impact trans individuals' sex lives, it's worth pointing out that everyone, regardless of gender identity, has been given different equipment and circumstances that impact their ability to participate in sex. Things like penis size, vaginal secretion levels, sex drives, sexual preferences, health conditions, and medications are factors that can affect anyone's sexual activity. Some cisgender men, for example, find it difficult or impossible to achieve an erection, and therefore pursue other avenues of sexual pleasure; similar circumstances may apply to a transgender person. Additionally, some cisgender women may experience pain or difficulty during vaginal intercourse, and the same can be true for some transgender people.

A trans woman—someone born with male genitalia and feminine gender identity—who hasn't had hormone therapy or genital surgery would therefore still have a penis. A functioning penis on a trans woman could become erect and ejaculate during orgasm. This transgender woman could also produce semen and possibly impregnate a woman. If that trans woman begins hormone therapy to increase some feminine aspects and reduce some masculine aspects, she will likely experience reductions in sexual arousal, sperm production, and ejaculation. In "When Transitioning Changes How We Have Sex," trans women report that after a few months of hormone replacement therapy, they stopped having nocturnal erections, had fewer orgasms, and noticed a decrease in semen during ejaculation. [198] If a transgender woman underwent genital surgery to remove the penis and replace it with a vagina, she could then have vaginal intercourse. The range of sexual pleasure from vaginal intercourse will vary from one transgender woman to another, just as it does from one cisgender woman to another.

A transgender man—someone born a biological female with the gender identity of a man—who is not undergoing hormone therapy and has not had genital surgery, would still have a vagina and uterus, and may be able to conceive children. If that transgender man begins hormone therapy to reduce feminine characteristics and increase male characteristics, the vagina and reproductive organs will experience changes such as the cessation of menstrual cycles. A transgender man can undergo hormone therapy and surgery to transform the vagina into what resembles and functions similarly to a penis.

> *My boyfriend chose to remove the clitoris. When this is done, it becomes more like a very small penis, and over time, it starts to take on that shape. They can get about four or five inches on what used to be the clitoris, which is now like a small penis. It gets erect, and it gets hard. All the tissue around it, where the scrotum would be [on a cisgender man], actually gets very firm too. They have an orgasm, much like a cisgender male would, except for the fact that they can't ejaculate. After they have an orgasm, it all just gets soft again.*
>
> –Raman

Based on Raman's description, her transgender partner's erect penis is the average size of a cisgender male's erect penis, which is approximately five inches. (Studies have shown that an erect cisgender male penis can range from about 3.5 inches to over eight inches.)

Testosterone can have other affects.

I would say he probably acts like a much younger man because of the testosterone injections, and he has a much stronger sex drive.

–Raman

Why do transgender people change their bodies instead of changing their gender identity?

Our bodies can be altered, however our gender identities cannot. There has never been any success in trying to change a person's gender identity, but there has been success in changing aspects of a person's body. Changing gender identity is not like changing personality traits and behaviors. We can develop our patience or punctuality or be more kind, but a person who is transgender, according to the experts, cannot become cisgender, and someone who is cisgender cannot become transgender.

Suggesting that a transgender person undergo therapy to change their gender identity assumes that being transgender is a choice or a mental disorder, which we have already established it is not. On the other hand, what is within our power to change is our physical appearance, which is what many trans people do. There is success in changing a transgender person's physical state and allowing that person to live as they see themselves. For trans people, the way to resolve gender dysphoria is to live according to their gender identity.

With gender dysphoria, it's stated for our happiness and our well-being that some of us need to have those physical changes to alleviate our gender dysphoria. That's where I'm at.

–Sabrina

Telling a transgender person to change their gender identity to match society's expectations shows a complete and total disregard for the individual. Why should any of us change who we are just to appease another person or society? Could you ever really be at peace or be happy if you couldn't be your true self? Our greatest loyalty and responsibility is to ourselves and not to other people. Each person must be allowed to determine their course of action to manage their particular set of circumstances. No one has the right to determine how another individual responds to the hand life has dealt them.

> *That's not their call to make. They don't get to say what my effective [path] is.*
>
> —Glenn

Transgender people are doing what many of us do—figuring out what we believe is best for us and our given situations. For some trans men and women, gender confirming treatments and/or surgery are what's best for them.

What is passing?

In the transgender community, passing refers to a person's ability to look like and live as their gender identity without it being obvious they are transgender. Janet Mock would be considered by many to pass because her physical appearance does not suggest she is transgender. Likewise, actor Brian Michael Smith would be considered by many to pass because his appearance does not hint that he is a transgender man.

> *Passing privilege is the ability to be viewed as cisgender. In other words, there's nothing about me that makes people assume that I'm a transgender woman. Nobody should be judged for that or mistreated for that, but many people are, and it's probably the single biggest source of difficulty in the world for trans people who do not have that ability. If you're fortunate enough, as I appear to be, to have passing privilege, eventually you learn that people aren't going to hassle you, and that's something you stop worrying about. I am acutely aware that not everybody has that ability though, and my heart really goes out to anyone who does have to deal with that.*
>
> —Glenn

Passing seems to be more difficult for transgender women. This is because, in many instances, it is difficult to femininize masculine features. If a transgender woman (male-to-female) had a square jaw or a protruding Adam's Apple prior to transitioning, those features could be minimized or softened with surgery. Other features, like broad shoulders or large hands and feet, will still be present even after hormones and surgery, which could leave a trans woman appearing masculine. The more masculine a trans woman appears, the less she is considered to "pass." Unfortunately, we live in a world where people judge us by our appearance, and there are cisgender women who are ridiculed as being men because they have certain masculine features. The world adores those who meet certain arbitrary and gendered standards of beauty; for those who do not, the world can be cruel.

> *The first thing I did was I started off with hormone treatment. I had some facial feminization surgery to try to help me look a little more feminine, and I've done breast implants. That helped some, but I've come to the realization that I'll never, ever be able to pass 100 percent, and it's just something that I'm going to have to live with and deal with, but that's okay. That's life.*
>
> –Sabrina

Why do people say it's brave to transition?

Brave is defined as "possessing or exhibiting courage."[199] Courage is defined as "the quality of mind or spirit that enables a person to face difficulty, danger, or pain."[200] That is exactly what a transgender person does when they decide to come out and to transition. That is why it's brave to transition, and it's why, in 2015, the ESPYs gave Caitlyn Jenner the Arthur Ashe Courage Award.

Bravery isn't limited to trans celebrities. Transgender people from all walks of life face difficulty, danger, and/or pain every day on a level that most cisgender people will never experience. In addition to the same difficulties all humans face, transgender children and adults suffer a myriad of difficulties that cisgender individuals are not forced to encounter.

They face the emotional pain of being ridiculed by society for being transgender. There are the dehumanizing instances of not being allowed to use the restroom when nature calls. The imminent danger of not being able to receive appropriate, or any, medical treatment when needed. The risk of being fired if they come out or transition. The heartbreaking reality of having spouses, children, loved ones, and friends pronounce, "You are dead to me," after they come out. Transgender people must face the intimidating question of how their gender identity will be received each time they enter a new relationship. Many also face the harsh reality of never having an intimate relationship because most cisgender people can't handle being in a relationship with a trans person. They face danger each time they walk out into the world as their true selves, never knowing if someone will assault or murder them for being trans. They also face the physical pain of surgeries necessary to make their bodies match their gender identities. Living as a transgender person is a daily act of bravery.

> *It's brave to be who you are, especially if that type of person isn't widely accepted in your society. That takes tremendous courage. It's got so many elements of bravery. It's not commonly accepted. It's something that is potentially risky. I think it's very brave.*
>
> –Dr. Lowell

If any other person were to share a story of enduring ridicule, fighting the status quo, being true to themselves, and coming out on the other end of it triumphantly, the world would applaud. It is hypocritical to withhold that applause when it comes to transgender people. Being true to yourself in a world that beats you down for being different sounds brave to me.

What is life like after transitioning?

Life after transitioning is a different experience for each person. No longer pretending to be a different gender allows many people to express their true identities, feelings, and personalities, which is liberating, as you might imagine. In the book *On Christopher Street: Transgender Stories*, one transgender woman named Bree says, "Obviously, it has been difficult. But it was as if, once I became Bree, all my fears went away. It's been just beautiful." Alex, a transgender man, tells the National Centers for Transgender Equality, "I am proud to be trans because I think life is too short to be anything besides what you are. This is who I am."[201]

Transitioning is not only about changing physical appearance and wearing different clothes. When a person transitions, they have given themselves freedom to think, feel, and behave according to their gender identity, which opens a vista of new emotions, behaviors, and experiences.

As Emily, my true self, I have always been a lot calmer and more thoughtful person. I relate to people a lot better. I have a much more compassionate side to me when dealing with people and society.

–Emily

Others also spoke of the emotional changes they experienced.

In a lot of ways, I'm the same, but Sabrina has experienced liberation and has a lot more joy. Donald was pretty negative most of the time, but Sabrina's a lot happier. Sabrina is a little lonely, but that's okay because getting to experience liberation and being yourself is an amazing thing. It's so incredible, and the acceptance that I've gotten from nearly everybody else is so, so far above... I can't explain it. It's been an amazing journey.

–Sabrina

There is also a feeling that even amidst the harsh realities, life is better now.

It is easier. I have a peace of mind that I never had before. A sense of wholeness, I would say.

–Glenn

Peace of mind and wholeness. Don't we all strive for and cherish these things? Shouldn't our love for humanity press us to want those things for others?

Many people also spoke of freedom.

I'm just overjoyed. It's like being set free. I am free to express all of the things that my mind enjoys, all of the smells, the things that interest me, the things that garner my attention. Now I'm free to follow my interests and follow those things that bring me joy and happiness and are close to my heart. Now, for the first time, I can express a full range of emotions that are mine that I could never do before. I could never go to that high range of feeling, the ecstasy of what it was like to see flowers, and soak in all that that meant to me. I could never cry at a movie, and now

*I can. My heart is just gripped, and I can cry and I can express
who I am inside and I couldn't do that before. I can wear the
clothes that express how I feel on the inside. I love to cook, and I
can do that, and I love to bake. Just all sorts of things. It's that
full expression of who I really am, and that is amazing.*

–Sabrina

I found myself smiling and crying as Sabrina spoke of feeling like she'd
been set free. The joy in Sabrina's voice made me want to hug her through
the phone. That sense of freedom is something many of us take for granted,
as is the feeling of being accepted.

*I am okay with who I am. I like me as a person, and I accept
me as a person. I am doing okay in life. I have been able to
make it work for me, but I wouldn't wish this on anyone else.
I wouldn't want them to have to go through and deal with all
of the things that I deal with being transgender and having to
live your life this way.*

–Emily

In addition to the physical adjustments that have been discussed,
transgender individuals must also manage the changing dynamics of
personal relationships with family, friends, coworkers, and potential
romantic interests. After coming out, in many instances, families of
transgender people become estranged because they refuse to accept the
trans individual's identity. Edanry Rivera, a twenty-seven-year-old trans
woman eventually opted to trade contact with family for the joy and
freedom of being themselves.[202] Others face similar ultimatums.

*This has cost me a lot. I lost all of my friends. I lost my family.
So, the cost is high, but the payoff is big. What's amazing to me
is the ones that supposedly love us the most, in my case, are the
ones who have rejected me the most.*

–Sabrina

It can be gravely disappointing and isolating to discover that family
members don't accept you. We might be able to brace ourselves for that

type of rejection from strangers, but how is one to deal with it from people we expect to love us unconditionally? Sadly, this is a reality many transgender people are forced to accept in order to maintain contact with family members.

In far too many families, love does not conquer fear, hate, religious beliefs, traditions, etc. How can that be? I was taught that loving someone includes wanting them to be true to themselves, even when we don't understand or agree with that person. That, however, is not the reality for many transgender youth and adults whose families kick them out of the house or sever contact with them. Faced with the prospect of losing contact with children and grandchildren, some trans men and women agree to temporarily place themselves back in the closet for family visits.

> When I am with my children and grandchildren, it is "Dad" and "Grandpa." That is their expectation. I will forever accommodate them to maintain the relationships with them. It's hard not being in a situation where I can be 100 percent open and honest with them, but I still have to make the accommodations.
>
> –Emily

Some trans individuals also say they become more aware of the different ways we treat people based on perceived gender. Thomas Page McBee, author of *Amateur: A True Story About What Makes a Man*, recalls, "A few months after I began injecting testosterone, I discovered that one of the startling new privileges of my male body was that I could silence an entire room just by opening my mouth… When I spoke, people didn't just listen, they leaned in. They perched their heads in their hands and tilted toward me for a better angle. It was as if whatever I said, however banal, was surely worth that strain of a neck or the hurried quieting of all other thoughts."[203] McBee recalls that as a woman, "I was frequently interrupted and talked over, especially by men, and especially at work. I had to fight harder to make a point. Early in my professional life, I was sometimes simply squeezed into silence." Brynn Tannehill, a Navy veteran, tells New York Magazine, "As an effeminate guy, if you want to come out of there with your point of view intact, you have to open up the meeting hard and fast to prove that you are the smartest motherfucker in this room. You make yourself look absolutely authoritative… Leadership has cultural and sociological aspects to it, and if a woman tries to lead just like a man, it's not going to go well."[204] She added that, "There are guy leaders who can just say, 'This is what we're doing.' That's great, but it's a much tougher sell as a woman."

Anderson was also struck by the difference in being received as a man instead of as a woman.

> *It is the first time in my life when I've not been physically in danger, because when I was read as a butch woman, I was constantly getting harassed by men and constantly in peril and always having to look over my shoulder and getting into physical fights.*

> *There is also just what it means to be a girl and a woman in our culture, and the fact that you are never left alone. You are never invisible. You are never allowed to just be.*

> *I think one of the really amazing—in both horrible and selfishly positive ways—one of the things about being read as a man, particularly a white man, is that all of a sudden you are like this is the bubble of safety that white men just walk around in all the fucking time. Right. Of course. But to really feel that is so jarring after a lifetime of not feeling that. I mean, obviously as a white person, I've experienced a level of safety that people of color don't experience, but as a queer person and as someone who was read as a woman, even that level of threat, of vigilance. I walk my dog at midnight in my neighborhood, and I see other men walking around, drunk, homeless guys around my neighborhood, and they just say what's up, brother, and keep on going. Walking through the park late at night, it's all good. I never would have done that. It makes me more angry about the world because I'm like, I know what it is like. So, all of that is to say my partner, I think, has been incredibly generous in her willingness to let me go wherever I need to go, which is why I'm with her. And I have tried to remember as much as possible what she is giving up by letting me do that.*

–Anderson

Can a transgender person change their sex on legal documents?

Yes. The male and female designation on a driver's license is referred to as a gender marker. Changing a gender marker is one of the legal aspects of transitioning. Most states require a court order to do so, and some states require verification of gender reassignment surgery. Some cities and states are changing these requirements. In 2018, New York City adopted legislation that, beginning in 2019, allows transgender people to change the gender on their birth certificates without an affidavit from a doctor or mental health professional.[205]

In a TED2014 Talk, transgender model Geena Rocero discusses how she decided to move to the US after learning she could legally change her gender marker from "M" for male to "F" for female. "I remember looking at my California driver's license, with the name Geena and gender marker F. That was a powerful moment. For some people, their ID is their license to drive or to get a drink, but for me, that was my license to live. To feel dignified." Some cisgender people might trivialize this matter by saying that a letter on a driver's license is insignificant. That trivialization may be because cisgender individuals take those markers for granted. But each of us seeks markers that reflect and support our self-image. When tempted to judge another person's validation, it might be helpful to try and imagine what it would feel like if our identity was denied or stripped from us.

As of 2017, Idaho, Kansas, Ohio, and Tennessee were the last four US states that do not allow gender markers to be changed on birth certificates. I understand that society and governments must have rules, but these restrictions seem to treat people as if they are not adults and are incapable of managing their own lives. Where does respect, compassion, and understanding for citizens come into play? In the case of transgender individuals, that compassion and understanding would translate into finding ways to ease a difficult situation. One of those ways is allowing a transgender adult to change their legal gender marker.

How do transgender people choose new names?

Names are a part of our identities. The name a person chooses usually has some personal significance, such as how a person sees themselves. Names are also chosen for sentimental value, to honor of a family member or favorite icon, or for some other reason. Those who want to keep some aspect of their original name might shorten it, use a different gendered or gender-neutral version of their birth name, or use initials. Some transgender people select a name during childhood, while others might wait to select a name when they begin thinking about transitioning. Walter Bockting, PhD, a professor of medical psychology and co-director of the LGBT Health Initiative at Columbia University Medical Center, observes that "most often, they have chosen a name a long time ago and initially kept this very private."[206]

> *It is connected to my mother's maiden name. I like the sound of it; I think it's distinctive without being so peculiar that it gets unwanted attention. And it's distinct enough from my birth name that it does a good job of marking the distinction between my former life and my current life.*
>
> –Glenn

The process can become complicated.

> *I mean, my dad has helped me with some of the ins and outs of the legal paperwork to get my name changed. My mom was very loving about the idea of me changing my name. My given name was after my grandmothers, and so I felt very sad about losing that connection to my history because I really loved my grandmothers. I also felt disrespectful to my parents. It felt like my name was a gift from my parents that then I was disavowing. I realized that I cared more about that than they did. They were like whatever, but I was like, I felt some kind of way about it, and so I wrote them a letter. I was just like this is what I want to do, and so I'm in the process of legally changing my name now. Changing it to one of my grandfathers' names, and that felt like a way to sort of honor my family and stay connected to my family, because one of the things I think is really important to me as a queer person and as a trans person is so many people queer and trans people don't feel that they can stay connected to their families when they come out or when they transition.*
>
> –Anderson

In the New York magazine article, "How Transgender People Choose Their New Names," Fred McConnell says he had initially collected names for the children he hoped to have. "Then I realized, I kind of always knew these were names I'd like for myself." One afternoon, Fred took the list of names out and cross-referenced them with family names, and the name Frederic stood out. Sophie Labelle says, "I kept changing my name, like, four times." She tried Emily and Genevieve, until finally the name Sophie felt right. She later discovered that had she been assigned female at birth, her parents would have name her "Sophie."[207]

The legal process of changing names can require a bit of work.

> *I mean, one of the things that I think a lot of cisgender people don't know is how it is to change your name, how hard it is that you still, in Georgia, to change your driver's license, need to have a letter saying you have had surgery; to get your passport, you need a letter from a doctor. There is so much about the standard of proof. Like we don't trust trans people to just be allowed to be who we are. If you are trans and you are changing your name, you have to put your name in the paper for thirty days with your full address… in the state of Georgia. If you get divorced, that's true too, but it is very easy to see who is trans.*

–Anderson

Relationships

How do transgender relationships differ from cisgender relationships?

Regardless of gender identity, humans are likely to have similarities in the types of relationships they have, as well as the dynamics and cycles of those relationships. We meet people, and they become acquaintances, friends, or lovers. We are drawn to and then grow apart from people for various reasons and seasons. These things can be true for everyone. The differences in transgender relationships versus cisgender relationships seem to hinge more on other people's perceptions and feelings about transgender individuals. Many transgender people experience greater difficulty in starting and maintaining relationships with cisgender people who don't want to engage in platonic or romantic relationships with transgender people.

Trans individuals may be more likely to discover whose friendship and love is unconditional and whose is not. We all have this experience at some point in our lives, however society's lack of acceptance of transgender people increases the chances of being rejected in relationships. This can leave many transgender people on shaky ground with family, close friends, and romantic interests, always fearing that being transgender will jeopardize old and new relationships. When it comes to dealing with parents, siblings, and children, many of us will never experience rejection. That is not the case for many transgender individuals. As mentioned earlier, fear of being rejected by family members is very real.

> *I guess my biggest fear relates to the family. My kids. My grandkids. The kids all know to some degree, and they are all perplexed and confused. It doesn't make a lot of sense to them. They are all accepting to some degree. My fear would be at some point in time I lose my kids and grandkids.*
>
> –Emily

Making platonic friends outside of the transgender community can also be challenging, and many will focus on building relationships with other transgender people.

> *I do a lot with guys and girls in the community that feel the only opportunity they have to get out in the world is within the transgender community. To me, they are shorting themselves on life because what you want to do is get out and be accepted by the whole world. It's important to me to have all avenues available to me and have as many friends, acquaintances, and interactions with everybody else in the world, but it's very, very difficult. I would say that 80 percent of the friends that I have only know Emily. There are some that don't know that Jim ever existed. There are a lot that know he used to be here. They don't really ask about him much, sometimes somebody might, but they just accept me as the person I am. There are no special*

accommodations that they have to make or that I have to make for them because we just are people who appreciate each other's friendship.

–Emily

Are transgender men treated differently than transgender women?

The overwhelming response to this question has been yes. Perhaps this should not come as a surprise in a world where cisgender women are treated differently than cisgender men. Women and men are held to different standards. Overall, women are more likely than men to be ridiculed for their appearance and behavior. Correspondingly, a transgender woman is more likely than a transgender man to be criticized for her appearance and behavior, particularly when it does not meet society's standard of femininity. Trans women have received the bulk of the news and media attention, as well as the bulk of the social ridicule. It can often be easier to identify a transgender woman than a transgender man, thus exposing trans women to much more attention, ridicule, and discrimination.

Transgender women have a rougher time, and I think people are uncomfortable with it because some don't "pass" very well, if we want to use that word. I also think that ignorance pretty much guides our reaction to people too, and if we don't understand, then we're going to avoid them or we're going to stare at them or we're going to think badly of them.

–Raman

More trans men pass as cis men than trans women pass as cis women because there is a greater rate of success transforming feminine features into masculine ones than there is transforming masculine features into feminine features. The result is that transgender men are less easily identifiable as transgender. Mark Seliger, a photographer and the author of a coffee table book on transgender men and women, discovered this while trying to find transgender men to participate in the book. He said finding transgender men to photograph was difficult because identifying them in public is impossible: "You usually have no idea." Trans men are, therefore, less likely to bear the brunt of the attention, questions, ridicule, and violence that is inflicted on transgender women.

Even though it's more difficult for transgender men to be identified, the possibility still exists for them to be treated differently than cisgender men.

> *People tend to treat transgender men like very young guys because they can look very young. Most don't have a lot of facial hair and most are short… They kind of pat my partner on the head because he's short, or they tend to let him know in other ways that they know he's trans by trying to open doors for him or by overemphasizing the "Hey, man," "Hey, bro," kind of thing. He would rather have natural interactions with people, but he knows many people are either over-compensating, or they're laughing at him.*
>
> –Raman

As Raman mentioned, in many cases, trans men resemble cis men who have small frames, short stature, and rounder facial features. Although these men are able to pass, there is still a good chance that they will face the same type of treatment as cisgender men who might not meet society's masculinity quotient. Each person is different. Some cisgender men are respectful, others are uncomfortable, and some can be verbally abusive or physically violent.

A cisgender man who is insecure with his manhood could find it unsettling to come face-to-face with a man he views as somewhat effeminate. That insecure man's response might be to pump up his perceived masculinity or to belittle what he perceives as feminine in the trans man. Some of what Raman has observed might be a function of what is referred to as a "pissing match" between men: their need to show which of them is the "dominant dog" in the pack. Or if those cisgender men are aware they're interacting with a trans man, their patronizing behavior could be their way of saying, "You're not really one of us." This is unfortunate, because this behavior further separates people and closes the door on discussing or enhancing our understanding of manhood, masculinity, and gender identity.

Not everyone shares Raman's perspective.

In my experience, most men don't give a shit about trans men. If you look like a dude, and you successfully perform masculinity, even if they know, men who know that I was born a woman, even guys who are super homophobic, super transphobic, would probably violently hurt a trans woman, they don't care as long as I follow the rules of straight masculinity. Even when men weren't 100 percent if I was a man or not, if I was successfully performing masculinity to whatever degree. Like strangers on the street, if I seemed masculine enough and I wasn't trying to talk to a woman that they were talking to, like I wasn't threatening them, but we were just both in line at the gas station or whatever, it didn't matter because masculinity is prized above all else.

–Anderson

How can someone be attracted to a person they know is transgender?

There are a number of reasons why any of us becomes attracted to someone. Our reasons include physical appearance, shared interests, personality, status, income, intellect, etc. When someone finds themselves attracted to a transgender person, it's likely for one or more of those reasons.

It was his connection with the people in the crowd. He's highly charismatic, and he's a storyteller. He's an old country man who talks about his life and uses that as an analogy to get a strong message out to the audience. He's an engaging speaker, and every person in the room feels like he's talking directly to them. That's what got my attention, his directness, his clarity. I loved listening to him speak. I loved the way he gave eye contact to people and the way he listened to people... I had this strong, strong urge to be around this person, and it wasn't sexually, it was just to be around him, to talk to him, to go watch movies with him, to be in his house, just to find out what kind of person he was and to be in his world. There was a strong need to be with this person, period.

–Raman

Perhaps what prompts some cisgender people to ask this question is that they assume everyone else shares their preferences, and because they cannot imagine themselves being attracted to a transgender person, they assume everyone else feels the same. We are all attracted to someone that another person would look at and think, "I would never be attracted to them." Many of us have found ourselves in a relationship with someone we never thought we could grow close to. In some instances, the hurdle might be age, race, religion, profession, or personal history. It may be a physical attribute like height, weight, physical impairment, or a medical condition. Conversely, there are situations where we are drawn to someone and later discover something about their body, past, or personality that we find difficult to accept. We begin to consider whether any of those things is a deal breaker. We consider if we will be happier with this person in our lives or without them. If the answer is happier with them, then we accept them for who they are and move forward. The same can be true upon the discovery someone is transgender. It is just one thing among many that we must consider when deciding whether to hitch our wagons to another living soul.

> *Early on, had I known he was trans, I would have said, "Forget it." Later, I thought, "I just want to get to know this person, and we'll take the rest of it very, very, very slow." I had just come out of a long marriage, so I had a good reason to take it slow anyway. I came to visit at his house every month for three or four months, and we just talked all those times. I said, "Look at yourself, Raman. You care so much about him, and yet you're putting this barrier between yourself and him because he was born with the wrong genitalia, and he's done everything he can possibly do in his life to change that, but he can't go back and get reborn." So, I had to go okay, did I mean what I said? And yeah, I did mean what I said, because I care very much for him, and the rest of it we got past. The rest of it we got through.*
>
> –Raman

The ways in which coming out and transitioning will impact their dating, sex, and love lives is a huge concern for transgender individuals. Many, like writer Juno Dawson, wonder if anyone will be interested in them. "I wrongly thought that neither gay nor straight men would be interested in a trans woman. But I thought it would be better to be single forever as Juno than to be a gay man for a moment longer."[208] Happily, Juno and others do find relationships, sex, and love after transitioning.

Though some would have us think only a sexual deviant could be interested in a transgender person, reality says otherwise. While there are some men who only turn to transgender women to fulfill sexual fantasies, there is more to the picture. There are also those who have relationships and build families with a transgender partner. They may be cisgender or transgender themselves. They are young and old, religious and non-religious, employed, self-employed, and retired. They are people who meet, like, and sometimes fall in love with someone who happens to be transgender.

Are transgender people straight, gay, or bi?

Transgender is a description of a person's gender identity, not their sexuality. A transgender person might be heterosexual, homosexual, bisexual, etc.

To better understand what it means when a trans person says they are straight, gay or some other sexuality, we must consider that person's transgender identity rather than the biological sex they were assigned at birth. For instance, TV host Janet Mock is a transgender woman who is attracted to men, and she is therefore considered heterosexual.

My friend Bryan also had something to say about this. "But wait a minute," he said, "If Mock is a biological male who is attracted to other males, then she's gay." No, she's not. A human sexuality educator explains it this way:

> **If you are transgender and see yourself as female and,**
> you like guys: then you are straight.
> you like girls: then you are lesbian.
> you like both: then you are bisexual.
> **If you are transgender and see yourself as male and,**
> you like guys: then you are gay.
> you like girls: then you are straight.
> you like both: then you are bisexual.
> *...No matter what your body looks like!*[209]

Many people also question the sexuality of someone who is dating, partnered with, or married to a transgender person. If a cisgender woman is in a relationship with a transgender man, what sexuality is the cisgender woman? Does the cis woman consider herself lesbian, straight, bi…?

> *I have absolutely no lesbian inclinations at all. I'm completely a straight woman, and even though I knew what was going to be there, it was still very different for me, not just mechanically but emotionally and everything, and I did have fears. I still have this tug-of-war inside of myself that yeah, I'm with a man. I know I'm with a straight man. He looks very male. He acts very male. He's a very physical person when it comes to being all male, but I still have those moments when I say, "Oh god, but he used to be called this, and he used to be considered a lesbian."*
>
> –Raman

Even though Raman only knew her partner as a man, her mind had trouble letting go of the fact that he was born a biological female. Raman's mind kept taking her back to what her partner used to be. It was telling her, "You're a woman who is attracted to someone who was born a biological female, and people who are attracted to the same sex are homosexuals." Raman's mind was questioning and challenging her sexuality. If Raman hadn't had an emotional and intimate connection to him, she might not have been able to quash those doubts and fears and be reassured that she was attracted to a transgender man.

That questioning and challenging can also happen when a heterosexual cisgender man discovers he is sexually attracted to a transgender woman. In some instances, that discovery doesn't get in the way of two people pursuing their attraction, and in others, that discovery has the cisgender man's mind tell him, "You're attracted to a man, and that makes you gay." That man may also see the transgender woman as a threat to his sexuality and his manhood. He may mistakenly feel his sexuality and manhood are under attack by the transgender woman he is attracted to. As many societies promote aggression in men, the cisgender man may feel inclined or even entitled to respond to the perceived threat by verbally or physically attacking the transgender woman. If he doesn't have an emotional connection with the transgender woman, like the one Raman shared with her partner, there is nothing to assuage the feeling that his manhood and sexuality are being challenged.

Another question about sexuality arises when a cisgender person is in a relationship with someone who comes out as transgender later in the relationship. Let's say Jane and John are married, and one day, John comes out as a transgender woman. If Jane stays in the relationship with a trans woman, does that mean she is now lesbian or bisexual? That question can only be answered by Jane. One woman from a *Thought Catalog* article reports that she married a biological male who later came out as a trans woman. The couple stayed together, and now the woman considers herself lesbian because she is in love with a transgender woman. Another woman experiencing the same situation and outcomes might identify as bisexual, heterosexual, or something else.

Marriage

Do trans individuals get married after transitioning?

Yes, some do. There is currently no data on the percentage of transgender people who get married after transitioning; however, trans people do find love and get married, as has been documented by countless newspapers, magazines, and books, like *On Christopher Street: Transgender Stories*, which profiles couples where one or both individuals are transgender.

It can be challenging for a transgender person to establish intimate relationships that evolve into marriage. It seems that most cisgender people are unwilling to accept transgender people and are not interested in forming romantic or loving relationships with them. This limits opportunities for relationships. As a result, many transgender people find themselves limited to dating other transgender people or pansexuals, who can be attracted to people regardless of gender identity or sexuality. Some transgender people are not interested in dating other transgender people, which further restricts their dating and marrying pool.

What happens to a marriage after one spouse comes out as transgender?

Some couples stay together, and others do not. Coming out and transitioning does not automatically dissolve the marriage. Very little information exists on the percentage of marriages that survive after transitioning; however, the US Trans Survey reports that 27 percent of transgender respondents say a spouse or partner ended the relationship because they were transgender. It also appears that the survival of relationships differs based on age, as 6 percent of people age 18-24 report relationships ending because of being transgender, while 19 percent of people 45 and older report relationships ending because of being transgender.

Boylan, who married her wife in the 1980s before Boylan's transition, says the important thing is that they love each other.[210] A *Thought Catalog* article shares responses from women whose spouses transitioned after marriage. Those who remained with a transgender spouse say they stayed because they loved their spouses, although they acknowledge that it wasn't easy. Mary says it was hard, but "anything worth doing is hard. My marriage is worth doing. My husband, now my wife, is worth doing. And I'd do it all over again if I had to."[211] Shellie says there was no way she could leave the relationship after learning what her spouse was going through. She also says "I will always miss aspects of Randi the man; that's just the reality. But there are so many things I love about Randi the woman." Georgia, another spouse says, "I kept coming back to the things I loved most about him: his passion, his loyalty, his wicked sense of humor, his intellect, his love for me and our kids. Life without him was unimaginable."

Coming out as transgender does not legally dissolve a marriage. According to Lambda Legal, if the marriage was legal at the time it was entered, then it remains legal after a spouse transitions. If the couple wants to divorce, they must follow divorce laws in their state.

One of the questions for transgender people who married before coming out is why they kept such a secret from their spouses. Just as there is no legal demand for disclosure of other secrets, there is no legal duty to disclose gender dysphoria before entering a marriage. People keep a variety of secrets from a spouse for a variety of reasons. Some people withhold information about past relationships, illnesses, addictions, and affairs for fear their spouse will think ill of them, or worse, use the information to hurt them or decide to end the relationship. The same fears can exist for a trans person who doesn't come out to their spouse. Finding the courage to reveal a secret may also take some time. Also, in many instances, we all wait for the proverbial "right moment" to reveal a secret. Waiting for a special occasion, whether it's to get a new job, move to a new house, send the kids away to college, etc., can turn into a pattern of putting off the truth.

Some hoped marriage would resolve their gender dysphoria. Tricia, who was known as Patrick when she and her wife got married, explains, "I didn't tell my wife because I believed I was going to shake this out of my system."[212] Before tying the knot, Tricia, vowed to no longer dress like a woman after the wedding and even marked the days that passed without expressing her gender identity. That lasted two weeks.[213] Eventually, Patrick came to accept his trans identity and came out to his wife.

Emily and Sabrina married their spouses at young ages, long before coming out as trans women, even though they knew they were trans. Part of their motivation for marrying was the hope that marriage might change them, making them cisgender instead of transgender.

I was thinking that if I fell in love with a woman and I got married, that would take these feelings away. I didn't get married just for that. I truly did love her. My thoughts were of getting married and falling in love. I thought that would make me go away, but it made it worse, because there were all of these feminine things that were right before me all the time.

–Sabrina

Some transgender folks say they desired marriage and felt staying in the closet was their only way of achieving that goal. Many trans individuals say they were also attempting to fulfill the expectation society has for us to lead what are considered "normal" lives—by getting married and having children. Emily and Sabrina told me they had dreamed of growing up to become wives and mothers. Neither, however, thought they could actually live those lives. What did seem within reach was to become husbands and fathers, so that's what they did.

Why I got married gets into the pressures of trying to conform with culture, society, and family. I think that a lot of transgender people always hold out the hope that there will be one thing that holds them back, and, for lack of a better word, fixes them.

–Emily

She also loved her spouse and longed to be a good husband.

My parents were always concerned that I wouldn't find the right girl. I dated some girls and had some relationships and it was never right for a lot of reasons, which had to do with me trying to put Emily in a box and set her aside. I eventually developed a relationship, fell in love, and got married. I tried to do all of the things to be a husband and a father and a provider. I think I did a pretty good job at all of those, but ultimately, Emily wasn't going away.

–Emily

I asked if she felt getting married before coming out as a transgender woman was a mistake.

I don't feel it was a mistake because my wife is a very special person. She is somebody that I fell in love with and I still love. I feel sad that at some level I disappointed her. People ask me what I regret most. It was probably that I was never confident enough that our relationship could withstand and accept Emily across the board. That is probably my biggest regret, and I don't regret a lot of things.

–Emily

In the beginning of relationships, it might be easy to hide something about ourselves, but over time, our true nature is bound to be revealed. This applies to anyone and everyone. In many instances, our spouse has some idea of what we've been trying to hide. Our mates catch glimpses of whatever it is we are trying to hide, or we grow weary of hiding or pretending and eventually 'fess up. Emily felt she did a good job of hiding herself for a while, but over time, it became more difficult, and her wife eventually figured it out.

My wife didn't know from the beginning. She learned bits and pieces of it over the course of years and became less and less comfortable with it. I always tried to talk about it to the point where I felt comfortable exposing Emily to her completely, and as I would approach that point, I could see how she was reacting to things and what her level of tolerance and acceptance was. I would back away, but she drew a lot from those conversations and discussions that eventually led her to identifying Emily.

–Emily

Spouses can also be good at looking the other way. For many of us, there are things we pretend not to see or choose to let slide because we love our mates and hope that "thing" isn't what we thought or that it will eventually pass.

Before I got married, in a very scary moment, I told her that I liked to dress in women's clothes, and I didn't give any explanation. I just felt an obligation. We were both attending a Bible college, and I felt this need for honesty, and so I wanted to tell her. She says she doesn't remember me telling her. I think she was so naïve and so in love that it didn't sink in. Then while married, I did some things that she should have understood, but I think she was in total denial. For example, she'd be painting her nails, and I'd say something like, "Why don't you do mine?" and she would say, "No," and I would say something else, and then she would do it. One of the things I got her to let me do was wear support pantyhose for my restless leg syndrome. She saw it as this medical issue. She just did not want to see it. She just did not want to accept it. That's all there was to it. She just didn't want to. She knew I was dressing in women's clothes and said I needed to stop pretending. She wanted me to go see a therapist to "get fixed" and to "stop this."

–Sabrina

Sabrina's story exemplifies how we can fall prey to hoping the other person will "figure it out." Sabrina felt that her wife should have been able to interpret the behavior and see through the smokescreens of medical excuses, etc. But it is never fair to make someone figure out what is going on in our hearts. The only way for them to know is through show and tell, and for a transgender person, that means coming out. Approximately 58 percent of married transgender men and women report being out to their spouse.[214]

Parenting

Can transgender people have children?

Yes. Some transgender people are capable of impregnating a woman, becoming pregnant, and/or giving birth, depending on factors like health, hormone therapy, and genital reconstructive surgery. A trans person can also adopt children, depending on state laws and adoption agency policies.

A transgender woman (someone who has transitioned from a man to a woman) does not have the internal physiology necessary to become pregnant, carry a fetus, or give birth. Genital reassignment surgery can provide a transgender woman with a functional vagina; however, it cannot give her the uterus, ovaries, fallopian tubes, etc. needed to conceive and bear children.[215] In answering a similar question, Christine Jorgensen said, "I can never have children. I am very much in the position right now of a woman who has a hysterectomy."[216] A transgender woman may, however, be capable of impregnating a woman. This can happen because a trans woman is someone who was born a biological male. That person could have a functioning male reproductive system with sperm that could fertilize a human egg.

It is also possible for a transgender man (someone who has transitioned from a woman to a man) to become pregnant. If that trans man has a healthy female reproductive system, has not had reassignment surgery, and is not taking testosterone, then he may be able to conceive and give birth.

In terms of adoption, many organizations and states have discriminatory practices that make it more difficult, or bar transgender adults from adopting children. As of 2018, only four states explicitly prohibited discrimination against foster and adoptive parent applicants based on sexual orientation and gender identity.[217]

Is it true that transgender people are more likely to molest children?

No. That is false. As discussed in the homosexuality chapter, the leading cause of child molestation is the mental disorder pedophilia, which has nothing to do with being transgender.[218] Studies show pedophiles, people who molest children, are predominantly heterosexual cisgender males.

How does being transgender impact the parent-child relationship?

Being transgender does not mean a person is unable to be a good parent. A person's gender identity does not impact their ability to parent.

Coming out and transitioning can, sometimes, impact the parent-child relationship, regardless of the child's age, however this does not always happen. The National Transgender Discrimination Survey reports that 58 percent of trans parents find relationships with their children to be better or the same after transitioning.[219] Thirteen percent report that some things are better and others worse. One in five trans parents say that at least one child stopped speaking to them after they came out. This happens more to trans women than to trans men, according to the survey, which found that 28 percent of trans women said a child stopped speaking to them, compared to 6 percent of trans men. Children seem to be more accepting of a mother transitioning to a man than they are of a father transitioning to a woman.

> *It was very bad with my daughter. I told her on April 26th, and when Father's Day rolled around, she wrote me a Father's Day card and told me that that would be the last Father's Day card and that I died to her on that day.*
> –Sabrina

I cannot imagine how devastating it must be for a parent to have the child they created, nurtured, and poured love into close the door on that relationship. When met with this type of reaction, many transgender parents must decide whether to deny their identity in order to stay in a relationship with their child, or be true to themselves even if it means losing the relationship. It's understandable that many trans parents choose to suffer in hiding, at least until their children are adults.

I also understand that, from the child's perspective, it can't be easy to have the man you've known as "Daddy," for instance, suddenly show up as a woman. In addition to dealing with the immediate physical appearance and name change, the child of a transgender parent may also have to build a new relationship with this familiar, yet unfamiliar, parent. I imagine that if either of my parents came out as transgender, it would certainly be shocking and disorienting, but I cannot imagine rejecting them or not loving them.

In some instances, a cisgender parent may try to take away the trans parent's legal rights. According to Lambda Legal, "Courts are generally only allowed to base custody or visitation rulings on factors that directly affect the 'best interests of the child.'"[220] Additionally, "If a transgender parent's gender identity can't be shown to hurt the child in some way, contact should not be limited, and other custody and visitation orders should not be changed because of a parent's transition."

CHAPTER TEN

INTERSEX

"Nature doesn't decide where the category of 'male' ends
and the category of 'intersex' begins, or where the category
of 'intersex' ends and the category of 'female' begins."
–Intersex Society of North America[221]

Intro

M any of us have been led to believe that there is a clear-cut distinction between the male and female biological sexes, and that those are the only two that exist. That is not the case for nearly two percent of the population.

A baby's sex is commonly assigned based on its genitalia. When the baby has what appears to be a vagina, the assigned sex is female, and the same box is checked on the birth certificate. Other female characteristics include clitoris, labia, XX chromosomes, and the hormones estrogen and progesterone. When the baby has what appears to be a penis, the sex assigned is male, and the "male" box on the birth certificate is checked. Other male characteristics include scrotum, testes, urethra, XY chromosomes, and the hormone testosterone.

In some people, however, these characteristics are ambiguous, or there are a mixture of male and female characteristics. When this occurs, that person may be identified as intersex. The prefix "inter-" means between. The term "intersex" suggests that biologically, that person's sex falls somewhere between male and female.

Human females are expected to have twenty-six sets of XX chromosomes and males are expected to have twenty-six sets of XY chromosomes. Doctors have determined that intersex individuals have a "misplaced" Y chromosome. When a Y chromosome is misplaced, that means it appears where an X was expected, or that it doesn't appear where a Y was expected. For instance, instead of there being twenty-six sets of XX, there might be twenty-five sets of XX and one set of XY. The cause of misplaced Y chromosomes has not yet been determined.

Chromosomes determine a person's biological sex, and things like genitalia, reproductive organs, hormones, etc.; therefore, a misplaced Y chromosome can have a drastic impact on the body's development. If in the midst of XX (female) pairs, an XY (male) pairing appears, it can lead to the presence of male hormones, male genitalia, and the development of other male physiology, where female hormones, genitalia, etc. would have appeared. If in the midst of XY (male) pairs, an XX (female) pairing is present, then that person might develop female genitalia or partially developed male genitalia, or a combination of male and female genitalia and reproductive organs, hormones, and other physiology. The Intersex Society of North America (ISNA) explains, "A person might be born appearing to be female on the outside but having mostly male-typical anatomy on the inside. An intersex person may be born with genitalia that seem to be between the usual male and female types—for example, a girl may be born with a noticeably large clitoris or lacking a vaginal opening, or a boy may be born with a notably small penis or with a scrotum that is divided so that it has formed more like labia."[222]

One condition associated with intersex is Turner Syndrome, which I learned more about after meeting Lianne Simon, a writer and intersex activist. Simon, a sixty-something-year-old woman who looks much younger, has Turner Syndrome and was assigned the male sex at birth and raised as a boy. Simon, who writes about intersex "in hopes of raising awareness about such conditions,"[223] explained some of the effects of Turner Syndrome:

> *What happens in Turner Syndrome is you have some cells*
> *that have a Y chromosome and some that don't. I have a Y*

chromosome in some of my cells and not in the rest. During fetal development, my development got confused. It resulted in a number of mild malformations of my kidneys, heart, thyroid, and reproductive system. It made me short and frail as a child. There's a characteristic, Turner Syndrome Facial Shape, which when you're a little kid, looks like an elephant. I have a visual motor and a spatial temporal deficit that keeps me from learning complex maneuvers. I wasn't able to do the sports kind of things that the boys did. Even in puberty, I didn't develop muscles to be able to wrestle or do any of the other strength things that boys do. The condition had a big hand in my physical and emotional makeup.

–Lianne Simon, writer and intersex activist, married,
intersex, heterosexual, 62 years old

It is estimated that there are more than 129 million intersex people worldwide, which equates to 1.7 percent of the world's 7.6 billion people.[224, 225] Applying that percentage to the US would mean at least 5.5 million of America's 325 million people are intersex. Those numbers are not, however, universally agreed upon.

An estimated 1 in 2000 births results in noticeably atypical genitalia that require a specialist in sex differentiation to be called; however, not all of these children are identified as intersex. This is, in part, because there are no universal guidelines for determining what qualifies as intersex. Some medical professionals say this lack of universal guidelines for what conditions and attributes qualify as intersex and what may be categorized as strictly male or strictly female make it difficult to calculate a reliable estimate of how many people are intersex.[226] Additionally, there are "babies born with subtler forms of sex anatomy variations, or variations that don't become visible until months or years later."[227] In many cases, an intersex baby is identifiable at birth; however, there are instances where the intersex status may not become evident until later. For instance, at birth, some intersex infants do not have ambiguous genitalia. For these children, intersex conditions may not become apparent until toddler years or even puberty.

Numerous conditions and biological and physiological characteristics are considered intersex. Each condition impacts what doctors see and use to assign a baby's biological sex. The Intersex National Association (ISNA) also says there are a number of different conditions associated with being intersex and that intersex anatomy and physiology presents differently in each individual. One condition, congenital adrenal hyperplasia (CAH), is characterized by the inability to produce an enzyme the body needs to make the hormones cortisol and aldosterone. "Without these, the body produces more androgens (male sex hormones). If the child is female, the raised androgen levels before birth cause the genitals to become more male in appearance."[228]

Additionally, as in Simon's case, many of the conditions are not related to genitalia and reproduction. Intersex is not solely categorized by genitalia, because the X and Y chromosomes impact other aspects of human development.

Not everyone prefers the label intersex. Some believe it to be "negative and sensationalizing." Some in the medical community believe the term intersex is stigmatizing and are replacing it with terms like "DSD" to represent both "disorders of sex development" and "disorders of sex differentiation," which they believe is a "more general and descriptive term."[229] The Intersex Society of North America (ISNA) began using "disorders of sex development" in 2005. Their website is careful to distinguish that "intersex itself is not a disorder, rather a variation." The term "disorders" refers to conditions that occur as a result of someone being intersex. The Intersex Society also explains that their use of "disorder" "refers to the underlying cause, not intersexuality itself, and certainly not to the whole person." Still, many people also find the DSD label offensive because it implies a defect rather than a natural state of being.

Do intersex people identify as "male," "female," or something else?

Intersex adults can identify as "intersex," "male," "female," neither male nor female, or both male and female. In *How Intersex People Identify*, Hida Viloria and Dana Zzyym, cofounders of Intersex Campaign for Equality, offer a breakdown of the three main ways intersex people identify: as the gender associated with the sex they were assigned at birth—some of whom consider themselves transgender and intersex; as the gender associated with the sex "opposite" the one they were assigned at birth; or as neither men nor women or both men and women.[230] Pidgeon Pagonis, who accidently found out about their intersex status in college, identifies as neither male nor female.[231] Viloria and Zzyym also offer that some intersex individuals who don't identify as male or female might use terms like "herms," or "intersex," or gender terms like "genderqueer," "genderfluid," "non-binary," and "non-binary intersex people."

An intersex person who doesn't consider themselves male or female may also prefer pronouns that are not gender-specific. Pagonis uses the gender-neutral pronouns "they," "them," and "their."[232]

Is hermaphrodite the same as intersex?

No. The word hermaphrodite originates from Greek mythology. Hermaphroditus was the son of Hermes and Aphrodite, and he possessed the physical traits of both male and female sexes. In biology, the term refers to organisms like earthworms or plants that have fully functioning male and female reproductive organs that enable them to reproduce without having sex with another organism.

Intersex individuals, unlike hermaphrodites, do not have complete male and female reproductive organs. Intersex individuals cannot reproduce by themselves. While intersex people may have some mixture of male and female anatomy and physiology, they often lack fully formed male or female reproductive systems, and as a result, most intersex people cannot reproduce. One of my early conversations with Simon included an explanation of why the term hermaphrodite is incorrect when referring to intersex.

> *Hermaphrodite is not really politically correct. The problem with the word "hermaphrodite" is it's often confused with the mythological term. I was born with a mixture of ovarian and testicular tissue, but I could never be both male and female or impregnate myself. I am not physically able to become pregnant or to impregnate someone else.*
>
> –Simon

Is intersex the same as transgender?

No. Intersex describes a person's biological sex. Transgender refers to a person's gender identity. An intersex person is someone born with some combination of male and female genitalia and/or reproductive organs and/or other biological factors.

What happens when an intersex baby is born?

In most instances, when an intersex baby is born, the doctor, midwife, etc. assigns the baby's sex as male or female. In the case of intersex babies, the prevailing approach has been to "pick one" even though the baby does not fit neatly into either sex designation. In the US, and many other countries, "male" or "female" are the only two available options on the birth certificate. In recent years, there has been a global push to add a third box to the birth certificate that would address children born with intersex characteristics. Germany was the first European country to offer a third sex option, which only exists for a baby born with a mixture of male and female characteristics. By leaving the male and female boxes on the birth certificate blank, the parents indicate they've selected an "indeterminate" gender. The new law is meant to avoid the need to label an intersex baby as male or female before the child is old enough to decide.[233] Once the person is old enough to know, the sex can be changed to male or female, if they desire. In 2019, New York City began allowing parents to choose the non-binary "X" for their newborns' birth certificates.[234]

Many health care professionals faced with the birth of an intersex child believe that by assigning either male or female sex, they are making it easier for the parents and the child to go on with their lives. That isn't always the case. Their rush to assign sex may make things easier for the parents, and even the child, at least in the early months and years; however, making this call without being able to consult the child adds a burdensome layer of complication to an already difficult situation.

The APA says most people born with intersex conditions are satisfied with their assigned sex, and that it's rare that people with intersex conditions feel their sex is opposite the sex they were assigned at birth. However, there doesn't appear to be any statistical data to substantiate or refute this statement. There are many documented cases of intersex teens and adults who assert they were assigned the wrong sex at birth. *Answers to Your Questions about Individuals with Intersex Conditions* says there is very little information about which intersex conditions, if any, are associated with an increased likelihood of dissatisfaction with one's assigned sex.

Some intersex individuals who believe their sex was mis-assigned do, at some point, begin to live the biological sex they believe should have been assigned to them.

When German model Hanne Gaby Odiele was born, doctors declared she was a girl based on her physical appearance, which is what occurs most often. A few months later, they discovered she had an XY chromosome and internal testes. Based on those discoveries, doctors then told Odiele's parents she was genetically male. They subsequently tried administering hormone therapy to supply her body with more male hormones in hopes of eliciting male physical development. That didn't work for Odiele, who like some other intersex people, has a condition that makes her body resistant to male hormones. Odiele does not have a penis, nor a uterus or ovaries, and says, "I am intersex, but I am much more female."

A story in *The Guardian* reports that blood tests and an amniocentesis led doctors to tell expecting parents that their baby was genetically male but that it didn't necessarily mean the baby was a boy. When born, the baby had testicular tissue, ovarian tissue, and genitals that could belong to either a boy or a girl. At the age of nine months, doctors discovered the child had a uterus and fallopian tubes that were incapable of producing children. [235]

Yet another story was about Dawn Vagos, who was born with testes and considered genetically male. Doctors assigned the male sex to Dawn because of XY (male) chromosomes, making Dawn genetically male. Dawn, however, has a condition called Complete Androgen Insensitivity Syndrome (CAIS), which makes the body unresponsive to the male hormone testosterone. For genetic males, those with a Y chromosome like Dawn, CAIS means genitalia don't masculinize and masculine secondary sex characteristics such as increased muscle mass, a deeper voice, and facial hair don't develop. [236] So although Dawn is genetically male, and doctors assigned the male sex, she developed female genitalia and has always appeared entirely female, even though she does not have ovaries or a uterus, and therefore cannot have children. [237] In these and other cases, although medical professionals assigned one biological sex at birth based on certain attributes, as the child developed, characteristics representing the opposite biological sex presented.

While we should not expect doctors to be perfect, medical professionals must be willing to admit when a mistake was made and work with the intersex individual to rectify that error. We also should not expect individuals to be beholden to the doctor's original choice of biological sex, especially when there is substantial evidence suggesting otherwise. Space must be held for the complete range of human biology when and as it presents itself.

Is there a way to "fix" or "correct" intersex children?

For many years, doctors tried to do what they perceived as "fixing" or "correcting" intersex babies. They often convinced parents that intersex babies needed surgery to make their genitalia and/or reproductive organs match the biological sex the doctors had selected for the child. These so-called "corrective surgeries" are increasingly frowned upon by the medical community and intersex individuals. The surgeries intersex children have been subjected to can be brutal and can have adverse physical and emotional consequences, including painful scarring, torn genital tissue, removal of natural hormones, possible sterilization, reduced sexual sensitivity, and the inability to have sexual intercourse.

In 2014, the adoptive parents of an intersex child filed a lawsuit against the Medical University of South Carolina and South Carolina Department of Social Services for cutting the baby's penis to make it look more like a clitoris. Doctors also cut the sixteen-month-old child's scrotum to form labia and removed the baby's internal testicle tissue.[238] Removal and alteration of the child's male genitalia and reproductive tissue was done because doctors wanted to make the baby a girl. Many people would agree that this type of invasive surgery should not be done without an individual's consent, which obviously a baby cannot give. It's also interesting that we as a society would condone a doctor and/or parents deciding that another human being should have genital reconstruction or some other invasive life-altering surgery, but we disapprove when an adult makes a similar decision for themselves.

When Dawn Vagos was a child, doctors told her parents that she would get cancer if her testes weren't removed. They performed a full gonadectomy, removing both of the eight-year-old child's testicles, which is the equivalent of surgical castration. Many refer to what was done to Dawn and the baby in South Carolina as "intersex genital mutilation"

(IGM). In Dawn's case, the doctors lied to her and the parents. "They said I would not survive puberty if I did not have the operation, and that wasn't true."[239] Sadly, it isn't uncommon for intersex patients and their parents to have surgery falsely presented as mandatory to supposedly treat or prevent cancer or some other ailment. Doctors also lied to Pidgeon Pagonis.[240] When doctors performed surgery to remove Pagonis's genitalia, they said it was to treat cancer. Later, when doctors decided to perform vaginoplasty, a surgery to construct a vagina, they again lied to Pagonis, saying it was to correct a urine drip issue.

Doctors are not always the instigators of these mutilating surgeries. In some instances, parents push doctors to perform so-called "corrective surgeries." Dr. Jay Hayes-Light, an intersex male who was assigned female and given medical treatment to make him female, acknowledged that it is often the fear of social rejection that motivates parents to choose surgery.[241] He believed parents just want their child to be what they consider "normal." Dr. Ian Aaronson, agrees: "Most parents are disturbed by the appearance of the genitalia and request that something be done as soon as possible so that their baby 'looks normal.'"[242]

Fortunately, these invasive, life-altering surgeries are being performed less frequently. In 2015, Malta became the first country to outlaw nonconsensual medical interventions on intersex people, including those too young to give informed consent. In January 2016, the Chilean government issued guidelines for doctors who oppose corrective surgery, allowing them to refuse parental requests without legal consequences. In March 2016, the United Nations condemned nonconsensual genital surgeries on intersex children, urging that they be classified as torture. Unfortunately, the UK, US, and Australia do not have national laws or guidance on corrective surgery.[243]

What is a child's perception of being intersex?

As you might imagine, being intersex can be emotionally and physically confusing and frustrating for a child. Similar to Simon, an intersex child's body might outwardly present as one sex, yet their thoughts and emotions represent the opposite sex. For others, their bodies might present some male and female aspects. Many intersex children also have ailments or developmental challenges that result from being intersex. All of these things can be even more confusing when a child hasn't been told they are intersex. This is often the case because some doctors advise parents to never speak of it, and many don't. Sometimes it's because they don't want to confuse the child, and sometimes it's because the parents are confused or ashamed.

Throughout much of her life, Simon was aware that something was different and that her mind and body were sending mixed messages, but she didn't know anything about being intersex, nor did her parents.

> *Growing up, I never really had a good handle on it. I was frail and had a cute face and was always small in size. I was always the smallest in my peer group. When I was nine, I wore 6X-size clothes, and my six-year-old sister was almost as tall as me because I was that small. On occasion, I would wear my younger sister's clothes. I knew that I had a syndrome that affected my facial shape. That's all that I knew when I was young.*
>
> *I had no clue what a penis, vagina, or clitoris was supposed to look like. I knew that at least between my legs was fairly masculine. I knew that because the shaft could get semi-rigid, but there was no erection. The rest of me was fairly feminine. I wasn't a boy and I wasn't a girl.*
>
> –Simon

Trying to live up to the sex they have been assigned can be difficult for an intersex person. Simon tried to be the male child the doctors and her parents insisted she was, even amidst the signs that suggested she wasn't.

> *When I was growing up, I thought that if I tried hard enough, if I was really good, kind of like Pinocchio, then God would make me a boy. I wanted very much to be a boy because it would simplify things and make everybody happy. I also wanted to be a girl because that's where my heart was at.*
>
> –Simon

It should not be surprising that intersex children and teens can have conflicting feelings about their biological sex and gender identity.

There was always a sense that I wasn't really a boy or a girl. I remember thinking it would be neat, if I was big and tall and strong, like my brother. I wasn't thinking in terms of identity as much as capability; that you had to be really strong and fast and all these other things. I thought in that context that, if I tried hard enough, God would make me a real boy.

I also wanted to be a mom when I grew up. I wanted to have babies and take care of them and nurse them and raise them. When I was in fifth grade, a new kid in class invited me over to his house to listen to this new group called the "Beatles." He sang the love songs to me. And for the next couple of days, all I could think about was marrying him and having his babies.

–Simon

An intersex person can spend all of their childhood, teens, and early adult years trying to reconcile their male and female aspects. There can be years of questioning what is going on or wondering, "What is wrong with me?" Years of trying to make themselves fit into the assigned sex, and as in Simon's case, years of praying God would fix it.

What recourse does an intersex person have when the wrong biological sex is assigned?

Once an intersex person comes to the realization and acceptance that they are not the biological sex the doctors chose for them, the next hurdle is deciding how to live the remainder of their lives. Some people, like Simon, take steps to correct the mistake; others do not.

Changing from the biological sex that was mis-assigned at birth can be a freeing experience for an intersex person, but that does not mean it is without pain or frustration. Intersex people who decide to correct their original sex assignment may require surgery to reverse the effects of surgeries performed when they were children. Or, if they were prescribed hormones to make them appear more like the sex assigned by the doctor, then they might stop taking those hormones in order for their bodies to function and appear more like their correct sex. Others will have to begin taking hormones to appear more like their correct sex. Other medical procedures and things like changing names and attire may also be involved.

What happens after an intersex person decides to change the sex they were assigned?

A major part of making changes includes handling the response of family and friends.

> *I needed one parent and one doctor to sign the paperwork to correct my birth certificate, and my mother agreed to do that. And she agreed she would loan me money for surgery. My dad, of course, forbid it and told me I had to go sleep with a girl first. I didn't explain to him that what I had between my legs wouldn't do that. My brothers were cordial about it; not extremely warm, but they were fine. Recently, my brother and sister and I have gotten a lot closer.*
>
> –Simon

For some, it can also involve becoming accustomed to presenting themselves as their correct biological sex and learning how to navigate the world in this way.

> *Ninety-nine percent of my harassment occurred when I was trying to live as a boy. It was catcalls and names and things like that in public and harassment in private. One of the things that surprised me after I made the change was that people were so unquestioning about my identity. They just accepted me. That helped me to relax, which I think made things go even easier because life became fairly natural-seeming to me, at that point. I still had things like walking to the wrong restroom, and when I went to see my father, I sometimes went into the mode of trying to hide who I was and go back to acting the way I always tried to act in front of him.*
>
> –Simon

Do intersex people seek psychological help to handle the challenges of being intersex?

An intersex person might seek the help of a mental health professional at different times in their life and for different reasons. Some might want help understanding what it means to be intersex and coping with this reality. Others might seek help dealing with how family, friends, and strangers treat them. Some people might seek counseling to cope with being assigned the wrong sex at birth or having surgeries performed that prevent them from having children. In general, therapy for intersex individuals can help sort and reconcile the conflicting physical, emotional, and social elements that exist for them. Simon was advised to see a psychologist in college.

> *After being caught wearing a dress in college, the dean summoned me to his office and said, "You can take counseling or you can go home." So, I took a bunch of psychological evaluation-type tests, which showed that I was under a little bit of stress and a little depressed and had a few gender issues. But I wasn't willing, at that point, to discuss it with school psychologists.*
>
> –Simon

Eventually, she did see a doctor.

> *Later, I went to see a psychiatrist who referred intersex patients to Johns Hopkins. The psychiatrist said I would have to have two years of counseling. Her first step was for me to go to the local gay bar and see how I liked having sex with a boy. I found an endocrinologist instead.*
>
> –Simon

Fortunately, Simon recognized that the psychiatrist's prescribed "treatment" was not appropriate and sought help elsewhere. Seeing an endocrinologist led Simon to realize there was a way for her to take control and right the ship that was her body and course-correct her life.

> *At first, he yelled at me because he thought I was anorexic. I wasn't. He then offered to make a stud of me with testosterone, anabolic steroids, and an exercise program. I asked if I could*

take estrogen instead. He said yes. Then, he said, I wouldn't have any trouble being accepted as a girl.

–Simon

Simon's experience highlights the unfortunate reality that some medical and mental health professionals are not prepared to treat intersex patients. It is important that intersex individuals seeking mental and medical help have access to professionals who understand intersex conditions, how those conditions impact individuals, and options to aid intersex people in living mentally and physically healthy lives.

Are intersex individuals able to have sexual intercourse?

Yes, many intersex people can have sexual intercourse. Odiele, the model, reported that she and her husband have a normal, active sex life. However, that is not the case for all intersex people. For some, sexual activity can be challenging, unpleasant, or impossible. Complications can include genitalia that isn't fully formed or does not function sexually, painful scars from childhood surgery, lack of sexual function due to surgery, or hormone therapies that reinforce the biological and behavioral development of one sex and dampen the other.

Pagonis said sexual intercourse with a boyfriend was difficult and painful. Later, they learned this was the result of the vaginoplasty surgery doctors performed and lied about. Pagonis soon came to associate almost any intimacy, including kissing, with the impending pain of penetration and found that any sexual desire evaporated the moment they were touched. The surgery and sexual trauma have proved a barrier to sexual pleasure and romantic relationships. Had the genitalia not been removed and replaced with a clitoris and vagina, Pagonis might be able to have pleasurable sexual intercourse instead of pain. Pagonis is forgoing relationships, for now, and trying to find peace and pleasure in their own body with the help of a therapist.[244] Katrina Karkazis, PhD, a senior research scholar at the Center for Biomedical Ethics at Stanford University says, "Imagine for a moment that you want to connect with someone sexually, and you feel nothing sexual in your genitalia. Or you feel pain. The door is closed before it's even opened. You can think you're so damaged that no one will be satisfied with you."[245]

Physical discomfort is not the only reason an intersex person might avoid sexual intimacy.

> *I didn't have any sexual activity until I got married. That was when I was in my forties. Part of that was because my hormone levels were so low. Earlier, it was because I didn't want to go into the sexual relationship with a boy where he perceived me as a boy. It would not have felt right. I wanted to do what a girl does with a boy. Also, what I had between my legs wouldn't work either way.*
>
> –Simon

Simon had genital tissue that appeared to be a penis but did not function sexually like a penis. As a young adult, she began taking hormones and later underwent genital surgery.

Each individual's situation is different, and it's up to each person to determine what their bodies will and won't do and if they want to be sexually active.

Do intersex people get married?

Yes. It might be more difficult for intersex adults to find loving and accepting partners, but as Simon and Odiele demonstrate, it is possible. Vagos says, "Doctors told my parents that I would never find a man who would love me, and I would never have my own family. I absolutely adore the fact that I am married and about to start a family. It proves you control your own life."

Why is intersex a part of LGBTQIAP?

Intersex has been added to the acronym by some because they believe there are shared issues and causes to be addressed. Some feel that, similar to other members of the LGBTQIAP community, including intersex in the group can help educate others and bring attention to concerns like societal prejudice and lack of proper healthcare.

There are differing opinions about whether intersex should be included in LGBTQIAP. Some in the intersex community don't believe they should be in the acronym or the movement. They believe that adding the "I" conflates two different issues: biological sex with gender identity and sexuality. PFLAG, an organization that supports parents and families of people who identify as LGBTQ, does not add the "I" because "there does not seem to be unanimity within the intersex community... about wanting to be included in or directly linked to the community that identifies as LGBTQ."[246]

Simon encouraged me to include intersex in this discussion.

CHAPTER ELEVEN

COMING OUT

"Everybody knows what they like to do
Whatever it is do it as long as it pleases you
Just take some time and relax your mind
Then do it, do it, do it 'til you're satisfied"
—B.T. Express[247]

Intro

Coming out is short for "coming out of the closet." Coming out is a process that people go through to begin living and expressing their true sexuality and/or gender identity openly in public and private spaces. The Human Rights Campaign describes it as a process of understanding, accepting, and valuing their identity. For centuries, fear of being ostracized, ridiculed, beaten, or even put to death led many people to deny or hide their sexuality or gender identity. Many pretended to be heterosexual and cisgender. Some trace coming out back to 1869 Germany, when gay rights advocate Karl Heinrich Ulrichs encouraged homosexuals to disclose their sexuality in order to help change public opinion. Coming out became an important part of the gay rights movement in the US in the 1960s.

Emmy-winning writer Lena Waithe says, "I think coming out is the most difficult thing anyone can do. And there's just nothing easy about it."[248] It is a personal process that can be mentally, emotionally, and physically challenging. Coming out can be frightening, liberating, confusing, and surprising for the person coming out and their family and friends. When it happens, how it happens, and how long it takes differ for each individual. It can be private, with an individual only coming out to themselves, and it can be public, as we've seen with comedian and activist Ellen DeGeneres, who came out on national TV. Most importantly, coming out is about being your true self.

The coming out process involves a number of steps, which have been described in different ways. The process can begin with an awareness of being different from the mainstream, perhaps not feeling heterosexual or cisgender. The next step can be for a person to come out to themselves. This is a personal acknowledgment of being lesbian, gay, bisexual, transgender, queer, intersex, asexual, pansexual, or something else. For some, this step may involve acknowledging a difference but not yet having a name for it. Another aspect of coming out involves learning more about that particular identity. This part of the process can include researching information, entering environments with people like themselves, talking to others about their identity, and establishing relationships with others who acknowledge their identity. Other aspects of coming out include adjusting attire, appearance, and behavior to better express their identity. The last phase of coming out is full acceptance of self.

One psychologist offered a perspective on how long it takes to come out.

> *A psychologist in Minnesota wrote a very famous paper where he looked at the coming out process and said for a gay person, it takes about twelve years. At first, there is recognition of same-sex attraction. Year six is where you would do that first coming out. From years six to twelve, you go from telling somebody else that you're gay to having a positive gay identity, and you feel good about being gay.*
>
> –Professor Wright

This psychologist's twelve-year coming out timetable is not a hard and fast rule for any sexuality or gender identity. It doesn't take everyone twelve years to move through the phases of the coming out. There are many factors, including personality, family, community, religion, maturity, age, and emotional stability, that influence how long it takes someone to move through the coming out process.

The most common image many have of a person coming out is when someone tells family and friends. In some instances, friends and family are completely caught off guard, and in other instances, they may have long suspected that their loved one was lesbian, gay, etc. You may find it surprising that only 54 percent of LGBT adults surveyed by the Pew Research Center said all or most of the important people in their lives know they are lesbian, gay, bisexual, or transgender.[249] The number is higher for gay men, 77 percent of whom say the important people in their lives know, while only 71 percent of gay women and lesbians say the same. One-third of bisexual women and only 12 percent of bisexual men say they have come out to those closest to them. The survey did not provide specific statistics for transgender, queer, pansexual, or intersex adults.

Is there a particular age or time for coming out?

The coming out process can begin at any age or time. It can occur during childhood, adolescence, adulthood, or even as a senior citizen. There are also people who never come out. Some determining factors can be generation, family, religion, geography, and the individual's personality. Some people only come out to themselves, while others may only come out to those closest to them.

A Pew Research Center survey investigated median ages for different phases of the coming out process.[250] Gay men reported ten as the median age when they first felt their sexuality might be something other than heterosexual, which can be the beginning of the coming out process. For lesbians and bisexuals that median age was thirteen.

Another step in coming out—being sure of one's sexuality—occurred at the median age of fifteen for gay men, eighteen for gay women, and seventeen for bisexual and transgender individuals. In terms of coming out to others, twenty was the median age at which LGBT respondents first shared this information with a family member or close friend.

The individuals I spoke with for this book reported coming out at different ages. Councilmember Wan came out to himself at the age of twenty-three, Commissioner Garner was in her late thirties, and Vicki was in her fifties. Fredis came out to family members when he was a teenager.

I think I was eighteen. My mom, I think, always knew. My grandmother always knew, but we would never talk about it. And at eighteen, one day, I was like, "Okay, enough's enough."

–Fredis

Dr. Lowell came out around the age of fourteen.

I came out at school first and then came out to my parents. My mom said, "Just make sure you have kids. You gotta have kids." And I was like, "I'm fourteen. I'll get to that eventually." The hardest thing was for me to confront my own internal homophobia; I wasn't quite expecting to be who I am. You know, we all grow up, I think, with some vague idea of living a "normal" life like all the "normal" people we see around us. I went from just assuming that my life would be like everybody else's around me to thinking, "Wait a minute, I kind of am on a different track. I don't feel as 'normal' as everyone else." It changed my view of things and of myself and where I fit into society. The high school that I went to couldn't have been cooler. There were several out students, some out teachers, and so there were role models and people to talk to.

–Dr. Lowell

Others come out in high school.

I came out to myself and my two closest friends. Part of the reason I came out as a kid was I thought it was a problem. I thought, "Well, it'll get solved by me coming out and accepting it." At my Catholic high school, I could identify that the principal and the associate principal might have been a couple. There was another gay man who was the head administrator. When I was in eighth grade, there was a lesbian couple that was one of the most powerful teaching teams there.

–Rev. Teague

Some people come out with the help of Facebook.

It was a slow process, but then more and more people were hearing about it. Word of mouth helped. And of course, with Facebook, that was great. Friends were easier to connect, not just by telephone but also they were able to chat via Facebook or social media, "So I heard this about Ryan, is this true?" And they would see some stuff that I was doing and the work I was doing with gay organizations, so I think that helped kind of solidify in people's mind what was going on. I didn't feel like I necessarily had to put a post on Facebook. The key people I wanted to know were going to know when I decided to tell them.

–Roemerman

There are others who were never closeted. Seventy-year-old Gloria in Chicago said, "I never was in the closet. The only time I was in the closet was to go in there and pick out a dress and come out of the closet and put it on."[251] Recently, an increasing number of individuals have been able to be "out" their entire lives and have never had to be "in the closet." It is my hope this number will continue to increase as more people understand human sexuality and gender identity, and all of our sexualities, gender identities, and biological sexes are recognized and accepted as "normal."

What are some reasons people come out?

There are many reasons for a person to come out. An article in *The Advocate* offered "13 Reasons Why You Must Come Out of the Closet." The list includes the observations that, "Keeping something so important a secret is bad for you"; "It gives you the most honest picture of life"; and, "It will reveal your allies." According to the report, employees who hide their identities languish in their careers, and those who feel safe coming out perform better and even advance more quickly in their careers. Studies also show that being out actually improves the productivity of non-LGBT colleagues, because being out creates trust while remaining closeted raises doubt. It is, however, very important to acknowledge that coming out can also end a person's career because, presently, no federal law explicitly forbids workplace discrimination against LGBTQIAP individuals.

There are other perspectives on why people come out.

*A lot of people don't make the formal announcement anymore;
they just start living their life. I wanted my mother to be aware
because she was putting a lot of pressure on me to go on dates
and bring home a girlfriend. For others, part of it is they want to
have acceptance. Some people just need the validation of others,
giving them a sense of their self. Just having clarity about who
you are can be very helpful. And so, in that regard, coming out
is a really powerful experience because it's sort of declaring who
you are, especially when you're young.*

–Professor Wright

Many people say they came out in part because they hoped it might
help other people in similar situations. Acer, a contributor on asexual.org,
says, "I am one of those people to whom asexuality is just a part of who I
am, not something I need to shout about for my own sake. I shout about
it for the sake of others." Apple CEO Tim Cook, who came out in a
Bloomberg Businessweek op-ed article in 2014, wrote, "If hearing that the
CEO of Apple is gay can help someone struggling to come to terms with
who he or she is or bring comfort to anyone who feels alone or inspire
people to insist on their equality, then it's worth the trade-off with my own
privacy."[252] The sense of responsibility is voiced often.

*People are really discriminated against, and we have had to live
our lives in the closet because it was dangerous. We are talking
violence. People had to protect themselves. When one can come
out and say, "This is who I am," then it breaks down a barrier.
For there to be change, you have got to make some friction;
you have got to make some noise. It's letting people know that
everybody is not the same. It is important to speak out.*

–Commissioner Garner

Often, people don't just come out for themselves.

*A lesbian activist once said, "We have to come out because we
are their brothers, sisters, daughters, cousins, aunts, uncles."
If they don't know that this is also a part of us, they're not
going to recognize that it's a very natural part of all of us as*

a human race. Once you come out, they can no longer say, "I don't know anyone who is LGBT." Because the moment you do know somebody who is LGBT, it's less easy to discount that community. That's the thing that needs to happen. I think it personalizes someone, and it takes it from the abstract and says, "Oh, so I know John down the street, and I've had this real visceral reaction to LGBT people all my life, but I've known John for a couple decades. He's been on the block, he's a great guy, he's a family person. Now that I find out he's LGBT, am I going to discount all those things? Probably not." It may not change all at once, but knowing that we're here and that we have been and we will be starts to change hearts and minds about what being LGBT means and what it means for them.

–Roemerman

Some people commit themselves to speaking to others about the process.

I stressed the importance of coming out and being out, if you can do so safely, and how important that is to show people that we are proud to be who we are, and we want to meet the rest of the world on our own terms. A college student told me that my words were inspirational to him and helped give him the courage to come out as transgender. That taught me the importance of my own words, how telling people to come out and be out is important for trans people themselves and the people around them.

–Glenn

Some people come out because they feel it's a matter of life or death— they are so miserable pretending to be a different gender that they would rather die.

I just couldn't go on. Life meant nothing to me.

–Sabrina

There's also another way to look at it.

Coming out is the best thing you can do for yourself. And you know, coming out to your friends and your family makes you a much more whole person and better able to live your life happily and find more love in your life.

–Rafshoon

Is coming out more difficult for any group of people?

The answer will differ depending on who is asked. In a perfect world, coming out would not be an issue, because every sexuality and gender identity would be accepted. Each group faces a different set of challenges, but there are also similarities.

A common thread is the apprehension of coming out to parents, even parents who have been loving and supportive. Children of any age are afraid of disappointing their parents, and of being rejected by their parents.

When I came out, I hid under a blanket because I didn't want to risk seeing the look of disappointment in their eyes. There was no doubt in my mind that my parents would support me, love me, and be okay with me once I told them. I had no doubt about that and never have. But I did think they might be disappointed.

–Rayna, self-employed, single,
    cisgender, lesbian, 28 years old

Most people look up to their parents, and many of us try hard not to disappoint them, because we desperately want their approval, though we may be unaware of it. Much of the tension that may exist between child and parent is often the result of a mutual desire for approval and appreciation. Children want their parents to be proud of them, and parents want to be proud of their children. It can be difficult and even frightening to reveal something about ourselves to a parent if we think it might change the way they view us or interact with us. Unfortunately, for many LGBTQIAP individuals, that fear is realized after coming out. Stories abound of children kicked out of their homes and adults banned from their families. While some are welcomed with open arms, many must go through a period of isolation, and some lose their families forever.

It appears that people are more likely to come out to mothers than they are to fathers. Overall, 56 percent of respondents to the 2013 Pew LGBT Survey say they've told their mother, while only 39 percent have told their father.[253] Of gay men, 70 percent report coming out to their mother, compared to 53 percent who came out to fathers. Sixty-seven percent of lesbians report coming out to their mothers, while only 46 percent are out to their fathers. Based on bisexuals responding to the survey, only 40 percent came out to their mothers and 24 percent to their fathers.

Research indicates that bisexuals are less likely to come out than homosexuals. Only 28 percent of bisexuals say they have come out to all or most of the important people in their life. This percentage suggests that bisexuals are much less likely than gay men or lesbians to come out to the important people in their lives.[254] The 2013 Pew LGBT Survey reports that the median age when bisexuals first told someone about their sexual orientation was twenty years old, but this obviously does not apply to every bisexual person.[255] In his book, *Bi America: Myths, Truths, and Struggles of An Invisible Community,* William Burleson recalls coming out to himself at the age of seventeen while riding the bus. In the book, he recounts, "I thought, 'That's it! I'm bisexual!'" It took him ten more years to come out to his friends and family.

For some bisexuals, there may never be a need to come out. Consider that when someone dates a person of the opposite sex, the world views that person as heterosexual. So as long as a bisexual individual is with a person of the opposite sex, then everyone, including the person they are in the relationship with, will likely assume they are heterosexual unless told otherwise. Similarly, when a bisexual person dates someone of the same sex, most people presume they are homosexual unless told otherwise.

Research shows that bisexuals live under intense pressures within both the heterosexual and homosexual communities. They experience higher rates of anxiety, depression, and substance abuse and are significantly more likely to engage in self-harming behaviors or attempt suicide when compared to heterosexuals and homosexuals.[256] This has been attributed, in large part, to the hostility and lack of acceptance bisexuals experience from heterosexual and homosexual people. Columnist Charles Blow says he came to realize that the world considered bisexuals as, "The hated ones. The bastard breed. The 'tragic mulattos' of sexual identity."[257] He goes on to say bisexual people are viewed as, "Dishonest and dishonorable.

Scandal-prone and disease-ridden. Nothing nice." If you have ever been on the receiving end of those types of feelings and opinions, then you know how painful, even crushing, it can be. It's no wonder that being ridiculed, belittled, and dismissed for something as core to your being as sexuality can lead to self-doubt, depression, anxiety, and attempted suicide. It's also why some bisexuals choose not to come out.

50 Great Myths of Human Sexuality explains that many "people don't come out as bisexual because they fear that neither heterosexuals nor homosexuals will accept them."[258] Bisexual activist Robyn Ochs tells the *New York Times*, "They said that bisexuals couldn't be trusted, that they would inevitably leave you for a man... But for me to say I was a lesbian would have required that I dismiss all of my previous attractions to men as some sort of false consciousness. So, I didn't come out."[259] Wisconsin state Representative JoCasta Zamarripa says, "Before the primary in 2010, I didn't have the valor and courage to come out."[260]

Blow believes that fear causes a person to hide their sexuality, and that, ultimately, this denial is harmful. For Blow, fighting his bisexuality consumed and almost ruined his life.[261] He concluded that fear can also become a reason to come out. R&B artist Frank Ocean, who came out on social media and in his lyrics, tells *GQ Magazine* that the fear that kept him and other bisexuals from coming out is crippling. "Know what fear does to your strength? You don't even feel smart or capable. You just feel broken—and not just your heart. Just a broken person."[262] One motivation Ocean provides for his coming out was the realization that there's "so much upkeep on a lie." He also says coming out changed his life. "It was like all the frequency just clicked to a change in my head. All the receptors were now receiving a different signal, and I was happy. I hadn't been happy in so long. There's just some magic in truth and honesty and openness."

Sophie Saint Thomas, who identifies as queer and bisexual, points out that LGBTQ individuals don't only come out to heterosexual or cisgender people. Not only does she have to come out in straight environments but also in LGBTQIAP environments, because people assume she is straight. In the *Cosmopolitan* article "Being Queer and Femme Means Constantly Coming Out," Saint Thomas explains that when people say "but you look straight," it can render "feelings of invalidation from which all queer people should be allowed to be free."[263]

There are also those who believe coming out is more difficult for pansexuals because the idea of pansexuality is relatively new to most people, and very few people understand it. Some who identify as pansexual report not initially being aware of the term pansexual and, as a result, come out as bisexual before discovering the term pansexual and realizing it as a better description of their sexuality. That was the case for Texas State Rep. Mary Gonzalez, who originally came out as bisexual when she was twenty-one.[264]

Some might say that coming out is most difficult for asexual individuals. Most individuals and societies expect sex to be a part of every adult's life and as a result might view asexual people as if they are weirdos or liars. Some asexual people will avoid coming out so they can avoid the judgment and stigma. There are also those who try to avoid dating in order to avoid sexual situations and to avoid coming out.

As mentioned earlier, some asexuals may come out to the person they're dating as a way to decline sexual advances. The general expectation that sex will occur early in a relationship can place greater pressure on asexuals to come out, often before they are ready. The downside is that coming out will probably end the relationship. According to The Trevor Project, coming out puts asexuals at risk of being rejected by a partner or love interest. Kissing, petting, and sexual intercourse can feel like natural parts of a relationship to those who are not asexual. When those sexual advances are rejected, it's not uncommon for sexual people to feel as if they are being rejected or as if the asexual person doesn't really like them. For these and other reasons, if an asexual person comes out to stop someone from pressing them for sex, then it's likely that person will end the relationship once they know sex is not forthcoming.

Consistent with other sexualities, some asexuals say they find it more difficult to come out to their families and people closest to them. In a post titled, "I'm… Coming… OUT!" one person comments that it's easier to be out to the world than it was to tell the people closest to them. "I've no problem being out to people all over the planet, but telling those I see every day is a different thing altogether. I know I'm not alone in feeling this way." There are many aspects of ourselves that we choose not to share with people with whom we have limited interactions or history as these connections do not require the heavy lifting that the intimacy of a closer relationship carries. One person on the site writes, "None of my family or friends know about my self-identification as an asexual… I just couldn't think of a good way of bringing it up." Another individual, Acer, writes, "I am 'out' on all my frequent websites online and to my brother and cousin but not to my parents because I know they wouldn't accept it. It's a lot easier to be 'out' online." Conversely, Cox told his mother soon after identifying himself as asexual. In an article for *The Guardian*, he writes, "I told my mother shortly after finding the asexual website, and she said: 'Well, as long as you understand the possibility that one of these days you'll meet someone and want to settle down with them.'"[265] In Cox's case, he did settle down, with a woman who is also asexual.

Of course, there are other asexuals who feel no need to come out. An anonymous writer on asexual.org says, "Sexuality—in all its myriad hues—is such an intimate subject some people (myself included) don't think every person on Earth needs to know about it."

Coming out as transgender might be the most difficult. Consider that a person's sexuality isn't on display every time they greet the world; however, an out trans person's identity is visible to those who knew them before coming out, and in many instances to new acquaintances. When a person comes out as homosexual or pansexual, for instance, we may not see a physical or visual change. Another consideration is that coming out as trans very often receives a hostile reaction from others, including physical violence, being fired, and not being able to secure a job. A forty-four-year-old trans person responding to a Pew survey writes, "Most people know me one way and to talk to them about a different side of me can be disconcerting. I have not told most people because of my standing in the community and my job, which could be in jeopardy."[266]

The coming out process can be difficult for most people. Much of the difficulty appears to stem from lack of acceptance and understanding from friends, family, and strangers.

How do intersex people explain their details to a potential mate?

Each person develops their own approach to this sensitive conversation. Most people have never heard the term intersex, and some have a negative opinion about intersex people, while others may confuse intersex with being transgender. That is the complex and ambiguous reality that an intersex person must consider before sharing this sensitive information.

Should something be revealed during the first phone call, the first date, or even the first month? Should they say it at the beginning of the date or the end of the date? Should they wait until things become intimate or until after they fall in love? Each person must decide for themselves when and if the information should be shared.

Bo Laurent, an intersex rights pioneer, advises clients like Jim Ambrose to share the information during the early stages of a relationship.[267] Jim was mis-assigned female at birth, and subsequently subjected to numerous surgeries and treatments to make him appear female, including reconstructing his penis into a vagina, and administering female hormones that eventually produced breasts. As a result, Jim says he is "a man who didn't have the penis that everyone was going to expect. And by 'everybody,' I mean that I was really focused on dating straight women. I wanted to date women who were going to desire me as a man... I wanted a woman to see me from across the room and say, 'Yeah, I want to f*** that guy,' before they knew anything about me." Many people can identify with Jim's inclination to be viewed as desirable, sexy, or attractive, particularly by those we find sexy or attractive.

Jim adopted Laurent's technique of presenting his story early and honestly. He tells prospective partners that he works at a bookstore, does advocacy work, workshops, and fundraising for an organization that works on behalf of intersex people. Jim then explains why he dedicates so much time to the cause, "Well, because it happened to me." This approach has worked for Jim who says, "It puts me in a position of somebody who is being proactive about their life. One who is acting in defense of myself and others." He believes it also conveys to a potential sexual partner that he cares what they think.

Laurent, also known as Cheryl Chase, was originally labeled a male at birth and given a boy's name. They had XX chromosomes and what doctors thought was a penis. At the age of one-and-a-half years, doctors reclassified the child's sex as female, after discovering ovaries and a uterus. A doctor performed a clitorectomy to partially remove or reduce what he determined to be a large clitoris. The child later developed ovotestis, a gonad with testicular and ovarian aspects. That sounds like a lot to tell a first date. Not surprisingly, Laurent avoided romantic and intimate situations for many years. Now approaching sixty, they have been married and divorced and reports being in a loving relationship with a woman who hadn't heard of intersex. "She wasn't familiar with those words or the story, but I did tell her about the clitorectomy. I was surprised and comforted at how well she took that."[268]

Full disclosure is, perhaps, a roll of the dice at any point in a relationship. Each may be surprised at the disclosure to come and the response to the disclosure made.

> *I only ever did that twice. I had a number of nonsexual relationships with boyfriends and had turned down a couple of marriage proposals. There was a man I got engaged to, and after we were engaged, I try to explain my history to him. His reaction was that he didn't feel like he could go through with the marriage. He still wanted to have sex together, which we had not yet had, and which I didn't really want to do just because he was interested. The second time I told someone, I knew a lot more about my medical stuff. I shared a little bit at a time, and each time, he reacted in a positive manner. So, I thought, well, I'll just tell him everything, and he'll go away and leave me alone. I sent him this long email, and he called me and said that he'd cried. He proposed about a week after that, and we got married in 2000. We are still married, and it doesn't bother him one way or the other.*
>
> –Simon

How does a transgender person come out to a spouse?

For transgender individuals, coming out to someone they've shared a life with, and possibly raised a family with, presents additional levels of complexity and difficulty.

> *My wife and I were what I thought was really kind of normal in many ways. One day she said, "We're just roommates," and that floored me. With that statement, I said, "Then why am I staying here? Why am I trying to hold all this together?" That*

gave me an idea that I need to think more about my happiness and where I needed to go with my life. I told my wife, "This is who I am," talking about I am a woman. She looked at me and said, "No, you're not." I said, "Yes, it is. This is who I am. For you and for everybody else, I've lived for who you think I should be, and I'm telling you, this is who I am, and this is who I've been inside all my life, and I cannot live as a man anymore. Life isn't worth living. I can't go on." And I couldn't. I couldn't do it anymore.

–Sabrina

There are, of course, other scenarios.

I guess there was never one particular minute where I came out and told her. It was an accumulation of events. It was her gaining an awareness of seeing me relate to other people and how I presented myself that just got her to the point where one day she looked across the table at me and said, "I know all about Emily." I said, "Well, what do you know?" She said, "I know enough about Emily to know I can't have her in our relationship and in my life." That is when things started to deteriorate, and I didn't know how we were going to resolve that. The resolution came to me when I came home from work one day and she was gone.

–Emily

How do family members respond when loved ones come out?

The emotions, experiences, and responses people receive are varied. Every family and family member responds differently. Some are supportive, and others are not. Some family members attempt to understand and accept the reality that someone they love is gay, bi, ace, pan, intersex, queer, or trans, and other families do not. There are always exceptions and surprises, but in many cases, the response from loved ones is likely to be consistent with the historical tone of the relationship. If the relationship has a history of being loving and kind, the response is likely to be loving and kind. If the relationship has been one-sided, selfish, and inconsiderate, the family member may respond as if they're being injured. In every relationship, coming out tests the mettle of what all parties are made of—both the giver and the receiver of this important news.

Some parents are accepting, but still have some difficulty with their child's coming out.

> *I waited about seven years before I told my parents. I set a mental deadline that I wanted to tell them before I turned thirty. My dad's answer was the textbook. "You're our son; we love you no matter what. Thank you for telling us." My mom was very quiet, for a long time, a couple weeks. My mom was not upset about the fact I was gay; she was upset with herself. She felt the way I told her reflected on how she had raised me; that I had lived in so much fear of telling them that I thought I was disappointing them. Her question was, "Why would he ever think that I wouldn't love him unconditionally?" I know I'm very lucky because not everyone has it that way. As soon as I came out to myself and my family, I felt like the hard part was over. From that point on, if anybody had any questions about it, I didn't think twice about it. I'm very open about it.*
>
> –Councilmember Wan

Although research shows that people are more apt to come out to mothers than fathers, that doesn't mean all mothers are accepting of the news.

> *My sister was fine; my mother not so much. It was not a pleasant conversation, and she just simply stopped talking to me. We didn't speak for six months.*
>
> –Tiffany

> *Most of my friends were great. I don't think I really lost any friends. Of course, you always worry about that. Finally, I came out to my parents. I explained what was going on, and they were very, very supportive. They then moved to Oklahoma about a year later, got a little evangelistic, and we didn't talk*

for a year. It was around the election of George W. Bush, and I said, "So Mom, who are you going to vote for?" She said, "George W. Bush." I'm like, "Oh, you're going to vote for a president who's going to deny your oldest son his basic human rights." And she said, "You and your special rights." And I said, "Okay. I think we're done." We didn't talk for a year, and actually, my next boyfriend encouraged me to get back in touch with her. Now we're fine. It takes time for people to get comfortable, and my mom did say a pretty good thing. She said, "You've had years to figure this out; I've had fifteen minutes, so give me some time." I said, "You know, that's totally valid; you're absolutely right."

–Roemerman

His mom raised an important point: families also have a process that has been referred to as a coming out of sorts. It includes acknowledging and accepting that a loved one's gender identity or sexuality, as well as acknowledging it to their friends, neighbors, coworkers, etc. The loved one of someone who has come out goes through a process that can include shock, confusion, denial, anger, and acceptance. The fact that a loved one might say, "I love you, no matter what," doesn't mean they don't experience some or all of those feelings. It takes time for family and loved ones to educate themselves, learn to live with their loved one's newly revealed identity, and eventually come to full acceptance. Sadly, some families never reconnect. Fortunately for Roemerman and Tiffany, the loss of communication with their mothers was temporary.

Commissioner Garner was also apprehensive about coming out to her mother, even though she was in her late thirties at the time and they had always had a good relationship. Rather than tell her mother, Commissioner Garner decided to show her.

I invited my mother down to visit. My mother and I always had an open relationship. We could talk about things but never like that. I just took her to meet my friends. They were all gay. After a couple of nights, she said, "You know Joanie, it's all right to be gay. My best friend in high school was gay. It is fine to be who you are." That really caught me off guard. That is how I came out to my mother. She had no questions. The only concern she had was, "Are you happy?" And I said, "Yes." She said, "That's wonderful."

–Commissioner Garner

Sometimes the response is to ask plenty of questions.

Probably the person I was most hesitant to talk to was my mother. And not so much because she would have a negative reaction but because my mother has this real need to understand. I knew she would be confused. My sister really urged me to talk to my mother sooner rather than later. I was going to wait, but based on that conversation, I made the decision to call her within the next couple days. She just kept asking me, "Is this your first relationship with a woman?" "How long have you known?" She was like really trying to figure out, "Who is my daughter? How does this relate to the person I am related to?" That lasted a couple of months. She would keep asking me the same kind of questions. She didn't always understand my answers, but she really wanted to understand.

–Jazmyn

At the other end of the spectrum are parents who make no effort to understand. A young pansexual woman posting on the website panpride. tumblr.com says her lesbian parents refused to accept her pansexuality, saying that if she was pansexual, then she "can go f*** a dog." The young woman who "expected a loving acceptance from them" has since given up trying to make her parents understand.[269] Another pansexual woman reports coming out to her mother, sister, friends, and coworkers with mostly positive responses, but says she has yet to tell her father, who referred to gay people as "fruit loops."[270]

There can be other surprises.

I came out to my dad, and he came out back to me, which was really surprising. I was not expecting that at all, and it really threw me for a loop. He kind of came out around the same time

I did to many people. He's still not out to everybody but mostly out to his friends and out in the family. My mom knew about it since before they got married.

–Dr. Lowell

Some parents wonder if they are to blame.

I didn't tell my dad until I was in my mid-to-late twenties, when I worked for Indianapolis Police Department. It just kind of happened in a phone call. I told him I was going on a ski trip with my friend and who we were going to stay with. He said, "Well, do those two girls have their husbands?" I said, "No Dad, they're girlfriends. They live together. They're partners." He goes, "What do you mean?" I explained it to him again, and he goes, "Well does that mean that you're gay too?" and I said, "Yeah, Dad, it does." Then he asked me a couple of questions, and he said, "Well, did I do something wrong?" I said, "No. Did you raise me to be honest and to be who I am supposed to be?" and he was like, "Well, yeah." I said, "Well, this is who I'm supposed to be, and this is what I'm supposed to be doing." He was like, "Did I play catch with you too much, or…" and I said "No, Dad. It has nothing to do with that." Once I kind of explained it to him like that, he didn't ask me any more questions about it; he was just supportive.

–Karla

One study found that conservative, religious families are more likely to reject children and other family members who come out.

My mother is Catholic, and when I told her she began praying. She prayed that I would change, and eventually, I sat her down and said, "Mom, you've got to stop. I'm not going to change, and praying isn't going to make me change. I need you to accept me." That's when she stopped praying for me to change and began moving toward accepting who I am.

–Conner, non-profit director, single,
   cisgender, gay, 35 years old

It occurs to me that instead of Conner's mother praying that he would come into his natural identity, she was praying for him to be who *she* wanted him to be. Unfortunately, this scenario is repeated in families all over the world.

> *When I connected with Kelly, I gave up everybody else for a time. My mother told my children I was going to hell when I got with a woman. She turned my children against me. All my girlfriends turned against me too. I had no one. My son asked, "Why are you doing this, Mom?" I said, "I don't know that I'm really doing it. This just seems to be my path. I'm just following my path."*
>
> –Vicki

The response to someone coming out as transgender can also be harsh and unaccepting. It's one thing to hear someone say, "I'm transgender," or, "I'm gender dysphoric," and quite another to see them appear as the opposite gender. Seeing the transition makes it harder for people to pretend their trans family member or friend never came out. It also dashes the hopes of loved ones who thought, "This too shall pass." Emily said the transitioning phase of coming out was very difficult for her siblings and adult children to accept.

> *I think, generally, all three of my girls are openminded enough to accept me as the person I really am, but they still have to disassociate that with the fact that they grew up knowing me as "Dad" and the male in the household. They all have questions, fears, and concerns that they have to deal with. As it goes from them to their children, you have a whole other level of understanding of how they are going to be comfortable. Of my two brothers and two sisters, my two sisters have met Emily. My oldest sister has this quiet acceptance and says, "If that is who you want to be, that is fine." My other sister just thinks that I am critically, mentally ill and deranged, and at some time in life, I will find out my life is not what I think it is and I will be healed and I will repent and I will get over it.*
>
> –Emily

Even loved ones who don't outright reject trans family members might display hostility or indifference. A twenty-nine-year-old trans man in the Transgender Survey says, "Some of my family still refers to me as 'she,' but when we go out, they catch themselves because of how I look; they sound foolish to strangers. When it's a bunch of family or old friends, they usually don't assign me a gender; they say my name. But I don't get too bothered by it; they are family, and well, that's a huge thing to have to change in your mind. For the ones that do it out of disrespect, I just talk to them one on one and ask for them to do better."[271]

Coming out to close friends and colleagues can also be emotional.

I am part owner in the construction company, and I had not come out to my business partner. I thought I would have to do something different for a living, even if I had to leave the state. I had a resume ready and had already researched companies that had non-discrimination policies that mentioned gender identity. My business partner is very, very conservative. I am talking very deep Republican, loves Donald Trump. I was scared to death. I thought, "When I tell him this, the ceiling is going to fall, the bottom is going to drop out," so I wrote him a letter. It was a page and a half. I just kind of did a quick synopsis from the time I was five, and I gave him the letter and said, "I want you to read this all the way through. Don't stop and say anything, don't stop and ask any questions, just read it all the way through, and then we'll talk." I stayed there while he read it. He read through it slowly. I could tell he was shocked. He had no idea. He was very surprised. Then he looked up at me and said, "I want you to know, it doesn't matter to me," and that shocked me. He said, "It doesn't matter to me if you're sitting over there with a vagina or a penis, you're the same person." I could not believe it. I was so relieved. I was ecstatic. I was floored with his response.

He was very concerned about our key employees and about the people with the city. He went around to all these people, let them know what I was going to do, and asked if they were all right with it, whether any of them would quit or if they were all going to hit the road or whatever. He was satisfied that the company

*would still survive with me as a woman. The relief for me was
like… I can't describe it. I cannot describe what it was like.
That moment was just like taking a million-pound load off me.*

–Sabrina

Sabrina wasn't the only one surprised by her business partner's response.

*My ex-wife was the bookkeeper for the company, and I think she
was mad. I think she wanted him to be on her side and wanted
him to be upset. I don't know why, because it was our livelihood.
She just couldn't believe that he had that attitude.*

–Sabrina

What are the risks of being "out?"

Coming out and being out can be dangerous, even deadly. Children, teens, and adults are at risk of having their property damaged and being emotionally abused, physically assaulted, or even murdered because of their sexuality or gender identity. Violence can occur just about anywhere, at any time—within families, schools, and neighborhoods, and among strangers. According to the Pew survey, 30 percent of LGBT respondents say they have been physically attacked or threatened, and 43 percent of those victims say they knew their attackers.[272] A 2016 report from the National Coalition of Anti-Violence Programs shows that of those who report violence, more than 50 percent of victims know the perpetrators, who were often landlords, neighbors, coworkers, employers, and relatives.[273]

Many of these crimes are not reported to the police, and of those that are reported, many are not classified as hate crimes by local jurisdictions.[274] HRC warns that the FBI reports do "not paint a complete picture of hate crimes against LGBT Americans because the vast majority of jurisdictions either fail to report their data or inaccurately report that they have had no hate crimes in their jurisdiction."[275]

The 2014 FBI hate crime stats reveal that 20 percent of hate crimes with a single motivation were based on sexual orientation or gender identity. The report explains that this means LGBT Americans are targeted in hate crimes 8.3 times more than would be expected based on their proportion of the population.[276] Another interesting point is that 32 percent of these hate crimes occurred in the "residence/home," which is higher than the 23 percent reported to occur on a "highway/road/alley/street/sidewalk."[277] Of the LGBT communities tracked in the FBI report, gay men face the greatest threat of hate crimes, with 10 in 100,000 hate-motivated physical assault crimes against gay men and 4 in 100,000 against lesbians.[278] The 2017 report reveals 15.8% of hate crimes were due to bias against sexual orientation, and 1.6% were because of gender identity bias.[279]

The Human Rights Campaign reports that in 2016, at least twenty-two transgender people in the United States were killed in violent assaults, the most ever recorded. These victims were killed by acquaintances, partners, and strangers.[280] In 2017, according to the FBI's report, 119 people were victims of anti-transgender hate crimes, double the number reported in 2014.

Additionally, trans women experience more violence than trans men..

I think it is important to say very clearly that trans women experience violence and anger and panic at a much higher rate than trans men. I think that's about misogyny. I think even the violence towards trans men is all very much grounded in misogyny and about the idea that if gender and sex are knowable and legible, then you can avoid accidentally doing "gay" shit. There is this idea that men are going to somehow, straight cisgender men, are going to accidently cross some gay line. Right? That's about patriarchy. That's about the tiny boxes that straight cisgender men are confining themselves to and that our culture confines men to. And then if they see a trans woman or someone they think they know is a trans woman, I think it is a dual thing that goes off in their head. One is, "Oh my god, I could be tricked by someone like her. I could be attracted to someone like her, and then what does that make me?" And then the other piece of it is, "I could never be that free." It is both of those things at once.

I think if we taught men how to live in their bodies and in their hearts in a way that allowed them a much freer range of expression around not just their sexuality, because I think we put too much emotion on that, but really around their emotions and being able to be physically affectionate with other men that they love, their fathers, their brothers, their best friends, that would really go a long way toward helping men not have such totally panicked violent reactions to expressions of difference in gender and sexuality.

–Anderson

Not all transgender individuals encounter violent situations.

For the most part, I have been pretty fortunate in my life to be able to see those situations develop and try to diffuse them early on. I have had one case where people have been physically violent with me. I have been exposed to people verbally attacking me and calling me names and making accusations. It's situational. It depends upon what the setting is, who the person is, who is around, and what the environment is, as to how you deal with that. Sometimes it is best to just turn and walk away. Sometimes it is a situation where you can try to reason with them. The best answer is to move away from it because you don't have the time or the energy to deal with that person. You don't have much of a success rate over a short period of time of changing how they feel and how they are going to react to you.

–Emily

One reason Emily may be less likely to be subjected to physical violence is that she is approximately 6'4" tall. But just as Emily's stature likely reduces the chance of someone assaulting her, trans women who are smaller in stature are more vulnerable to physical violence. While size may reduce physical attack, most visibly trans people, regardless of size or height, are subject to insult and the possibility of injury.

Some believe that in order to address hate crimes against transgender women, we must address the violence between men and women.

If we help men deal with their own violence and their own inability to access their emotions and all those things and deal with interpersonal violence between men and women, that shifts more broadly what happens to trans people. Trans people are

*collateral damage in the war between men and women and the
war frankly between men and themselves.*

– Anderson

The risk of physical assault is even greater for trans women of color.
Among the 53 known transgender victims between 2013 and 2015,
87 percent were transgender people of color, according to HRC.[281]
Among those, at least 39 were African American and 6 were Latino.
Correspondingly, HRC reports that "fatal violence disproportionately
affects transgender women of color, and that the intersections of racism,
sexism, homophobia, and transphobia conspire to deprive them of
employment, housing, healthcare, and other necessities, barriers that make
them vulnerable."[282]

Why is violence against LGBTQIAP individuals still a problem?

"As the majority of society becomes more tolerant of L.G.B.T. people, some
of those who are opposed to them become more radical,"[283] according to
Mark Potok, a senior fellow at the Southern Poverty Law Center. Gregory
M. Herek, an expert on anti-gay violence and a psychology professor at
the University of California, adds, "The flipside of marriage equality is
that people who strongly oppose it find the shifting culture extremely
disturbing. They may feel that the way they see the world is threatened,
which motivates them to strike out in some way, and for some people, that
way could be in violent attacks."[284]

The fact that violence remains prevalent in a time when it seems
people are becoming more accepting keeps me mindful that improvement
and progress should not be misconstrued with total acceptance or total
equality. There is the chance that violence and hate crimes might continue
to rise as the number of people living "out" continues to increase. One
way to halt the rise of violence is for families, neighborhoods, churches,
law enforcement, and governments to send the message that former NFL
player and gay activist Esera Tuaolo spreads: "Hate is wrong." We must
send a clear message that we, as a civilized society, do not accept hate or
violence.

Why do some people stay in the closet?

There are a number of reasons why a person would not come out. Some people don't come out because they have not accepted their sexuality or gender identity. Others don't come out because they believe they shouldn't have to publicly divulge such personal aspects of their lives. Another reason is fear of physical harm, ridicule, rejection, and loss.

The threat of loss accompanies each coming out because there's always someone who isn't accepting. Many people do not come out, because they are not willing to accept losing family, friends, careers, social standing, and more. Approximately 39 percent of LGBT people say that at some point in their lives, they were rejected by a family member or close friend because of their sexual orientation or gender identity.[285] For some, especially earlier generations, staying in the closet guarded them from such loss. Dr. Lowell believes her father didn't come out sooner because he thought it would mean losing the opportunity to build a family.

> *My dad knew he was gay since he was a kid and just never dated men. He really wanted to have kids, so he got married and had kids. My mom knew about it since before they got married. He told her he was gay and still wanted to get married. She just absolutely adored him, and so they got married. I wouldn't quite recommend that, but that's what they chose to do, and I think they were, more or less, happy. They made it work. They really loved each other very much.*

–Dr. Lowell

One of my friends never came out to her parents for fear it would be too much of a burden for them, and she delayed coming out to others because she worried what they would think about her.

> *I worried about people thinking that was just gross and terrible. It had to do with being judged poorly. I didn't love the idea of being out to people who would judge me severely, and there were a few who did in those earlier years. I didn't talk to my family about it for years. They were the last. In fact, I never told my parents. I would have told my sister and my brother*

and their kids and their spouses sooner, but I was afraid they would tell my parents. I didn't tell my brother and my sister until both parents had passed on. Mostly, my parents would have been frightened for me. They would not have disowned me or anything like that, but they would have thought, "Oh my god, I can't believe it." My dad had gone broke; they totally changed their lifestyle, so they were devastated in their living, so I couldn't add to their problems. There just never was a time, and in the much later years, when there might have been a time, both of my parents, one after the other, suffered from Alzheimer's. First my dad, and my mom was taking care of him. There was no way I wanted her to hear this then. Although, there's some possibility that she guessed by then. I don't think she ever did, but I don't know that.

–Marilyn

Even after Marilyn had fully accepted her sexuality, she felt the need to protect her parents by not coming out to them. In doing so, she continued to place her sexuality, and herself, in the closet.

Rejection by family is not the only fear that might prevent someone from coming out. Some people fear rejection by peers because it can result in loss of social network or social standing. Others fear rejection by their religious community, which can lead to a perceived loss of God or a relationship with God, as well as the loss of a church family and social network.

As indicated earlier by Charles Blow and Kendrick Lamar, fear of rejection is a reason many celebrities don't come out.

I think most people don't come out because of the fear of being alienated or rejected. For celebrities, there are so many different reasons, but the biggest thing is financial. Obviously, when you're that well known and you're a cash cow for so many people, they will guard that with their life. That goes with the music industry—there's so many rappers out there that people know are gay, but they will never come out because they think they will never sell another record again. It's like playing with fire—you want the fame and money, but you will always have to hide who you really are.

–Fredis

Oscar-nominated filmmaker Paul Weitz believes actors might be reticent to come out because, "The fear is that if you come out, will you not be able to play straight characters."[286] Actor and comedian Lily Tomlin says, "I wasn't totally forthcoming. Everybody in the business knew I was gay, and certainly everybody I worked with and everything like that. I just never had a press conference to announce it." She tells the Washington Post, "I wanted to be acknowledged for my work. I didn't want to be that gay person who does comedy. I wonder if I'd come out on that '75 cover of *TIME* if I would have had as long a career as I've had."[287]

Celebrities aren't the only people reluctant to come out in the workplace for fear that it will adversely affect their ability to earn a living and provide food and shelter for themselves and their families. Discrimination is still a major concern. There is no US federal law protecting LGBTQIAP individuals from employment, housing, and public accommodation discrimination, and 28 states lack any statewide LGBTQ protections.[288] An article on thinkprogress.com stated that more than half of LGBT workers hide their identities in the workplace because they fear unfair treatment.[289]

The possible loss of livelihood and income also affects LGBTQIAP entrepreneurs:

> *I haven't told my clients. I am not as comfortable with that. I don't want that aspect of me to be an issue, no matter what. I am not interested in entering anything into the business relationship that puts the client relationship at risk. It is my livelihood. I wish I didn't think it might be an issue, but I work in some pretty conservative environments.*
>
> –Jazmyn

It doesn't seem fair that a coming out should jeopardize a person's life or livelihood.

CHAPTER TWELVE

THE ISSUE OF EQUALITY

"The things that make us different, those are
our superpowers… the world would not be
as beautiful as it is if we weren't in it."
–Lena Waithe[290]

Intro

Equality is based on the premise that everyone is of like value and merit. The presumption is made that, in terms of our humanity, we are all equal and deserving of the same rights, opportunities, and protections. Sadly, too many people add restrictions and exclusions to their notion of equality, which, of course, means they don't really believe in equality. For instance, if everyone in a society does not have equal protection under the law, then equality does not exist. If everyone in that society does not have equal access to employment, housing, education, and healthcare, then equality is just a myth.

What is the best way to achieve equality?

There are differing ideas about how to achieve equality for those who identify as LGBTQIAP. When Pew Research asked about the best way to pursue equality, approximately half of the LGBT respondents said, "The best way to achieve equality is to become part of mainstream culture and institutions like marriage."[291] The other half said they should be able to achieve equality "while maintaining a distinct culture and way of life."

While LGBT Americans agree that discrimination is a problem, there is substantial disagreement over the causes and how to eradicate it. This comes from a poll conducted by National Public Radio (NPR), the Robert Wood Johnson Foundation, and the Harvard T.H. Chan School of Public Health. One interesting observation is that survey respondents over the age of fifty tend to blame discrimination on individual prejudice, while younger generations point to both individuals and biased laws.[292]

Additionally, some people think it's more important to combat individual prejudice, while others believe that new laws will be more effective and efficient. This might explain the differences in opinion expressed by fifty-seven-year-old Louis Mitchell and twenty-seven-year-old Edanry Rivera in an NPR "Morning Edition" segment.[293] Rivera, a transgender woman, says, "I can't change people who are so deeply rooted in their values, so the only thing I can do is to focus on policy and legislation because we're always going to have a bias, but we need policy in place to reflect our values now in 2017." Rivera says that many transgender people in their twenties and thirties focus on implementing change through the government and its policies and laws. Some believe this is because that generation expects more from the government, such as student loans, healthcare coverage, and employment assistance. Rivera believes, "Our dependence on the government is making us much more in tune as to the laws and policies in place that have put us there." Mitchell, a transgender male, has a different perspective. "We've also seen where the policy changes have not necessarily made all of us safer." He adds, "I want to work on every heart that I can find to say, hey, it's me. You loved me yesterday. Why are you not loving me now?"

What we have observed through this and other struggles for equality is that both approaches are needed if change is to occur. Sometimes, reaching out to individuals pushes them to action that changes public policy and laws, and sometimes, changes in public policy and laws prompt individuals to accept the humanity in others and treat them as equals.

Is the LGBTQIAP community bullying politicians to get what they want?

I was surprised to hear elected officials and others lob this accusation. The answer is no. Bullies use their strength or power to intimidate or harm those who are weaker. LGBTQIAP communities and individuals use their strength to help people, and LGBTQIAP communities are "weaker" in terms of equal treatment, freedoms, rights, and protections under the law. Based on the definition of bully, it is more accurate to say the bullies are anti-LGBTQIAP elected officials who propose and pass discriminatory laws against lesbian, gay, bisexual, transgender, queer, intersex, asexual, and pansexual people. We could also consider anti-LGBTQIAP religious leaders and other groups as bullies when they use their power, influence, and money to proposition and pressure elected officials to propose and pass discriminatory laws.

It's not uncommon for people in power to disparage those who are trying to get out from under their thumb. Use of the word "bully" is an attempt to make the pursuit of civil and human rights sound like a bad thing and to make the people pursuing those rights sound like bad people. Several people shared their perspectives.

I mean, it is the same as all the stuff that's happening now where somebody with more power will strike out at someone with less power, and then act persecuted although they started it.

–Anderson

We are fighting for fairness. It's not about bullying. It's about having a right to be who you want to be, and who you want to be in love with, and not have repercussions and be looked down upon because of who you are. It's about fairness and equality.

–Fredis

Yes. And the straight community has bullied the American people and officials into getting what they want too. You know, showing political strength is not bullying. I mean, I don't see how raising your voice politically is bullying. We've made amazing progress over the last forty years, and we will continue to do so in the fight for equal rights.

–Rafshoon

The LGBTQIAP community and its allies use their voices, votes, and money to oppose laws, elected officials, products, and companies that are against their interests and agendas, and to support those who work to improve their well-being and advance equality.[294] This is another example of the similarities we share as humans. Many of us belong to a group of people with a history of banding together to fight for equality, whether that group is women, Irish, Chinese, Jewish, etc. It is the human thing to do.

Why do some people equate hate speech with free speech?

It seems that those who equate free speech with hate speech misunderstand what freedom of speech actually is. Free speech or freedom of speech refers to the concept that neither federal, state, nor local governments can punish you for saying something—in most instances—even if what you say is false, misleading, or hateful. Freedom of speech only refers to what the government can do in response to your words. Protection under freedom of speech does not guard you from backlash from others such as your non-government employer, community, family, social media friends, or anyone else.

Yes, you can say almost anything you want, but as Sir Isaac Newton discovered, every action has an equal and opposite reaction. The right to say or write what you want does not preclude anyone else's right to respond to what you've said or written. If you make an anti-LGBTQIAP statement, then you should expect a response, from those who agree with you as well as those who disagree. Those who disagree with you have the right to say publicly that you are wrong, to boycott you or your business, to suspend your social media account, or to fire you from your job.

My question for anyone eager to espouse hate speech is, "Why not use your words to speak out for everyone's freedom to pursue life, liberty, and happiness?"

What is the "gay agenda"?

There has been much talk about the "gay agenda" agenda. When you think about it, we all have or have had agendas, because an agenda is simply a list of things to be considered, discussed, or done. Agendas can be broken down into three categories: 1) achieving something for self; 2) helping others achieve; and 3) preventing others from achieving.

Some would have us believe there is a sinister gay agenda that must be stopped. Others would have us believe there is a righteous agenda that must be advanced. The concept of an agenda is not intrinsically negative or positive. The purpose, tenor, and validity of a particular agenda may be viewed as positive by those setting it and negative by those opposed to it. We should be mindful of this as we consider how different people shape what some refer to as the gay agenda.

Throughout history, oppressed groups fighting for freedom, equality, and fairness have been painted with a dreadful brush by their oppressors, who attempt to discredit what they interpret as a threat to their power and the status quo. When any group establishes an agenda for better, fair, civil, or equal treatment, there will probably be a larger or more powerful group to label that agenda as bad, unnecessary, immoral, unpatriotic, or some other negative description. For example, when the American British colonies fought the Revolutionary War, Great Britain described their agenda as unpatriotic. When women fought for the right to vote, men tried to invalidate their agenda as subversive. When the agenda included legalizing same-sex marriage, those opposed labeled it immoral or unchristian. Now, as transgender children and adults seek the right to use public restrooms, their agenda is being characterized as perverted, among other things.

For those who feel or believe an agenda for fair and equal treatment is a bad agenda, I must ask, "How can an agenda based on treating other humans civilly and equally be bad? How can an agenda based on freedom, equality, fairness, safety, and love be wrong?"

Perhaps the most prominent agenda item was the right of same-sex marriage, but there are other rights to achieve. "Marriage alone is not a silver bullet," as Danielle Moody-Mills, an advisor for the Center for American Progress, says.[295]

Politics. Marriage. Employment non-discrimination. Health, AIDS, HIV. I think people are concerned in our community about the internet taking over our lives, that there's not as much face-to-face contact, and it's harder to get people out and about to events and out at social functions. They're concerned about violence and getting beat up. Hate crimes. It really depends where you live. I mean, if you go—even in New York, there are some hate crimes out there. There's some in Atlanta. I mean, it's not something that we think about that much, but it is an issue out there. Some of us are concerned about the same issues that everybody else is, you know, racism, anti-immigrant stuff. I think these days, we have a lot of the same concerns everybody else in the world does.

–Rafshoon

Elected officials also have agendas that might reflect their personal concerns and those of their constituents.

Moving the gay agenda forward means a lot of different things to different people. I know what it means to me, and it doesn't always line up with everybody else. The LGBT community is so diverse, just like the general population is, and I don't know that any representative of any community is always going to be 100 percent aligned with anybody in that community. My focus has been on our civil and human rights and fighting discrimination. Getting municipalities and businesses to recognize our community and treat us equally, and then working legislatively in the city of Atlanta and also at the state and federal level for equality. There are others who would add things like sexual freedom and freedom of sexual expression, which I don't oppose; it's just not one of the priorities for me.

–Councilmember Wan

What is the LGBTQIAP agenda?

The agenda will vary among groups of people and among individuals. As Moody-Mills also offers, "We're a rainbow, right? So, we have a rainbow of ideas and a rainbow of opinions." It shouldn't be surprising that there are different views on what is needed, which concerns should take precedence, and how change should be sought and implemented. Most who identify as LGBTQIAP agree that there are many areas where fair and equitable treatment is yet to be achieved, including housing, education, employment, income, adoption, and healthcare.

Organizations like the LGBTQ Institute at the Center for Civil and Human Rights have specific agendas.

> *This is about making sure that everybody in society has an equal shot at happiness. Laws that are specifically geared toward discriminating against a certain population, that's not the American way. Any time we can get closer to our ideal of having a society where we truly care about our freedoms and protections for all people, that's where we need to go. We're looking at poverty. We're looking at LGBT and aging issues. Some of these things have gotten some airplay but not to the extent that they need to be. And then it may become a national safe-school law that protects LGBT kids, along with a host of other minority youth, in a more sincere way. But once we get past those really big-kind-of-ticket-item issues, it's transitioning from the idea of legal equality to lived equality, and that takes work and that takes time and that takes having a variety of folks.*

–Roemerman

Adoption is one of the many concerns shared across most LGBTQIAP identities. Each state has the authority to create its own adoption laws, which for some states includes discriminating against would-be parents because of their sexuality or gender identity. Florida and New Hampshire, for example, have laws expressly denying adoption to lesbian and gay parents, and Arkansas's laws prevent lesbian and gay adults from becoming foster parents.[296] In 2018, only California, the District of Columbia, New Jersey, and Rhode Island explicitly prohibited discrimination against foster and adoptive parent applicants based on sexual orientation and gender identity.[297, 298] Additionally, only Maryland, Massachusetts, New

York, Oregon, and Wisconsin prohibited discrimination against foster and adoptive parent applicants based on sexual orientation.[299] No federal adoption law exists to protect prospective parents against this type of discrimination.

Some states, like Georgia, have even tried to pass laws giving faith-based adoption agencies permission to discriminate without fear of lawsuits while still collecting government funds. People like Georgia Republican State Senator William Ligon claim their ultimate goal is to provide loving homes for children. If this were true, then wouldn't they expand the pool of loving homes rather than restrict it? If their true mission was giving every child a loving home, then they would not add the caveat "unless that home is gay, trans, bi, etc." How can having two loving female parents or two loving male parents be worse than having no parents?

It's been discussed earlier that a parent's sexuality or gender identity does not have a negative impact on a child. On the other hand, studies show that foster care negatively impacts children. Adoptive Families reports that children in foster care are twice as likely to have a learning disability, three times more likely to have hearing and vision problems, five times more likely to have anxiety, six times more likely to have behavioral problems, and seven times more likely to have depression.[300] We should also be mindful that "a child stuck in permanent foster care can live in twenty or more homes by the time she reaches eighteen."[301] Also, "long-term foster care is associated with increased emotional problems, delinquency, substance abuse, and academic problems."[302] Another study finds that "foster care predicts higher adult criminality for males first placed during adolescence (ages 13–18)."[303]

Additionally, the Academy of Pediatrics concludes, "Many factors confer risk to children's healthy development and adult outcomes, such as poverty, parental depression, parental substance abuse, divorce, and domestic violence, but the sexual orientation of their parents is not among them."[304]

Given these facts, it does not appear that lawmakers, states, and agencies with these restrictions are acting in the best interest of parentless children. Sadly, many states and adoption agencies put their prejudices above the child's welfare instead of being concerned with placing each child in a stable, loving home environment. Most importantly, we should think about the children. It should be considered a form of child abuse to condemn them to a life of orphanages, foster care, and possibly abuse when a safe, loving, nurturing home awaits them, just because the potential parents are not cisgender heterosexuals.

> *What's most important is a child has a warm bowl of oatmeal and a hug before they go to school and a hug when they come home.*

–Joe

Lack of morals or responsibility makes for a bad parent, not sexuality or gender identity. A person's sexuality only advises us about who they are sexually and romantically attracted to, and gender identity simply tells us which gender a person identifies with. They do not inform us about a person's ability to nurture, love, protect, guide, discipline, and support a child. It's unfair, to parents and children, to restrict parenthood based on sexuality or gender identity.

> *God forbid we go to some sort of economically depressed part of our community and find some kids either raising themselves or in an environment that's not suitable, with no love whatsoever, and you have an option to put them in a loving environment. Whether it's two guys, two women, one guy, one woman, one grandparent, it doesn't matter, as long as the child is cared for, loved, and encouraged to go out and do good things. The dynamic doesn't change who the kid is going to be. The dynamic changes if you put them in an environment where they're abused or neglected. I teach my kids how to love and be honest. That's really all you can do as a parent is love them and hope they make the right choices when that comes around.*

–Karla

Fortunately, there are agencies like AdoptUsKids, a national project of the US Children's Bureau that connects children with families and provides "support to lesbian, gay, bisexual, transgender, and queer/questioning (LGBTQ) families who are seeking to foster or adopt children from foster care."

Do LGBTQIAP individuals earn less money than heterosexual cisgender people?

Data, surveys, and studies confirm that lesbian, gay, bisexual, and transgender individuals and families are more likely to have lower incomes than the overall population. Note that, as of 2019, data on queer, intersex, asexual, and pansexual has not been compiled.

The Gallup poll finds startling disparities between LGBT and non-LGBT income and financial well-being, which includes standard of living, ability to afford basic necessities, and financial stress. There is also a disproportionate risk for poverty and food insecurity, according to the Williams Institute.[305] In 2017, a single-person household in the US with annual income of $12,060 or less was considered to be living in poverty. Fifteen percent of heterosexual men lived in poverty that year. The rate for gay men was 20 percent, and the rate for bisexual men was 26 percent.[306] Among women, 21 percent of heterosexual women lived in poverty, compared to nearly 23 percent of gay women and 29 percent of bisexual women.

The difference is even more dramatic for transgender people in America, according to a Williams Institute poverty study. The poverty rate for transgender people is more than twice the national rate. When the overall poverty rate for Americans was 14 percent, it was 29 percent for transgender Americans.[307]

The poverty rate is worse for trans people of color: 43 percent of trans Latinos, 41 percent of trans American Indians, 40 percent of trans multiracial people, and 38 percent of trans black people. Additionally, the survey reports that 16 percent of respondents turned to underground employment, "including 11 percent who turned to sex work because they could find no other job."[308]

> Many transgender people have to become street workers just to eat and to pay for the things that they need to get by. And that's a trade that unfortunately, there're a lot of men out there who prey on them.
>
> –Raman

Heterosexual married couples experience a nearly 6 percent poverty rate. It's 14 percent for same-sex couples.[309] We should also be mindful that the conditions that create greater poverty rates for same-sex couples also impact their children. The children of married heterosexual couples have a poverty rate of 12.1 percent, while 29.8 percent of the children of same-sex couples are in poverty. African American children in same-sex male households have the highest poverty rate, 52.3 percent, of any children in gay or straight households. Poverty and low income are also important agenda items that are direct offshoots of discrimination and unemployment.

Even when higher incomes are examined, there is disparity. For instance, 34 percent of the overall adult population earns more than $75,000, while only 20 percent of LGBT adults reach or exceed that income level, according to an American Community Survey.

Over the years, I've heard people insist that gay people earn more money than heterosexuals. The lesbian and gay people I spoke with were surprised to learn that some people hold this belief.

> *There are a lot of poor people out there. I am an elected official, so I make nothing. I had a business, but I am devoting my time now to being an elected official, so I don't make a lot of money.*
>
> –Commissioner Garner

Where, then, did the perception arise that gay people are better off financially than straight people? A deeper dive reveals that the perception is more specifically applicable to gay men.

> *There are two thoughts. On average, it's probably cheaper to be a gay man because we may not have the family structure that straight people often have. Also, things are a little bit more difficult for gay people, and I think there's a case for a lot of gay people to prove themselves. I suffer from this. I have some need to win in life because I feel like maybe I've been dealt a more difficult hand than some of my straight counterparts. In my case, I wanted to make sure that I was very successful in whatever career path I took. In part, I think that was to compensate for not being able to have the traditional family life that some of*

my straight counterparts were experiencing already in their early twenties.

–Perry

Perry also suggested that some gay men might be more driven to achieve career success, for various reasons. The need to be better or to prove to the world and self that you can succeed is not uncommon in marginalized groups, and depending on the field and other factors, can lead to a lucrative career and more money. Certainly, there are men of other races and women of all races who are members of marginalized groups and are also driven to achieve success. They typically face discriminatory barriers that white men do not encounter.

White heterosexual men are likely to earn more money than black heterosexual men, white heterosexual women, black gay men, Hispanic gay men, Native American gay men, white lesbians, black lesbians, Hispanic lesbians, Native American lesbians, and transgender men and women of any race. The only group that might, in some instances, have a higher income than white heterosexual men is white gay men.

It's already been shown that poverty rates for gay men are higher than for straight men; however, at higher income levels, homosexual men have been able to outperform incomes of heterosexual men. This becomes more obvious when we compare couples. One reason why white, gay, male couples might have more income and financial well-being than heterosexual couples is that same-sex male couples do not include a woman. It has been repeatedly shown that, in general, women earn less than their male counterparts. Therefore, any couple that includes a woman is likely to experience the gender pay gap that often befalls women. Male same-sex couples are also less likely than heterosexual couples or female same-sex couples to have children. This might be due to the fact that men can't get pregnant, have a harder time adopting, and are less likely to want children than other couples. Male couples without children don't have to spend money on expenses related to raising children, and therefore, have more of their income available for other purchases like a house, investments, apparel, and travel. This has contributed to the perception that a same-sex male couple earns more than a heterosexual couple, even if they actually earn the same or less.

Which issues are priorities for the transgender community?

While there are common concerns, such as fair treatment and protections under the law, there are also issues that only impact the transgender community.

Restroom Access

One major issue specific to the transgender community is playing out across the country in numerous lawsuits and legislative actions attempting to restrict transgender children and adults from using the restroom or locker room that matches their gender identity. Placing these restrictions on transgender individuals seems discriminatory, punitive, cruel, and inhumane. These laws are also intrusive and invasive. They are society's attempt to look under a trans woman's skirt and unzip a trans man's pants before allowing them to answer the call of nature. Can you imagine walking into a restaurant restroom and having another person say, "You must prove to me you belong in here before I will allow you to empty your bladder or move your bowels?" It's a safe bet you would be appalled and offended, as would I, and as are transgender men and women.

Some people claim the need for discriminatory laws is to prevent transgender women from revealing their genitalia in the women's restroom or locker room. For the sake of argument, let's say a trans person in a locker room decided not to cover up while going to the shower or getting dressed. No one is going to die or go blind because of it. The worst that will happen is people might be confused or curious, which opens an opportunity for learning.

As a woman who has used locker rooms for nearly fifty years it has also been my experience that most women cover their bodies on the way to and from the shower, and some seek privacy behind a curtain, when available rather than dress in front of others. Women are often shy about showing their bodies for many reasons, and it's very likely that a trans girl or woman would also be inclined to follow similar behavior, and would therefore probably not show their genitalia. The same holds true in the lady's restroom. I have never seen anyone walk out of the bathroom stall with their pants down or skirt up to reveal their genitalia. That is not how things work in the lady's room. It is no more likely that a trans girl or trans woman would walk out of the bathroom stall revealing their genitalia than it is that any other person in a public bathroom would reveal themselves. I have been in bathrooms with people who appeared to be transgender women, and I didn't feel threatened, unsafe, or uncomfortable. We were both there to answer nature's call. Once we each step into a stall and close the door, no one sees what's underneath our clothes. And once that business has been handled, we wash our hands, refresh our makeup, primp our hair, and head back out the door. What is the harm or threat in that?

> *Trans people are not trying to peep on you or do anything to you. They are just trying to live their lives. I think that's the main thing.*
>
> –Anderson

In discussing these bathroom laws, much of the focus is on which facility transgender women should use. Sabrina pointed out that little consideration was given to the fact that enforcing these laws would also force trans men into the women's restroom.

> *Here in Florida, when all of that started, they didn't consider trans men. That wasn't even on their radar. It didn't stop them, but it opened their eyes when they started realizing they were going to send trans men, who they never would have been able to tell the difference, who were very masculine, they were going to be sending these men into the ladies' room. What's your wife gonna do, Senator, when this guy shows up in the ladies' room? Do you understand that? What's going to happen then? It's not just trans women in this world; there's trans men.*
>
> –Sabrina

Sabrina also shared the concerns she faced when travel plans unexpectedly placed her in a North Carolina airport where a law passed in 2016 declared "transgender people who have not taken surgical and legal steps to change the gender noted on their birth certificates have no legal right under state law to use public restrooms of the gender with which they identify."[310]

I had a six-hour layover in Charlotte, North Carolina. I thought, "Oh my goodness, what am I going to do? What am I going to do when I hit North Carolina?" Then I said, "First of all, I am not going to have my birth certificate with me. If they want to get my birth certificate, they're going to first have to find out who I used to be. They're going to have to find out my old name, and good luck with that, and every document that I'm going to carry with me—my passport, my driver's license—is going to say, 'Sabrina, female.' So, let them do whatever they want to do because I'm going to walk into the ladies' room, and I'm going to use the ladies' room.

I think this is such a stupid discussion, such an unbelievable thing. If they were just to open their eyes, take a serious look, most people aren't standing in the restroom saying, "Can I see your genitals please?" People walk in, close the stall door, do their thing, and walk out.

–Sabrina

Requiring a trans woman—someone born a biological male, who identifies as a woman, who looks like a woman, lives like a woman, and behaves like a woman—to walk into a men's restroom places the trans woman at risk of bodily harm. That trans woman, who is dressed like a woman, appears to be female, and feels like a woman, is now surrounded by men. It's reasonable to presume she would be uncomfortable, as would any woman who is forced to use a men's restroom. The situation could quickly become dangerous for her if the men in that restroom are fearful or uncomfortable with her presence. That fear and discomfort could lead men to physically assault the transgender woman, as has been known to happen. Many transgender youth and adults are forced to confront similar situations, due to restrictive bathroom and locker room laws.

Jennifer Finney Boylan believes the bathroom bills that require transgender women to use men's restrooms and transgender men to use lady's restrooms will increase the possibility for physical attacks. "I have been on the receiving end of violence; I have been on the receiving end of prejudice, but in some ways, I've never felt quite as at risk since this HB2 business began in North Carolina… So technically, even though I am by all impressions, rights, and reasons female, I would be required to use a men's room, and that puts me in danger. And so, in some ways, the laws of certifying gender are in fact making people like me less safe rather than more safe."[311]

To those who say, "I don't feel safe around transgender people," I urge you to consider why that is so. Have you been attacked by a transgender person? Is your feeling based on conjecture that transgender people are bad people? Is it based on a lack of knowledge about transgender identity? I would also urge you to consider that the likelihood of a trans man or woman randomly attacking or molesting someone in the bathroom or anywhere else is close to zero. Heterosexual cisgender men are the most likely offenders, and most often, these are Caucasian men who are married, educated, employed, and religious.[312] If the concern is women's safety or lack of safety, we must look at the real problems.

> *I think a lot of women have legitimate safety concerns about bathrooms and things like that. But oftentimes, we frame things in terms of safety and put the onus on trans people instead of looking at our broader culture that makes women unsafe.*
>
> –Anderson

Boylan believes the restroom controversy is "not about bathrooms. Really. It's about people thinking that the one thing in the world they could depend on, gender, as a constant, as something stable and unchanging, turns out in fact to be the opposite. It turns out to be malleable and morphable. And so, this is frightening to people who have never considered this truth before."

For many people, it's a matter of human dignity.

> *It is mindboggling, but it is really dangerous. I don't even know what I want to say about that except I just see that happening so much, this idea that trans people are predators who want to destroy how the world works. If trans people were that powerful, lord, so many things would be different, but trans people are not that powerful. Trans people just want to be able to pee and eat like everybody. I mean, I think that's the thing. The question of*

public accommodations, that's always where it comes up around human dignity.

–Anderson

For those concerned about what children might see, I suggest that children aren't likely to see anything, unless they intrude on that person's stall or forcefully disrobe the transgender person. In terms of being in a school restroom or locker room, consider that most children are self-conscious about being different, don't want to be seen as different, and don't want to draw attention to the things that make them different. For this reason, it is highly unlikely that a trans child in the locker room would want to show their genitals to anyone. But let's say they do, then what? Then that's an opportunity to learn. That's an opportunity for parents and the school to explain cisgender, transgender, and the importance of mutual respect among all human beings.

This is an opportunity for us all. As Boylan states, "Going about creating a world that is more accepting and fair of all of the variations in human experience makes this a better world. So, I know people are nervous about the world not being as simple as they thought it was. But in fact, if the world is not as simple as we thought, the world is also more wondrous and full of variety and miracles. And we should celebrate that."[313]

Legal Documents

Another daily challenge for transgender people is having identification that doesn't match their trans identity. As mentioned earlier, there are state laws controlling if and when a transgender person can change their name and gender marker on state IDs. A national survey indicates that 40 percent of transgender men and women report being harassed in situations that require they present an ID that does not match their gender identity/expression. In those situations, 15 percent report being asked to leave, and 3 percent report being attacked or assaulted.[314]

Healthcare and Health Insurance

Another agenda item for trans people is lack of access to healthcare, which can be life-threatening. Something as simple and necessary as accessing healthcare professionals who are willing and able to treat them becomes a tremendous challenge. Many medical professionals and their staff are uncomfortable treating transgender patients. Even worse, many healthcare professionals refuse to treat transgender children and adults. This means transgender people are less likely to receive healthcare, including regular checkups and preventative care. As a result, they are more likely to develop fatal illnesses, like cervical or prostate cancer, owing to lack of early or timely diagnosis or no diagnosis at all. In a humane society, shouldn't there be a moral imperative that every human being has access to affordable, quality medical care?

> *A patient told me once that they had a sore throat, and they had to go to five different doctors to find one who would even accept them as a patient to see them for a sore throat. Also, pap smears for trans men is a huge obstacle, and so the only people in this country really who die of cervical cancer anymore are trans men because they just don't have anywhere to go. Most people need screening for things that they would rather not even think about. Like, everybody still has a heart, there's still a risk for heart attack, high blood pressure, all the regular stuff. But then who's going to do the primary care for these patients? Right now, what's happening is there's sort of a siphoning off: "Oh, you have this issue that I don't understand." Most primary doctors are saying, "I don't understand your medical needs because you're on hormone therapy that I don't usually prescribe, so go see the endocrinologist." And that's fine, except then you're saying, "You have this special problem that needs a specialist to take care of." That's what I think is really not acceptable, that physicians feel like they can say, "I don't understand this one aspect of your health; therefore, I'm not going to see you for anything."*
> –Dr. Lowell

Sixty-five percent of transgender patients do not seek care when they should, even when they may be critically ill, according to Dr. Lowell. In the past year, one in four adults who identified as transgender avoided a necessary doctor's visit because of fear of being mistreated, according to the National Center for Transgender Equality.[315]

It appears that many medical professionals have forgotten their oath. Around the world, various forms of the Hippocratic Oath include the promise, "I will remember that I remain a member of society, with special obligations to all my fellow human beings, those sound of mind and body, as well as the infirm."[316] They also swear, "May I always act so as to preserve the finest traditions of my calling, and may I long experience the joy of healing those who seek my help." Medical professionals who honor this oath would not deny treatment to a patient because of gender identity or sexuality.

Some in the healthcare profession believe the medical community should provide better treatment and service for transgender patients.

For trans people, it is a lot harder to find doctors even if you are going for something that is totally unrelated to your trans status. My wife is a social worker, and she gets people writing in trying to find a specialist willing to take care of a trans patient because they have been to multiple doctors and can't find one that is comfortable taking care of them. It is depressing how behind we can be in the medical profession. I think it is going to be the next big push. I think the emphasis is going to turn toward health because there are a lot of disparities in that realm. I am an emergency physician. We are way behind. There has been very little training up until this time in medicine. As early as possible, treating trans patients should be worked into the curriculum, the standardized patients that medical students see and the case studies. The more exposure you have the better, and the earlier the better because you have the language. I also think it is easy for medical professionals to get in ruts. Once you have been doing something for five, ten, fifteen years, you need to go back and learn a new language, a new way to communicate with a certain patient population. I don't think people are very motivated to do that.

–Anne

Others say they have been fortunate to have respectful doctors, but not all doctors' staff members follow suit.

Most of the doctors I received treatment from have been very respectful and sensitive. That has not always been the case with doctors' staff. Their receptionists and other support personnel who work with them are sometimes not as considerate as I'd like them to be.

–Glenn

And he is admitting me, and I said can you put a preferred name in there because I've not changed my legal name and so my assigned name. The waiting room is packed, and they are going to call my name. I was like can you please not call it. He was like no, we can't do that. My sister, who had done her nurse training there, was like you sure can do that. And he was like no, no, we can't. Then the doctor came in and he was like yeah, we can. No problem. And put it in there…

–Anderson

While these experiences may not seem egregious, that is not the case for other trans patients.

I have friends who have been horribly mistreated and made fun of and had bad things happen to them while they were under anesthesia.

–Anderson

Additionally, many trans individuals face substantial issues surrounding health insurance coverage. A trans person is less likely than a cisgender person to receive adequate healthcare coverage.

In order to become a man, he has to have testosterone, but because he has female organs, he also has to have pap smears, pelvic exams, and breast exams. He needed an ultrasound because he was having problems with pain and some kind of engorgement in the ovarian area, so we were concerned there might be something wrong with the ovaries, like cysts or God forbid a cancer. The insurance company said, "Well, you can't be both, you have to be one or the other." They chose that he's male, so that covered his testosterone, but that meant his ultrasounds aren't covered, his pelvic exams aren't covered, his breast exams aren't covered, mammograms aren't covered. And then, if we decide to fight them, then they say, "Well, we won't cover your testosterone."

–Raman

Employment Discrimination

Transgender men and women are not the only people to experience employment discrimination, however it may be more pronounced. A National Transgender Discrimination survey reports nearly 90 percent of trans people have experienced harassment or mistreatment on the job.[317]

Employers can legally fire a person for coming out as transgender or for transitioning. Employers can also legally refuse to hire someone because they are trans. "Transgender people face pervasive mistreatment, harassment, and discrimination in the workplace and during the hiring process," according to authors of the US Transgender Survey. Emma Green, the senior associate editor at *The Atlantic,* says, "There is no federal law that says it's illegal for an employer to fire a person when they go through a transition, for example. Some states do outlaw that, and some cities do outlaw that on a local ordinance level. But there is still a very, very long way to go in the United States before it is actually even illegal to discriminate against transgender people."[318] In a land where we claim to believe every able-bodied person should work and have the right to work and get paid fairly, we should be ashamed and appalled that this right is denied to transgender individuals.

In October 2007, Glenn informed her employer at the Georgia General Assembly that she intended to transition. Glenn thought she was being a responsible employee by giving her boss advance notice. Her dutifulness was not rewarded. She was fired. Glenn's boss described her intent to transition as "inappropriate" and subsequently had her ejected from the state capitol building in Atlanta.

A trans person has the right to transition without getting fired. It was made clear to me, in no uncertain terms, that I was to vacate the capital and with all deliberate haste… Getting fired from my job was the most difficult part of transitioning.

–Glenn

Believing she had been unjustly and unlawfully terminated, Glenn decided to take legal action on behalf of herself and other transgender employees.

> *What happened to me was wrong, and I wanted to do what I could to keep it from happening to anyone else. I filed a lawsuit. It established at the Eleventh Circuit Level, which covers Georgia, Alabama, and Florida, that it is unlawful to terminate a government employee for being transgender. In other words, the equal protection clause, the Fourteenth Amendment, applies to transgender people because transgender discrimination is the same as any other sex discrimination. That is the precedent that was set by the Eleventh Circuit panel that heard my case.*
>
> –Glenn

Glenn won the court case and got her job back. The court victory provided protection to transgender state government employees in Georgia, Alabama, and Florida. However, government agencies in any states other than those three were still free to discriminate against transgender employees, as were any federal government employer, private corporations, and small businesses.

In September 2009, Glenn became the first transgender person to address a Congressional committee when she was invited to the Labor Committee of the US House of Representatives to discuss her case and urge passage of the Employment Non-Discrimination Act (ENDA).[319] If it becomes a law, ENDA would ban US employers from firing, refusing to hire, or otherwise discriminating against employees based on sexuality or gender identity. Though, as of 2018, no federal law explicitly prohibits this discrimination, Glenn's regional court victory for government employees was expanded in 2012.

> *In April 2012, the Equal Employment Opportunity Commission expanded on that ruling to apply to all trans people nationwide in public or private employment. So, the letter of the precedent, it's somewhat limited because it only applies to public employees in Georgia, Alabama, and Florida, but it was a precedent that*

*was decided by the EEOC later to apply to all trans people
nationwide.*

–Glenn

The EEOC cited "Glenn v. Brumby" as a precedent when it ruled that discrimination against transgender people is illegal sex discrimination covered under Title VII.[320] This ruling means that transgender people in the US have the right to not be fired for being transgender, even in states that don't specifically provide this protection. Although it gives legal recourse to trans men and women who believe they've been fired because of gender identity, it doesn't mean they won't be fired for that reason. It is important to note that until ENDA becomes a law, there is no federal law providing workplace protections that extend to sexuality and gender identity.

> *Once they say, "I'm a transgender woman," nobody wants to interview them because they might have male booming voices, they might have large hands, sometimes they still have hairy faces. So, they're already discriminated against. To come into mainstream society and to be accepted and to be given a great job, it's a dream that doesn't happen very often.*
>
> –Raman

The Workplace Equality Fact Sheet reports that 27 percent of transgender people who held or applied for a job in the last year report being fired, not hired, or denied a promotion due to their gender identity.[321] Jeff Graham, the executive director of the LGBT rights organization Georgia Equality, says the lack of state-specific protections is a problem. "Employees will file a grievance with the EEOC," he says, "and that's when they find out there are no explicit (state) protections."[322] In 2018, the American Association of Pediatrics also reported that "only eighteen states and the District of Columbia had laws that prohibited discrimination based on gender expression when it comes to employment, housing, public accommodations, and insurance benefits."[323]

Workplace discrimination isn't just about the individual victims; it also negatively impacts their families on multiple levels. Imagine what might become of you and your family if you were fired because of who you are or the way you look. And that no one else will hire you—not a fast food chain, a retail store, or a toll booth—for the same reasons. How are you going to earn a living? Where are you going to lay your head? What are you going to eat? How will you pay for healthcare when you get sick? For many transgender people, particularly trans women who do not easily "pass," the outcome is dire.

Workplace discrimination can lead to unemployment, the solving of which is another agenda item shared by many LGBTQIAP individuals, but it is an especially acute problem for those who are transgender. The unemployment rate for transgender people is triple the national rate, as reported by the US Transgender Survey. The unemployment rate jumps up to 20 percent for black transgender adults.

Housing

The United States government also allows housing discrimination against transgender people. One in five transgender people (19 percent) in the United States has been refused a home or apartment because of their gender identity. More than one in ten (11 percent) have been evicted because of their gender identity, according to The Movement Advancement Project.[324] Once a transgender person is without a job and a home, they are most likely homeless. One in five transgender people have experienced homelessness at some time in their lives because of discrimination or family rejection. Transgender people facing homelessness also face discrimination from agencies that should be helping them, with nearly one in three (29 percent) reporting being turned away from a shelter.

Slow progress is being made. A small, but growing number of municipalities are beginning to pass protective laws. On June 19, 2018, the Augusta-Richmond County Commission voted to pass a resolution adding sexual orientation and gender identity to the list of discrimination protections for municipal employees. This vote expands Augusta's EEO Policy to broaden the sex discrimination definition to include acts of gender stereotyping and to prohibit discrimination based on gender, gender expression, gender identity, and sexual orientation.[325]

A handful of states have protective laws. The governors of Indiana, Kentucky, Michigan, New York, and Pennsylvania have issued executive orders banning discrimination against transgender state workers.

California, Colorado, Connecticut, Delaware, Hawaii, Illinois, Iowa, Maine, Maryland, Massachusetts, Minnesota, Nevada, New Jersey, New Mexico, Oregon, Rhode Island, Vermont, Washington, and the District of Columbia all have such laws. In 2019, the New York state senate passed a bill including "gender identity and gender expression as protected classes in New York's human rights and hate crimes laws, and prohibit[ing] discrimination in several areas, including housing, employment, and public accommodations such as restrooms."[326] Each state's protections vary. For example, Nevada's law bans discrimination in employment, housing, and public accommodations like restaurants, hospitals, and retail stores; Maine's law covers those categories plus access to credit and education.[327] Shouldn't these laws exist in every state and cover every aspect of our lives?

To those who think denying a person a job or a roof over their heads is justifiable, please consider what your existence would be like if, for some reason, society decided you were not worthy of these protections. What would it do to your psyche and self-esteem to have no place to live because someone doesn't approve of something personal about you? How crushing would it be to have to return home to your childhood bedroom in your parents' house or to ask a friend if you could crash on their couch, indefinitely? What if your family and friends have turned against you for the same reason, and the only place left to lay your head is the concrete pallet of a sidewalk or alleyway?

I don't understand how any human being could wish that on another human. Yet that is exactly what is happening. As of 2019, federal law allows discrimination against transgender people on every front with little to no protection. This pervasive discrimination blocks their ability to pursue and achieve the things we all hold dear: education, employment, healthcare, housing, religion, using public restrooms… This is why ENDA should be on all of our agendas, because every human being should have the right to live without discrimination.

Does the trans community feel celebrities like Caitlyn Jenner help or hurt their cause?

The transgender community is not monolithic and, therefore, has differing thoughts and opinions about Caitlyn Jenner and other celebrity transgender men and women. The Olympic medalist, formerly known as Bruce Jenner, had a very public coming out and transitioning that included television and magazine interviews, as well as a reality TV show, which some people viewed positively, and others did not.

I can relate very closely to what she has gone through all these years. First and foremost, I think she was very brave in coming out the way she did. I think she was in a position that she had to come out in a way that allowed her to have a little more control over the way people saw her and related to her. You saw all of the paparazzi and articles about growing her hair and what happened to the Adam's apple and all the speculation and rumors and it was just escalating. I think the right thing to do was defuse the situation and take control of it... For the transgender community as a whole, it is a good thing in that there is someone who has come out and had that prominent dramatic impact on the world. I think there is a lot of awareness and a lot of openness that is coming out of this.

There are a lot of potential issues as well. I don't begrudge her a bit the fact that she has the money and the resources to be able to come out as gracefully as she has, to be able to come out to the world in a magazine spread where you have had your hair and make-up done by the best of the Hollywood make-up artists. How much fun is that? The average transgender girl doesn't have the means to do that. They are struggling to decide if they can someday come up with ten, fifteen, twenty thousand dollars to have facial feminization surgery, let alone the cost of breast implants, let alone the costs of sexual reassignment surgery that can run tens of thousands of dollars. I think it can be very frustrating. It can also be frustrating from the fact that Caitlyn has transitioned so well and comes across as being such a beautiful person that she has set this artificial standard of some expectation of beauty and femininity that transgendered girls are going to be measured against. It is this media beauty type thing, and most don't live up to it. It is a whole different reality. Cisgender women deal with that on a daily basis anyhow, and now, it's transgendered women who are going to be put in the same situation. It is unfortunate that at a time where we struggle just to be accepted, now that is going to be layered on top of it.

–Emily

Another perspective comes from someone who works on behalf of transgender communities.

It's all part of the consistent drumbeat that we need to keep beating, and every person that's high profile just helps us beat that drum a little bit louder. It's the voice of the community that they're speaking for and on behalf. It's not about Caitlyn Jenner. It's not about Chaz Bono. It's not about Jazz Jennings. It's about the people who they represent. The celebrities just happen to be the louder voice that gets heard. They're heroes, but the ones who are unseen, the ones who have to live on the street, the ones who are stuck being sex workers just to survive, and the ones who are homeless, the unemployed, those are the people who, in my mind, are heroes. They're the ones who pay the price. They're the victims of a society that doesn't understand them, so if these big players can draw attention to them and can improve their lives, then keep it going. We've got to keep that drumbeat going until we don't need it anymore.

–Raman

What motivates some people to become activists?

Eleanor Roosevelt believed, "One's philosophy is not best expressed in words, it is expressed in the choices one makes."[328] I interpret this to mean that the best way to exhibit and embody a philosophy is to put it into action. If you say your philosophy is love, but you never love anyone or anything, then there's a pretty good chance love is not really your philosophy. If equal rights is your philosophy, then you will extend equal rights to others, and if you or others are being denied those rights, you will take action to secure those rights. Of course, there are other ways to look at it.

Hunter Shafer, a model and plaintiff in the American Civil Liberties Union's lawsuit against North Carolina's House Bill 2, says, "I don't know if I would call myself an activist, as much as someone who's just vocal about being trans, which sometimes can feel like activism because just existing as a trans person can often be hard enough, particularly for people of color or people who don't pass."[329]

Each person I spoke with expressed a different reason for actively working for equality, including personal circumstances, religious beliefs, and humanitarian reasons.

> When I was in high school, I wasn't out, and I remember there was a guy named Ben who had been picked on and harassed all the time. He was called "faggot" and all these different kinds of things in the locker room, and I'd not say anything. I remember the morning the principal came on with an announcement letting us know that Ben had killed himself. I thought to myself, "If only I had said something." But I didn't, because I didn't want to become the new target. Later, when I went to college and heard Judy Shepard, the mother of Jeremy Shepard, speak, it was just so moving that I went up to her and said, "Judy, I want to work with LGBT youth; I want to help them feel safe and secure." I immediately came out after that, in March, and by that summer, I was helping start a nonprofit. I came out and then went into activism pretty quickly. I came up with the idea of Safe School Certification, and later, I created Iowa Gay Straight Alliance Day.
>
> –Roemerman

> I would like it to be a better place. The reason I get involved is I want to make it better and easier for guys and girls that are ten, fifteen, twenty, twenty-two years old that are growing up and dealing with and confronting all the issues that I have been through. I would like it to be an easier journey for them. I would like to know that at some point in time, maybe through some conversation that I have had with a girl or a guy, that it has helped to keep them from being the one out of three transgender people who take their own lives. The outreach things that I do with some of the schools, colleges, universities are really to set a

platform from which we can educate people and create change. Change that is needed is not going to happen overnight. It is going to be a change that happens over generations. The more we can do to educate early in the process, the more successful it is going to be… I do a lot of things in the transgender community, and I do a lot of things beyond the transgender community, working with various humanitarian groups and efforts. The struggles are the same; it's just the situation that you are in, who you are, and what your specific problems are that change.

–Emily

Everyone has their own cause, motivation, and way of participating. One common thread is the realization that activism is crucial for change to occur. During his last days in office, President Barack Obama brought home the importance of activism. He stated, "The primary heroes in this stage of our growth as a democracy and a society are all the individual activists and sons and daughters and couples who courageously said, 'This is who I am, and I'm proud of it.' And that opened people's minds and opened their hearts and eventually laws caught up. But I don't think any of that would have happened without the activism, in some cases, loud and noisy, but in some cases, very quiet and personal."[330]

What are some organizations that work on behalf of LGBTQIAP individuals and communities?

There are local, regional, and national organizations working with and for lesbian, gay, bisexual, transgender, queer, intersex, asexual, and pansexual people. They provide information resources, legal services, health care, housing, and more. The LGBT Institute, established in 2014 as part of the Center for Civil and Human Rights in Atlanta, Georgia, is one of those organizations.

You can't talk about civil and human rights without talking about LGBT and how that fits. So that's why we're doing this. The Center for Civil and Human Rights was always careful not to call themselves a museum, and the point was that it was meant to be a platform for engagement. It was meant to be a jumping-off point for discussion, and the institutes can do that through their programming.

Our point is that we want to bring some of the greatest minds from around the world to talk about LGBT issues and provide a platform for that, to have that discourse and help create a national movement strategy. For the first time, there's an actual physical location these LGBT groups can come to and have a platform to discuss things. There's nothing like this on the East Coast, certainly nothing like this in the South. The highest proportion of LGBT people out of all the regions in the country—Midwest, Southeast, et cetera—is based in the South. We have more LGBT people than any other region of the country. We also have more LGBT people raising families than any other region of the country. The only other institutes that are kind of like us are the Williams Institute out of UCLA in California, and the Movement Advancement Project. UCLA does a lot of study around demographics around LGBT. The Movement Advancement Project takes a lot of different studies and puts them into bite-sized chunks for movement leaders.

–Roemerman

THEA+ is a 365-day-a-year support organization who intends to be there for the community all the time. We're forming alliances with other organizations that share our values, so although we focus on the trans community, we work very closely with the LGBT community. We need them as much as they need us to change society, change public policy, make the strong impact that these are people and they deserve the same rights every other person has, and they deserve the same healthcare and quality of care and jobs and acceptance in society that every other person in this world, in this country, gets.

–Raman

Prominent national entities working on behalf of LGBTQIAP individuals and communities include GLAAD, HRC, and the American Civil Liberties Union (ACLU). There are many others. Equality Federation is a strategic partner to state-based organizations advocating for LGBTQ people. The National LGBTQ Task Force advances full freedom, justice, and equality for LGBTQ people. The National Resource Center on LGBT Aging touts itself as the country's first and only technical assistance resource center aimed at improving the quality of services and supports offered to lesbian, gay, bisexual, and/or transgender older adults. The Anti-Violence Project helps survivors of violence and allies become advocates for safety. They participate in community education and outreach, development of organizing campaigns, and the creation and support of city, state, and national coalitions too.

There are also medical centers and clinics like the ones established by Dr. Lowell who believes "life is not fair. But healthcare should be." In addition to launching a clinic at Emory University Hospitals, Dr. Lowell established and operates QMed, a clinic that utilizes telemedicine services to provide care for transgender and gender-nonconforming patients in Alabama, Georgia, North Carolina, South Carolina, and Tennessee.

> *During residency, I spent a week at the Mazzoni Center, an exclusively transgender clinic in Philadelphia, learning about what they do and some of the services that they provide. That really exposed me to the amount of need that there is in this country. There's a huge transgender population and so few places to get medical care of any kind, let alone hormone therapy, surgery, all that stuff. I think there are probably a handful of physicians who treat transgender patients at all, and very few who manage hormones and things like that. I'm a primary care physician, and so I thought, well, I can do this. I can set up a clinic and really focus on serving a completely unmet need in Atlanta.*
>
> –Dr. Lowell

More extensive lists of national, local, and regional entities are offered at websites like glaad.org, and pflag.org.

CHAPTER THIRTEEN

THE HOLY WORD AND RELIGION

"Whoever does not love does not know God, for God is love."
–I John 4:8 (Good News Translation (GNT))

Intro

At this point of the discussion, we've worked our way through research, biology, psychology, and history that support the existence of different human sexualities and gender identities. I recognize that for some people, none of that matters if it doesn't align with the Bible.

I was raised in a Protestant home and educated in Catholic schools from kindergarten through college. This fostered my general trust in religious leaders and cultivated a belief that they know the Bible better than the rest of us. As a result, I was inclined to believe religious leaders who claimed the Bible condemned homosexuality. There was no need for me to double check their work, because I believed they wouldn't teach it if they hadn't studied it and verified it.

Years passed without me examining this doctrine against homosexuality, until one day, I wasn't so sure anymore. That was the day I saw "God hates fags" on a church sign. This statement, posted by the pastor of a Christian church, forced me to take a closer look at those claiming to preach God's

Word and examine what the Bible actually says. What I discovered didn't match what has been taught.

Reconciling some of the differences between biblical text and the teachings of some faith leaders requires an examination of the Bible and those who enter religious professions. Faith leaders come to the profession with varying levels of education and preparation, intellect, prejudices, and motivations. Some have spent years studying biblical texts, and some have not. Some have earned their designations as "pastor," "reverend," "doctor," and "bishop," while others have bestowed those titles upon themselves without the benefit of seminary school, theological training, or any attempt at learning and studying the Bible. Their backgrounds inevitably impact what they believe and what they preach.

Some faith leaders have spent numerous years studying at universities and seminaries. A few have dedicated themselves to continued research and study of the Bible's ancient text, language, and societies. There are also those who simply got "the calling" one day and started preaching the next. Then there are those who enter the profession because they are good orators or storytellers and believe preaching is a good way to put those talents to work. Others start churches because they didn't agree with what the pastor of their church was teaching and decided to branch out on their own. Some church leaders saw pastoring as an alternative way to earn money after other careers had tanked. This leaves us with too many faith leaders around the world teaching and preaching without the benefit of careful study of biblical text and history and culture. Instead, many faith leaders preach not based on the Word, but based on personal beliefs, biases, prejudices, and emotions. "For we know in part, and we prophesy in part," Corinthians 13:9 (King James Version (KJV)). That is why it's possible for some religious leaders to have taught that enslaving black people was their god's will, that Jewish people are the devil, or that women are not equal to men. If God's Word and the Bible were distorted to proffer these beliefs, then we should question whether the same has been done with homosexuality. We should question if claims that homosexuality is a sin, that "God hates fags," and that marriage should only be between a man and a woman are the product of biblical text or personal bias.

This chapter is dedicated to exploring what the Old and New

Testaments actually say about sexuality and gender identity, as well as how religious leaders and communities should treat LGBTQIAP individuals.

Should we believe that "God hates fags?"

Not if you believe God is love. Not if you believe that God is the creator of all life. Not if you believe biblical text, which speaks nothing of hating homosexuals. The Bible does, however, reinforce the importance of love: "Whoever does not love does not know God, because God is love," I John 4:8, (New International Version (NIV)). When Jesus was asked which commandment is the most important of all, the Bible reports that Jesus said: "Love the Lord… The second most important commandment is this: 'Love your neighbor as you love yourself.' There is no other commandment more important than these two." Mark 12:31 (Authorized King James Version (AKJV)). Jesus went on to say, "On these two commandments hang all the law and the prophets," according to Matthew 22:34-40.[331] In other words, this edict of love is most important, and everything else stems from it.

We should also wonder if a God who is the Ultimate Being would ever stoop so low as to use a derogatory term like "fags." It doesn't add up. We should be alarmed that anyone claiming to be a "man or woman of God" would promote such an ungodly notion. Preaching "God hates fags" sounds like blasphemy. How can anyone side with a blasphemous Christian leader? I was taught that God is love. I was also taught that God is our Father and that all humans are God's children. If these things are true, then how can there be room for God to hate homosexuals? I could not resign myself to the belief that God, the Supreme Being, the Creator of all life would hate the life He created.

I am not the only one who cannot reconcile a loving God that would also hate homosexuals.

> If God is loving, then God doesn't hate anybody. If God is about love, then shouldn't God love everyone? Shouldn't the congregation love everyone?
>
> –Jennie

> I've always believed that all faith and all religion are about love. The fundamental concept and teachings are all about

love. It's not about hate. It's not about exclusion. It's not about discrimination. It's about how you treat other people. I find it ironic and hypocritical that folks use religion to condemn LGBT communities. It goes against the very fundamental tenets of Christianity and all major organized religions.

–Councilmember Wan

I had a cousin, Craig, who I grew up with, and Craig was probably gay. He used to play with Barbie dolls and braid their hair and paint nails better than we ever could. It was just who Craig was, and I don't believe that God hated Craig. No one ever said that God hated Craig. Even old Momma Chris, who used to babysit all of us, never said anything. She sat on the porch all day with that Bible, but she never sent those messages growing up. I just don't believe in a God that would make that child and then say, "I hate you for it. You're wrong for it."

–Tiffany

To those who are parents, I ask, "Do you hate any of your children?" No one I've ever talked to has answered yes to this question. You may not like your child's behavior at times, or you may wish they had chosen a different path, were more successful, or would call you more often, but there is nothing your child could do to make you hate them. Even two metro-Atlanta parents whose two sons beat them and left them for dead stood before television cameras and professed undying love for those young men. If these imperfect humans could not reach the depths of hating their children, then why would a perfect God hate any of His children?

Genesis 1:27 says, "So God created mankind in his own image," (Complete Jewish Bible (CJB)). There's no caveat that says, "some of mankind." And if humans were created in God's image, then why would God hate mankind? Wouldn't that be akin to God hating Himself?

Some of these contradictory beliefs have led me to believe that we've created a God that resembles our image instead of the other way around. Religious scholar and author Reza Aslan has also remarked that "we have fashioned God in our image, not the other way around." Aslan also says, "Everything that's good or bad about our religion is merely a reflection of everything that's good or bad about us." When a religion is hateful, it's not because God is hateful; it's because the people propagating that religion are hateful. Just as when a religion is discriminatory, it's because the people are discriminatory. Instead of reaching up to grab some of God's love and spread it around, those who believe God hates gay people, or any other group of people, are assigning their personal biases to God. That's not a reflection of trying to be like God. It's more about trying to transform God into a version of ourselves. It's about fashioning God in our image instead of the other way around. Aslan, who has a degree in Religious Studies, focusing on the New Testament; a Master of Theological Studies from Harvard University; and a PhD in the Sociology of Religions, suggests, "We implant God in our own emotions and our personalities, our virtues and our vices. We bestow upon God not just all that is worthy in human nature: our capacity for love, our empathy and compassion, but all that is vile in it: our aggression and greed, our bias and bigotries, our penchant for extreme acts of violence."

What does the Bible say about sexuality?

Biblical scholars, historians, and linguists—those whose job is to study the original text, languages, and meanings of the Bible—insist there is no mention of what we refer to as homosexuality. New Testament scholar Victor Paul Furnish declares, "There is no text on homosexual orientation in the Bible."[332] Members of Presbyterian Seminaries biblical faculty conclude that "the concept of homosexuality as now understood may not appear at all in the Bible," and that the issue does not arise at all "in important sections of the Bible—the Ten Commandments, the prophets, the teaching of Jesus."[333] These men and women who have studied the Bible, its original language, and the culture, religions, and societies of the people in the Bible, are adamant that homosexuality— same-sex relationships and marriages—is not addressed anywhere in the Bible. In fact, the word homosexual did not appear in any translation of the Christian Bible until 1946?

They also advise against using the Bible to make judgments about homosexuality. Robin Scroggs, of Union Seminary, says the Bible should not be used to make judgments against homosexuality "because it does not address the issues involved."[334] Presbyterian biblical faculty also caution "against any hasty conclusion that these passages present instructions for us on what we know as homosexuality today."

If homosexuality is never addressed in the Bible, then how does one reasonably use the Bible to support the position that the Bible and God say homosexuality is wrong? At this point, you are likely to have even more questions. Is it true that homosexuality is never addressed in the Bible? If so, then why was it inserted in 1946? If the Bible does not address homosexuality, then why do so many religious leaders use it to rail against homosexuality?

To find the answers, I initially consulted the Ten Commandments and Jesus's teachings. Surely if being gay, lesbian, bisexual, or transgender is a sin, then God would have told His two top guys, Moses and Jesus, and they would have told us. From there, I dug deeper into the Old and New Testaments for passages that have been referred to as "clobber passages" or "clobber verses"—the biblical texts most often used to condemn homosexuality. I explored the most common ones, as listed by Evangelicals Concerned Inc., which are Genesis 1:27, Genesis 19 (Cf. 18:20), Leviticus 18:22 (20:13), Deuteronomy 23:17-18, Romans 1:26-27, I Corinthians 6:9, and Timothy 1:10.

Old Testament

Is there anything in the Old Testament about homosexuality?

"There is nothing in the Old Testament that corresponds to homosexuality,"[335] according to Calvin Theological Seminary Old Testament scholar Marten H. Woudstra. Others agree, including Peter J. Gomes, former Plummer Professor of Christian Morals at Harvard Divinity School and Dr. Ralph Blair, the founder of Evangelicals Concerned Inc.

Why have so many biblical scholars, theologians, and religious leaders reached the conclusion that the Old Testament does not address homosexuality? They have attempted to understand the meaning of the original text and the culture of the times, as well as the changes and distortions that have occurred with subsequent translations. We should strive to do the same.

The Old Testament is a written compilation of Jewish oral stories, history, and laws told over thousands of years before humans learned to write. Stories were told and passed on by kings, shepherds, prophets, and holy leaders. Once humans began to write, Jewish leaders recorded these oral histories, laws, and stories to stone, then leather scrolls, then papyrus. They were eventually compiled into books and painstakingly replicated in Hebrew. Regrettably, the subsequent translations used today were not given the same attention.

The Hebrew Bible, the *Tanakh,* is what Christians refer to as the Old Testament. The books of the *Tanakh,* and therefore the Christian Old Testament, were originally written in Hebrew and Aramaic. The replication of these books was known to have been carried out with a meticulous system of scribes who developed intricate and ritualistic methods for counting letters, words, and paragraphs to ensure that no copying errors were made. These scribes dedicated their entire lives to preserving the accuracy of the holy books.

Complete manuscripts of the original Hebrew Old Testament, composed of thirty-nine books, were completed around 500 BC. Then, somewhere around 250 BC, scholars of the Hebrew language translated these thirty-nine books into Greek. The next translation was to Latin in AD 382. By AD 500, the books had been translated into more than 500 languages. Later translations were not given the same duty of care that the Jewish scribes applied, and when these books were later translated by Christians, the attention to detail and meaning was abandoned. With each subsequent translation, the meanings of original Hebrew words were distorted, changed, and in some instances, completely obliterated, giving us some of the versions of the Bible we use today. This is how we have arrived at words like homosexuality being introduced in place of original words that held different meanings.

Based on the experts' conclusions, use of the word homosexuality appears to be a product of a twentieth-century translation and does not represent the original intent of the Hebrew or Aramaic words Jewish scribes painstakingly replicated each time they made copies of the Bible. Remember, the word homosexuality didn't exist until 1880 and wasn't inserted into the Bible until 1946. That's more than 3,000 years *after* the first five books of the Old Testament were committed to writing.

Those who have searched the Hebrew and Aramaic languages of the original oral stories and text, and the Greek language of the first translation, have found no words that equate to homosexuality, homosexuals, or homosexual relationships. It has also been revealed that words in the original text that were replaced by "homosexuality" have different meanings.

For instance, the Hebrew words *kedeshah*, *qadesh*, or *qadash* were replaced with homosexual. These words are derived from a word that means "holy" or "separate" and referred to men who were involved in religious rituals.[336] Some Canaanites and Egyptians considered them to be male devotees to idolatry and a sacred people. Similar words are used to refer to women in these sacred positions. Because they were paid to perform these religious sexual rituals with men and/or women, others, including Jews, referred to them as temple prostitutes. For these holy people, sex was a normal part of a religious ceremony, as was paying someone to have sex as part of a religious ritual. These sexual acts were considered religious rituals, regardless of the biological sex of the participants. The sex that occurred was not about same-sex attraction or same-sex relationships. It was about religion and ritual. Therefore, scholars and linguists say that replacing these words with "homosexual" is an inaccurate translation.

It has also been asserted that disapproval of this behavior was not about sexual orientation. Victor Paul Furnish, PhD, University Distinguished Professor *Emeritus* of New Testament, at Southern Methodist University explains that it was "not because they have sexual relations with other men but because they serve the alien gods of the Canaanite and Babylonian fertility cults."[337]

Modern translations of the Bible have also mistakenly equated other practices with homosexuality. One practice, pederasty, describes a sexual relationship between an adult male and a young boy. An adult male having a sexual relationship with a boy should not be defined as homosexuality, just as an adult male having sex with a young girl would not be defined as heterosexuality. Homosexual relationships are consensual and occur between two peers, not between a boy and a man. Therefore, calling pederasty the same as homosexuality is inaccurate and reckless.

Another example of misappropriating the word "homosexual" is found in the case of male-on-male rape. As discussed in the homosexuality chapter, it was not uncommon for male captors to rape their male captives to humiliate and emasculate them. Rape is about power and aggression, not sexual attraction. A soldier who rapes a male or female captive is not expressing sexual, emotional, or romantic attraction. Rape is not indicative of any sexuality. The translation of these biblical male-on-male rape instances into homosexuality is also incorrect.

If biblical scholars, linguists, and historians are correct in their assertion that homosexuality—consensual same-sex relationships *not* involving religious rituals, prostitution, children, or rape—was never mentioned in the original Old Testament scriptures, then why was it inserted thousands of years later? Several reasons have been offered. Some suggest it was a simple misunderstanding of the original text. Others believe it was done intentionally to send a message that homosexuality is abhorrent behavior. Both scenarios are likely. Regardless of the intent, it is important to recognize that rape, pederasty, and prostitution are not examples of homosexuality. Based on this information, the original Old Testament scriptures did not refer to homosexuals or homosexuality. It is therefore misguided to use those scriptures to condemn homosexuals and homosexuality.

What do the Ten Commandments say about homosexuality?

To many people, the Ten Commandments are revered as God's ultimate list of dos and don'ts, the overarching rules we should live by.

When it comes to things we shouldn't do, the Ten Commandments say: "Do not steal"; "Do not covet"; "Do not murder"; "Do not commit adultery"; "Do not bear false witness"; "Do not have any other god before me"; "Do not make yourself an idol"; and, "Do not take the Lord's name in vain." The Ten Commandments don't include a rule that says, "Do not be homosexual"; nor do they prohibit being bisexual, transgender, queer, intersex, asexual, or pansexual. They also don't mention, let alone forbid, same-sax marriage.

If it was important to God that we only be heterosexual, then why didn't it make His top ten list of rules to live by? Were these rules absent from the Ten Commandments because Moses ran out of room on the stone tablets? Or are they absent because God looked at LGBTQIAP people and said, "It's all good"?

Did God say that homosexuality was the sin of Sodom?

No. "As I live says *Adonai Elohim* (the Lord God)… The crimes of your sister S'dom (Sodom) were pride and gluttony; she and her daughters were careless and complacent so that they did nothing to help the poor and needy," (Ezekiel 16:48–49 (CJB)). There is no mention of homosexuality in the Hebrew version or translated versions of this scripture. The NIV says, "This was the sin of your sister city of Sodom: she and her suburbs had pride, excess of food, and prosperous ease but did not help or encourage the poor and needy. They were arrogant, and this was abominable in my eyes." The claim that God destroyed Sodom because of homosexuality is false.

We should ask how it benefits faith leaders to manufacture a reason that God did not offer. Even if you were to add homosexuality to the above list of God's reasons, you would still have to explain why, of all the other "sins," homosexuality gets highlighted and the others fall by the wayside.

There are also those who point to the story of Sodom, in Genesis 19, as proof the men of Sodom were homosexuals who tried to have sex with some foreign men staying at Lot's house. Reviewing the different versions, translations, and interpretations of this scripture helps us see why this belief has been perpetuated. The English Standard Version (ESV), for instance, says, "Where are the men who came in to you this night? Bring them out unto us, that we may know them." The New International Version (NSV) reads, "Bring them out to us so that we can have sex with them." The Living Bible (TLB) says, "Bring out those men to us so we can rape them."

How are we to determine which is an accurate recounting of the story? "We may know them" in the ESV could mean they want to know who the foreigners are. It could also, as some have interpreted, mean they want to know the men carnally. To "have sex with them," as the NSV states, makes it sound like the Sodomite men stopped by Lot's house for an evening of consensual sex with his male guests. The TLB's "we can rape them" is clearly about rape and aggression.

Dr. Richard Hayes of Duke Divinity School says, "There is nothing in the passage pertinent to a judgment about the morality of consensual homosexual intercourse."[338] He and others have reached similar conclusions that exploring the language, history, and culture of the times can lead us to a better understanding of this story.

Getting to the truth of this text requires some understanding of the culture, customs, people, and era in which the story occurs. At the time, it was not uncommon for "YHWH, the God of Israel" and nations to send out spies to explore a territory before attacking it, according to Randall C. Bailey, the Andrew W. Mellon Professor of Hebrew Bible at Interdenominational Theological Centre.[339] Bailey points out, "When new men come into a city, they are often suspected of being spies by the local inhabitants and leaders." He also says the common response was to send the military to investigate suspected spies. As in many instances, including present-day America, foreigners are not welcomed and are likely to be treated hostilely, suspected of nefarious purposes, and attacked or dragged off to jail. Other biblical scholars and historians have concluded that the Sodomite people who arrived at Lot's dwelling were not citizens out looking for a sexual encounter; they were in fact part of the military force there to find out if Lot's guests were spies.

The next point to consider is what the soldiers intended to do with the potential spies. In many warlike or hostile environments, captors do things to humiliate their captives. There are other instances in the Bible where spies are captured and treated in ways that humiliate and shame the men, and as Bailey points out, "For this reason, many commentators regard these acts as emasculation of the emissaries." Some scholars and experts therefore say this story reflects the rape culture sometimes present in hostile situations. If we are to believe that the Sodomite soldiers mentioned sex with the potential spies, then the sex they spoke of was not amorous or consensual. The sex would not have been about attraction, but about subduing and demeaning their captives.

To further understand whether the soldiers simply wanted to investigate the spies or rape them requires an examination of the original Hebrew text, which used the word *yada*. This word appears in other scriptures and has different meanings, including "to have awareness or knowledge of someone or something," "to have sexual relations with someone," and "to sexually assault someone." Bailey is skeptical that the original text was describing consensual sex because a different word meaning "to lie down with" or another word meaning "to go into" was more often used when referring to consensual sex. The scholar is inclined to support the use of *yada* in this scripture as "to have knowledge of something" and points out the many other times *yada* appears in the Bible with this meaning. Other biblical scholars have concluded that *yada* refers to capturing Lot's guests and raping them. Dr. Robert Blair agrees: "The men of Sodom tried to dominate the strangers at Lot's house by subjecting them to sexual abuse. Such attempted gang-rape is about humiliation and violence, not same-sex affection."[340] Dr. Robert Gagnon of Pittsburgh Theological Seminary concluded, "The story does not deal directly with consensual homosexual relationships; it is not an 'ideal' text to guide contemporary Christian sexual ethics."[341]

Why are homosexuals called Sodomites or sodomites?

The answer to this question lies in the misuse of words. Some people mistakenly believe sodomite and/or Sodomite are the same as homosexual; however, that is incorrect. A "Sodomite" with an uppercase 'S' is a person—man, woman, or child—from Sodom, like an American is a person from America. A "sodomite" with a lower case "s," is not a synonym for "homosexual,"[342] according to biblical scholars like Catholic priest Peter Gomes. Scholar Victor Paul Furnish, agrees and notes that the term "sodomite" is not used in the Old Testament Hebrew text, not even to refer to a resident of Sodom.[343] When "sodomite" does appear in the New Testament, it "refers almost exclusively to a male prostitute," according to Gomes.

The conclusion is that neither term, Sodomite nor sodomite, was intended to refer to a homosexual person.

Does the Bible say homosexuality is an abomination or a sin?

If the original scripture never refers to homosexuality, then there is also no scripture that proclaims homosexuality is a sin or an abomination. Much like homosexuality was inserted into modern bibles, so is the case for abomination. Jewish scholars, linguists, and biblical scholars report that abomination replaced a Hebrew word that held a completely different meaning. For instance, it was inserted to replace the Hebrew word *to'evah*, which Dr. Blair explained is "not about a moral or ethical issue."[344] It refers to something that Jews considered "ritually unclean."

According to biblical scholar John Boswell, *to'evah* "does not usually signify something intrinsically evil, but something which is ritually unclean for Jews, like eating pork or engaging in intercourse during menstruation, both of which are prohibited in the same chapters."[345] If a person was ritually unclean, it meant they could not enter the temple until a certain length of time had passed or until they did something to become clean again.

Sassoon and other scholars have the understanding that this word refers to taboo or error, and that it was used specifically in reference to ritual prostitution, not homosexual relationships. According to Jewish law, having sex as part of a spiritual ritual made a person ritually unclean, regardless of whether it was with the same sex or the opposite sex. A man having sex with a woman as part of a spiritual ritual was unclean, and a man having sex with a man was unclean for the same reason. Rabbi Debra Kolodny explains, "Leviticus is merely describing a pagan ritual practice prohibited to Jews." If someone asks if it's okay for two men to engage in homosexual relations, she responds, "Are you engaging with pagan ritual? If not, it's not prohibited—the Torah doesn't speak to it."[346] It is also important to note that there is no reference to same-sex relationships or marriages being *to'evah*.

What, then, is the meaning of abomination? According to the dictionary, an abomination is "something that causes disgust or hatred; detestable; loathsome; very unpleasant; disagreeable." When someone says they consider homosexuality an abomination, what they are really saying is homosexuality disgusts them. Disgust is a personal, visceral reaction. Disgust for homosexuality is a feeling; it is not a scriptural teaching. It is incorrect to blame this personal feeling on Scripture.

The word "abomination" has also been falsely equated with the word "sin." Each word has a different meaning. Labeling something an "abomination" means it is disgusting. Labeling something a "sin" means it is a transgression against God or divine law. Also, something can be disgusting without being a sin. Just because something disgusts you, that does not make it a sin. Something can also be a sin without being disgusting.

For argument's sake, let's say the original scriptures did refer to homosexuality as an abomination (which they do not) and abomination as a sin (which they do not). The question would remain: "Why single out homosexuality as the one abomination or sin that cannot be tolerated, while we give a pass to other things that have been labeled as abominations or sins?" Let's consider the other abominations that we commit daily such as wearing clothes made of mixed materials or shaving a beard. There's also the abominations of lying and cheating, which are serious trespasses that harm other people. Yet many who say homosexuals are going to hell wouldn't say that all liars, thieves, and cheaters are going to hell. Many religious leaders who rail against homosexuality are themselves liars and cheaters, yet they give themselves a pass on those abominations. They don't ban themselves from leadership positions the way many churches exclude homosexuals. Why is one so-called abomination more severe than another?

The biblical list of what is now referred to as abominations was not weighted. It does not say one is better or worse than the other. Also consider that we cannot choose to be homosexual or heterosexual, but we can choose whether to tell the truth, shave a beard, or wear clothing made of mixed materials. We can choose whether to swindle someone out of their money. Yet many Christians are willing to ignore many or all of the "abominations" they commit while pushing homosexuality to the front of the line. This practice seems more a reflection of human double standards than of God's laws.

Those who believe homosexuality is an "abomination" while ignoring all the other "abominations" have decided to take God's words into their own hands. Why have we made a distinction that God did not make? It could be that we want to give ourselves a pass for the things we choose to do so we don't have to think of ourselves as abominable. It allows us to find comfort in pointing the finger at another person while pacifying ourselves that our actions are acceptable. It's easier to convince ourselves we're not so bad if we can point to someone else and say, "Look at what they're doing. At least I'm not doing that! I'm not 'that' bad." It seems that sexuality is an easy target because we are uncomfortable with sex, and we don't understand sexuality. That makes it easier to turn homosexuality into this thing that is taboo instead of recognizing it as natural.

What does the Deuteronomy clobber passage say about homosexuality?

Deuteronomy does not mention homosexuality. Deuteronomy 23:17–19 is about pagan ritual sex and prostitution, not about homosexuality. The general teaching is that no one should pay for a ritual prostitute or lend anyone money for a ritual prostitute. Ritual prostitution, be it by male or female, heterosexual or homosexual, was considered *to'avat*, not pleasing to God.

The Orthodox Jewish Bible (OJB) says there shall be no *kedeshah*, or *kadesh*, "involved in ritualized sexual activity associated with temple worship."[347] According to Dr. Hacham Isaac Sassoon, PhD, "Deut 23:18 does reference a professional *kadesh* who, whether attached to a shrine or not, offered his services to men. The parallel to *kedeshah*, which involves heterosexual intercourse, implies that the problem is not the kind of sex but the circumstances, whether because the act is (problematically) religious, commercial, or promiscuous. Hence it may be inferred that homosexuality *per se* is not one of Deuteronomy's concerns."[348] Dr. Sassoon insists that "the focus seems to be idolatry, sacrilege, and fraud."

Do the Old Testament scriptures address gender identity or intersex people?

It doesn't appear that Old Testament scriptures directly address gender identity or intersex people. Some people, however, point to the mention of eunuchs as an example of God's approval of transgender, genderqueer, and intersex people.

A eunuch is a male born without testes or external genitals, or a male whose testes have been removed (castrated) by force or by choice. The Bible refers to people who were born eunuchs, chose to be eunuchs, or were forced to be eunuchs. According to Isaiah 56: 3–5, God expressed approval of eunuchs: "For thus says the LORD, 'To the eunuchs who keep My Sabbaths, And choose what pleases Me, And hold fast My covenant, To them I will give in My house and within My walls a memorial, And a name better than that of sons and daughters; I will give them an everlasting name which will not be cut off.'"

A eunuch who is born without testes and/or without external genitals matches the description of some intersex children, therefore it is believed that some eunuchs mentioned in the Bible may have actually been intersex. Recall that in some intersex cases, a missing Y chromosome results in a lack of testes and/or external genitalia. Eunuchs are often viewed and portrayed as lacking virility because the testes impact a man's sex drive, ability to achieve an erection, and ability to produce sperm.

There are other reasons for the comparison. Males without testes do not produce testosterone, the hormone that promotes male physical development. Therefore, a eunuch born without testes, or for whom the testes were removed at a young age, would likely have a smaller body frame, softer facial features, no facial hair, and perhaps a more feminine voice.

Sabrina pointed out what a eunuch born without testicles might look like physically.

> *What is a man who is born without testicles, or in other words, without testosterone, going to be like? He's going to be very effeminate; the voice is not going to change at puberty. At puberty, all these masculine characteristics aren't going to happen because the testosterone is not there to do that.*
>
> –Sabrina

That means their gender would likely appear to be ambiguous, or even feminine, as is the case with some intersex people, and some who identify as genderqueer. Recognizing this has given fuel to the belief that the Bible's position on eunuchs also refers to genderqueer individuals.

Lastly, the Bible speaks of eunuchs who chose to legally change their gender, which some believe is akin to a transgender person who transitions.

New Testament

While the Old Testament was written by the Jews and for the Jews, the New Testament was written by followers of Jesus Christ, which included Jews, Christians, and people of other religions. Because the New Testament also includes laws and rules issued by Jesus, I was eager to see what Jesus said.

What did Jesus say about homosexuality?

Not a single, mumbling word. Jesus issued at least 50, and as many as 147 statements or commandments, including "Judge not, lest ye be judged,"

Matthew 7:1–2 (KJV); "So in everything, do to others what you would have them do to you," Matthew 7:12, (NIV); and, "Beware of false prophets," Matthew 7:15.[349, 350]

If Jesus disapproved of homosexuality, then surely it would be mentioned in one of His commandments? It was not. Contrary to what some religious leaders preach, Jesus never said homosexuals should be stoned or that homosexuality is wrong or that homosexuality is an abomination or a sin. In fact, it appears that Jesus never talked about homosexuality or any other sexuality.

Those using Jesus's name to preach against LGBTQIAP individuals have been putting words in Jesus's mouth. They have been behaving as the false prophets Jesus warned about. People like "Pastor" James David Manning, who claimed Jesus called for us to "stone homos,"[351] are lying on Jesus. When it came to throwing stones, the Bible quotes Jesus as saying, "He that is without sin among you, let him first cast a stone at her," John 7:53 (KJV).

Why do Christians say homosexuality is a sin?

This feels like an important question that Christians should want to address. If Jesus Christ is the center of your religion, and He never condemned homosexuality, then why would you condemn homosexuality? If you strive to be like Jesus, and He never hated, castigated, or discriminated against homosexuals, then why should you?

Some anti-gay Christians point to the words of Paul to justify their beliefs. Specifically, they turn to translated versions of 1 Corinthians 6:9–10, 1 Timothy 1:9–10, and Romans 1:26–27, which are believed to have been authored by Paul. These epistles list activities that are supposed to be unrighteous or unworthy of God's kingdom. Paul's list included things like idolatry, infidelity, premarital sex, and prostitution. He also includes thieves, murderers, and people who get drunk.

Some modern versions of these scriptures have added homosexuals to the list, although the original text did not. They have incorrectly connected homosexual to the words *pornoi*, *arsenokoitai*, and *andrapodostai*, which appear in the original writings. Linguist Dale Martin concludes that *arsenokaoitai* referred to "some kind of economic exploitation, probably by sexual means: rape or sex by economic coercion, prostitution, pimping, or something of the sort."[352] Biblical scholar John Boswell says the sin listed in Paul's writings refers to prostitution, not homosexuality. He also says it refers "rather specifically to the male prostitute, who could serve heterosexual or homosexual clients."[353] Pastor John Shore, author of *UNFAIR: Christians and the LGBT Question,* says Paul "wrote about promiscuous, predatory, non-consensual same-sex acts between people whom he understood to be heterosexual."[354] Shore does not believe Paul could have been writing about homosexual relationships and marriages. "We can be confident that Paul was not writing to, or about, gay people, because he simply could not have been, any more than he could have written about smartphones, iPads, or televisions," he writes.

But what if these scholars are wrong, and Paul really was railing against same-sex relationships instead of male prostitution and rape? The question still remains: Should Christians place Paul's word above Jesus's? If Jesus's Word is the ultimate word for Christians, and Jesus did not condemn anyone's sexuality, then it would follow that Christians would not condemn anyone's sexuality. And if Jesus never spoke against homosexuality, why would Paul go off-script? Lastly, if Paul did stray from Jesus's teachings, why would Christians give Paul's words more credence than the words of Jesus Christ?

Did Jesus say marriage should only be between a man and a woman?

No. Contrary to what some people teach and believe, there is no biblical record of Jesus teaching that marriage should only occur between men and women, or that marriage should be between one man and one woman. We often hear legislators, clergy, and others opine, "I believe that marriage should be between a man and woman." Let's consider that when someone tells you what they believe, they are telling you what they believe but not necessarily what is just, true, and accurate. That seems to be the case here. These personal beliefs do not align with Jesus's teachings.

This teaching that Jesus condemned same-sex marriage stems from Mark 10:6–9 (ESV). A closer look at this scripture reveals that Jesus is answering the specific question of whether it is lawful for a man to divorce his wife. The question being asked has nothing to do with homosexuality, nor is Jesus's response about homosexuality. Jesus says, "But at the beginning of creation, God 'made them male and female. For this reason, a man will leave his father and mother and be united to his wife, and the two will become one flesh.' So, they are no longer two but one flesh. Therefore, what God has joined together, let no one separate." In answering whether a man and his wife can divorce, Jesus tells the Pharisees that a man and his wife become one in marriage, and that no human being should separate a union God has created.

The Pharisees question was not about same-sex marriage, and since there are no stories in the Bible about same-sex marriage, it doesn't seem likely Jesus would have had occasion to discuss same-sex marriage. Nowhere in this scripture does Jesus say only men and women should marry, and those who teach this are twisting Jesus's words to say what they believe rather than what Jesus taught.

The conclusion is that use of this scripture or any other part of the Bible to insist marriage is between one man and one woman is unfounded. Marriage between one man and one woman is not a rule of the Old or New Testaments. Let us remember that it was acceptable and common for men to have more than one wife. The Old and New Testaments include many instances of men having multiple wives. Many of the prominent men of the Bible practiced polygamy and had concubines or sex slaves. According to 1 Kings 11, Solomon, reputed to be the wisest man who ever lived, had 700 wives and 300 concubines! It was also acceptable for single men to have concubines or sex slaves.

According to the Bible, marriage between one man and one woman is not a rule from God or Jesus.

What did Jesus say about transgender people and gender identity?

There are no statements in the New Testament that specifically refer to transgender people or gender identity. Jesus did, however, speak of eunuchs, which as stated earlier, bear some resemblance to those who are transgender, genderqueer, and intersex, in some instances.

In Matthew 19:11–12 (ESV), Jesus says, "For there are eunuchs who have been so from birth, and there are eunuchs who have been made eunuchs by men, and there are eunuchs who have made themselves eunuchs for the sake of the kingdom of heaven." There is no record of

Jesus condemning any of these eunuchs, regardless of how they came to be that way. Some argue that this scripture sets the example of how Jesus would view intersex, transgender, and genderqueer individuals today, and that Christians who strive to be Christ-like should also accept them as Jesus did.

> *Jesus talks about three different types of what He calls "eunuchs." Jesus doesn't condemn any of those three. He doesn't differentiate between intersex and trans, the ones who are that way from their mother's womb, and those who become that way later.*
>
> –Simon

Sabrina, a former ordained Southern Baptist minister, explained further.

> *If Jesus says people are going to be born this way, then that means things are going to happen "wrong" in the womb. So, what makes us think that what's happened to me can't happen in the womb? I think it can. Our problem is the church thinks that anything that's sexual is evil and so off-limits that we won't even acknowledge it, we won't consider it, but we know it happens.*
>
> –Sabrina

Jesus acknowledges differences in the way people are born, and He accepts it.

Another scripture in the New Testament depicts Phillip's encounter with a eunuch. In Acts 8, Phillip meets an Ethiopian eunuch and teaches him about Jesus. When the eunuch asks if he can be baptized, Phillip replied, "If you believe with all your heart." We should note that Phillip does not offer the baptism so the man would no longer be a eunuch. Nor does Phillip condemn the man for being a eunuch or say God doesn't accept him.

> *Phillip baptizes the Ethiopian eunuch. He doesn't say, "You're bad for being a eunuch." He doesn't require anything of the eunuch, other than faith in Christ. He doesn't heal the eunuch, even though earlier in the chapter, he has performed a bunch of*

miracles. What we know, because of what Romans says, is that the eunuch's condition was for his good and God's glory, because he's a believer, and believers have that promise. If you look at even the Old Testament, God has made special promises to eunuchs who are faithful. He says that he'll give them a heritage better than sons and daughters. So, if you look at all that combined, God's fairly positive about physical sexual differences and about those who change their legal gender status.

–Simon

This discussion of eunuchs, many of whom were effeminate, androgynous men, also brings to mind the ways Jesus is depicted. He is often shown with delicate, even feminine features—long hair, kind eyes, rosy cheeks, smooth features, and demure expression. Rarely is Jesus shown as a rugged, virile, masculine, "manly" man.

Mary McClintock Fulkerson, a theology teacher at Duke Divinity School, notes that there have been Christian movements to masculinize Jesus, like "Muscular Christianity," associating muscles and strength with masculinity. Fulkerson also mentions a movement to view Jesus as a "Tender Warrior," with warrior also being a masculine trait. This tinkering with Jesus to dial up his masculinity appears to be evidence of our need for men to look and act a certain way. Fulkerson suggests that "if Jesus doesn't fit our notion of what a man should be, we would be better off broadening our understanding of gender roles."[355] If we can't accept Jesus's femininity, it's no wonder we're hard-pressed to accept any man's femininity. Yet many images depict Jesus as a non-masculine being.

The effeminate imagery of Jesus does not fit the masculine gender traits many people cling to and use as a measuring stick for manhood. Why do we accept this in Jesus but not in our fellow humans? When a man who looks and behaves the way Jesus is depicted walks among us today, that man is likely to be ridiculed as being effeminate or gay. There are also Christian songs that romanticize Jesus as the ideal mate, yet when many Christian women meet a man who looks the way Jesus is portrayed, those women are more likely to shun that man for being "soft." If it was good enough for Jesus, then why do we demean people who resemble Him?

Does the book of Revelations say gay people are going to hell?

No. The OJB says those without faith or those who are cowardly, murderers, fornicators, sorcerers, idolaters, or liars will burn in fire. There is no mention of homosexuals. The KJV provides a similar list that also fails to mention sexuality or gender identity. The KJV and other versions do mention the "abominable," however, as discussed earlier, this was not a word used in the original text, and it is a mistake to equate "abominable" with homosexual.

Old & New Testament Summary

I recognize that it's impossible for any of us to be 100 percent sure of what God wants. As Dr. E. Dewey Smith writes, "Religion and Biblical interpretation will always be laden with challenges because it involves humanity's attempt to understand the mind and methods of the Divine."[356] We can't know for sure. It is possible that God is hate, but it's not likely. It's possible that God hates His children, but it's not likely. I cannot be 100 percent sure that God never addressed homosexuality in the Bible, even though biblical historians, scholars, and linguists can find no evidence. On the flipside, I ask, "How can you say with 100 percent certainty that the Bible says homosexuality is a sin, even after learning that biblical historians, scholars, and linguists say no such text exists?"

According to many biblical scholars, nothing in the Bible condemns sexuality or gender identity. On the few occasions when the Old Testament mentions men having sex with men, it is in reference to rape, pederasty, pagan sex rituals, or ritual prostitution, which are not synonymous with homosexuality. There is no mention of homosexual relationships, love, or marriage. Biblical scholar Gomes concludes that the only exposure biblical writers had to same-sex interactions was "prostitution, pederasty, lasciviousness, and exploitation." He asserts that defining "contemporary homosexuals only in these terms is a cultural slander of the highest order."[357]

It has also been proven that the original biblical text has been replaced with words that have completely different meanings. For various reasons, words that meant "prostitute," "rape," "sexual religious ritual," and "pederasty" have been replaced with the term "homosexual." Jack Rogers, author of *Jesus, the Bible, and Homosexuality*, says that "the Bible has been used inappropriately to oppress people who are homosexual," and that the Bible passages used to condemn homosexuality "are pulled out of their biblical context to justify that oppression."[358] He also writes, "Most Christians have been told at one time or another that the Bible condemns all homosexual relationships. That view is simply incorrect." Dr. Donald W. Haynes, author of *On the Threshold of Grace—Methodist Fundamentals*, writes, "Holy Scripture never refers to homosexuality in the context of a loving relationship between two consenting adults whose sexual orientation might be naturally homosexual, and who have a committed, monogamous relationship or marriage. Is our condemnation of such relationships on the basis of rather scant scriptural references somewhat like the justification of slavery until the nineteenth century? Is it like the subordination of women until the 1960s and, in some instances, still today?"[359]

Distorting biblical texts to justify condemning a group of people does not serve God; it only serves the agenda of those who want to oppress others. The findings point to God's Word having been misunderstood at best, and more likely, deliberately co-opted at worse. According to Dr. Haynes, "Many of our convictions about homosexuality are rooted in our own culture more than in the overarching biblical message."[360] Rev. Dr. Otis Moss III wrote, "For the clergy to hide from true dialogue with quick dismissive claims devised from poor biblical scholarship is as sinful as unthoughtful acceptance of a theological position. When we make biblical claims without sound interpretation, we run the risk of adopting a doctrinal position of deep conviction but devoid of love."[361]

It would appear that both God's and Jesus's words have been hijacked and re-purposed to satisfy personal biases and fears. Thus, those who truly want to adhere to biblical teachings are duty-bound to reevaluate their understanding of the Bible with regard to sexuality and gender identity.

Additionally, I encourage those who believe in the Bible to review 1 John 4:19 -21, "We ourselves love now because he loved us first.[20] If anyone says, "I love God" and hates his brother, he is a liar. For if a person does not love his brother, whom he has seen, then he cannot love God, whom he has not seen.[21] Yes, this is the command we have from him: whoever loves God must love his brother too," (Complete Jewish Bible (CJB)).

Religious Communities

I also wanted to explore how religious leaders, churches, and religious communities are addressing sexuality and gender identity. The response is diverse. There are religious faiths and leaders who embrace God's message of love and who believe we are all God's creation. For example, Presbyterians, Universalist Unitarians, and Reform Jews recognize the natural human diversity of sexuality and gender identity. The Reform Jews say they are "committed to the full participation of gays and lesbians in synagogue life as well as society at large."[362] In 2009, a pastor appearing on Oprah's Soul Series on Oprah & Friends Radio told a call-in viewer that "being gay is a gift from God."[363]

Reverend Teague, who grew up in a church that made it clear they didn't approve of homosexuality, is now an ordained minister in the Unitarian Universalist church, which accepts gay clergy and members.

> It's not an issue for me religiously to be an out gay man because I'm affirmed as who I am in my religion. The Quakers, that's where we were married, under the care of the Friends, were also wrestling with this in the sixties and seventies. The fact that David wanted to bring me, his partner, to his religious community and say, "We want to affirm our relationship," was not a new thing. It wasn't an odd thing; it was something they already had been doing for a long time. Unitarian Universalism affirms human rights and how we treat each other. We had outwardly gay ordained clergy in 1968.
>
> –Rev. Teague

In this aspect, the Unitarian Universalists seem to practice what they preach. The denomination professes to have "a deep regard for intellectual freedom and inclusive love." Their seven guiding principles include "affirming and promoting the inherent worth and dignity of every person"; "justice, equity, and compassion in human relations"; and "a free and responsible search for truth and meaning." According to Rev. Teague, Unitarian congregations live up to these principles by fully accepting people who are not cisgender heterosexuals.

Karla and her wife are members of a United Church of Christ (UCC) in Atlanta and have had a positive experience with their church.

> *We go to a UCC church, and the message is about love. The Bible is a book of stories and parables, it's about lessons learned. It's about following your moral compass and doing what's right and helping other people. It's about action; it's about giving; it's about what you're doing in your community to give back and help other people.*
>
> –Karla

As we have seen, there are also religious leaders of various faiths who believe God does not approve of anyone who is not heterosexual and cisgender. There are Christian leaders who follow the modern translations of the Bible that incorrectly say God does not approve of anyone who is not heterosexual and cisgender. Some denominations have gone to the extremes of formalizing doctrines that state they will not accept homosexuality, transgender identity, etc. These religions seem designed to disconnect people from their faith and each other. Sabrina, an ordained Southern Baptist minister, commented on the "Southern Baptist Resolution on Transgender Identity," which prompted her to leave the church.

> *The Southern Baptist Convention did a resolution in 2014 on transgender identity, so I knew exactly what the stance would be, and it was not favorable. I was concerned about everything else I would be facing personally, and I didn't think I was going to change the Southern Baptist Convention. I decided to leave my position as an ordained minister.*
>
> –Sabrina

As stated earlier, some religious leaders refer to homosexuals using derogatory terms and proclaim that God hates people because of their sexuality. I can't help but wonder how they reconcile this with the scripture that reads, "Those who say, 'I love God' and hate their brothers or sisters are liars," I John 4:16b–21.

The God of the Christian Bible says anyone who does not love does not know God. Jesus says loving God and loving one's neighbors are the two most fundamental laws of Christianity. Don't Christian leaders then have the duty and obligation to teach this, model this, and encourage this behavior? As Dr. Smith, senior pastor of a church in Atlanta, GA, writes, "When theology fails to unite us, affirmation of each other's humanity and intrinsic value should be the underlying resolve and resounding declaration. The goal can't be merely about determining who is 'right' but, instead, living by a mandate to treat each other righteously."[364] Preaching hatred and exiling people from church is not a loving way to treat Christians who identify as LGBTQIAP and leaves many feeling hurt, confused, and dejected.

> *It's really disconcerting to have a religion that you've used to guide you through your life be used against you as a weapon. Churches are recognizing that LGBT people are people too. They're God's children too.*
>
> –Roemerman

Shouldn't faith communities be places of love and healing rather than discord and divisiveness, places where members exhibit love rather than hate? It seems that if religions and the religious were focused on love, they would accept all of God's children and let their personal biases fall by the wayside. It seems that if those who rely on the Old and New Testaments spent time delving into the true meaning of the scriptures, they would find no justification for categorizing any sexuality, sex, gender, or gender identity as sin. If all Christians would follow God's and Jesus's directives of love, there would be no room left for hate.

As the Bible advises, "If anyone says, "I love God" and hates his brother, he is a liar. For if a person does not love his brother, whom he has seen, then he cannot love God, whom he has not seen.[21] Yes, this is the command we have from him: whoever loves God must love his brother too." (1 John 4:19 -21 Complete Jewish Bible (CJB))

Should religious leaders advocate for and preach in favor of all sexualities and gender identities?

There are some faith leaders who believe it is their duty to welcome and support all of God's children. The Religious Institute, a multi-faith organization, states, "People of faith and religious leaders must help to create new understandings of sexual and gender diversity and promote justice for LGBTQ people in all areas of religious and public life." In 2017, 300 religious leaders, educators, and activists from all major Christian denominations signed a statement that read, "We affirm that every human being is created in the image and likeness of God and that the great diversity expressed in humanity through our wide spectrum of unique sexualities and gender identities is a perfect reflection of the magnitude of God's creative work." This statement was issued after Rev. Paul Brandeis Raushenbush, senior vice president and editor of *Voices* at Auburn Seminary, called on faith leaders across the US to show solidarity with the LGBTQ community and to denounce an anti-LGBT statement issued by a group of anti-LGBT Evangelicals.

It is encouraging that the number of religious leaders and communities supporting LGBTQIAP people continues to grow. In 2014, Rev. John C. Dorhauer, the general minister and president of the UCC, officiated the first legal same-sex marriage in Arizona. Along with more than one hundred other faith leaders, Rev. Dorhauer signed a letter opposing a proposal that would give religious organizations permission to discriminate in LGBTQ hiring.[365] In 2015, Imam Daayiee Abdullah, a Muslim leader, said, "We do not limit people by their gender or their sexual orientation, or their particular aspect of being Muslim or non-Muslim. They're there to worship."[366] In 2017, 200 American Jewish leaders and institutions urged the Israeli government to end discrimination against same-sex couples who want to adopt children. Signers of the letter were from Hillel International, the Central Conference of American Rabbis, and the Union of Reform Judaism, as well as prominent Jewish LGBT leaders and over sixty US rabbis. While Pope Francis, head of the Catholic church, has said opposite-sex couples were the only ones able to form families, he also reportedly told a young gay man, "God made you like that, and he loves you like that…"[367]

According to Lydia Meredith, the ex-wife of now openly gay pastor Reverend Dennis A. Meredith, "The church needs a new kind of ministry— one steeped in the ministry started by Jesus—free of bias, discrimination, hate, or prejudice."[368] If we believe God is love, and that whoever does not love, does not know God, shouldn't we advocate for loving all of humanity? If we believe we are all children of God, and as such, are all accepted by God, shouldn't we insist that we treat one another accordingly? Christian leaders specifically have the responsibility to emulate Christ, who declared that loving God and loving each other are our primary objectives. Those who believe this are obligated to set the example. Jesus was an activist, going out into the world and acting on what He taught. Likewise, Christian leaders are obliged to be activists on behalf of Jesus's teachings of love.

> *I think their job is to be mindful of, "What is love? What is God? What really is God?" That, to me, is what their responsibility is, to really teach about love.*
>
> –Tiffany

Commissioner Garner said she believes it is important for religious institutions to talk about and demonstrate love for all human beings.

> *My church is a very welcoming congregation. There are a number of congregations in Atlanta, and around the country, that openly accept lesbian and gay people for who they are. I think when we can have an honest conversation about being loving human beings and demonstrate that, then we are much healthier. I think that our religious institutions, as well as other institutions, need to be more thoughtful about that.*
>
> –Commissioner Garner

It is not only our institutions that must be more thoughtful, it is also our communities, our families, and ourselves. Imagine how much better the world would be if we were more mindful about being loving human beings. How many of us can honestly say we practice the love that we preach?

Should we have the "religious freedom" to discriminate?

Let's first consider what religious freedom is and means. Religious freedom does not mean we get to impose our religious beliefs onto other people. In fact, it means the opposite. Religious freedom means that an individual has the right to practice any religion, or no religion, without persecution.

It means no one gets to force their religious beliefs on another person in public spaces such as work environments, public schools, libraries, restaurants, stores, or government buildings. Because we have religious freedom, we can be Catholic, Protestant, Muslim, atheist, etc. without being punished, persecuted, discriminated against, or imprisoned. It means you can participate in activities related to your beliefs, such as going to a place of worship or celebrating holy days.

Because of religious freedom, you can be an Evangelical store owner and hold whatever beliefs make you feel good; however, you do not have the right to impose those beliefs on employees or customers. Nor does anyone have the right to deny service or employment to people with different religious beliefs. It means, for example, that a Catholic person cannot fire a Protestant for not observing Catholic customs or for being Protestant. It means a Protestant can't refuse to sell paper towels to a Jewish customer, and so on and so forth. It also means a government clerk cannot refuse to issue a marriage license to a gay couple. Religious freedom gives a bakery owner the right to be anti-gay, but it does not give them the right to refuse to make a wedding cake for a gay couple. A person who chooses to believe homosexuality is a sin is free to embrace that belief and to practice whatever religion espouses that belief. They are free to not engage in homosexual activities and same-sex marriage. What they are not free to do is restrict the rights of others based on these personally held beliefs. Denying a marriage license to a gay couple is denying them a legal right, and it is the gay couple whose religious freedom is being violated in these situations.

Refusing to provide a service or product to someone because they are a member of a particular group is discrimination. It's discrimination when it happens to women, Jews, blacks, Indians, Muslims, and members of the LGBTQIAP community. Individuals, states, and municipalities across the United States have pushed to create laws that would allow business owners to refuse service to a customer whose sexuality or gender identity opposes their religious beliefs. Those pushing for such laws claim that "religious freedom" gives them the right to discriminate. It does not.

Reverend Teague worked with Georgia Equality in their efforts to prevent Georgia from passing The Religious Freedom Restoration Act (RFRA),[369] which would have given businesses and organizations the right to discriminate based on sexuality or gender identity.

> *The Restoration Act was a smoke screen. It was masking people's presumed right to discriminate against certain groups of people. That was disheartening that there were people in this state who were actually proud of the fact that they were going to discriminate against somebody.*
>
> –Rev. Teague

Professor Wright also shared his thoughts about this recent spin on religious freedom to discriminate against people.

> *As long as your religion is yours, and you're not forcing it on anybody else, that's one thing. But when you start forcing your religion on others through the denial of services, that bothers me. We're a country that's supposed to be founded on this notion of separation of church and state.*
>
> –Professor Wright

Professor Wright's comments raise another important point. In the US, we claim to separate church and state, yet these types of laws rely on the state, the government, to support and enforce one religious belief over another. At the end of the day, discrimination and freedom cannot coexist; one cancels out the other. Where there is freedom, discrimination cannot exist. Where there is discrimination, freedom does not exist.

Where does the saying "God doesn't make mistakes" fit in?

This is another area where two different meanings are applied to one statement. When I hear that phrase, it means that all the human variety that exists on this planet was created by God, and since God is the ultimate, all-powerful being, all of His creations have God's stamp of approval. It means that even though humans may view some of God's creations as flawed, God does not. If God doesn't make mistakes, then each of us exists the way God intended. God did not make a mistake in creating me heterosexual, Fredis homosexual, Vicki bisexual, Simon intersex, etc. God created each person as they should be.

While that makes sense to me, religious anti-LGBTQIAP folks would disagree. They say God intended everyone to be cisgender and heterosexual, and anyone who isn't has altered God's plan. Let's recall what God and Jesus said about eunuchs. According to Christian and Jewish bibles, some people are born that way. If God is the creator of life, then doesn't that mean God created them that way? So, God created eunuchs. If you say eunuchs are imperfect, then you must acknowledge that, in fact, no human being is perfect. When and why do we decide one attribute is a mistake or flaw, while another condition is a blessing?

If we look around at all of humanity, we see people with different bodies, ailments, abilities, disabilities, physiological traits, etc. There are little people, albinos, geniuses, super athletes, child prodigies, etc. There are asexual, heterosexual, homosexual, and bisexual people. Amid all these varieties and expressions of life, it seems ridiculous to think, let alone insist, that God intended for us all to be cisgender and heterosexual.

In responding to a Facebook post, a thirty-eight-year-old transgender woman named Serra wrote, "Okay, if God does not make mistakes, that means he made us transgender intentionally. Now I have to ask, 'Who the hell are you to question God's intentions?'" Sabrina shared a similar opinion.

> When something looks different or doesn't fall into the norm, it is presumptuous to say God messed up. When a person is born with one blue eye and one green, did God make a mistake? If someone has an above-average IQ, did God make a mistake? Why then is it a mistake when a person is born to love someone of the same sex? Some people say it's not God who made the mistake, it's the person's choice to be attracted to or love someone of the same sex. Then I would ask, "How successful have you been in controlling who you're attracted to and who you fall in love with?"
> –Sabrina

Tiffany agreed.

> "God made us" is always my answer. God made us, and God made us as we are.
> –Tiffany

Why do humans think they know which human conditions are God's will and which are not? Would we not be better served to acknowledge that God does not make mistakes, but humans do? Perhaps the most egregious mistake a human being can make is to pretend to be something other than what God created. To deny who they are, to live as someone they are not, that would be a mistake, and that, to me, is the equivalent of denying God.

We should also reconsider our arbitrary assignment of certain human conditions as good and bad, natural and unnatural, normal and not normal. There are certain human conditions that some societies choose to revere and hold up to the light as trophies, celebrating their rarity. For example, why are blond hair and blue eyes prized in some cultures, even when they are not the norm, or perhaps *because* they are not the norm? In some cultures, having bowed legs is considered an attractive trait, while others would consider it a defect. The same is true for sexuality and gender identity. In some cultures, other sexualities and gender identities are revered because they are different, and that difference is associated with a special connection to the Creator. Yet in other cultures, a person's sexuality is condemned if it is not the norm. Similarly, Sabrina sees hypocrisy in approving of certain surgeries that change a person's condition while disapproving of others.

> *They'll have a prayer meeting praising that God has given man the ability to do a transplant and that this miracle took place. But if I walked in there and said, "I want to praise God because He's given man the ability to give me a sexual reassignment surgery, and I can be happy." Then, all of the sudden, I'm playing God. It's just so selective.*
>
> –Sabrina

This parsing of labels for good, desirable, evil, unacceptable, etc. seems arbitrary and very unfair.

Conclusion

Janelle Monae offers what appears to be sound advice: "If your religion is causing you to spew out words of hate, [to] judge, or look down on others because of who one loves then you need to change it… If the religion don't make you a more loving or better person, ditch it."[370]

What is the harm in treating our fellow humans with love and respect? Most religions speak to love—of a god, of self, and of our fellow humans. As spiritualist Eckhart Toley explained, "Loving your neighbor as yourself is recognizing your neighbor in yourself or yourself in your neighbor." Let us love one another.

Christians might also keep in mind what Anderson offered.

> *There are tons of trans Christians who would love to be seen in their whole dignity and worth as children of God.*
>
> –Anderson

CHAPTER FOURTEEN

GUIDANCE FOR LOVED ONES

"It's hard to carry on, when no one loves you."
–Tupac[371]

Intro

When a person we love comes out, one temptation might be to make it primarily, or all, about us. Instead of focusing on the other person, our attention might turn inward. There can be a tendency to get caught up in our stuff—our shock, our fears, our pain, our difficulties, our dreams. Some people wonder, *Why is this happening to* me? *Oh Lord, what will I tell the usher board? Will I ever walk my child down the aisle? Will I ever have grandchildren?* We might even say to our loved ones, "I can't believe you're doing this to *me*," or "You're ruining my life," or "I can't support you in this." These kinds of responses have everything to do with our egos and absolutely nothing to do with giving our loved ones what they need most from us: love and support.

> *Start with love and end up with support. First and foremost, they're your kid, and you love and support your kids and want them to be successful. Just be supportive, because if you don't provide a learning and loving and safe environment, they're*

going to seek it elsewhere, which could be dangerous. Or they're going to ask the wrong people for advice; or God forbid, they shut down and want to hurt themselves or feel like they're a disappointment to the parent.

–Karla

One mother, whose son came out to her in a phone conversation, said she had been tempted to ride the train of her own feelings but quickly realized it wasn't about her.

A few weeks before his twenty-fifth birthday, my son called and told me he was gay. I wanted to ask, "How long have you known?" "Why didn't you tell me before?" "Do you have a boyfriend?" But the first thing I wanted to know was, "Are you happy?" He said, "Yes, Mom. I am happy." For me, that's what is most important; that's what I want for my child.

–Stephanie, retired nurse, widowed,
cisgender, heterosexual, 65 years old

Doctors and researchers have found that when adults and children lack the support of loved ones, it can increase feelings of isolation, low self-esteem, devastation, fear, depression, and a diminished will to live. In other words, your loved one may not survive without evidence of genuine emotional love and support from you.

It has been shown that people who feel supported and loved by others feel better about themselves and fare better during difficult times. People with support tend to handle personal crises better than those who have been rejected by loved ones. People with a good support network tend to be emotionally better off than those without one. People with support also tend to have stronger platonic and romantic relationships.

The benefits of a strong support network apply to all humans, regardless of biological sex, gender identity, or sexual orientation, but those things become crucial for a person who has come out as lesbian, gay, bi, trans, queer, intersex, asexual, or pansexual. This is because LGBTQIAP individuals are far more likely than cisgender heterosexuals to face daily opposition and rejection from the outside world. A safe haven and a support system make all the difference in a person's ability to face these challenges and emerge with their physical, mental, and emotional beings intact.

Love and support are especially critical for LGBTQIAP children. Dr. William Pollack, a specialist in childhood development, insists that immediately upon learning of a child's feelings or identity, it is critically important to let them know they are "still loved through and through, that [their] sexual orientation will not in any way diminish how much [they are] admired and respected."[372] Pollack, author of *Real Boys: Rescuing Our Sons from the Myths of Boyhood*, says this affirmation of love, admiration, and respect is what that child needs to hear most. He warns that "to refrain from saying [these things] is to risk placing a [child] in serious emotional—even physical—jeopardy. And to risk losing him, in one way or another." I would go a step further to say that this is what we all need to hear, regardless of age, sex, gender identity, or sexuality. Children and adults need and want to hear that they are loved for who they are, as they are. If we as adults need to hear and feel loved and supported, then it shouldn't be difficult to understand how crushing it is for a child to have their parents, guardians, or siblings withhold these things because of the child's sexuality or gender identity.

TransUp Pulse Project found that 70 percent of transgender youth "with parents strongly supportive of their gender identity and expression reported positive mental health."[373] That percentage dropped "to a staggeringly low 15 percent when parents were not strongly supportive." They also found that trans youth whose parents were strongly supportive of their gender identity and expression "were 72 percent more likely to report being satisfied with their lives than those without supportive parents." Anyone inclined to minimize this notion of feeling "satisfied with their lives" should consider the implications of a young LGBTQIAP person who feels dissatisfied with their lives because they lack family support. For those young people, the dissatisfaction resulting from lack of love and support can intensify confusion, depression, loneliness, and loss of hope.

> *We looked at some data that showed if the kids had one supportive adult in their life, their mental health was a lot better, even if they had really lousy relationships with their family. It's kind of like a lifeline.*
>
> –Professor Wright

There is also the shock of being rejected by her family.

> *You think a parent's love is supposed to be unconditional. And then you find out there's all these conditions.*

–Laura, laser technician, divorced,
  cisgender, bisexual, 40 years old

Although Laura said she had never contemplated suicide, she has experienced sadness, depression, and isolation over realizing her parents' love was, in fact, conditional. Rather than accepting and loving her for who she is, they rejected her because of who she is. Fortunately, Laura survived to reach adulthood and is better equipped to handle her family's lack of support. Many children and teens are not as fortunate.

Throughout our lives, many of us have needed and received a lifeline— that someone who shows up at our lowest moment and provides a refuge or salvation from a difficult situation. For many of us, the first place we turn to for that lifeline is parents, family, and loved ones.

Raman believes support and love made the difference for her transgender son, who was depressed and exhibited suicidal tendencies.

> *One of the things I know made life easier for my trans son is having a very supportive, understanding group of siblings around him. He had a brother and two older sisters who went through their own battle of seeing their sister turn into their brother, but they loved him so much, and they knew that he was so unhappy that they were willing to do whatever it took to make him happy and to give him a quality of life that they had. They rallied around him and they supported him and they lifted him up. They helped him buy clothes and helped him do his hair and helped him try to become the man that he is. They did everything they could possibly do. I think having a supportive family around you is something that's unmatched, and whether it be a natal family or a family that's blended or a family of your choosing, whatever you call family, that's what you need, and you need to hang onto them real tight.*

–Raman

Youth whose families reject them are forced to seek that love and support from others.

> I worked with an organization called IYG. They created a couple of drop-in homes where kids could go and live with supervision if they got thrown out of their houses. That worked for a while, but what was instrumental is they really needed to have adults in their life who were accepting of who they are as individuals. I think we often forget that youths need us. I think sometimes we sort of throw them out into the world, and we don't give them enough support. There are people who are self-identified gay Moms and gay Dads, and they'll take homeless kids in. The kids manage to survive because they've got these people who are willing to be parental figures in their life.
>
> –Professor Wright

When a child is kicked out of their family home, they may wind up in the foster care system. Unfortunately, the foster parents may only perpetuate the rejection.

> Our leader, who was a vocal supporter of LGBT youth, said that there are a disproportionate number of gay kids in the system because their families don't want them. And then foster families don't always treat them right either.
>
> –Clarice, foster parent, married,
>   cisgender, heterosexual, 40 years old

At no point does any of us stop needing and wanting our parents' and family's love. If the people who created you aren't on your side, life becomes infinitely more difficult.

An article from *Atlanta PFLAG* titled "Our Daughters and Sons: Questions and Answers for Parents of Gay, Lesbian, Bisexual People" advises, "The fact that your son or daughter told you is a sign of his or her love and need for your support and understanding... and shows a very strong desire for an open, honest relationship with you."[374] Many children, even adult children, want parental approval, love, and support. We all want to be accepted as who we are, especially by the people we love

What are the commonalities between straight and LGBT youth/young adults?

Many people tend to focus on differences and try to use those differences to make loved ones feel bad about who they are. One key to supporting your loved one is to recognize the similarities we all share.

> *There's really very little difference. They all want a family of some sort. They want to have opportunities to experience the world in a pleasurable way. One other thing that's kind of been striking to me about this particular generation is they all seem to be really striving for a sense of fairness that I don't remember seeing very much of. Some demographers suggest that they're really motivated by social justice. That's a core issue. Also, right now, they show interest in, "When am I going to get a job?" and "When am I going to be able to make ends meet?" They want a sense of security, I think, whether it's income, social support, or having somebody who loves them, whether biological family or maybe chosen.*

–Professor Wright

These sound like the types of things we all desire or are concerned with. I can't help but return to the premise of shared humanity. We are all humans and, as humans, we all have the same basic needs: love, connection, contact, acceptance, fulfillment. That doesn't change because of sexuality or gender identity.

Why won't my loved one come out to me?

As mentioned in an earlier chapter, it is estimated that only 56 percent of LGBT respondents say they have told their mother about their sexual orientation or gender identity, and only 39 percent have told their father.[375] There are a number of reasons your child, sibling, spouse, parent, etc. hasn't come out to you. It could be they are trying to figure it out for themselves before announcing it to you or anyone else. It could also be they are worried about how it would affect their relationship with you. The second-most common response given by LGBT adults in explaining why they did not tell their mother or father is that they assumed their parent would not be accepting or understanding.[376] Fear is a major concern on both sides of the table. They might be afraid you won't approve of them or that you won't love them as much after they come out to you. Fear of disapproval and fear of being rejected are primary reasons people are hesitant to share their identity, even with those closest to them.

Your loved one might be reluctant to tell you because they don't want to make you uncomfortable. That doesn't seem fair to me. Why should someone not be who they are or hide who they are just because it makes others feel uncomfortable? Shouldn't the people we love be able to trust that our love for them has no bounds and that we want them to be open and honest with us? A 52-year-old trans man named Preston says, "I never thought that I would actually transition while my parents were alive. I thought, 'Well, it's gonna break their hearts.' That was what I was putting on myself."[377]

Another reason some people don't come out to family and friends is because they think you should know without them having to say it. This isn't fair. No matter how much we know someone or love someone, we cannot read minds. The only way we can truly know is if they tell us.

Some parents beat themselves up, thinking, "I should have known." This seems like a lot of pressure for a parent to put on themselves, particularly with such a personal issue. We can't ever really know unless a person shares this information with us. Until that happens, many parents make assumptions about what is happening.

"In the experience of our group, most parents of gay teenagers have no idea that their children are gay," according to The Presbyterian Church of Mt. Kisco.[378] The typical parent-child dynamic is not very conducive to divulging such personal information once a child becomes a teen or adult. How much of your sex life did you reveal to your parents as a young adult? As a cisgender heterosexual, I tried to hide as much as possible from my parents, and I was operating within society's expected norms. Most kids don't want their parents to know anything about their sex lives, which can be compounded by the societal stigma of being different from what is considered the norm and the frequent messages that being different is somehow wrong. This can create an environment where a child, teen, young adult, or full-grown adult will put a lot of energy into hiding whom they are for as long as they can. A male acquaintance said his forty-five-year-old boyfriend still hadn't come out to his family.

If my child is wearing weird clothes, does that mean they're gay, queer, or something else?

A person's apparel is not a reliable indicator of sexuality or gender identity. Clothes don't make a person gay any more than they make someone straight. This can be difficult for us to process because we have been socialized to believe that men wear certain types of clothes and accessories and women wear a different set of clothing and accessories. While women have much greater leeway with these rules—being able to wear "boy" jeans, slacks, ties, and jackets—there are still some clear gender and sexual orientation expectations.

When a woman makes a habit of wearing traditionally masculine apparel, especially without feminizing it with jewelry, makeup, or high heels, the public's assumption is that she is a lesbian. When it comes to boys and men, the expectations are much stricter. A few years ago, a male friend wore a kilt to a party. He wasn't Scottish nor was he dressing up for Halloween. This simple apparel choice placed his sexuality in question for many of the people at the party, even though he never seemed to have a problem attracting female dates or girlfriends. Some party-goers were saying, "I knew he was gay," when in fact, the only thing they really knew for sure was that he decided to wear a kilt that day.

For generations, young people have dressed in ways older folks don't understand or approve of. It is not unusual for parents to disapprove of or question the way their children dress. If your child's attire concerns or troubles you, perhaps you should consider why. Is it simply that you don't like the way they look, or is it something else? Are you worried about what the neighbors will think? If their apparel isn't unsanitary, obscene, or dangerous, then what is the harm? If the attire won't lead to them getting arrested or kicked out of school, then perhaps you shouldn't make a big deal about it. If your concern is about their sexuality or gender identity and not the clothes, then find a way to talk about those things instead of making assumptions.

Should I ask my loved one about their sexuality or gender identity?

No one can answer that question for you. While deciding what to do, consider factors such as your relationship, the trust level between you and your loved one, your motivation for wanting to ask, and what you plan to do with the information.

In deciding whether to question a loved one, it might also be helpful to consider the danger of assuming you know what that person's sexuality or gender identity is. PFLAG cautions that assuming a straight child is gay "can be equally harmful as not accepting a gay child."[379] Instead of asking a child explicitly if they are gay, PFLAG advises parents, "If you've created an open dialogue with your child and you feel safe doing so, you can ask them how they feel about other sexualities and if they think they might be something other than heterosexual."

When broaching these personal and delicate matters, it might be helpful to keep in mind that asking the right questions is important. The value of questions is that they can open the dialogue and create a greater opportunity for learning and understanding. The question asked, and the way it's asked, can influence the type of response you receive. For instance, if the underlying intent is to make a judgment about someone, then that intent will likely be revealed by the question and by your tone of voice, choice of words, and body language. The person you're talking to will see, hear, and sense this, and is likely to shut down or become defensive or evasive. On the other hand, if the intent is to learn how the other person thinks and feels and how you might support them, then that will also come through in ways the other person can sense and will make them more likely to respond from the heart. This doesn't necessarily mean they will immediately open up and tell you everything on the first try, but it can cultivate fertile ground for discussions.

Did I do something to make them this way?

No. It's important to reiterate that doctors and scientists agree that a person's sexuality and gender identity are not determined by their parents' or anyone else's actions. "Homosexual orientation is not caused by parents or family," as stated in "Frequently Asked Questions about LGBT," a publication of The Presbyterian Church of Mt. Kisco."[380] Researchers and health care professionals believe our sexuality is determined before birth and is caused by multiple factors. Also consider that if your child's sexuality is your "fault," then everything else about them is your "fault" and everything about you is your parents' fault and everything about your parents is their parents' fault and so on.

That's a general question that a parent would ask. Now as a parent, I get it. If you want to say it's your fault because you created me, then so be it, but it is what it is. It's there from the start. It wasn't a choice I made. [My parents] didn't do anything "wrong."

–Karla

Trying to figure out who to blame seems like wasted energy. Assessing fault or blame does not change the reality of your child's sexuality or gender identity. As a parent, your energy might be better spent doing what you can to ensure your child is happy, productive, and loved.

What are some of the mistakes parents and others make?

Most parents do what they believe is the right thing at the time. No one is perfect; thus, no parent is perfect. Mistakes are inevitable; it's part of being human. And many parents make the mistake of trying to "fix" their children, which Dr. William Pollack, a specialist in childhood development, says might appear to be uncaring behavior.[381]

Pollack also says that parents who withhold love "probably believed that if they withheld their love and affection from their son, somehow he would 'decide' he was no longer homosexual. But sexual orientation is… not a 'decision' that we can control or that can be changed by or for our parents."[382] It is imperative for parents or any other loved one to realize that there is nothing they can do to change someone's sexuality or gender identity. Withholding love and support is more likely to severely damage or sever the relationship permanently.

Professor Wright, who has many years of experience working with gay youth, also shared some insights and observations regarding how parents respond to gay kids.

Parents can do some bad things to their gay kids. Kids get thrown out of their houses on a regular basis because they're gay. There's a famous book called Sexual Preference *where they did a path analytic model and showed that when children engage in gender-atypical behavior, the same-sex parent would actually distance themselves socially because they would see them as 'you're not like me.' This occurs particularly for boys, not so much girls, but it happened to them too. The parent would do subtle things like making fun of them or just raising their eyebrows, shaking their head, things like that. As small children, that causes pretty profound reactions. Parents do that partly to help socialize the children, but sometimes, those can have really bad effects too when making judgments at the same time as telling them what's appropriate and what's not appropriate. Parents with young children develop all sorts of scripts about how they expect their children's lives to unfold, and when they don't unfold that way, as they age, whether it's their kid's gay or their kid is not as smart as they wanted them to be, the parents feel this grief or disappointment. You also get over-controlling parents who try to control their lives. My mother was one of those. But then you get the other, which I think is more common, the laissez-faire "well they'll figure it out eventually." That was my dad.*

–Professor Wright

Even parents who try to support their children can make mistakes.

We made the assumption our child was gay. It was like a matter of deduction—she doesn't show any interest in boys, she doesn't ever talk about being interested in anybody, so we're going to make this decision for her, and we've judged her, and we've decided that it's a sexual thing, not an identity thing, and there's a huge mistake in doing that... I always thought I was very insightful and prided myself on being progressive and being there to anticipate a lot of my children's needs, so when I heard I had a transgender child, and I didn't know it, I just wanted to kick myself.

–Raman

One of the most detrimental mistakes is forcing a loved one into so-called "conversion therapy." There has been a resounding cry from mental health professionals that these types of therapies cannot and will not alter a person's sexuality or gender. Mental health professionals are also adamant that conversion therapy harms the people subjected to it. Ann Lazaroff, mental health counselor, says, "It takes years to undo the damage done by that so-called therapy. This idea that a child needs to be changed from who they innately are is ludicrous and it contributes to the stigma that's attached to being LGBT."[383] Psychiatric literature unequivocally proves that treatments attempting to change sexual orientation are ineffective. Additionally, the risks are great, including depression, anxiety, and self-destructive, even suicidal, behavior.[384]

Sexuality and gender identity cannot be altered by internal or external forces. If a loved one is lesbian, gay, bisexual, transgender, queer, intersex, asexual, or pansexual, then that is who they are. They were never straight or cisgender, and therefore can't be made "straight again." Nothing can "make" a person straight if they are not. No amount or type of conversion therapy will change them, just as nothing can change a person who is straight. Conversion, reversion, and reparative therapies are part of the denial and coercion approach rather than acceptance and support. These programs have all been rejected by the American Psychological Association and the American Medical Association. They are so detrimental that state and federal governments are trying to pass legislation to ban them.[385] The consensus is that rather than reject, deny, or defy a loved one's sexuality or gender identity, the best approach is to accept, support, love, and learn.

Isn't it normal that a parent would have a hard time accepting that their child isn't heterosexual and cisgender?

Whether it's normal would depend on your definition of normal. Perhaps it's more productive to examine why a parent might have difficulty accepting their child's sexuality or gender identity, and then finding a way to move toward acceptance.

If you are a parent having difficulty accepting your child's identity, it might be helpful to ask, "Am I rejecting them because of who they are or because of who *I* am?" We all have expectations of ourselves and others, especially our children. Our expectations, wishes, hopes, and dreams for loved ones are often tied to unfulfilled dreams we had for ourselves. It is imperative that we realize our children have their own dreams to pursue. We should not try to project our intentions upon them.

As a parent, you may desperately want your child to be happy, but your perception of happiness is not theirs. We forget or ignore the fact that happiness looks different to different people. Happiness is tied to our individual sense of self. We should want loved ones to be happy based on *their* definition of happiness and fulfillment, not ours. As Kahlil Gibran writes, "Your children are not your children... though they are with you, they belong not to you... You may give them your love but not your thoughts... You may strive to be like them but not seek to make them like you."[386]

> *I think a lot of parents are afraid because of what other people may think and because they think their child doesn't know themselves the way that we believe they do. Some parents don't have the trust in their child's sense of self or their knowledge about themselves. I think we all tend to assume that teenagers get involved in too many fads, or they get convinced about things, or they look for extreme fads to be involved in, and we don't have the faith in them that we should have. The other thing is, I think a lot of parents are not risk takers, because you have to be a risk taker to make this kind of a change in your life. A lot of parents are afraid because of what other people may think. "How will it affect me and my friends and my family and my colleagues and the people in my community if my child is this outcast?" Sadly, my child was always the outcast, whether he was being bullied, or whether he was failing in school, whether he had difficulty maintaining continence because he could not walk into a girl's bathroom, ever. He was always an outcast, one way or the other. I figured if he's going to be the one that stands out in the crowd, let's at least make him the one that stands out with his head held high and be proud of himself, and so we went that route.*
>
> –Raman

Isn't that what we should want for those we love, for them to be able to hold their heads high and be who they are?

My mom recently shared that a neighbor came to her seeking advice about what to do after his son revealed he was gay. My mother said, "He is your son and will always be your son. You have to find a way to accept this and love him, no matter what."

There's a difference between accepting something out there, accepting people for who they are, and your child not living up to what your dreams are for them. I think she wanted to believe that it was a choice, and it wasn't what she, and my father to an extent, wanted for their child. You know, if it's more like that, "This is not what we want for your life," it wasn't, you know, in any way based in religion or homophobia; it was just that this wasn't what they wanted for their child. And I think they were going to try to do what they could to try to dissuade me.
–Rafshoon

A parent's hopes, concerns, and beliefs might impact their response.

My mother thought it was absolutely wrong religiously and in terms of her idea of what is right and how the world works. She thought, "You find a man, you marry a man, and you have children. You don't go and have a relationship with a woman. It's not right." She was thinking in terms of "What's going to happen? How can you raise your child? What are you doing? You're too young to make this decision, and you don't know what you want. This may be a phase. Why don't you just see if this is a phase before you make this declaration?" Also, the shame, you know. I can imagine from her perspective, the absolute shame of it.
–Tiffany

Sometimes, it is necessary to remind adults to remember what the child needs.

There are parents saying, "How could you do this to me? Do you realize what this does to me?" I was working with a young transgender kid who is in high school who just simply wanted to use the bathroom that matched his gender identity. And the principal kept saying, "Do you realize how hard this is for me?" I had to say, "Listen, just to be clear, this is not about you. This is about your student and what you're going to do for your student to make sure he feels safe. This is about this young kid who just wants to go to the bathroom."

–Roemerman

Parents can also carry most of the worry and seek most of the control.

The parents are coming up with all the worries and problems. Most parents are concerned with wanting to do what's best for them. Most parents in the trans clinic cry. They are beside themselves with worry for their child, with hope, with fear, with having gotten bounced around the medical system already, and about fertility. Parents are concerned about social repercussions—what's Grandma going to think? They are mourning the loss of the boy or girl they thought they had. I think that's a huge piece of it. Growing up with this boy who's now a girl, and you've gained a daughter, but you've lost a son, is sort of how they think of it. But the person is the same; it's the same person who's existing in different ways.

–Lowell

Parents of intersex children also have a difficulty accepting their child's status. The discovery their child has a condition that does not fit into the parameters of a "normal" baby is frightening. As you might expect, there is shock, disbelief, and confusion. It raises many doubts and uncertainties. There are health and medical issues that will have to be addressed. One of the things that seems to occupy most parents of an intersex child is the uncertainty of the immediate and distant futures. Simple things like assigning a male or female name, telling family and friends, "It's a boy" or "It's a girl," or buying clothes, toys, and books to reflect the child's gender can become problematic. As does dreaming about who the child will be in the future, because for many parents and families, all of those things are contingent upon knowing the baby's biological sex. Parents of intersex children might also believe their dreams for that child have been crushed;

that marriage, children, and having a family are no longer possible. They wonder what others will think. They wonder how others will treat them and their child. Being intersex can also carry a social stigma for the parents and the child. People might look at the parents and wonder if they did something to cause this. Others will consider the child a "freak" and shun both child and parents.

Intersex rights pioneer Bo Laurent said her parents were traumatized and frightened. The doctors told them to move to another town and not tell anyone where they were going and to never tell Bo what happened. She said it affected her parents' relationship with her and "made it hard for them to relate normally to me."[387] This happens even if the intersex status isn't known. Though neither Simon nor her parents seem to have known she was intersex, her medical conditions and non-gender conforming behavior created some strain and tension.

> *Initially, my parents wrote my lack of development off, just my being late and frail and all that. They didn't have a name for it. I'm not sure they connected all the different things that were wrong with me into a single unified syndrome. My parents were loving and supportive but pretty firm on the boy thing. They were fairly typical in their outlook regarding pink and blue for girls and boys, and what you should and shouldn't play with. None of that was really an issue for them, until I reached fifth or sixth grade. When I was young, I was allowed to have dolls and tea sets. Those sorts of things were okay when I was five. I even had an Easy Bake Oven. When I was about nine, my parents started becoming much more aggressive about enforcing gender behavior. They started getting concerned about using my hands when I spoke or wearing a dress. They were always concerned about my hair, keeping it very short, because my dad felt that I looked like a girl if my hair was allowed to grow at all. One of the things that my father told me after my mom died was that she thought, perhaps, they should have intervened when I was very young. My father kind of had this idea that it was his fault.*
>
> –Simon

It is understandable that parents might experience a range of emotions upon learning a loved one is lesbian, gay, bi, trans, queer, intersex, asexual, or pansexual. It may not be easy, but it seems that one of a parent's primary duties is to give their child the tools and the freedom to be who they are. My mother once told me, "Live your life. I've lived mine." Children cannot and should not live their lives for parents. Part of a parent's job is to prepare a child to live their own lives.

What's the worst that could happen to someone who is rejected by family?

The worst outcome is that your child, sibling, parent, or spouse could attempt suicide, or worse, succeed in committing suicide.

Children and youth rejected by family "are *more* likely to hurt themselves, use illegal drugs, drop out of school, run away, experience homelessness, and attempt suicide," according to health care professionals and LGBTQIAP support organizations like TransPulse Resource.[388] Suicide becomes a greater possibility for any youth who is rejected by family, but that risk is dramatically increased when the young person is LGBT.

Suicide Prevention Education Awareness for Kids (SPEAK) confirms that suicide is the leading cause of death among gay and lesbian youth. PFLAG reports that gay teens are more than eight times more likely to report having attempted suicide "compared with peers from families that reported no or low levels of family rejection." Compared to the general population, gay males are six times more likely to commit suicide, and lesbians are twice as likely, according to the AAS. Family rejection is part of the "experiences of stigma and discrimination" that are risk factors for attempted suicide among LGBT people according to "Talking About Suicide and LGBT Populations," a resource provided by the Gay and Lesbian Alliance Against Defamation (GLAAD). PFLAG also reports that "LGBT youth are three times more likely to use illegal drugs" when they experience higher levels of family rejection during adolescence. Gay teens with low or no family support are almost six times "more likely to report high levels of depression." Make no mistake, there are definite life-threatening ramifications when parents and families reject LGBTQIAP children, teens, and young adults.

Raman recalls that her child's coming out as transgender was accompanied by a declaration of wanting to die. She also believes that her family's immediate response of verbal and physical support was influential in helping her child alleviate suicidal thoughts and feelings.

> *As puberty hit, that's when my child's world kind of came crashing in, and she didn't associate anymore with the boys or with the girls. She was bullied and became very withdrawn, had learning issues, physical problems, and then began failing in school and became very introverted. When she was eighteen, I was worried she would kill herself or put herself in a situation where somebody else would hurt her. I asked, "What's wrong with you?" and she said, "What's wrong with me is something that people can't live with, so I have to die. In my head, I'm a boy, but my body says I'm a girl, and it doesn't make sense to me." The next day, we were on a bus going to get the first testosterone injection and to get a haircut and to buy new clothes.*

–Raman

Transgender people who are rejected by their families or lack social support are much more likely to consider suicide and to attempt it than trans people whose families support who they are. Numerous studies have confirmed this fact. When strong parental support is present, suicide attempts for transgender youth go down by 93 percent.[389] Trans youth with strong familial support are 82 percent less likely to attempt suicide than those without support, according to one recent study. A Huffington Post article quotes another study that showed transgender youth whose parents reject their gender identity are 13 times more likely to attempt suicide than transgender youth who are supported by their parents.[390] Darlene Tando, a licensed clinical social worker and gender therapist, says it's been "shown over time that kids who have family support… have a very similar statistic of suicidality… as the general population. So, the family support is so important."[391]

The rate of suicide and attempted suicide among transgender people is at least nine times higher than the national average. Compared to the 4.6 percent of the overall US population that have attempted suicide, 41 percent of trans or gender-nonconforming people have attempted suicide.[392] According to Youth Suicide Prevention Program over 50 percent of transgender youths attempted to commit suicide at least once before reaching the age of twenty.[393] That is an astronomical rate. The American Foundation for Suicide Prevention and The Williams Institute also show that the numbers can be higher depending on race and ethnicity. More than 50 percent of American Indian, Alaska Natives, and mixed-race/ethnicity trans respondents have attempted suicide. The percentage is 45 percent for black and 44 percent for Latino respondents.[394]

That attempted suicide rate for homosexuals is 10 percent and for bisexuals it is 20 percent, according to The Williams Institute, the National Center for Transgender Equality NCTE, and the National LGBTQ Task Force.[395]

For some families, the worst thing that happens is that their relationship is irreparably severed. When parents or other family members refuse to accept a person's sexuality or gender identity, the loved one may feel their only recourse for survival is to get away from the toxicity, permanently. That's what a young man named Evan did after his father refused to talk to him and his mother said, "You're no longer my son." Evan says, "The only way I could cope was to stop seeing my parents at all." Now that his parents are elderly, they have tried reaching out, but Evan says, "As much as they want to see me now, I just can't get myself to do it. It hurts a lot."[396] Whether the emotional and psychological damage is immediate and acute, or subtle and chronic, it can be devastating and have long-term effects.

Even years and decades after leaving their parents' homes, many adults often attempt to recreate the relationship dynamics of their youth with other parental figures, for better or worse, and mostly unconsciously. When a person is forced to seek support and acceptance elsewhere, they are at risk of being killed or hurt, physically and emotionally, by someone outside of the family. They may fall prey to an adult who sees their vulnerability and uses it to take advantage of them by coercing them into abusive relationships, prostitution, selling drugs, or some other illegal or physically and emotionally harmful activity.

Why does rejection increase the chance of suicide?

The American Association of Suicidology (AAS) says being rejected by the people closest to us contributes to a feeling of isolation. Socially isolated people are generally found to be at a higher risk for suicide.

Many LGBTQIAP folks are socially isolated, on some level, because of their biological sex, sexuality, or gender identity. That social isolation can be compounded by self-doubt or confusion about their sexuality, biological sex, or gender identity and whether it is right or wrong to be who they are. When social rejection and isolation are merged with familial rejection and isolation, the risk for suicide sharply increases. An individual might begin to believe, "If my parents don't love me, then I must not be loveable. I must not be worth the air I breathe. So why should I keep breathing?"

Psychologists and psychiatrists working with transitioning transgender men, women, children, and teens say the high transgender attempted suicide rate is because they experience more of the factors that lead people to attempt suicide. They explain that the risk of suicide among trans youth increases is higher than the overall youth population due to rejection by family or lack of social support, discrimination, physical abuse, internalized transphobia, or being a member of a racial minority. One of these conditions by itself might be manageable for a young person, but experiencing several or all of them on top of the other stresses and insecurities of teen life can feel insurmountable.

Rejection and inability to transition appear to have led seventeen-year-old Lelah Alcorn to commit suicide by walking in front of a tractor trailer in Warren County, Ohio early one Sunday morning. Lelah's last words, written in a note left on Tumblr, mentioned that her Christian parents did not accept her true gender identity, and that they took Lelah to Christian therapists, who said she was "selfish" and "wrong" for being transgender. The teen's note also said her parents wouldn't give consent to begin transitioning. Lelah wrote, "My death needs to mean something. My death needs to be counted in the number of transgender people who commit suicide this year. I want someone to look at that number and say, 'that's fucked up,' and fix it. Fix society. Please."[397]

If you are struggling to find it in your heart to love, accept, and support a lesbian, gay, trans, bi, queer, asexual, or pansexual child, teen, or young adult, please consider that your choice to accept or reject them could be a matter of their life or death.

Do kids really run away if they're not accepted by family?

Yes, children and teens really do leave home as a result of family rejection or conflict. The most frequently cited factor for LGBTQIAP youth running away from home is family rejection based on sexual orientation and gender identity, according to The Williams Institute. The second most common reason is "being forced out by their parents after coming out." This corresponds with reports that more than one in four are thrown out of their homes.

Professor Wright has had first-hand experience working with youth who've been kicked out or abused. His work included counseling this population and conducting research in hopes of identifying and resolving some of their needs.

> *The majority of them are actually told to leave. Kids get thrown out of their houses because they're gay on a regular basis. Many kids face physical, mental, and emotional abuse from family and peers. Some of them are sexually abused. There was a widely publicized case in the Atlanta area about a teen whose family beat him more than once before he ran away from home.*

–Professor Wright

When a child runs away from home, the outcome is not likely to be a safe return home and a happy ending. Many do not return. Many join the growing ranks of homeless children and youth. Of the one million reported homeless youth in the US, LGBT youth constitute at least 40 percent or 400,000 of these children and teens. That number is disproportionately high considering they only represent seven percent of the youth population, according to The Covenant House and True Colors Fund, two organizations that help homeless youth in America.

Additional factors, like homophobia and transphobia, can contribute to a young person's feelings of isolation, insecurity, and lack of value that can lead them to run away. This can be particularly significant depending on where a person lives. For example, a youth living in New York City or San Francisco is less likely to encounter pervasive homophobia, because those cities have larger homosexual populations, openly gay and lesbian elected officials, and city residents who are generally more accepting of homosexuality. On the other hand, a young person growing up in rural Bible Belt areas like Georgia, Alabama, or Mississippi is more likely to be openly subjected to religious persecution and verbal and physical assaults because of their sexuality or gender identity. Even if their home life is tolerable, that young person may suffer while at school, church, or athletic events, and while out in the community. The emotional toll of constantly and consistently being subjected to homophobia or transphobia can cause a youth to run away from home. Their search for a place where they can feel safe and free to be themselves might lead them to the least safe environment they have yet to experience—living on the streets.

Sadly, LGBTQIAP youth are also disproportionately likely to remain homeless because of the same sort of discrimination that pushed them to the streets in the first place. The website nationalhomelessness.org reports that widespread discrimination in federally funded institutions exacerbates the growing rates of homelessness among LGBT youth. On the street, the dangers an LGBT young person faces increase dramatically, much more so than if they were straight.[398] They are more likely than their straight counterparts to use hard drugs, seven times more likely to be the victims of a crime, "more than three times more likely to engage in survival sex, for which shelter is the payment more often than cash, and more likely to be arrested for survival crimes."[399]

What does support look like?

Saying loudly and clearly, "I love you and accept who you are," is one of the first signs of support. "Supporting transgender people means letting them be who they are," according to a middle school student whose sister is transgender.[400] Support looks like showing up, being present at critical moments, even if it's uncomfortable or inconvenient. It looks like communication. It looks like having your loved one's back. When I asked a father why he accompanied his teen son to a PFLAG meeting, the man said, "My job as a parent is to love and support my child, no matter what. So, when he came out to me, that's what I did."

Love and trust are also important aspects of support.

> *Your child is coming to you in an act of love and trust. They believe that you are on their side because otherwise they would not tell you, and so the most important thing you can do is see it as an act of love even if you don't get it, even if there is stuff that you think is totally out there. The most important thing you can do is hear their disclosure as an act of generosity of spirit in trusting you that you are going to get enough of it to be on their side. And they are prioritizing the connection to you over their own privacy or sense of safety sometimes.*

> *There is this idea that it is this very flippant kind of thing. All the discussion around stuff about phases. It is like parents have to be vigilant against these phases, and I would challenge parents to imagine that actually even if it is a phase, which it almost never is, but how much harm is done by assuming it is a phase than by trusting your child? I think there is so much more harm by approaching it as if your child doesn't know their own heart. So, it is most important that you trust your child. So, if your kids come to you, even if you think they are making the wrong decision, they are likely going to seek this out one way or another. They are going to find their own path, and they can do it with you or they can do it without you. And I think it is much better that they do it with you.*

–Anderson

Support for an LGBTQIAP loved one can look a lot like support for a straight loved one who is experiencing something unfamiliar to you. It involves being present, listening, asking questions, empathizing, and avoiding judgement. It also involves open-mindedness, compassion, patience, sensitivity, and loyalty.

Listening can be hard, especially in an era where we've become accustomed to interrupting other people and insisting that our thoughts are more important than theirs, but it's imperative we try. It can also be difficult to listen to something we don't understand or don't approve of. If you've ever had first-hand experience sharing your deepest thoughts, feelings, fears, or doubts, only to have the person you love dismiss them as insignificant, or worse, reject you for having them, then you know how defeating that can feel.

One of the keys to understanding anyone who may be different from us in any way is to have an open mind. Opening our minds to the possibility that someone is having an experience completely different than anything we've had helps to push our egos out of the way and makes it easier to be non-judgmental and accept that their experience is just as valid as ours. Being compassionate, patient, present, careful, and non-judgmental are also important, as is empathy. You may not be able to relate to your loved one's sexuality or gender identity, but perhaps there is some emotion or aspect of the process of self-discovery, or need for authenticity, that you can empathize with. If while listening and having conversations something is said that you don't understand, then try saying something like, "I'm not sure I understand. Can you try explaining it to me again?"

Roemerman, who came out in college and has since spent many years working with LGBT youth, offered some specific language that can be helpful.

Let them know that they have a place to come to talk regardless of the topic and that they're supported and they'll always be loved no matter what. Say, "I don't know where you're at on your path, but I just want to let you know I love you regardless of whether you're straight or gay or bisexual, transgender, whatever. I just want to let you know I love you." Another thing I would do is use gender-neutral terms and not make assumptions about someone's gender or sexuality. Make the questions you're asking be gender-neutral, so it doesn't seem like you're projecting on them an expectation. For example, as someone who is gay, my ears would always perk up when I heard a teacher say, "How's your significant other? Are you seeing someone?" instead of saying, "How's your girlfriend?" We immediately pick up on those things. We think, "This is someone who might be a little bit more aware of the fact that not everyone is straight." I think those kinds of things are very helpful, and I suggest that to teachers as well, to do those kinds of things in their classrooms.

–Roemerman

Karla offered one specific piece of advice about what not to say when communicating with your child or loved one.

Do not use the word "tolerate" because tolerate means that you just kind of put up with it, and you still don't approve of it, and that's not fair.

–Karla

Support must also go beyond words and take the form of important action. Raman discussed one of the ways she made her support visible.

Helping him get the testosterone shots was the most important thing, in my mind, and I think in my son's mind too. That was my message of complete acceptance and understanding. I think that was the strongest message I could have given him that I'm supportive.

–Raman

Commissioner Garner explained her idea of supporting children and some additional work parents should do.

Be there as a support and let that child know, "We are here for you and you can come to us and ask questions." Just be accepting and available and don't push them. It's when we push our kids, and want them to go in a certain direction, that we just lose touch, and it is no longer authentic. I would also say to parents to get themselves ready because they are going to have to come out as well. They should get an education, talk to other gay people.

–Commissioner Garner

The coming out for parents, family members, and other loved ones that Commissioner Garner referenced is also a form of support that can involve learning more about biological sex, sexuality, or gender identity. A loved one's support can include reading books and articles, joining support groups, and attending meetings and conferences.

Child psychiatrists and pediatricians say lack of acceptance from family, and especially parents, can lead to depression, drug use, suicide attempts, and running away from home. They urge parents to demonstrate immediate and early acceptance and support of gender dysphoria as the best and only way to raise a well-adjusted, healthy child.

Sabrina offered advice for those who learn that their child is transgender.

> *First of all, I would say, get informed. Soak up all the information you can. Become an expert on transgender identity, and then believe your child when they tell you that their brain is not matching their body. Don't blow that off. Do the right things. Get the counseling, but don't dismiss it. Do not dismiss it. Be cautious, but take it seriously, and be as informed as you can possibly be, and then support them and love them and be there for them.*
>
> –Sabrina

That's exactly what the Whittington family did after initially trying to ignore it when, at the age of three, their child began saying they were a boy. Once it became evident that ignoring the situation wasn't going to make it go away, Mr. and Mrs. Whittington paid more attention and began gathering information about gender dysphoria. Learning that 41 percent of transgender people attempt suicide when not accepted by loved ones was the turning point. "Would we rather have a living son or a dead daughter?" Mr. Wittington said in a CBS interview. "We weren't willing to play with that statistic—we'd rather have a living son." The parents now say they do everything they can to support their transgender child and help him lead a happy life.

Another family, the Wilsons, said they didn't understand what was happening with their child and wondered how far they should let their child go with expressing a girl's gender identity. The parents eventually sought counseling and learned their child was transgender.[401] Mr. Wilson was reluctant to accept the notion of his child being transgender. At some point, the father realized that by clinging to the notion of having a boy child he was "holding onto something that wasn't there." Mr. Wilson eventually accepted that he has a transgender daughter and said, "I never looked back; I really didn't. It changed my relationship with Tracey; it completely changed it."

Raman also didn't know anything about transgender identity before learning her teen was trans.

> Originally, we assumed my daughter was gay. Ignorance is what helped us make that assumption. I just did not know. In my mind, at that time, there was no transgender person. There was a transvestite, which was, I thought, a crossdressing entertainment-type person or a fetish-type person. I did not know that there were people who had a gender dysphoria. I was completely ignorant of that.
>
> –Raman

Even though, at that moment, Raman didn't know anything about transgender identity, she immediately accepted her child, and then went about educating herself.

Loyalty is another form of support. Loyalty is important, because even when we don't understand or don't know exactly what to do, our sense of loyalty to a person will push us into action. If we are loyal, we will not abandon a loved one or join in on the joke when someone is ridiculing "those people." Loyalty will not allow us to remain silent when the world is beating them down.

Where can I obtain more information about LGBTQIAP?

A good place to start is with your loved one. But don't stop there. The amount of information a loved one can share depends on where they are in their coming out process and what they've learned about themselves and their sexuality or gender identity. It can also depend on their relationship with the person asking questions and their level of comfort or discomfort in talking about biological sex, sexuality, or gender identity. It may be presumptuous to think that someone represents a group with which they identify. Just because a person identifies with a group doesn't mean they can stand as a representative for that group or any other group in the acronym. For example, a gay person should not be expected to represent all gay people, and may not be able to answer questions about other sexualities or gender identities.

Quite a few resources exist to provide additional information, services, and support.

> *Parents, Families and Friends of Lesbians and Gays, PFLAG, is a great resource. It's literally friends and allies of people who are LGBT. They have amazing amounts of resources for people in terms of how to talk to your child or your father or your mother or whoever else. Human Rights Campaign has good resources, as well as the Gay Lesbian Straight Education Network, GLSEN. They have great resources too, for coming out, how to be an ally, and other things.*
>
> –Roemerman

National organizations like PFLAG, GLAAD, and HRC have local chapters that offer different levels of resources to families and advocates of LGBTQ individuals. They produce informational publications, and offer lists of other local and national entities, organizations, and events. Local PFLAG chapters also offer meetings and other activities for families and loved ones. Additionally, institutions like Pew Research produce insightful and timely studies and reports about LGBTQ individuals and communities in the US.

CHAPTER FIFTEEN

BREATHING THE SAME AIR

"It's your thing. Do what you want to do.
I can't tell you who to sock it to."
–Isley Brothers[402]

Intro

We all have a different set of circumstances, which I like to think of as our individual expressions of humanity. Human characteristics like race, sex, religion, sexuality, and gender identity should neither elevate our status in society nor should they diminish it. For me to believe my humanity is on equal standing with anyone else's requires me to think and act as if no other human warrants better or worse treatment than I do.

Every human being should have the freedom and safety to live their truth and express their humanity without being discriminated against, attacked, punished, or killed for it. David Letterman once asked, "Who are you to throw a log in the road of someone who has a different set of difficulties in life?" None of us has that right. None of us has the right to make life difficult for another human being just because their circumstances and realities differ from ours. None of us has the right to tell someone they shouldn't be themselves. We also don't have the right to tell consenting adults who to love, or as the Isley Brothers put it, "Who to sock it to."

What motivates fear and hatred of people who identify as LGBTQIAP?

Psychologists say hatred can be driven by differences, and more specifically, by love of the group we belong to and aggression toward groups that differ from ours. In early humanity, in times of scarce resources, this might have been helpful for the survival of tribes, clans, families, etc. I wonder how well that serves us now, considering that differing sexualities and gender identities do not encroach upon our survival. Psychologists also say we don't just hate because things are different; we hate because we *fear* things that are different.

Fear of homosexuals has been named "homophobia," a term coined in the 1960s by heterosexual psychologist George Weinberg. The Pride Resource Center at Colorado State University describes homophobia as pervasive and irrational. Internalized homophobia refers to homosexuals whose self-hatred and self-denial of homosexuality are a product of being taught to view themselves as sick, sinful, and criminal. Homophobia includes fear of mannerisms, actions, or feelings that might suggest homosexuality and a corresponding desire to suppress or wipe out homosexuality. Homophobia can be exhibited by a person of any sexuality.

> *Something deeper inside you triggers hatred toward others. A lot of times, it's someone who is hiding their sexuality, and they hate homosexuals because they see too much of themselves in that person. You see things, traits of your personality, that you don't like about yourself, so therefore, you immediately feel as if you don't like the person. Otherwise, why would you care who I sleep with? Why would you instantly hate on somebody just because of their sexuality?*
>
> –Fredis

"The things people hate about others are the things that they fear within themselves," according to clinical psychologist Dana Harron.[403] This doesn't necessarily mean every person who hates homosexuals fears they are homosexual. It could mean they recognize some personality traits or characteristics within themselves that might stereotypically be identified with homosexuality. For instance, a man who likes to dress, speak, or behave in a way that has been associated with homosexuality might be fearful that people will presume he is homosexual, even if he isn't. Because he doesn't want to be presumed homosexual, he might respond negatively to seeing those same traits in a gay man. Some people react negatively to homosexuals because they want to make sure others won't think they are homosexual.

> *Once, while at a club with my husband, a dancer asked if I wanted a lap dance. I was so uncomfortable with this idea of a lesbian interaction, or that she thought I might enjoy it, I got angry with the girl, and I snapped at her. I felt threatened because I didn't want people in that bar to think that I was a lesbian.*
>
> –Raman

Anne shared her opinions on why people express fear, hate, or discomfort about gender-nonconforming people.

> *I think that there are probably a number of things. One is we live in a culture where we have these nice neat boxes of man and woman, as opposed to some other cultures where they might have a third gender box. We live in a place that has a very rigid gender idea. I think that makes it hard as Americans. Some of the North American native people have two-spirit persons who embody both genders. Another place is Southeast Asia where there is more flexibility. Additionally, I think it is an experience that has not been very shared, so it is something that people don't know about, and they don't have any experience with. It is something that is incredibly hard to talk about. I can say from my own experience it is incredibly difficult to bring this up with people. Thirdly, I think there is just a general lack of language around it. People don't know how to ask questions about it.*
>
> –Anne

Glenn shared her perspective on why some people have difficulty accepting transgender people.

Gender and sex is something that hits people at a very deep level. There's something in our reptile brains that makes people uncomfortable with that and hateful toward any sort of gender nonconformity. It's basically a phobia. When we were a primitive species living in savannas, we lived in tribes, and you liked the people in your own tribe, but it was safe to dislike people outside your own tribe. I guess, just because gender nonconformity is unfamiliar to most people, it makes it uncomfortable, and it makes them hateful.

–Glenn

Demetrius offered another perspective.

It's like an alien to them, and they don't understand. And things that we don't understand, we shy away from and look at from afar instead of trying to understand what we're about.

–Demetrius

Creating lies and stereotypes is one of the tools we use to feed our fears and hatred of others. They help us to create further separation between ourselves and others. Lies and stereotypes give us more reasons to view others as less than human—less than worthy of love, compassion, and understanding.

I think the most damaging misconception is that we are different, that we are outside of what is normal, that we are somehow defective. The whole stigma of mental illness that was cast upon us for so many years has only recently started to be pulled away. I think that is the most damaging part of it… People being exposed to it and thinking and believing those things.

–Emily

Fear has been our pattern for responding to the unknown. Fear can be a rite of passage if we use it to make ourselves smarter and better people. Conversely, clinging to fear can make us ignorant and hateful, with appalling results. Clinging to fear rather than seeking true understanding led to the Salem witch trials. Little girls and young women were hanged because people feared their unexplained "fits" and convulsions. We now look back on that era with shame, knowing that this mysterious behavior was the product of natural physiological functions. How will we feel about ourselves upon realizing that a person's sexual orientation or gender identity is simply a matter of natural physiological functions?

The antidote to fear and hate is compassion for ourselves and others. The key to overcoming fear of the unknown or unfamiliar is information and education.

> *It's probably just lack of understanding, or reflects what they've been taught to think about people who are different. It would be helpful if everybody could understand that their reactions to other people are coming from themselves, not from the other person, in anything, whatever it is. It would be helpful to get to the root of it by asking, "Why do I feel this way about that person, even though they've done nothing to me and aren't planning to?" Unless somebody is coming after you with a knife or something, that's different, but to hate somebody who has no way of possibly harming you doesn't make sense. My partner and I can't harm anyone by doing what we want in our own house. It would be helpful to recognize that the response, whatever response we are having to somebody who's not able to harm us in any way, is coming from purely within ourselves. We would all be better off if people could see that and start from that place, in terms of trying to interact with that person and learn about them, and ask, "What is causing this from within me? Where am I getting this? And why and what does it actually have to do with that person?"*
>
> –Dr. Lowell

Glenn believed overcoming fear and hate could be as simple as recognizing our commonalities.

> *We're just like them, and we want nothing more than to be treated as the ordinary people we are.*
>
> –Glenn

Professor Wright agreed that more people recognizing their sameness would eliminate the fear that drives hatred and phobias.

> *There's a lot more commonalities in our differences than we realize, and if we can find a way to embrace them and not necessarily fear them, then I think that would go a long way. I'd love it for our society.*
>
> –Professor Wright

What is the harm in accepting all sexualities and gender identities?

It's tempting to simply answer, "There is no harm," and move on to another question. Instead, I would like to address some of the reasons why people would say there is harm.

Family Values

One argument offered is that acceptance of LGBTQIAP people harms family values. Let's examine this for a moment. What are "family values?" Generally, values are principles or standards of behavior. When we talk about family values, we refer to principles and standards of behavior for families. Perhaps the first and most important topic in a discussion of family values is valuing family. If we say we value family, then doesn't that mean that having a family is important to us? If we value family, then shouldn't each member of the family be important to us? Additionally, if we profess to value family, then keeping the family together should be important. If we claim to value family, then isn't it contradictory to want to *prevent* people from having a family, raising a family, and taking care of a family? If we say we value family, then we should encourage people to build families. If we value family, then the harm comes in preventing the building and nurturing of families.

Let's also consider that marriage can be a gateway to family, and that disallowing marriage for a segment of the population is also anti-family.

> *If you at all believe that discrimination is inherently bad, then why would you completely disallow a population to have the ability to be happy in a society that revolves around having*

a family, and having children, seeing your children grow up, and knowing that they're going out into the world to replace you, when you're gone? Your legacy. How could you disallow that to an entire population? If family values are what built the country, then great, let us have families. If you say, we're a nation based on family values, then, let us have a family.

–Perry

Valuing family is not the sole domain of heterosexual cisgender people. People of any sexuality or gender identity can value family. There is no data-based or factual support for the belief that sexuality or gender identity could prevent people from valuing family. Families led by one or two people who identify as LGBTQIAP are just as healthy, happy, or dysfunctional as families led by heterosexual cisgender people. That's because sexuality and gender identity don't determine how much a person loves their family or how well they are able to care for their family. We've seen enough heterosexual and cisgender dead-beat dads and abusive moms, for instance, to know that being gay, bi, trans, etc. isn't what makes a bad parent or spouse.

Another way to interpret the term "family values" is that it refers to the values that individual families hold. Every family has a right to its own set of values. Some of your family's values are likely to differ from some of my family's values. Does that mean my families' values are good and correct and yours are bad and wrong? Not necessarily. Each family is free to define their own values as long as they do not encroach on the values and well-being of others.

Moral Decay

A claim has also been made that the acceptance of LGBTQIAP individuals contributes to a decline of morals. Let's take a look at this. The general definition of morals explains it as a standard of behaviors or beliefs about what is acceptable behavior. Morals impact how we behave in society. They dictate things like whether we think it's okay to lie, steal, rape, pillage, plunder, kill, or commit adultery. Heterosexual cisgender people have been known to commit heinous and immoral acts without the help or influence of LGBTQIAP individuals. There is no evidence that LGBTQIAP individuals commit these acts with a greater frequency than heterosexual cisgender people. In fact, when it comes to immoral acts like rape and child molestation, heterosexual cisgender males are the predominant perpetrators. How is it then that being homosexual, transgender, or queer, for instance, is tagged as cultivating immorality but heterosexuality is not?

Plot Against Black Males

There has also been a growing cry among some African Americans that homosexuality is a harmful plot to destroy black males. There is no truth to this. A black person's sexuality is not a plot, secret plan, or scheme to accomplish an especially hostile, unlawful, or evil purpose. Homosexuality is a naturally occurring sexuality. Additionally, sexuality does not harm or diminish a person's race. On the contrary. Not being allowed to be yourself is what destroys a human being. Being gay, bi, or trans does not prevent a person from being black, white, Asian, or any other racial construct. A black male who is homosexual is still black. A black male who is homosexual is still male. Most importantly, an openly gay black man is a person who can love himself. He is a person who can live a productive life, build a family, and contribute to society.

Threat to Cisgender Women

There are also heterosexual and lesbian women who believe that transgender women pose a threat to cisgender women. This came to my attention when a Facebook friend posted that transgender people are delusional.

> *That group of women who consider themselves radical feminists is called by other feminists 'terfs' or 'trans-exclusionary radical feminists,' and basically, they believe that trans women in particular are trying to, like, ape femininity, mock femininity, are trying to take women-only space, are trying to destroy sacred, divine, feminine stuff. This all has come to a head over many years. I mean it is interesting because this is, like, a very lesbian feminist infight that then straight people got wind of. The Michigan Women's Music Festival was sort of like the ground zero of this fight. The Michigan Women's Music Festival was part of a broader movement but was the most successful of these*

kinds of festivals that were about lesbian and women separate in space. There are many things about this that were really beautiful. It was, like, women need a place to go to be away from male violence, to not to have to deal with patriarchal culture for a little while. And Michigan lasted for forty-five, forty-six years and was very, very successful in lots of ways. A lot of lesbian feminists felt like that was a utopian ideal, but they had a non-transwoman policy. They did not have a no trans men policy. To be specific, they had a women-born-women-only policy. And a lot of people were, like, it is really fucked up for you to decide who is a woman based only on gender roles... All of these ideas, it is a very essentialist and frankly negative way, I think, to a certain extent of thinking about womanhood... It is this very backwards and monolithic of thinking about who trans people are, mostly who trans women are, but it is a very painful fight as a feminist institution, for us, seeing sister feminist institutions with a lot of history go down in flames because they can't accept trans women has been really, really hard and really sad... They look at trans women and they are like, you are making a mockery of femininity. You are making a mockery of us. It is, like, no, actually. These women are more invested in womanhood than just about anybody because they are trying so fucking hard to live their truth. They are more your sisters than anybody.

–Anderson

We are all trying to live our truths. I can live my truth without negating your individual truth. My truth as a woman is not the same as your truth, but that doesn't negate either of our realities. My truth as a heterosexual is not impacted by another person's truth as lesbian, gay, bi or pan. My truth as a cisgender person is not impacted by another person's truth as queer or trans.

Harmful to Children

There are also those who claim that accepting LGBTQIAP identities is harmful to children. This is also unfounded. Children are not negatively affected by interacting with LGBTQIAP individuals. Nor can a child's sexual orientation be changed by interacting with someone who is LGBTQIAP. As stated earlier, we are born with our sexuality and gender identity. If a child is heterosexual, they cannot be "turned" into some other sexuality. If a child is cisgender, their gender identity will not be altered by interacting with someone who is not cisgender. It is also important to restate that children are much more at risk of being molested by a heterosexual cisgender male than by someone of any other sexuality or gender identity.

The bottom line is there is no harm in accepting all sexualities and gender identities. The sexuality or gender identity of another human being has no adverse impact on my life or yours. Two women having sex in the comfort and privacy of their home does not harm me or you or anyone else. My neighbor's sexuality doesn't stop me from going to work or walking the dog or loving my family. A transgender woman's presence in the women's bathroom does not stop me from using the restroom. The presence of LGBTQIAP individuals does not impact my or your ability to earn a living, raise a family, take a vacation, buy a home, etc.

Is there any harm in not accepting LGBTQIAP?

What is the harm in discrimination and prejudice against LGBTQIAP individuals? According to the APA, individuals and society are harmed. And "any discrimination based on gender identity or expression, real or perceived, is damaging to the socioemotional health of children, families, and society," according to the AAP.[404] On the social level, prejudice and discrimination are reflected in the everyday stereotypes that persist even though they are not supported by evidence. These stereotypes can be most harmful when they are used to condone unequal treatment, diminish the quality of people's lives, and deny civil liberties, housing, employment, healthcare, etc.[405]

Even if an individual learns to cope with the social stigma against their sexuality or gender identity, a pattern of prejudice can gravely affect their health and wellbeing. Sexual prejudice, sexual orientation discrimination, and antigay violence are major sources of stress for LGBTQ people and are significant mental health concerns. It has been shown that people who don't come out can have higher degrees of stress and mental health challenges than those who do come out. The child subjected to verbal ridicule at school or at home and the adult who is demeaned at work because of sexuality and/or gender identity is likely to experience emotional stress and lowered self-esteem. We've already discussed how these situations can lead to mental health problems, cutting, running away from home, and suicide. Unfair treatment like job and housing discrimination also heightens an individual's stress, fuels self-doubt, diminishes quality of life, and erodes faith in humanity. Physical violence that stems from prejudice has obvious health concerns such as internal and external injuries, and worst of all, death. Lack of acceptance can lead to an ever-present threat of violence that adversely affects children and adults.

"The real harm to individuals and society occurs when people are not accepted for who they are," according to Shankar Vedantam, host of *Hidden Brain*.[406] He goes on to say, "Stereotypes are powerful because the stories we tell about ourselves are powerful. They shape how we see the world and how the world sees us. But in the end, they are only stories, and stories, we can rewrite them." My hope is that we stop writing and telling stories that demean a group of people because they differ from us in some way. Instead, let us turn toward stories that help us all be happy, hopeful, kind, and loving.

Is acceptance of LGBTQIAP increasing?

Some, including President Barack Obama, believe it is. He says, "American society has changed; the attitudes of young people in particular has changed."[407]

Research supports the belief that acceptance is increasing. Ninety-two percent of LGBT adults surveyed by Pew Research say society is more accepting of transgender, gay, lesbian, and bisexual people than it was ten years ago. Overall, homosexuality is more accepted in the US now than at any time in the past, according to General Social Survey (GSS), National Opinion Research Center (NORC) at the University of Chicago, Gallup, and Pew Research. Additionally, one survey showed that in 1993, 63 percent of Americans thought homosexuality was "always wrong." By 2010, more than 50 percent of the population thought homosexuality was "never wrong." Another indicator of increasing acceptance is seen in perceptions about employment. Support for equal rights in job opportunities increased from 56 percent in 1977 to 89 percent in 2008. The percentage of people who believed that school boards should be able to fire teachers who are known homosexuals went from 51 percent in 1987 to 28 percent in 2009.

Most LGBT individuals attribute the changes to a variety of factors, including people knowing and interacting with someone who is LGBT, advocacy on their behalf by high-profile public figures including celebrities and non-LGBT leaders, and the growing visibility of LGBT adults raising families.[408]

The people I spoke with also felt there is definitely an increased acceptance and visibility.

> *When I started teaching thirty years ago, when I asked a question about homosexuality, I had people say overtly in class, "I hate fags. All gay people should be dead," and things like this. Two weeks ago, in class, I asked a similar question and the students didn't seem to have any negative conceptions about LGBT people. So, something's shifting really dramatically. When you look back over thirty years, it really is a dramatically different place... A transgender person in my study group said somebody who was transgender a generation ago would never have thought about coming out as quickly as she did because she didn't see the same negative social consequences to doing what she was doing. It's interesting how the world really is changing or being more open-minded. I also think this may be a stressful period as we're sort of trying to grapple with diversity in a new way.*
>
> –Professor Wright

> *I wish I would've been born two generations after me, because people are accepting this now, to a certain degree. Not everybody, but the conversation is out there. They're killing some of us, but it's not like it was.*
>
> –Sabrina

Sabrina's chilling and tragically true statement, "They're killing some of us," serves as a reminder that hazards continue to exist. There is still work to be done as long as LGBTQIAP children and adults are being assaulted, murdered, discriminated against, and oppressed. While attitudes are changing and conditions are improving, there are still plenty of people who feel justified in setting a gay teenager on fire or murdering a transgender woman. Progress has been made, but as President Obama also cautioned, "That doesn't mean there aren't going to be some fights that are important. Legal issues, issues surrounding transgender persons. There is [sic] still going to be some battles that still need to take place."[409]

According to GLAAD, 14 percent of the US population still disapproves of LGBT people, and 33 percent remain unsure. Statistics also show that conservative, religious people are more likely to disapprove. The South tends to be less accepting, and its states are less likely to have laws that prevent discrimination.

> *While other parts of the country have been gaining rights, that has not taken place in the South. When you look at the most recent polling that asks "Are you okay with gay marriage?" the places where acceptance is less than 50 percent are in the South. Also, when you look at where funding goes for LGBT efforts, the South has the least amount of funding going toward research. The highest proportion of LGBT people out of all the regions in the country—Midwest, Southeast, etc.—are based in the South. We have more LGBT people than any other region of the country. We also have more LGBT people raising families than any other region of the country. However, if you look at the fourteen states that make up the US South, none of those states have had any statewide non-discrimination policy that protects LGBT people [as of 2017].*
>
> –Roemerman

Professor Wright, who moved from the Midwest a few years ago, was surprised at the level of anti-gay sentiment he has experienced in the South.

> *What I've been befuddled by here in Georgia is the people who are anti-gay are really anti-gay and are willing to be out there on the internet or in your face. That's kind of striking to me because I really thought there was this Southern politeness thing going on here.*
>
> –Professor Wright

The South has a long history of mistreating people they consider outsiders based on religion, race, sexuality, gender identity, and so on. However, this is not a Southern issue; it is a universal issue. Acceptance remains a challenge that must be addressed.

If you don't identify with LGBTQIAP, then why should you care about how they are treated?

"Until we are all free, none of us are free."[410] Or as actor Asia Kate Dillon says, "Until the most marginalized among us, black, indigenous, and people of color, especially trans, intersex, and genderqueer folks, are held up as essential assets toward the survival of us all, no one will be free."[411] As long as LGBTQIAP individuals are discriminated against, marginalized, and denied full rights and protections under the law, they are not free, and therefore, none of us are. How can we claim to live in a free society when a segment of that society is not free?

Think about what it feels like to be on the receiving end of discrimination. As actress Jameela Jamil suggests, "I think it's very important that if you know what it feels like to be left out for any reason, that you start to think about all the other people who are left out, even those who don't look like you or who aren't like you."[412] If that still doesn't do it for you, then consider a family member or friend who has considered or attempted suicide because their sexuality or gender identity isn't accepted by family, friends, and society. Do you have some duty to try and ensure their well-being, survival, and happiness?

If you are wondering how one person can make a difference without joining a march or giving money to an organization, look to your immediate surroundings. There's a good chance that a situation will arise among your family, friends, and coworkers to make it known that you don't support discrimination against LGBTQIAP individuals, or that you don't agree with stereotypical or anti-LGBTQIAP statements. It doesn't require challenging anyone to a duel or citing a list of data. It can be as simple as saying, "I haven't found that to be true," or asking, "Why do you believe that to be true?" For myself, I think, "If this is something that I believe with my heart and soul, and I do and say nothing, then I am not living up to my philosophy, values, and morals." When I'm in a room and I hear someone make an ugly statement, then it is my duty to question or challenge the statement. In that setting, it can be much more impactful coming from me than the person being disparaged. It's more difficult for my family, friends, or associates to dismiss me because I'm inside their group; I'm one of them. Sometimes that makes people stop and think about what they're saying and what they feel and believe. If nothing else, it makes them reluctant to spew hate speech, which is a start.

> *The biggest thing straight people might be able to do is help their straight friends understand it better. It's very powerful when someone who is not the subject of the prejudice stands up for that person. It's one thing for a gay person to say, "Don't hate me because I'm gay." It's a cool and slightly different thing for a straight person to say, "You shouldn't talk to that person that way because they're the same as we are."*
>
> –Dr. Lowell

We all need allies to stand up for us at some point in our lives.

What is a straight ally?

A straight ally is a heterosexual cisgender person who is an advocate for lesbian, gay, bisexual, transgender, queer, intersex, asexual, and/or pansexual people and their rights. I didn't know what a straight ally was, or that I was one, until I came across WeAreStraightAllies.com, an organization founded by an associate of mine, Chevara Orrin. We Are Straight Allies works to end the discrimination and violence directed at the LGBT community.

A GLAAD survey reports that at least 53 percent of the US population are LGBT allies. Straight allies are found in all walks of life and include people like Beyoncé, Willie Nelson, A$AP Rocky, Jay-Z, Brad Pitt, and Cindy Lauper. Writer and comedian Larry Wilmore says, "I realized it's important for me to be an advocate for issues that aren't necessarily my own... I'm not a homosexual, but if I can be an ally for that issue, I think it's fantastic."[413]

Like Larry Wilmore, I believe it's important for me to advocate for issues that aren't necessarily my own. Some people are puzzled by this. Some assume I am on the verge of coming out. To them I say, I am coming out as a straight ally. I know that in some instances I will be misunderstood or viewed as peculiar. That's okay with me. I accept that, "If you're going to stand up for what's right, sometimes you got to stand apart."[414] I cannot allow the judgment and perceptions of others to interfere with this work. I am willing to "stand apart" if it means that one day, we can all stand together. I am willing to "stand apart" if it means that one day, everyone, regardless of sexuality or gender identity, will have equal rights to life, liberty, and the pursuit of happiness.

The APA suggests that there are a number of ways heterosexual cisgender individuals can help eradicate discrimination, starting with "examine their own response to antigay stereotypes and prejudice."[415] Other suggestions include working with these individuals and communities to combat prejudice and discrimination and to encourage nondiscrimination policies that include sexual orientation and working to make coming out safe. It has been proven that straight allies can have an impact.

> We're also starting to find an ally marketplace. It's friends and family who won't frequent businesses and restaurants and things like that if they're not LGBT friendly. That is five times as large as the LGBT community, so it's a huge segment of the population, which is why we're seeing—for example, when Indiana tried to find a way not to deal with gay couples and screen against them, you saw businesses immediately responding because the tipping point has occurred.
>
> –Roemerman

Historically, we have seen the value of involvement by those who may not be directly affected by the discrimination of another group. When the larger community becomes involved and flexes its muscles on behalf of the oppressed group, it can provide efficient and effective leverage.

What will it take to change perspectives about LGBTQIAP?

As heartbreaking as it is for me to admit, some people will never change their perspectives. Fortunately, for humanity's sake, those people are not the majority.

Changing perspectives must be addressed on numerous fronts. Danielle Moodie-Mills, former Center for American Progress Advisor for LGBT Racial Policy and Justice, believes it's important to present positive images of LGBT people and that policies need to evolve with our cultural shift, especially employment nondiscrimination.

Respect and compassion for basic matters, like identification, are necessary.

> *I think treating everybody with respect is what it comes down to. Just trying to get regular care, there are huge barriers. A patient of mine couldn't change her name on her insurance card, so she's in the waiting room waiting to see me, and then they call out "Jim," and she has to stand up and say, "That's me." Things like that and changes to the whole check-in process are needed. So now we have a form that says, "preferred name," and then my nurses know to call that name. That solved it in my office, but not in other offices that didn't think about that. That's just one example of all the different minefields that there are, and it can be dangerous for somebody in a large group of people, in a waiting room, to be identified as someone with a name that doesn't match their gender. They could be at risk going out to their car later, you know? There are higher stakes to some of these things than is readily obvious. There are so many barriers like that to coming to the doctor.*
>
> –Dr. Lowell

Some of these issues need to be addressed legally or legislatively to implement change in policy to then influence personal thoughts and behavior. Making it illegal to ask an employee about their gender identity could dissuade employers and service providers from asking invasive questions. Employers, staff, and service providers would think twice about doing so if they knew there were legal ramifications that would impact their businesses and jobs. It has been proven that laws can impact how we extend to others the respect and compassion we all desire for ourselves.

Anne reiterated the belief that focusing on what we as humans have in common can overcome the negativity toward LGBTQIAP people.

Mostly, there is more sameness than difference. The same comfort they get to feel at being their authentic selves is the same comfort and need that we get in being our authentic selves; people living their authentic lives.

–Anne

Anne also expressed a belief that straight people having more personal interactions with LGBTQIAP individuals could be a primary agent for changing hearts and minds.

There is nothing that changes someone's mind like having someone in their life, who they really love, who is gay or queer or trans. There is nothing that changes people's minds more than that.

–Anne

This is not just wishful thinking. According to the APA, "Studies of prejudice, including prejudice against gay people, consistently show that prejudice declines when members of the majority group interact with members of a minority group."[416] The APA also stated that having personal contact with an openly gay person is one of the most powerful influences on heterosexuals' acceptance of homosexuals. Antigay attitudes are far less common among members of the population who have a close friend or family member who is lesbian or gay, especially if the gay person has directly come out to the heterosexual person.

For me, what it is about is coming to the table. The more we demonstrate that we are human beings and have one-on-one conversations, I think that will help. I have to credit Mayor Maynard Jackson. He was the first to say, "I want you be on this board and I want you to do that and I want you to be the liaison." He said, "Get out there and do it," and I had to do it. I think people's perceptions will change when they have real experiences. It takes building those personal relationships and demonstrating who you are. A lot of laws get changed because of people.

–Commissioner Garner

Changing our perceptions also permits people to shift in the direction of greater inclusion, more justice, and more peace. I turn to David Letterman again, who says, "Look, you're a human; I'm a human. We're breathing the same air. We have the same problems. We're trying to get through our day."[417] As humans, we should allow for and embrace each individual's expression of humanity. When we see and treat each other as equals on this plane of humanity, then the fear, hatred, stereotypes, and discrimination are washed away.

For me, it all starts about humanity and being a humanitarian. We are all part of this great big brotherhood of humanity. Whether we are male or female, whatever our race, religion, gender, sexual orientation, we are all part of humanity, and we are all brothers and sisters at some level. We all need to find ways to strive to give love and get along with humans; that is a big part of it. It is important to understand that being transgender, our expectations are that we would like to be accepted and loved, to live our lives in cultured society. This is the same with most groups that are ostracized by societies.

–Emily

It's not surprising to me that everyone I spoke with expressed similar thoughts and feelings.

I want people to see me as a human being first and then as a woman, African American, lesbian. I can put any of it first. I am African American. I am a lesbian. I am a woman. I can do any of them in any order. Asking me a question about my sexuality sort of put me in a box that I don't want to be placed in. I want to know who you are, and I want you to know who I am as a person and what I bring to the party and what I bring to the work that I do; and then, out of that, we develop a relationship.

–Commissioner Garner

Another core desire is that people be allowed to be who they are, which I believe is something we all want for ourselves. Meg Zulch says, "We're not asking you to completely understand the ins and outs of our identity or know every piece of lingo regarding gender-nonconforming identities. Just validate our existence by acknowledging our right to be here and to be seen as we are."[418] That shouldn't be too much to ask for. Nor should respect. Krysten Sinema, US Representative (D-Arizona) and out bisexual, says, "We're simply people like everyone else, who want and deserve respect." I suppose we all feel we deserve respect, yet there are plenty of folks who feel they don't have to extend respect to other people. Since we desire respect, why not extend respect to others? Let us take advice from Tommia Dean, a college student, who says, "Eventually if you respect each other, you will understand each other."[419]

Another common desire is to be treated like everyone else.

> *I don't want anybody to treat me different or special because I'm gay or whatever; I just want to be treated like anybody else.*
> –Dr. Lowell

There are hopes for self, family, and the future.

> *It matters to me and my family how we get treated and perceived in the world. I am really invested in pushing people to rethink their long-held ideas. It is really important that people have some facts. I really like the idea that you are using your privilege and your understanding as a straight person in the world to help dispel some of the myths. I don't think we are all that different, and some of those things that people are holding on to, if they spent the day in my shoes, it wouldn't feel any different. That's the truth.*
>
> –Anne

Even though you may think you deserve to be treated like everyone else, there is likely some person or some group that would look at you and say you don't. At any moment in human history, there has always been a group or groups of people being denied the full benefits of membership in society. There is always a segment of the population committed to maintaining dominance over those groups. Fortunately, there is always a segment who believes everyone should be afforded equality. And there is yet another group of people who aren't sure what to think or believe. Over time, the undecided and uncommitted move in one direction or another. It seems that in each modern era, more people move to the side of fairness and equality. That does not happen without agitation in the forms of communication, grassroots activism, advocacy, financial support, and legislation.

Let us seek to understand each other better rather than hide behind our differences. Let us recognize our sameness. Let us acknowledge that we each have different ways of expressing our humanity. Let us embrace the truth that no one is better than anyone else and no person is less valuable than another. Let us allow each human being equal access to education, healthcare, housing, employment, protection, freedom, and love.

Let us go there.

"Love's in need of love today
Don't delay
Send it in right away
Hate's goin' round
Breaking many hearts
Stop it please
Before it's gone too far"
—Stevie Wonder[420]

ACKNOWLEDGEMENTS

Thank you to...

My parents, Barbara and Eddie Coyt, for their enduring, unquestionable love and support; for showing me that silence is not an acceptable option in the face of hate and discrimination; and for the constant and consistent example of treating people with kindness and respect.

My twin brother Todd, who always has my back.

The Man of My Dreams for assuring and reassuring me that this was a book *I* had to write.

The sincere and courageous people who allowed me to interview them: Councilmember Alex Wan, Dr. David J. Thurman, Rev. Duncan E. Teague, Professor Eric R. Wright, E.R. Anderson, Dr. Isabel Lowell, Commissioner Joan Garner, Lianne Simon, Lisa Raman, Philip Rafshoon, Ryan Roemerman, and Vandy Beth Glenn. As well as Angelia, Anne, Conner, Demetrius, Emily, Fredis, Jennie, Jazmyn, Joe, Karla, Lisa, Marilyn, Nancy, Omar, Perry, Rayna, Sam, Sabrina, Sheila, Stephanie, Tiffany, Timothy, and Vicki.

The Atlanta Writers Club non-fiction critique group: Aimee, Chuck, Glenn, Greta, Marilyn, Quinn, Rebecca E., and Tiffany.

Carlos Collins, Deanna Turner, Doug Shipman, and Don, Lois, and Jackie Reitzes.

Everyone who has offered support and encouragement.

VOICES

Interviews that appear in this book have been minorly edited for grammar and spelling. Some names were changed upon request.

Alex Wan (Atlanta City Council Member, married, cisgender, gay, 48 years old), in discussion with the author, audio recording, May 2014, Chapters 3, 11, 12, 13.

Anne (emergency physician, married, genderqueer, queer sexuality, 35 years old), in discussion with author, audio recording, June 2015, Chapters 2, 3, 4, 8, 12, 15.

Angelia (truck driver, engaged, cisgender, bisexual, 27 years old), in discussion with author, October 2015, Chapter 5.

Clarice (foster parent, married, cisgender, heterosexual, 40 years old), in email to author, February 2018, Chapter 14.

Conner (non-profit director, single, cisgender, gay, 35 years old), in group discussion with author, March 2016, Chapter 11.

David J. Thurman, MD (epidemiologist, Centers for Disease Control (CDC), married, cisgender, gay, 65 years old), in discussion with author, audio recording, June 2015, Chapter 3.

Demetrius (analyst, single, cisgender, gay, 50 years old), in discussion with author, audio recording, December 2013, Chapters 3, 4, 15.

Duncan E. Teague, MDiv (Founder, Abundant Love Unitarian Universalists Congregation of Atlanta, cisgender, gay, 54 years old), in discussion with author, audio recordings, June 2015, Chapters 3, 4, 11, 13, 15.

Emily (engineer, separated, transgender, heterosexual, 60 years old), in discussion with author, audio recording, June 2015, Chapters 9, 10, 11, 12, 15.

E.R. Anderson (non-profit executive director, long-term monogamous relationship, trans masculine, queer sexuality, 36 years old), in discussion with author, audio recording, August 2018, Chapters 8, 9, 11, 12, 13, 14, 15.

Eric R. Wright, PhD (Sociology Professor, Georgia State University, married, cisgender, gay, 53 years old), in discussion with author, audio recording, December 2015, Chapters 3, 4, 5, 11, 13, 14, 15.

Fredis (makeup artist, single, cisgender, gay, 35 years old), in discussion with author, audio recording, September 2014, Chapters 2, 3, 4, 5, 11, 12.

Isabel "Izzy" Lowell, MD (Founder, QMed, married, genderqueer, lesbian, 35 years old), in discussion with author, audio recording, June 2015, Chapters 2, 3, 8, 9, 11, 12, 14, 15.

Jazmyn (entrepreneur, committed relationship, cisgender, bisexual, 61 years old), in discussion with author, audio recording, January 2015, Chapters 3, 4, 5, 11.

Jennie (entrepreneur, committed relationship, no labels, 49 years old), in discussion with author, audio recordings, October 2014, January 2015, Chapters 3, 5, 13.

Joan P. Garner (Fulton County Commission Co-Chair, married, cisgender, lesbian, 63 years old), in discussion with author, audio recording, September 2014, Chapters 2, 3, 4, 11, 12, 13, 14, 15.

Joe (retired, single, cisgender, heterosexual, 58 years old), in discussion with author, May 2014, Chapters 4, 12.

Karla (Lieutenant, metropolitan police department, married, cisgender, lesbian, 39 years old) in discussion with author, audio recording, December 2014, Chapters 3, 4, 11, 12, 13, 14.

Lianne Simon (writer and intersex activist, married, intersex, heterosexual, 62 years old), in discussion with author, audio recordings, December 2014, Chapters 10, 11, 13, 14.

Lisa Raman (Cofounder and Co-President, Transgender Health and Education Alliance Plus (THEA+), committed relationship, cisgender, heterosexual, 52 years old), in discussion with author, audio recording, June 2016, Chapters 9, 12, 14.

Laura (laser technician, divorced, cisgender, bisexual, 40 years old), in discussion with author, February 2018, Chapter 19.

Marilyn (speech-language pathologist and author, single, cisgender, lesbian, 75 years old), in discussion with author, audio recording, December 2014, Chapters 3, 11.

Nancy (esthetician, divorced and in a relationship, cisgender, bisexual, 35 years old), in discussion with author, December 2013, Chapter 3.

Omar (production manager, single, cisgender, gay, 23 years old), in discussion with author, audio recording, February 2014, Chapter 3, 4.

Perry (realtor, single, cisgender, gay, 31 years old), in discussion with author, audio recording, May 2014, Chapters 3, 12, 15.

Philip Rafshoon (founder of Outwrite Bookstore, married, cisgender, gay, 53 years old), in discussion with author, audio recording, December 2014, Chapters, 4, 5, 11, 12, 14.

Rayna (self-employed, single, cisgender, lesbian, 28 years old), in discussion with author, February 2018, Chapter 11.

Ryan Roemerman (Executive Director, LGBT Institute, Center for Civil and Human Rights, cisgender, homosexual, single, 32 years old), in discussion with author, audio recording, June 2014, Chapters 4, 11, 12, 13, 14, 15.

Sabrina (construction project manager, ordained minister, divorced, transgender, heterosexual, 60 years old), in discussion with author, audio recording, October 2016, Chapters 8, 9, 11, 12, 13, 14, 15.

Sam (entrepreneur, single, cisgender, gay, 45 years old), in discussion with author, February 2016, Chapter 4.

Sheila (entrepreneur, engaged, cisgender, sexually bisexual, romantically lesbian, 59 years old), in discussion with author, audio recording, July 2015, Chapters 3, 5.

Stephanie (retired nurse, widowed, cisgender, heterosexual, 65 years old) in discussion with author, March 2016, Chapter 14.

Tiffany (realtor, married, cisgender, lesbian, 45 years old), in discussion with author, audio recording, December 2014, Chapters 3, 4, 11.

Vicki (office manager, divorced and engaged, cisgender, bisexual, 59 years old), in discussion with author, audio recording, July 2015, Chapters 3, 5, 11.

Vandy Beth Glenn (writer, single, transgender, lesbian, age undisclosed), in discussion with author, audio recording, January 2016, Chapters 2, 9, 12, 15.

Yvette (writer, single, heterosexual, cisgender, 49 years old), in discussion with author, January 2017, Chapter 3.

Consultant: Joe Barry Carroll
Copy Editors: Nadene Seiters, Diana Anderson-Watson
Proofreader: Dylan Garity
Layout & Design: Madison Lux
Cover Design: Mirko Pohle

ENDNOTES

1. Clayton, Meg Waite, "Beautiful exiles" pg. 142, location 1422, Lake Union Publishing, Aug 2018.

2. Berger, Thomas, source unknown, accessed http://orrt.org/berger/index.asp

3. Boylan, Jennifer Finney, "Evolving Perspectives on Gender and Sex," in an interview on *The Diane Rehm Show*, WAMU 88.5 American University Radio, dianerehm.org, August 30, 2016.

4. Manseau, Peter, "The apparition this: a tale of phantoms, fraud, photography and the man who captured Lincoln's ghost," Houghton Mifflin Harcourt, 2017.

5. "LGBT demographics of the United States," Wikipedia, updated August 16, 2018, https://en.wikipedia.org/wiki/LGBT_demographics_of_the_United_States.

6. Schneider, Margaret. "Answers to your Questions About Individuals with Intersex Conditions." APA Task Force on Gender Identity, Gender Variance, and Intersex Conditions. American Psychological Association. 2006.

7. Klein, Fritz, MD. *The Bisexual Option*, Second Edition. (Hawthorne Press, 1993).

8. "Average Height for Men by Country," AverageHeight.co, accessed February 27, 2018, http://www.averageheight.co/average-male-height-by-country.

9. "The Ten Most Spoken Languages in the World," Babbel, accessed February 27, 2018, https://www.babbel.com/en/magazine/the-10-most-spoken-languages-in-the-world.

10. "The Ten Most Common Languages," Accredited Language, accessed February 27, 2018, https://www.accreditedlanguage.com/2016/09/09/the-10-most-common-languages/.

11. "Sexual Orientation and Homosexuality," American Psychological Association, accessed https://www.apa.org/topics/lgbt/orientation.aspx

12. Piphus, LaTierra, "Sexual Orientation vs. Sexuality," Agents For Liberation, University of Wisconsin, Parkside, August 2018, accessed November 29, 2018, https://campusconnect.uwp.edu/news/3419

13. "Sexuality," Options for Sexual Health, accessed 2016, https://www.optionsforsexual health.org/sexual-health/sexuality.

14. "Sexual Orientation & Gender Identity 101," Unitarian Universalist Association, Accessed Https://Www.Uua.Org/Lgbtq/Identity

15. Frankowski, B.L., American Academy of Pediatrics Committee on Adolescence, June 2004, "Sexual orientation and adolescents," *Pediatrics*, 113(6):1827–32, doi:10.1542/peds.113.6.1827, PMID 15173519.

16. *Dictionary.com*, accessed January 24, 2018, https://www.dictionary.com/.

17. McNally, Victoria, "Bill Nye F*cking Gets It, You Guys," April 24, 2017, http://www.pajiba.com/tv_reviews/bill-nye-gets-that-gender-and-sexuality-is-a-spectrum.php.

18. Herek, Gregory M, PhD, "Facts About Homosexuality and Mental Health," http://psychology.ucdavis.edu/rainbow/html/facts_mental_health.html.

19. Shapiro, Lin, "This Bill Could End 'Gay Conversion Therapy' In The U.S.," *Huffington Post*, May 19, 2015, updated Feb 02, 2016, accessed Aug 12, 2016, https://www.huffingtonpost.com/2015/05/19/conversion-therapy-ban_n_7322828.html.

20. Parker, Kim, "Among LGBT Americans, bisexuals stand out when it comes to identity, acceptance," Pew Research Center, February 20, 2015.

21. Decker, Julie Sondra, "How to Tell If You Are Asexual," *Time*, June 18, 2014.

22. Klein, *The Bisexual Option*, ebook, Foreword LOC 68.

23. Gary Gates, *LGBT Parenting in the US* accessed December 23, 2016, https://williamsinstitute.law.ucla.edu/wp-content/uploads/LGBT-Parenting.pdf.

24. "Overview of Lesbian and Gay Parenting, Adoption, and Foster Care," ACLU, accessed December 27, 2017, https://www.aclu.org/fact-sheet/overview-lesbian-and-gay-parenting-adoption-and-foster-care

25. "Overview Of Lesbian And Gay Parenting, Adoption, And Foster Care," ACLU, accessed December 27, 2017, https://www.aclu.org/fact-sheet/overview-lesbian-and-gay-parenting-adoption-and-foster-care.

26. Perrin, Ellen C., Benjamin S. Siegel, the Committee on Psychosocial Aspects of Child and Family Health, "Promoting the Well-Being of Children Whose Parents Are Gay or Lesbian," *Pediatrics*, April 2013, Volume 131, Issue 4, The Academy of Pediatrics, accessed October 28, 2018, http://pediatrics.aappublications.org/content/131/4/e1374.

27. Herek, G. M., "The Psychology of Sexual Prejudice," *Current Directions in Psychological Science*, 9, 19-22 (2000).

28. Ellen Pompeo, "Interracial Marriage with Ellen Pompeo," *Red Table Talk*, December 10, 2018, accessed December 11, 2018, https://www.facebook.com/redtabletalk/

29. *Godless*, "Homecoming," Season 1, Episode 7, Netflix, 2017.

30. Meek, Will, PhD, "Romantic vs. Committed Love," accessed February 2018, http://www.willmeekphd.com/romantic-vs-committed-love/.

31. Shakespeare, William, "Polonius," *Hamlet*, Act 1, scene 3, 78–82, accessed http://shakespeare-navigators.com/hamlet/H13.html.

32. Fisher, Helen, E., Brown, Lucy L., Aron, Arthur, Strong, Greg, and Mashek, Debra, "Reward, Addiction, and Emotion Regulation Systems Associated With Rejection in Love," *Journal of Neurophysiology*, July 1, 2010, p 56, doi: 10.1152/jn.00784.2009, PMID: 20445032.

33. Doobie Brothers, "Long Train Runnin'" *The Captain and Me*. Warner Bros. 1973.

34. Christopher Hitchens, accessed https://www.allgreatquotes.com/gay_homosexual_quotes.shtml

35. Ward BW, Dahlhamer JM, Galinsky AM, Joestl SS. "Sexual orientation and health among U.S. adults: National Health Interview Survey," *National Health Statistics Reports*, no 77 (2014), National Center for Health Statistics.

36. Gates, Gary J. "How many people are lesbian, gay, bisexual, and transgender?" April 2011, Williams Institute, University of California School of Law.

37. Lopez, German, "Ta-nehisi Coates has an incredibly clear explanation for why white people shouldn't use the n- word.," *Vox*, November 9, 2017, accessed November 11, 2017, https://www.vox.com/identities/2017/11/9/16627900/ta-nehisi-coates-n-word.

38. Kosciw, Joseph G, PhD, "The 2015 National School Climate Survey," accessed March 29, 2018, https://www.glsen.org/article/2015-national-school-climate-survey.

39. New Progressive Party of Puerto Rico (NPP), derived from the conservative Republican Statehood Party.

40. Waithe, Lena, "The Chi Creator Lena Waithe Says Television 'Taught Me How to Dream'," interviewed by Terry Gross on *Fresh Air*, NPR, January 11, 2018.

41. Sivakumaran, Sandesh, "Sexual Violence Against Men in Armed Conflict," *The European Journal of International Law*, Vol. 18, no 2 (2007), pp. 253-276.

42. Pun, Big, "When you awaken, your manhood will be taken," *The Dream Shatterer*; Dog, Snoop, "I'm hollin one-eight-seven with my dick in yo mouth beeyatch," *Dre Day*; DMX, "Motherf**ka, "I'll rip your butthole outta place," *Here Comes the Boom*

43. Johns, Kate, "Many prison inmates are 'gay for the stay'," *Independent*, May 6, 2013.

44. Lumpkin, Jincey, "11 things you've always wanted to know about lesbian sex but were afraid to ask," *Huffington Post*, December 10, 2013, accessed December 12, 2013, https://www.huffingtonpost.com/jincey-lumpkin/10-things-youve-always-wa_b_4414539.html

45. Stone, Richard, "Sex Drive: How Do Men and Women Compare?" https://www.webmd.com/sex/features/sex-drive-how-do-men-women-compare#4.

46. "FAQ–Frequently Asked Questions about LGBT," PFLAG Atlanta, http://www.pflagatl.org/lgbtfaq/.

47. "Are gay and lesbian people more likely to molest children than heterosexuals are?" Presbyterian Church of Mt. Kisco (PCMK) Blue Book, via PFLAGATL FAQ.

48. "FAQ–Frequently Asked Questions about LGBT," PFLAG Atlanta.

49. "FAQ–Frequently Asked Questions about LGBT," PFLAG Atlanta.

50. Kort, Joe, PhD. Homosexuality and Pedophilia: The False Link 10/05/2012 11:46 am ET | Updated Feb 02, 2016.

51. *Obergefell V. Hodges*, 576 U.S. ___ (2015)

52. Pew Research Center, *A Survey of LGBT Americans*, "Chapter 4: Marriage and Parenting," 68.

53. "Same-Sex Marriage Law Prior to Obergefell," FindLaw, accessed December 19, 2018 https://family.findlaw.com/marriage/developments-in-same-sex-marriage-law.html

54. Pew Research Center, "Gay Marriage Around the World," June 26, 2015.

55. Planas, Roque, "Prohibiting Gay Marriage 'Tortures People Needlessly,' Says Weed-Legalizing President, *The Huffington Post*, updated March 10, 2014.

56. Lerner, Adam B., "The Supreme Court's most memorable quotes on gay marriage," June 26, 2015.

57. Bertsche, Rachel, "Once 'Father' and 'Son,' Now a Married Couple," *Yahoo Parenting*, May 27, 2015.

58. "Gay marriages up 33% in year since Supreme Court ruling by Richard Wolf," *USA Today*, June 22, 2016.

59. Pew Research Center, *A Survey of LGBT Americans*.

60. Roberts, Dan, "Ruth Bader Ginsburg eviscerates same-sex marriage opponents in court," *The Guardian*, April 28, 2015.

61. Moss, Otis, III, "Challenges Fellow Black Clergy On Marriage Equality For Gays And Lesbians," May 28, 2012 11:00.

62. American Psychological Association, "Sexual orientation and homosexuality," February 5, 2011, accessed https://www.milehighpsychology.com/wp-content/uploads/2016/07/material_personal_sex_orient.pdf.

63. "Overview of Lesbian and Gay Parenting, Adoption, and Foster Care," ACLU, accessed October 28, 2018, https://www.aclu.org/fact-sheet/overview-lesbian-and-gay-parenting-adoption-and-foster-care.

64. Haynes, Freddie, 100 Black Men of America 32nd Annual Conference, June 2018.

65. "What is bisexuality?" Bisexual Resource Center, 2018, http://biresource.org/resources/youth/what-is-bisexuality/.

66. Klein, *The Bisexual Option*, Chapter 1: The Threat.

67. "Health survey gives government its first large-scale data on gay, bisexual population," *Washington Post*, accessed March 20, 2015.

68. "Understanding Bisexuality," American Psychological Association, accessed December 21, 2018, https://www.apa.org/pi/lgbt/resources/bisexual.aspx

69. Michelson, Noah, "28 Stars You Probably Didn't Know Are Bisexual," *Huffington Post*, August 10, 2015, accessed June 13, 2018.

70. Carlton, Vanessa, Nashville Pride concert, June 19, 2010.

71. Driscoll, Emily V. (July 2008). "Bisexual Species: Unorthodox Sex in the Animal Kingdom". *Scientific American*.

72. Thorpe, J.R., "A Brief History of Bisexuality, From Ancient Greece and The Kinsey Scale To Lindsay Lohan," *Bustle*, September 23, 2014, https://www.bustle.com/article s/40282-a-brief-history-of-bisexuality-from-ancient-greece-and-the-kinsey-scale-to-lin dsay-lohan.

73. "Are 'Heteroflexible' and 'Homoflexible' Shades of 'Bisexual'?" By Joe Kort PhD, HuffPost

74. "Heteroflexible, Bi-Curious, But Mostly Straight" By Zachary Zane, January 20 2016, Pride.

75. "AM I BI?" American Institute of Bisexuality, *Bi Magazine*, *Journal of Bisexuality*, http://bisexual.org/am-i-bi/.

76. Klein, *The Bisexual Option*.

77. Dingle, Charlotte, "12 Things To Never Say To A Bisexual Woman," *Curve*, 3/31/16.

78. "Chapter 5: Identity and Community" in *A Survey of LGBT Americans: Attitudes, Experiences and Values in Changing Times*, Pew Research Center, (Washington, D.C.: The Pew Charitable Trusts, June 2013), 8.

79. Pew Research Center, *A Survey of LGBT Americans*, "Chapter 5: Identity and Community," 8.

80. Michelson, Noah, "28 Stars You Probably Didn't Know Are Bisexual."

81. Klein, *The Bisexual Option*, Chapter 1 LOC 157 in ebook.

82. Klein, *The Bisexual Option*.

83. Nathan, Sara, "Neil Patrick Harris Tells Struggle to Come to Terms with Sexuality," October 14, 2014, *Daily Mail*, http://www.dailymail.co.uk/news/article-2791578/neil-p atrick-harris-tells-struggle-come-terms-sexuality-lip-lock-burt-reynolds-convinced-gay. html#ixzz4hBpd5TXd.

84. Martin, Rachel, "Sorting Through The Numbers On Infidelity," July 26, 2015, *Weekend Edition Sunday*, NPR, accessed Marcy 13, 2018, https://Www.Npr. Org/2015/07/26/426434619/Sorting-Through-The-Numbers-On-Infidelity.

85. Bielski, Zosia, "The Truth About Infidelity: Why Researchers Say It's Time To Rethink Cheating." *The Globe And Mail*, February 11, 2016, updated March 25, 2017, accessed March 13, 2018, https://www.theglobeandmail.com/Life/Relationships/The-Truth-Ab out-Infidelity-Why-Researchers-Say-Its-Time-To-Rethink-Cheating/Article28717694/.

86. Pew Research Center, *A Survey of LGBT Americans*, "Chapter 4: Marriage and Parenting,"

87. Samin, Suzanne "11 Things Not to Say to a Bisexual Woman," *Huffington Post*, October 23, 2014, updated December 6, 2017. https://www.huffingtonpost.com/bustle/things-not-to-say-to-bisexual-woman-women_b_5901128.html.

88. Klein, *The Bisexual Option*, Chapter 1: The Threat, ebook LOC 171.

89. Marusic, Kristina, "Why Do So Many Bisexuals End Up In "Straight" Relationships?" *Slate*, May 4, 2016, http://www.slate.com/blogs/outward/2016/05/04/over_80_ percent_of_bisexuals_end_up_in_straight_relationships_why.html.

90. Klein, *The Bisexual Option*, Foreword, ebook LOC 68.

91. Dingle, "12 Things To Never Say To A Bisexual Woman."

92. Wikipedia, "LGBT demographics of the US."

93. Marcotte, Amanda, "Anna Paquin's Bisexuality for Dummies," *The Daily Beast*, August 5, 2014.

94. Marusic, "Bisexuals in 'Straight' Relationships?"

95. Parker, Kim, "bisexuals stand out."

96. Marusic, "Bisexuals in 'Straight' Relationships?"

97. Cox, Paul, "We're Married, We Just Don't Have Sex," *The Guardian*, September 7, 2008, accessed June 2, 2017, https://www.theguardian.com/lifeandstyle/2008/sep/08/relationships.healthandwellbeing.

98. Miller, Anna Medaris, "Asexuality: the Invisible Orientation?" *U.S. News & World Report*, May 4, 2015, https://health.usnews.com/health-news/health-wellness/articles/2015/05/04/asexuality-the-invisible-orientation.

99. Sexual Attraction vs Sexual Arousal," Asexuality New Zealand Trust, 2018, accessed December 22, 2018, https://asexualitytrust.org.nz/what-is-asexuality/attraction-vs-arousal/.

100. Sexual Attraction vs Sexual Arousal," Asexuality New Zealand Trust, 2018.

101. "About Asexuality: Overview: Arousal," The Asexuality Visibility & Education Network, https://www.asexuality.org/?q=overview.html.

102. Paterson, Beck, "Asexuality and Having Children," My Kid is Gay, 2015, accessed September 6, 2017, http://mykidisgay.com/asexuality-and-having-children/.

103. Paterson, Beck, "Asexuality and Having Children," My Kid is Gay, 2015, accessed September 6, 2017, http://mykidisgay.com/asexuality-and-having-children/.

104. Cox, "We're Married, We Just Don't Have Sex."

105. "Asexuality: Love Doesn't Have to Equal Sex," The Trevor Project, September 1, 2017, accessed June 2, 2017, http://www.thetrevorproject.org/pages/asexuality.

106. Cox, "We're Married, We Just Don't Have Sex."

107. Cox, "We're Married, We Just Don't Have Sex."

108. Evans, Daniel, "What is Pansexuality? 4 Pan Celebs Explain in Their Own Words," GLAAD, September 23, 2015, accessed November 14, 2018, https://www.glaad.org/blog/what-pansexuality-4-pan-celebs-explain-their-own-words

109. Weigle, Lauren, "What Is a Pansexual? 5 Fast Facts You Need to Know," Heavy.com, August 28, 2015, https://heavy.com/entertainment/2015/08/what-is-a-pansexual-miley-cyrus-flags-colors-pansexuality-definition-omnisexuality-bi/.

110. Savin-Williams, Ritch C., PhD, "Who and What is Pansexual," *Psychology Today*, November 6, 2017.

111. Papisova, Vera, "Pansexuality and Being Pansexual: Everything You Need to Know: It's less confusing than you think," *TeenVogue*, November 17, 2015.

112. Papisova, "Pansexuality and Being Pansexual."

113. Papisova, "Pansexuality and Being Pansexual."

114. Evans, Daniels, "What is Pansexuality? 4 Pan Celebs Explain in their Own Words," September 23, 2015, https://www.glaad.org/blog/what-pansexuality-4-pan-celebs-exp lain-their-own-words.

115. Evans, "What is Pansexuality?"

116. Anas, Brittany, "5 Things You Need to Know About Pansexuality," *Women's Health*, May 23, 2017, accessed June 3, 2017, https://www.womenshealthmag. com/sex-and-love/a19994281/pansexuality/.

117. Morandini, James S., Blaszczynski, Alexander, and Dar-Nimrod, Ilan, "Who Adopts Queer and Pansexual Sexual Identities?" *The Journal of Sex Research*, December 2, 2016, p 911-922.

118. Khan, Farhana, "I'm pansexual–here are the five biggest misconceptions about my sexuality," *Independent,* September 1, 2015.

119. Savin-Williams, Ritch C, PhD, "What Everyone Should Know About Pansexuality," *Psychology Today*, November 6, 2017, accessed June 2, 2017, https://www. psychologytoday.com/us/blog/sex-sexuality-and-romance/201711/what-everyone-sho uld-know-about-pansexuality.

120. Papisova, "Pansexuality and Being Pansexual."

121. Papisova, "Pansexuality and Being Pansexual."

122. Ostrow, Ruth, "Hello, is anyone out there still straight?" *The Australian*, April 27, 2015.

123. Papisova, "Pansexuality and Being Pansexual."

124. Khan, "I'm pansexual."

125. Papisova, "Pansexuality and Being Pansexual."

126. Ziyad, Hari, "3 Differences Between the Terms 'Gay' and 'Queer' — and Why it Matters," *Every Day Feminism*, March 1, 2016, accessed November 14, 2018, Https://Everydayfeminism.Com/2016/03/Difference-Between-Gay-Queer/.

127. Higgins, Marissa, "Is The Word 'Queer' Offensive? Here's a look at the LGBTQIAP+ Community" *Bustle*, February 4, 2016, bustle.com, retrieved January 9, 2018.

128. Croom, A. M., "Slurs," *Language Sciences*, 33(3): 343–358, doi:10.1016/j.langsci. 2010.11.005.

129. Snyder, Mark Daniel, "Tranny," *Queer Today*, February 3, 2009, retrieved September 23, 2010.

130. Queer Nation, "Queers Read This," June 1990.

131. Barrie, Zara, "What to Ask If You're Questioning You're Sexuality," EliteDaily.com, January 20, 2017, accessed June 2, 2017, https://www.elitedaily.com/dating/questioni ng-your-sexuality/1759249.

132. Jones, Michal 'MJ', "Coming Out as Genderqueer Non-Binary (Outside of and Within the Queer Community)," *Everyday Feminism,* April 18, 2015.

133. "What Do We Mean By 'Sex' And 'Gender'?" World Health Organization (WHO), accessed November 26, 2015, http://www.who.int/gender-equity-rights/under standing/gender-definition/en/.

134. Rafferty, Jason, "Ensuring Comprehensive Care and Support for Transgender and Gender-Diverse Children and Adolescents," American Academy of Pediatrics Policy Statement, *Pediatrics,* October 2018, Volume 142,/Issue 4, accessed November 11, 2018, http://pediatrics.aappublications.org/content/142/4/e20182162

135. "Gender identity and gender role," medscape.com, accessed June 21, 2018, https://emedicine.medscape.com/article/917990-overview.

136. "Gender Terminology," genderspectrum.com, accessed June 29, 2015, https://www.genderspectrum.org/quick-links/understanding-gender/.

137. Rafferty, Jason, "Ensuring Comprehensive Care and Support for Transgender and Gender-Diverse Children and Adolescents."

138. Rafferty, "Ensuring Comprehensive Care and Support for Transgender and Gender-Diverse Children and Adolescents."

139. Rafferty, "Ensuring Comprehensive Care and Support for Transgender and Gender-Diverse Children and Adolescents."

140. Rafferty, Jason, "Ensuring Comprehensive Care and Support for Transgender and Gender-Diverse Children and Adolescents."

141. Zulch, Meg, "7 Things Genderqueer People Want You to Know," *Bustle,* December 3, 2015.

142. Clements, K. C., "What Does It Mean to Identify as Genderqueer?" Healthline.com, accessed April 12, 2018, https://www.healthline.com/health/transgender/genderqueer#takeaway.

143. Clements, "What Does It Mean to Identify as Genderqueer?"

144. "Key Terms and Concepts in Understanding Gender Diversity and Sexual Orientation Among Students," American Psychological Association, Divisions 16 and 44, 2015, 20.

145. Higgins, "Is the Word 'Queer' Offensive?"

146. Samin, Suzanne, "12 Questions About Non-Binary Gender Identity You've Been Afraid to Ask, And Real Answers," *Bustle*, June 10, 2015.

147. Jones, "Coming Out as Genderqueer Non-Binary."

148. Weiss, Suzannah, "9 Things People Get Wrong About Being Non-Binary," *TeenVogue*, February 15, 2018, accessed April 8, 2018, https://www.teenvogue.com/story/9-things-people-get-wrong-about-being-non-binary.

149. Papisova, Vera, "Here's What It Means When You Don't Identify as a Girl or a Boy," *TeenVogue*, February 12, 2016, accessed March 4, 2018, https://www.teenvogue.com/story/what-is-non-binary-gender

150. Abrams, Mere, "What Does it Mean to Identify as Nonbinary?" Healthline.com, accessed September 21, 2018, https://www.healthline.com/health/transgender/nonbinary.

151. Hess, Monique, "When no gender fits: A quest to be seen as just a person," *The Washington Post*, September 20, 2014.

152. Weiss, "9 Things People Get Wrong About Being Non-Binary."

153. Samin, Suzanne, "12 Questions About Non-Binary Gender Identity."

154. Booker, Lauren, "What it means to be gender-fluid," CNN, April 13, 2016, accessed April 12, 2018, https://www.cnn.com/2016/04/13/living/gender-fluid-feat/index.html.

155. Booker, "What it means to be gender-fluid."

156. "EJ & Cookie Johnson: Daring to be Different," *Red Table Talk*, Season 1, Episode 7, June 18, 2018, Jada Pinkett Smith, Westbrook Studios, Very Tall Productions.

157. Owen, Liz, "About the Q," PFLAG, 2018, accessed April 12, 2018, https://www.pflag. org/blog/about-q.

158. "Gender and Sexual Identity," University Library, University of Illinois at Urbana-Champaign, accessed April 12, 2018, http://guides.library.illinois. edu/lgbtq/queer.

159. "Answers to your questions about transgender people, gender identity, and gender expression," American Psychological Association, 2011, accessed March 20, 2017, http://www.apa.org/topics/lgbt/transgender.aspx.

160. Grady, "Anatomy Does Not Determine Gender, Experts Say."

161. Grady, Denise, "Anatomy Does Not Determine Gender, Experts Say," *The New York Times*, October 22, 2018, accessed November 10, 2018 https://www.nytimes. com/2018/10/22/health/transgender-trump-biology.html

162. Rehm, Diane, "Evolving Perspectives on Gender and Sex," in an interview on *The Diane Rehm Show*, WAMU 88.5 American University Radio, dianerehm.org, August 30, 2016.

163. Graham Davies, Sharyn, *Challenging Gender Norms: Five Genders Among Bugis in Indonesia. Case Studies in Cultural Anthropology.* (Thomson Wadsworth, 2006), xi.

164. CBS This Morning story 031716

165. Flores, A. R., Gates, J. L., and Brown, T. N. T., *How Many Adults Identify as Transgender in the United States?* (Los Angeles, CA: The Williams Institute, 2016).

166. Herman, J.L., Flores, A.R., Brown, T.N.T., Wilson, B.D.M., & Conron, K.J., "Age of Individuals Who Identify as Transgender in the United States," The Williams Institute. (2017), accessed November 12, 2018, https://williamsinstitute.law.ucla. edu/wp-content/uploads/TransAgeReport.pdf.

167. "Gender Dysphoria: DSM-5 Reflects Shift In Perspective On Gender Identity," By: Wynne Parry, 06/04/2013, LiveScience

168. "Glossary of Terms–Transgender," GLAAD, accessed April 15, 2018, https://www. glaad.org/reference/transgender.

169. Soldani, Bianca, "Here's exactly why the word 'transvestite' is offensive," SBS, July 29, 2016, accessed April 15, 2018, https://www.sbs.com.au/topics/life/article/2016/07/29/he res-exactly-why-word-transvestite-offensive.

170. Soldani, "Why the word 'transvestite' is offensive."

171. Soldani, "Why the word 'transvestite' is offensive."

172. PFLAG, "Our Trans Loved Ones, Questions and Answers for Parents, Families and Friends of People Who are Transgender and Gender Expansive," 2008, 17.

173. Westervelt, Eric, "At Age 3—Transitioning from Jack to Jackie," July 4, 2015, 09:25 ET.

174. Wallace, Kelly, "When your young daughter says 'I'm a boy'," CNN, Updated June 2, 2015, 11:10 ET.

175. "The Moment A Mom Realized Her Trans Daughter Wasn't 'Going Through A Phase': Jazz was 2 when her mom realized she wasn't 'just going through a phase,'" OWN, February 16, 2016, 07:57.

176. Rose, Charlie, "Brain Series Three, Episode Three, Gender Identity," PBS, June 19, 2015.

177. Wallace, "When your young daughter says 'I'm a boy'."

178. "The guide to being a trans ally," PFLAG, 2014, accessed June 11, 2015, https://www.pflag.org/sites/default/files/guide%20to%20being%20a%20trans%20ally.pdf.

179. Rafferty, Jason, "Ensuring Comprehensive Care and Support for Transgender and Gender-Diverse Children and Adolescents."

180. Rafferty, "Ensuring Comprehensive Care and Support for Transgender and Gender-Diverse Children and Adolescents."

181. Rehm, "Evolving Perspectives on Gender And Sex."

182. Raypole, Crystal, "What Does It Mean for a Transgender Person to Transition?" GoodTherapy.org, June 29, 2016, accessed May 28, 2017, http://www.goodtherapy.org/blog/what-does-it-mean-for-transgender-person-to-transition-0629167.

183. "Bruce Jenner–The Interview," with Diane Sawyer, *20/20*, ABC, April 24, 2015, accessed April 28, 2015, https://abc.go.com/shows/2020/episode-guide/2015-04/24-bruce-jenner-the-interview.

184. Raypole, "Transgender Transition."

185. Unger, Cécile A., "Hormone Therapy for Transgender Patients," *Translational Andrology and Urology*, December 2016, 5(6): 877–884, accessed March 5, 2018, 10.21037/tau.2016.09.04 https://www.ncbi.nlm.nih.gov/pmc/articles/PMC5182227/.

186. Christine Jorgensen Biographical Notes, ChristineJorgensen.com, accessed October 10, 2016, http://www.christinejorgensen.org/MainPages/biography.html.

187. Christine Jorgensen Biographical Notes, ChristineJorgensen.com, accessed October 10, 2016, http://www.christinejorgensen.org/MainPages/biography.html.

188. Coleman, Nancy, "Transgender man gives birth to a boy," CNN, August 1, 2017, accessed April 21, 2018, https://www.cnn.com/2017/07/31/health/trans-man-pregnancy-dad-trnd/index.html.

189. Raypole, "Transgender Transition."

190. Reuters, "U.S. Gender Confirmation Surgery Up 19% in 2016, Doctors Say," *NBC News*, May 22, 2017, accessed January 2018, https://www.nbcnews.com/feature/nbc-out/u-s-gender-confirmation-surgery-19-2016-doctors-say-n762916.

191. Scutti, Susan, "What Is the Difference Between Transsexual and Transgender?" Medical Daily, March 17, 2014, accessed March 5, 2018, http://www.medicaldaily.com/what-difference-between-transsexual-and-transgender-facebooks-new-version-its-complicated-271389.

192. Reuters, "U.S. Gender Confirmation Surgery Up 19% in 2016, Doctors Say," NBCnews.com, May 22, 2017, accessed https://www.nbcnews.com/feature/nbc-out/u-s-gender-confirmation-surgery-19-2016-doctors-say-n762916

193. "What is the Cost of Breast Augmentation?" American Society of Plastic Surgeons, accessed March 5, 2018, https://www.plasticsurgery.org/cosmetic-procedures/breast-augmentation/cost.

194. "Sex Reassignment Surgery Cost," www.Health.Costhelper.com, accessed March 5, 2018, http://health.costhelper.com/sex-reassignment-surgery.html.

195. Bhojani, Fatima, "Watch Katie Couric's Offensive Attempt to Interview 2 Transgender TV Stars," motherjones.com, January 7, 2014, http://www.motherjones.com/mixed-media/2014/01/katie-couric-transgender-laverne-cox.

196. Bhojani, "Couric's Offensive Interview."

197. Nikkelen, Sanne W. C., and Kreukels, Baudewijntje P. C., "Sexual Experiences in Transgender People: The Role of Desire for Gender-Confirming Interventions, Psychological Well-Being, and Body Satisfaction," *Journal of Sex & Marital Therapy*, 2017, DOI: 10.1080/0092623X.2017.1405303.

198. Verman, Alex, "When Transitioning Changes How We Have Sex," The Establishment, March 29, 2017, accessed April 19, 2018, https://theestablishment.co/when-transitioning-changes-how-we-have-sex-af579cb02120.

199. "Brave," dictionary.com, https://www.dictionary.com/browse/brave?s=t.

200. "Courage," dictionary.com, https://www.dictionary.com/browse/courage.

201. "An introduction to Transgender People," National Centers for Transgender Equality.

202. "New Generation of Transgender Americans Wants to Change Laws, Not Just Minds," November 28, 2017, *Morning Edition*, NPR, retrieved November 30, 2017.

203. McBee, Thomas Page, "My Voice Got Deeper. Suddenly, People Listened." New York Times, Aug. 9, 2018, accessed August 14, 2018 https://www.nytimes.com/2018/08/09/style/transgender-men-voice-change.html.

204. Marotta, Jenna, "Women and Power" *New York Magazine*, "Brynn Tannehill Leads Better As a Woman Than She Did As a Man," *The Cut*, October 14, 2018, accessed October 22, 2018 https://www.thecut.com/2018/10/women-and-power-chapter-one.html

205. Associated Press, "New 'X' Gender Option Added to NYC Birth Certificates," NBC New York.com, September 12, 2018, accessed September 13, 2018, https://www.nbcnewyork.com/news/local/New-X-Gender-Option-Added-to-NYC-Birth-Certificates-493087431.html?_osource=SocialFlowFB_NYBrand

206. Dahl, Melissa, "How Transgender People Choose Their New Names," nymag.com, June 3, 2015.

207. Dahl, "How Transgender People Choose New Names."

208. Dawson, Juno, "I Can't Be a 24-hour sexual fantasy," *The Guardian*, May 19, 2017, accessed April 19, 2018, https://www.theguardian.com/society/2017/may/19/juno-dawson-cant-be-24-hour-sexual-fantasy-dating-trans-woman.

209. "How Does Sexual Orientation Work Wen You're Transgender?" *LGBT Teens Expert*, gayteens/about.com, updated January 27, 2016, retrieved July 10, 2017.

210. Rehm, "Evolving Perspectives on Gender And Sex."

211. Winters, "How Marriages Changed After Unexpected Transition."

212. Herring, Chloe. "Couple struggles after husband comes out as transgender after three decades of marriage." *The Florida Times Union*. Aug 20, 2015 | updated Fri, Aug 21, 2015. Accessed January 7, 2018. http://www.jax-cdn.com/news/metro/2015-08-

213. Herring, "Couple struggles after husband comes out as transgender."

214. "Outness to Family and Friends," US Transgender Survey 2015.

215. Herman, Joanne, "Can Transgender People Bear Children?" Huffington Post, March 28, 2011, accessed May 31, 2017, http://www.huffingtonpost.com/joanne-herman/can-transgender-people-be_b_839703.html.

216. Hadjimatheou, Chloe, "Christine Jorgensen: 60 years of sex change ops," BBC World Service, 30 November 2012.

217. "Foster Care" Movement Advancement Project, July 10, 2018, Accessed October 25, 2018, https://www.lgbtmap.org/img/maps/citations-adoption-foster.pdf

218. "The Abel and Harlow Child Molestation Prevention Study," *The Stop Child Molestation Book*, 2001, revised April 2002.

219. "FAQ About Transgender Parenting," Lambda Legal, accessed May 31, 2017, https://www.lambdalegal.org/know-your-rights/article/trans-parenting-faq.

220. "FAQ About Transgender Parenting."

221. "What is Intersex," Intersex Society of North American (ISNA), accessed March 28, 2015, http://www.isna.org/faq/what_is_intersex

222. "What is Intersex," Intersex Society of North American (ISNA), accessed March 28, 2015, http://www.isna.org/faq/what_is_intersex.

223. "About Lianne Simon," liannesimon.com, Accessed Dec 4, 2015, http://www.liannesimon.com/about-lianne/#.

224. "What Is Intersex?" Intersex Society of North America, 2008, http://www.isna.org/faq/what_is_intersex.

225. Hida, "How Common is Intersex? An Explanation of the Stats," Intersex Campaign for Equality, April 1, 2015, https://www.intersexequality.com/how-common-is-intersex-in-humans/.

226. Dreger, Alice Duramat, "'Ambiguous Sex'—or Ambiguous Medicine? Ethical Issues in the Treatment of Intersexuality," *The Hastings Center Report*, May/June 1998, Volume 28, Issue, 3, 24–35.

227. "How common is intersex?" Intersex Society of North America, 2008, http://www.isna.org/faq/frequency.

228. "Disorders of Sex Development," National Health Service (United Kingdom), accessed March 3, 2018, https://www.nhs.uk/conditions/disorders-sex-development/#types-of-dsds.

229. Kim, Kun Suk, and Kim, Jongwon, "Disorders of Sex Development," *Korean Journal of Urology*, January 2012, 53(1): 1-8, accessed March 3, 2018, https://www.ncbi.nlm.nih.gov/pmc/articles/PMC3272549/.

230. Viloria, Hida and Zzyym, Dana, "How Intersex People Identify," Intersex Campaign for Equality, July, 10, 2015, accessed September 4, 2017, http://oii-usa.org/2719/how-intersex-people-identify/

231. Kinsman, "Intersex dating."

232. Kinsman, "Intersex dating."

233. Chappell, Bill, "Germany Offers Third Gender Option on Birth Certificates" The Two-Way, November 1, 2013, 13:37, www.npr.org.

234. "New 'X' Gender Option Added to NYC Birth Certificates," NBC NewYork.com.

235. 'We don't know if your baby's a boy or a girl': growing up intersex" Jenny Kleeman, July 2, 2016, The Guardian.

236. Kinsman, Kat, "Intersex dating: Finding love across the intersection," CNN, April 15, 2014, accessed September 6, 2017, https://www.cnn.com/2014/04/15/living/intersex-dating-relate/index.html.

237. Kleeman, Jenny, "We don't know if your baby's a boy or a girl: growing up intersex," The Guardian, July 2, 2016.

238. Greenfield, Charlotte, "Should We 'Fix' Intersex Children?" July 8, 2014, The Atlantic.

239. Kleeman, "growing up intersex."

240. Kinsman, "Intersex dating"

241. Kleeman, Jenny, "'We don't know if your baby's a boy or a girl': growing up intersex," The Guardian, July 2, 2016, accessed September 1, 2017, https://www.theguardian.com/world/2016/jul/02/male-and-female-what-is-it-like-to-be-intersex

242. Greenfield, Charlotte, "Should We 'Fix' Intersex Children?" The Atlantic, July 8, 2014, accessed September 2, 2017, https://www.theatlantic.com/health/archive/2014/07/should-we-fix-intersex-children/373536/

243. Kleeman, "growing up intersex."

244. Kinsman, "Intersex dating."

245. Kinsman, "Intersex dating."

246. Owen, Liz, "About the Q," PFLAG, 2018, accessed April 12, 2018, https://www.pflag.org/blog/about-q.

247. B.T. Express, "Do It ('Til You're Satisfied)" Express, Scepter, 1974.

248. Waithe, interview on Fresh Air.

249. Pew Research Center, A Survey of LGBT Americans.

250. Pew Research Center, A Survey of LGBT Americans.

251. Naughton, Jake, "A visual record of the joys, fears and hopes of older transgender people," The New York Times, August 20, 2018, accessed https://www.nytimes.com/2018/08/20/lens/older-transgender-people.html

252. Cook, Timothy Donald, "Tim Cook Speaks Up," Bloomberg Businessweek, October 30, 2014, accessed September 5, 2016, https://www.bloomberg.com/news/articles/2014-10-30/tim-cook-speaks-up.

253. Pew Research Center, A Survey of LGBT Americans.

254. Parker, Kim, "bisexuals stand out."

255. Pew Research Center, *A Survey of LGBT Americans.*

256. Marusic, "Bisexuals in 'Straight' Relationships?"

257. Blow, Charles, "Up from Pain," *New York Times*, September 19, 2014, accessed July 1, 2017, nytimes.com.

258. Schwarts, Pepper, and Kempner John, Martha, *50 Great Myths of Human Sexuality*, First Edition, (2015, Wiley & Sons Inc.), 47, https://books.google.com/books?id=p0go BgAAQBAJ&pg=PA45&lpg=PA45&dq=Pew+Study+–+40%25+of+LGBT+identify+as +bisexual&source=bl&ots=22gsMQoq8v&sig=2_5aisGnLdZti58Xi38b-MgLo_8&hl =en&sa=X&ved=0ahUKEwiRopuEn7fLAhVDQCYKHTpmDsYQ6AEISzAH#v=on epage&q=Pew%20Study%20–%2040%25%20of%20LGBT%20identify%20as%20 bisexual&f=false.

259. Schwarts and Kempner John, *50 Great Myths of Human Sexuality*, 47.

260. Pabst, Georgia, "State Rep. Zamarripa says she's bisexual," *Milwaukee Wisconsin Journal Sentinel*, July 25, 2012, accessed March 10, 2016, http://archive. jsonline.com/news/milwaukee/state-rep-zamarripa-says-shes-bisexual-156843q- 163805696.html

261. Famous Bi People, http://bisexual.org/famous/.

262. Powers, Anne, "A Close Look at Frank Ocean's Coming Out Letter," *The Record*, July 5, 2012, NPR Music.

263. Saint Thomas, Sophie, "Being Queer and Femme Means Constantly Coming Out," *Cosmopolitan*, September 8, 2017, accessed January 30, 2018, https://www. cosmopolitan.com/sex-love/a12200016/queer-femme-essay/.

264. Pugachevsky, Julia, "What Does It Mean to be Pansexual?" *Cosmopolitan*, April 26, 2017.

265. Cox, "We're Married, We Just Don't Have Sex."

266. Pew Research Center, *A Survey of LGBT Americans.*

267. Kinsman, "Intersex dating."

268. Kinsman, "Intersex dating."

269. xAcidGhostx, "Gender Fluid, Pansexual," *LGBT+ True Coming Out Stories*, Wattpad.com, https://www.wattpad.com/238446775-lgbt%2B-true-coming-out-stories-genderfluid.

270. @rikkiatia, "On Coming Out," panpride.tumblr.com http://panpride.tumblr. com/post/122915249463/on-coming-out.

271. Pew Research Center, *A Survey of LGBT Americans.*

272. Wile, Rob, "It's still dangerous to be gay in America. Here are the statistics that prove it," *Fusion*, June 12, 2016.

273. Waters, Emily, "Lesbian, Gay, Bisexual, Transgender, Queer and HIV-Affected Hate Violence in 2016," National Coalition of Anti-Violence Programs, New York, 2016, Accessed http://avp.org/wp-content/uploads/2017/06/NCAVP_2016HateViolence_ REPORT.pdf.

274. Park, Haeyoun and Mykhyalyshyn, Iaryna, "L.G.B.T. People Are More Likely to Be Targets of Hate Crimes Than Any Other Minority Group," *New York Times*, June 16, 2016.

275. "Violence Against the Transgender Community in 2017," Human Rights Campaign, 2017, http://www.hrc.org/resources/violence-against-the-transgender-community-in-2017.

276. Koeze, Ella, "Hate Crimes Against LGBT People Are Sadly Common," FiveThirtyEight, June 14, 2016, accessed October 21, 2016.

277. Koeze, "Hate Crimes Against LGBT People."

278. Stotzer, Rebecca L., "Comparison of Hate Crime Rates Across Protected and Unprotected Groups–An Update," (Manoa: University of Hawaii Press, The Williams Institute, January 2012).

279. Uniform Crime Report, "Hate Crime Statistics, 2017," Federal Bureau of Investigation, U.S. Justice Department, Released Fall 2018, Accessed February 20, 2019, https://ucr.fbi.gov/hate-crime/2017/topic-pages/victims

280. "Violence Against the Transgender Community in 2017," Human Rights Campaign, 2017, http://www.hrc.org/resources/violence-against-the-transgender-community-in-2017.

281. "Addressing Anti-Transgender Violence," Human Rights Campaign, 2016.

282. "Violence Against the Transgender Community in 2017."

283. Park and Mykhyalyshyn, "L.G.B.T. People More Likely Hate Crime Targets."

284. Park and Mykhyalyshyn, "L.G.B.T. People More Likely Hate Crime Targets."

285. Pew Research Center, *A Survey of LGBT Americans*.

286. Lily Tomlin interview by Ryan Buxton, *HuffPost Live*, April 20, 2015.

287. Lily Tomlin interview by Ryan Buxton, *HuffPost Live*, April 20, 2015.

288. Smith, Gwendolyn, "Statewide protections for transgender people pass in historic New York vote," LGBTQ Nation, January 15, 2019, accessed January 15, 2019, https://www.lgbtqnation.com/2019/01/statewide-protections-transgender-people-pass-historic-new-york-vote/?utm_campaign=wp-to-twitter&utm_medium=twitter&utm_source=twitter&fbclid=IwAR3u38JqDe6Eo4yxcz4G9nzoDcjFYsHYNtwyJq Svy3wDROU_sQT7hCrUWug.

289. Ford, Zack, "Rand Paul Answers Question About LGBT Workplace Discrimination by Telling Them to Find Another Job," Think Progress, October 15, 2015, http://thinkprogress.org/lgbt/2015/10/15/3712626/rand-paul-lgbt-employment/.

290. Lena Waithe, "The Chi Creator Lena Waithe Says Television 'Taught Me How to Dream'," interviewed by Terry Gross on *Fresh Air*, NPR, January 11, 2018.

291. *A Survey of LGBT Americans*, (Pew Research Center).

292. "New Generation of Transgender Americans Wants to Change Laws, Not Just Minds," Morning Edition, *NPR*, November 28, 2017, retrieved November 30, 2017.

293. "New Generation of Transgender Americans Wants to Change Laws," (*NPR*).

294. *A Survey of LGBT Americans*, (Pew Research Center).

295. Comcast Newsmakers, June 13, 2014, accessed December 12, 2017, https://www.youtube.com/watch?v=sJKIMh7pfGY.

296. "Overview," ACLU.

297. "Foster Care" Movement Advancement Project, July 10, 2018, accessed October 25, 2018, https://www.lgbtmap.org/img/maps/citations-adoption-foster.pdf

298. "FAQ About Transgender Parenting," Lambda Legal.

299. "Foster Care," Movement Advancement Project.

300. Janice Rodden, "News Brief: Children in Foster Care More Likely to Have Health Problems," Adoptive Families, accessed October 25, 2018 https://www.adoptive families.com/resources/adoption-news/children-in-foster-care-more-likely-to-have-health-problems/.

301. "Overview," ACLU.

302. "Overview," ACLU.

303. Matthew J. Lindquist, Torsten Santavirta, "Does Placing Children in Foster Care Increase Their Adult Criminality?" *Labour Economics*, Volume 31, December 2014, 72-83, accessed October 25, 2018, https://www.sciencedirect.com/science/article/pii/S0927537114001146#!

304. "Promoting the Well-Being of Children Whose Parents Are Gay or Lesbian," *Pediatrics*, April 2013, Volume 131, Issue 4,

305. Gary J. Gates, "LGBT Americans Report Lower Well-Being," Gallup, accessed October 26, 2014, http://news.gallup.com/poll/175418/lgbt-americans-report-lower.aspx.

306. National Survey of Family Growth.

307. S. E. James, J. L. Herman, S. Rankin, M. Keisling, L. Mottet, and M. Anafi, *The Report of the 2015 U.S. Transgender Survey*, (Washington, DC: National Center for Transgender Equality, 2016), accessed August 27, 2017.

308. Ford, "Rand Paul."

309. M.V. Lee Badgette, "New Patterns of Poverty in the Lesbian, Gay, and Bisexual Community," The Williams Institute, June 2013.

310. Michael Gordon, "Understanding HB2: North Carolina's newest law solidifies state's role in defining discrimination," *The Charlotte Observer*, March 26, 2016, accessed March 29, 2018, http://www.charlotteobserver.com/news/politics-government/article68401147.html.

311. Rehm, "Evolving Perspectives."

312. *The Abel and Harlow Child Molestation Prevention Study* and the *1999 U.S. Census Statistical Abstract*.

313. Rehm, "Evolving Perspectives."

314. National Center for Transgender Equality NCTE and the National LGBTQ Task Force, 2011.

315. James S. E. Herman, *The Report of the 2015 U.S. Transgender Survey*, National Center for Transgender Equality, 2016.

316. Peter Tyson, "The Hippocratic Oath Today," *Nova*, PBS, accessed March 5, 2018, http://Www.Pbs.Org/Wgbh/Nova/Body/Hippocratic-Oath-Today.html.

317. Ford, "Rand Paul."

318. Rehm, "Evolving Perspectives.

319. Vandy Beth Glenn, "About," Fibonacci Spiral, The Web Home and Blog of Vandy Beth Glenn.

320. "Know Your Rights: Transgender People and the Law," American Civil Liberties Union, June 1, 2017.

321. 2017 Workplace Equality Fact Sheet," Out and Equal, accessed May 30, 2018, http://outandequal.org/2017-workplace-equality-fact-sheet/.

322. Maya T Prabhu, "Study: Georgia second for occurrence of LGBT workplace discrimination," *The Atlanta Journal-Constitution*, August 20, 2018, accessed August 20, 2018, https://politics.myajc.com/news/state--regional-govt--politics/study-georgia-seco nd-for-occurrence-lgbt-workplace-discrimination/EjlXMWbzZLy5CKwKX4YNNN/

323. Rafferty, "Ensuring Comprehensive Care."

324. "Transgender Americans Face Staggering Rates of Poverty, Violence," The Movement Advancement Project, February 18, 2015.

325. "Augusta Commission Unanimously Passes Employment Non-discrimination Measure," Georgia Equality, June 19, 2018.

326. Gwendolyn Smith, "Statewide protections for transgender people pass in historic New York vote," LGBTQ Nation, January 15, 2019, accessed January 15, 2019, https://www.lgbtqnation.com/2019/01/statewide-protections-transgender-people-pass-historic-new-york-vote/.

327. "Transgender People and the Law," American Civil Liberties Union.

328. Eleanor Roosevelt, *You Learn by Living: Eleven Keys for a More Fulfilling Life*, 1960.

329. Kate Dwyer, "From Transgender Activist to Runway Model," *New York Times*, May 30, 2018, https://www.nytimes.com/2018/05/30/style/hunter-schafer-transgender-acti vist-model.html.

330. President Barack Obama, "Final Presidential Press Conference," January 18, 2017, White House.

331. Donald W. Haynes, "A Biblical analysis of homosexuality," *Wesleyan Wisdom with Donald Haynes*, February 17, 2016, http://unitedmethodistreporter.com/2016/02/17/ha ynes-a-biblical-analysis-of-homosexuality/.

332. Ralph E.C. Blair, "Clobber Passages." Evangelicals Concerned, Inc. http://ecinc.org/clobber-passages/

333. Bryan K. Blount, et.al. "What Do Biblical Scholars Say About Homosexuality and Scripture?" in *Frequently Asked Questions About Sexuality, The Bible and The Church*, edited by Ted A. Smith, (Covenant Network of Presbyterians, 2006), 119.

334. Ralph E.C. Blair, "Clobber Passages," Evangelicals Concerned, Inc. http://ecinc.org/clobber-passages/

335. Blair, "Clobber Passages."

336. Chaim, Word Study–Prostitution–זנה," February 28, 2015, http://www.chaimbentorah. com/2015/02/word-study-prostitution-זהנ/.

337. Peter J. Gomes, "The Use and Abuse of the Bible," in *The Good Book*, (William Morrow and Company, 1996), 151.

338. Rick Brentlinger, "Awaiting the Redemption of Our Bodies," quoting Dr. Richard Hayes, Christian 101, https://www.gaychristian101.com/Sodom.html.

339. Randall C. Bailey, "Why Do Readers Believe Lot? Genesis 19 Reconsidered." Old Testament Essays 23.3 (2010), 519-548.

340. "The story of Sodom and Lot's duty of hospitality to his guests," Evangelicals Concerned Inc.

341. Dr. Robert Gagnon, "The Bible and Homosexual Practice," Gay Christian 101, http://www.gaychristian101.com/Sodom.html.

342. Gomes, "Use and Abuse," 159.

343. Jack Rogers, *Jesus, the Bible, and Homosexuality*, (Westminster: John Knox Press, 2006).

344. Dr. Ralph Blair, "Clobber Passages: Leviticus 18:22 (20:13)," Evangelicals Concerned, Inc., http://ecinc.org/clobber-passages/leviticus-1822-2013/.

345. John Boswell, *Christianity, Social Tolerance, and Homosexuality*, (Chicago: The University of Chicago Press, 1980), 100.

346. Greg Tepper, "The queering of Leviticus, or how a rabbi permits gay sex," *The Times of Israel*, December 4, 2014, http://www.timesofisrael.com/the-queering-of-leviticus-or-how-a-rabbi-permits-gay-sex/.

347. Hacham Isaac Sassoon, PhD, "What Does Deuteronomy Say about Homosexuality?" Project TABS (Torah And Biblical Scholarship), accessed November 1, 2018, https://thetorah.com/what-does-deuteronomy-say-about-homosexuality/

348. "What Does Deuteronomy Say about Homosexuality?" Project TABS

349. Bill McGinnis, "Welcome to The Commandments of Jesus: The Complete List," accessed March 15, 2018, https://www.loveallpeople.org/pearl-thecommandmentsofjesus.html.

350. J. S. McConnell, Evangelist, "Commandments of Jesus," 1925, http://www.wowzone. com/commandm.htm.

351. "ATLAH Pastor James David Manning Says He's 'Absolutely' Been Tempted by the 'Gay Lifestyle'," http://www.huffingtonpost.com/2015/01/30/starbucks-james-david-manning-_n_6579966.html.

352. Rogers, *Jesus, the Bible, and Homosexuality*.

353. Bruce L Gerig, "The Clobber Passages: Reexamined HOMOSEXUALITY AND THE BIBLE, Introduction A 'letter to a friend' takes a quick look at the key verses," http://epistle.us/hbarticles/clobber1.html.

354. Pastor John Shore, "The Bible Does NOT Condemn Homosexuality" an excerpt from *UNFAIR: Christians and the LGBT Question*, The Progressive Christian Alliance.

355. Mary McClintock Fulkerson, "Is gender complementarity essential to Christian marriage?" in *Sexuality, the Bible, & the Church*, edited by Ted A Smith, (Covenant Network of Presbyterians, 2006), 65.

356. E. Dewey Smith, "5 Thoughts on Religious Freedom & Kim Burrell's Viral Video," Joy105.com, January 16, 2017, accessed January 17, 2017, http://www.joy105.com/soc ial-media-firestorm-over-dr-e-dewey-smiths-comments-about-kim-burrells-video/.

357. Gomes, *The Good Book*, 162.

358. Rogers, Jack, *Jesus the Bible and Homosexuality*, 70.

359. Haynes, "Biblical analysis."

360. Haynes, "Biblical Analysis."

361. Moss, "Black Clergy."

362. "What is Reform Judaism?" Reform Judaism, Religionfacts.com.

363. Staff writer, "All Saints, Pasadena, bids farewell to rector Ed Bacon after 21-year tenure," *The Episcopal News*, May 4, 2016, accessed December 2, 2014, http://episcopalnews. ladiocese.org/dfc/newsdetail_2/3178977.

364. Smith, "Religious Freedom."

365. Tracy Wolf, and Claire Markham, "12 Faith Leaders to Watch in 2017," *American Progress*, January 18, 2017.

366. Azmat Khan, "Meet America's first openly gay imam," Aljazeera America, December 20, 2015, http://america.aljazeera.com/watch/shows/america-tonight/ america-tonight-blog/2013/12/20/meet-america-s-firstopenlygayimam.html.

367. Olivia Rudgard, "Vatican recognises 'LGBT' for the first time," *The Telegraph*, June 19, 2018, accessed June 19, 2018, https://www.telegraph.co.uk/news/2018/06/19/vatican-r ecognises-lgbt-first-time/.

368. Yvette Caslin, "Atlanta church first lady's husband and son come out as gay," *Rolling Out*, October 12, 2016.

369. Gerald Weber and Zack Greenamyre, "Liberty and Justice in Georgia," Georgia Unites Against Discrimination, 2017, August 28, 2018, https://georgiaequality. org/issues/nondiscrimination/.

370. Janelle Monae, via Instagram, December 31, 2016.

371. 2Pac, "Thugz Mansion," *Better Dayz* 2002.

372. "FAQ–Frequently Asked Questions about LGBT, What happens when well-meaning parents initially reject their children?" PFLAG Atlanta.

373. "Impacts of Strong Parental Support for Trans Youth," TransPulse, October 2, 2012, transpulseproject.ca.

374. "Our Daughters and Sons: Questions and Answers for Parents of Gay, Lesbian, Bisexual People" PFLAG Atlanta, 2006.

375. *A Survey of LGBT Americans*, (Pew Research Center).

376. *A Survey of LGBT Americans*, (Pew Research Center).

377. Jake Naughton, "A Visual Record Of The Joys, Fears and Hopes Of Older Transgender People," *The New York Times*, August 20, 2018, accessed August 21, 2018, https://www. nytimes.com/2018/08/20/lens/older-transgender-people.html

378. Karen Ellen Kavey and Michael D. B. Kavey, "Do Families Know if Their Children Are Gay," in *FAQ –Frequently Asked Questions about LGBT*, Tenth printing, (New York: The Presbyterian Church Mt. Kisco, August 2007), http://www.pflagatl.org/lgbtfaq/.

379. "When You Think Your Son or Daughter is Gay," PFLAG Atlanta (PFLAG ATL), accessed June 4, 2017, http://www.pflagatl.org/when-you-think-your-son-or-daughter-is-gay/.

380. Kavey and Kavey, *FAQ about LGBT.*

381. "FAQ about LGBT," PFLAG Atlanta.

382. Kavey and Kavey, *FAQ about LGBT, 38.*

383. Daniel Demay, "Seattle bans gay conversion 'therapy'," https://www.seattlepi.com/local/article/Seattle-bans-gay-conversion-therapy-9009149.php, updated August 1, 2016.

384. The American Medical Association, 1998.

385. Demay, "Seattle bans."

386. Kahlil Gibran, "On Children" in *The Prophet,* (Alfred A. Knopf, 1923).

387. Kinsman, "Intersex dating."

388. "Trans PULSE Resource Guide Survey," Trans PULSE Project, 2010.

389. "Impacts of Strong Parental Support for Trans Youth," TransPulse, October 10, 2012, accessed June 4, 2017, http://transpulseproject.ca/research/impacts-of-strong-parental-support-for-trans-youth/

390. Brynn Tannehill, "The Truth About Transgender Suicide," *The Huffington Post*, November 14, 2015.

391. Wallace, "I'm a boy."

392. Luke Malone, "Transgender Suicide Attempt Rates Are Staggering," *Vocativ*, March 5, 2015.

393. Paula Mejia, "Suicide of Transgender Teen Sparks Heightened Advocacy for Trans Rights," December 30, 2014.

394. Malone, "Transgender Suicide Attempt Rates."

395. National Center for Transgender Equality NCTE and the National LGBTQ Task Force, 2011.

396. pflagatl.org.

397. Meija, "Transgender Teen Suicide."

398. Alex Morris, "The Forsaken: A Rising Number of Homeless Gay Teens Are Being Cast Out by Religious Families," *Rolling Stone,* September 3, 2014.

399. Morris, "Homeless Gay Teens."

400. "An Introduction to Transgender People," video on National Centers for Transgender Equality, http://www.transequality.org/about-transgender.

401. Mia Sheldon, and Jill Krop, "From Trey to Tracey: One child's journey to be herself."

402. Ronald Isley, O'Kelly Isley, Jr., and Rudolph Isley, "It's Your Thing," *It's Our Thing,* T-Neck, 1969.